OLIVER STONE'S USA

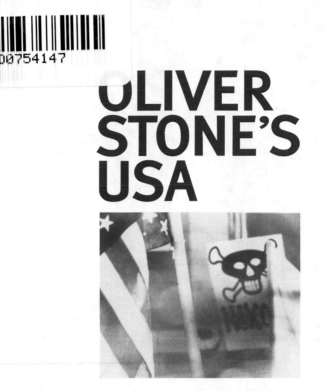

OLIVER STONE'S USA

Film, History, and Controversy

Edited by
Robert Brent Toplin

University Press of Kansas

Published by the University Press of Kansas (Lawrence, Kansas 66049), which was organized by the Kansas Board of Regents and is operated and funded by Emporia State University, Fort Hays State University, Kansas State University, Pittsburg State University, the University of Kansas, and Wichita State University

© 2000

by the University Press of Kansas

"Oliver Stone As Historian," p. 26, © 2000 by Robert A. Rosenstone

"Heaven and Earth," p. 178, © 2000 by Le Ly Hayslip

"Stone on Stone's Image (As Presented by Some Historians)," p. 40, "On Seven Films," p. 219, "On Nixon and JFK," p. 249, © 2000 by Oliver Stone

Library of Congress Cataloging-in-Publication Data

Oliver Stone's USA : film, history, and controversy / edited by Robert Brent Toplin.

p. cm.

Includes bibliographical references and index.

ISBN 0-7006-1035-9 (cloth)   ISBN 0-7006-1257-2 (pbk)

1. Stone, Oliver—Criticism and interpretation.   I. Toplin, Robert Brent, 1940–

PN1998.3.S76 O45 2000

791.43'0233'092—dc21   00-021665

British Library Cataloguing in Publication Data is available.

Printed in the United States of America

10   9   8   7   6   5   4   3   2

Contents

PART I
FRAMING THE DEBATE

Introduction

When planning a session on film and history for the American Historical Association's 1997 meeting, I decided to attempt something dramatic. I sent
a speaking invitation to Oliver Stone, Hollywood's most controversial creator
of movies about the American past. As chair of the session, I asked Stone to
talk about his film *Nixon* to a large audience of professional historians, with
the understanding that many thousands more would see the program in a
national broadcast of the event on C-SPAN.

The effort looked like Mission Impossible, and I did not expect to get a
positive response. Why would one of the nation's busiest and most successful
filmmakers want to fly across the country to New York to speak to scholars
about his treatment of history? Stone would receive no compensation for the
trip, and his performance at the meeting was not likely to enhance the marketing of his movies and videos. In fact, the visit might damage the reputation
of his productions. Critics from the profession would be on hand ready to attack him for factual errors, for distorting the historical record, or for manipu-
lating evidence. Historians might attempt to ambush Stone for his intrusions
onto their professional turf. The meeting could result in bad publicity for the
artist and his productions.

To my surprise, Oliver Stone accepted the invitation. In a long-distance
telephone conversation before the meeting, I sensed that Stone understood the
risks. He wanted to know about the format for the discussion and the manner
in which questions and answers would be handled. Stone asked me if I thought
some people in attendance would be eager for a fight about his historical interpretations. I confessed that such an assault was quite possible. The director
expressed serious concern about the harshness of the criticism he might encounter, but he did not back off from the challenge I presented to him. He came
to New York and defended *Nixon* before a packed room of nearly a thousand
scholars.

When introducing Stone at the session, I observed that he was straying far
from the familiar halls of Hollywood. I said, "Many filmmakers have tried their
hand at history, but only in a hit and run fashion. They have produced movies,

talked a bit with the press to help promote their products, and then disappeared into their commercial studios to work on their next productions. Very few have displayed the guts to enter a large meeting of professional historians in order to discuss their film's relationship to history." We were likely to dispute many of his views of the recent past, I said, but at least we could appreciate his courage in stepping up to the microphone.

Stone received both praise and criticism at the conference. Former Democratic presidential candidate George McGovern and Arthur M. Schlesinger, Jr., a distinguished historian and former adviser to President John F. Kennedy, delivered the verdicts on Stone's film *Nixon* (revised and expanded versions of their remarks appear in this book). McGovern was enthusiastic about the movie, applauding Stone for composing a brilliant, multidimensional portrait of a politician McGovern knew from firsthand experience. Schlesinger found some virtues in the film but generally scolded the director for his imaginative excesses (especially the segments dealing with conspiracies). When it was time to receive questions and comments from the audience, Stone again encountered a mixture of reactions. Some in attendance offered praise; others raised penetrating questions. The thrust of remarks from the audience was generally positive, however. Members of the historical profession were impressed that Stone had been willing to face his inquisitors and defend his movie. The *Chronicle of Higher Education* later summarized reactions with the headline "Oliver Stone Wins Some Converts at a Meeting of Historians." The *Chronicle* reported, "Appreciation and relief showed on [Oliver Stone's] face when the audience gave his presentation sustained applause."

I now realize that I should not have been surprised that Oliver Stone would walk straight into the wolves' den of historians, for he has faced controversy directly throughout his career. More than any other filmmaker, he has been willing to participate in public debates about the controversial aspects of his movies. He has argued aggressively in defense of *JFK*, for example, the movie that raised doubts about the Warren Commission's conclusions on the Kennedy assassination. Stone outlined his thesis in op-ed articles for the *New York Times* and other publications and in numerous television appearances. In these spirited presentations, Stone assumed the role of a passionate historian who was determined to persuade listeners of the wisdom of his particular spin on the past. He tried to punch holes in the arguments of his critics and cited detailed evidence in support of his own conclusions about the assassination. Stone also engaged in heated arguments about other issues addressed in *JFK*, particularly the question of whether President Kennedy intended to withdraw U.S. forces from Vietnam (Stone argued that Kennedy intended to take troops out and suggested that America's tragedy in Vietnam probably would not have occurred if there had been no assassination).

Stone is not only Hollywood's leader in making controversial movies; he is also the most prolific creator of motion pictures that deal with recent American history. In 1986 he released *Salvador,* an implied criticism of U.S. endorsement of right-wing politics in the Central American country of El Salvador. Stone also received an Academy Award for Best Picture for *Platoon* (1986), which provided a dark view of the American combat experience in Vietnam. *Wall Street* (1987) offered critical perspectives on insider trading and power brokering in the securities business of the 1980s, and *Born on the Fourth of July* (1989) examined the way American culture made youngsters enthusiastic about war and contributed to the country's tragic involvement in the Vietnam War. *Born on the Fourth of July* brought Stone an Academy Award for Best Director. *Talk Radio* (1988) dealt with the murder of Denver's caustic talk-show host Alan Berg by neofascists, and *The Doors* (1990) looked at the life of the late-1960s music icon Jim Morrison in an age of sex, drugs, and rock 'n' roll. *JFK* (1991) excited reconsideration of the Kennedy assassination. *Heaven and Earth* (1993) followed the real-life story of a Vietnamese woman who left her war-torn country, married an American, and moved to California. *Nixon* (1995) presented a psychological portrait of a corrupt and flawed president, and *Natural Born Killers* (1994) examined connections between criminal violence and the media's glamorization of it. All these films made pointed statements about American life and American foreign relations from the 1960s to the present.

IS OLIVER STONE A "HISTORIAN"?

Can movies do history? Is Stone really a historian? Should we talk about his motion pictures as if they represented significant *historical* interpretations?

Stone acknowledges that many of his films deal with historical issues. He identifies himself as a lover of history and an avid reader of history books. His history-oriented productions have focused on the recent past, the period of Stone's own youth and adulthood. Often these stories have deep personal meaning to him. *Platoon* draws on some of his experiences as a soldier in Vietnam, and *The Doors* explores the life of one of his favorite musicians, Jim Morrison. Stone has also considered development of a motion picture around the story of Alexander the Great, and he has given consideration to making a film about George Armstrong Custer. These explorations demonstrate that his interest in movie themes has moved deeper into history, to eras far removed from his own times.

Movies that deal with the past can stir an audience's thinking and arouse people's interest in reading books, says Stone, but drama cannot produce the same kind of investigation of the past as scholarship. Movies give us a "first draft" on history, he says, a treatment that suggests broad lines for thinking and feeling. It is not the same as written history, Stone stresses, and the film-maker should not be called a historian. Stone insists that he is a dramatist first and foremost and that he never claimed to be a historian (he outlines this argument in "Stone on Stone's Image (As Presented by Some Historians)."

Some writers have claimed that Stone identified himself as a "cinematic historian" in the early years of his directorial career. Stone counters that such claims are false and have unwisely encouraged viewers to judge his films as if they were evaluating historical scholarship. As a result, he contends, his work has been misunderstood and unfairly criticized by historians and others who have approached his films with this flawed model of analysis. Instead, he advocates an approach to his work grounded in the understanding that he considers himself to be first and foremost a dramatist or docu-dramatist.

Some scholars and journalists are reluctant to treat products of the popular cinema as examples of history. They complain that movies come too close to fiction to count as legitimate works of historical interpretation. Moviemakers, they say, enjoy too many opportunities for artistic license. Writers and directors such as Oliver Stone invent scenes, dialogue, and characters; compress the time in which events occur; collapse several personalities into a few representative figures; and participate in other manipulations that compromise truthfulness in order to make their stories dramatically compelling. Furthermore, moviemakers grossly simplify the historical record. Hollywood artists tend to suggest single explanations for events that have complex causes, and they often attribute change to the actions of one or two heroic figures, namely, the principal characters in their movies. To learn about history, go to a book, not a movie, argue these critics. Scholarship aims to discover truths through complex understanding; moviemakers are far more interested in portraying the past simplistically in order to entertain audiences, make money, and advance their personal agendas.

Those who defend Stone and other Hollywood artists who deal with history tend to argue for a more expansive definition of the term "historian." They observe that the opportunities to bring history to the public are much broader today than they were decades ago. We no longer obtain our views of the past almost exclusively from individuals who teach students and publish books and articles. The past comes to life for us through the activities of many other presenters of history. "Public historians," professionals who instruct outside the classroom, educate us, too. They organize museum displays and programs, renovate historic buildings, give talks at historic sites, and create dramatic reenactments in which actors play the roles of historic figures.

Documentary filmmakers such as Ken Burns and David Grubin are also working as "historians" on PBS television, interpreting the record of the American Civil War, the American presidents, and other subjects through the production of popular documentary films. Cable television, too, makes a contribution, through programs on the History Channel, the Arts and Entertainment Network, the Learning Channel, and other stations. The World Wide Web is also exploring a tremendous variety of ways to engage the public in history — from providing chat stations devoted to discussions about the past to facilitating access to historical databases. And, of course, there is history by Hollywood, of which Oliver Stone is the nation's most famous and controversial practitioner.

In his essay in this book, Robert A. Rosenstone suggests ways that Oliver Stone is also a significant contributor to our thinking about history. Stone produces something different from written history, says Rosenstone, but his productions do offer a form of historical analysis. Rosenstone reminds us that nobody can be a *pure* historian, not even the writer of a distinguished book. Everyone who deals with historical evidence must make personal judgments. They have to shape disparate evidence into an interpretation. Making sense of complex information involves "fiction, invention, creation," says Rosenstone, even for the scholarly writer. When the author of a book talks about "revolution," "evolution," or "progress," he or she imposes these constructs on the evidence. The terms are not necessarily "true" (indeed, scholars often dispute their validity). These terms are inventions designed to symbolize the historian's personal understanding of what happened in the past. In a different but related manner, Oliver Stone employs fiction, invention, and creation. He designs stories for the screen that attempt to make sense of our past — or at least to communicate his own sense of our past. The scenes in Stone's movies about real people from history may not be precisely correct, notes Rosenstone, but the more important question is, Does Stone identify larger truths? Rosenstone warns us about the danger of becoming too picayunish about the filmmaker's exercise of creative license. "The Historical film will always include images that are at once invented and, at best, true," says Rosenstone. "True in that they symbolize, condense, or summarize larger amounts of data; true in that they impart an overall meaning of the past."

A DIFFERENT KIND OF FILMMAKER

What does Stone try to communicate? Which "truths" does he attempt to discover? Does he distort the truth? To many viewers and critics, his messages are strongly political. Far more than other moviemakers, they say, Stone attempts to deliver strong opinions about America's government and foreign policy. His films make judgments: the United States backed the wrong people in El Salvador, the United States should not have pursued the brutal war in Vietnam, Kennedy was an impressive president, the Warren Commission erred in judging the causes of Kennedy's assassination, Richard Nixon participated in appalling abuses of power.

Interestingly, Oliver Stone is America's leading designer of the kind of movies that Hollywood executives prefer to avoid. Historical and political cinema is supposedly deadly at the box office. Audiences want to be entertained, say the executives; they do not want their minds stretched and their ideas challenged. The public does not want "message movies." As one Hollywood mogul said decades ago, if you want to send a message, use Western Union. Yet, amazingly, Stone has built his reputation around the very genres that Hollywood's investors consider a bad bet — movies that carry strong historical and political interpretations.

Stone also bucks a current trend in movie production by making viewers uncomfortable. Whereas most filmmakers design stories with upbeat themes and happy endings, many of Stone's films examine the dark side of American life and leave audiences uncomfortable. They show failure of leadership, deceptive policy making, immoral practices, weakness of character, personal corruption, and self-destructive behavior. *Salvador* revealed American support for political figures behind the "death squads" of a Central American country. *Platoon* showed American soldiers indulging in drugs, destroying Vietnamese villages, and killing Asians with little sense of remorse. *Wall Street* exposed practices in the securities business reminiscent of the scandals involving traders such as Ivan Boesky and Michael Milken. *Born on the Fourth of July* delivered disturbing messages that questioned America's gung-ho approach to combat in Vietnam. *The Doors* studied the deterioration of a rock star who abused booze, drugs, and women. *JFK* suggested that government leaders had lied to the American public about the true nature of the Kennedy assassination. *Nixon* showed the deterioration of a president who was waist-deep in corruption. *Natural Born Killers* examined the mindless violence of young people who went on a killing spree. These productions are very different from the "feel-good" movies that often come out of Hollywood. They are also quite distinct from the familiar fare of action-adventure films that display movement and noise but are weak on ideas. Stone's films carry opinions, and the lessons are often painful to contemplate.

The issue-oriented character of Stone's work emerges, in part, from his extensive personal involvement in his motion picture projects. Stone is not simply the director–as–hired gun, a role played by many artists in Hollywood's industry. Often producers and studio executives — and even actors — take a particular interest in a project and shepherd it along toward production. They put together packages that combine funding with teams of writers, technicians, and actors. Eventually they choose a director who, they believe, can handle their project effectively (often they select someone who has already directed a successful picture of the genre). Stone, however, frequently develops his *own* projects. He pursues subjects that excite his personal interest. Once he has identified the story for a movie, he buys the rights to an important book on the topic and collaborates with someone who is familiar with the material. In the case of *JFK*, for example, Stone teamed up with Zachary Sklar, cowriter with Jim Garrison of *On the Trail of the Assassins* (the book that provided the basic framework for the movie's story). Stone then writes the scripts with his collaborators. This puts him in a unique position. Few Hollywood artists are consistently listed as both cowriters and directors of their movies. Not many have such an extensive beginning-to-end personal and emotional investment in their projects.

Stone's involvement, his selection of controversial topics, and his ability to defend his movies in public forums have made him one of the most recognizable public faces among the many Hollywood artists behind the camera (along with Steven Spielberg and Woody Allen). Typically, movie directors are less well known as *faces* than the actors they counsel on the set. Moviegoers can easily recognize Tom Hanks or Julia Roberts in a crowd. They find it much more difficult to pick out accomplished directors such as James Cameron, Martin Scorsese, Peter Weir, or Francis Ford Coppola. If moviegoers know their faces at all, it is often from seeing the directors express thanks at the Academy Award ceremonies. Stone, however, is truly a *public* figure. He has spoken about his movies in numerous television appearances and has argued about his historical and political interpretations in many public forums. It is not surprising, then, that Stone got to play himself in the movie comedy *Dave* (1993). In that cameo, he acted as a guest on a television talk show who claimed that a conspiracy was afoot in the White House. Most moviegoers implicitly understood the humor, for they recognized Hollywood's master of conspiracy theories.

Oliver Stone has also achieved distinction for his innovations and experimentation. His movies are not conventional productions. Often Stone boldly explores a variety of modern artistic techniques, using the medium brilliantly to arouse viewers' emotions and to stimulate their interest. David Halberstam, who covered much of the Vietnam War as a reporter for the *New York Times*, points to this achievement in his review of *Platoon* published at the time of the movie's release and in the essay he prepared for this volume. Halberstam reminds us of the way Stone employed the camera imaginatively to communicate a sense of the frightening experience of night patrol in Vietnam. The movie takes audiences into a rain-soaked jungle, where the soldiers have to wait as lookouts. The men's task is to surprise enemy intruders who may attempt an ambush of their camp. Against the menacing backdrop of heavy foliage, the American soldiers seem as much the hunted as the hunters. They can hardly see the approaching Vietnamese communists. The men appear alone and exposed in the dark jungle. Stone's camera works like the eyes of the nervous servicemen, scanning the environment, attempting to discern movement. Suddenly, the enemy is upon the Americans, and the jungle explodes into a confusing and bloody nighttime firefight. In this emotionally taxing scene, Stone delivers an important lesson. He shows how soldiers from the most powerful nation in the world could feel like underdogs in a foreign environment. Imaginative photographic techniques communicated that message.

In a very different way, *Natural Born Killers* is also avant-garde in its style. David T. Courtwright notes in the discussion in this book that the movie contains "upward of 3,000 shots, weird camera angles, multiple formats, morphing, cartoons, avant-eclectic sound track, and headache-inducing montage." He observes that Stone and his associates worked for eleven months after principal shooting, carefully crafting the configuration of frames to create an impressionist feeling. Courtwright points out that such a boldly experimental format could easily become a commercial and critical disaster in the hands of a filmmaker less talented than Stone.

Stone also experiments boldly in his more overtly political movies. In *JFK*, for example, he presents a lengthy study of more than three hours that bombards viewers with a plethora of words and images. Borrowing the quick-cut style of MTV, *JFK* flashes evidence by the audience at such rapid speed that viewers hardly have time to ponder what is true, what is speculation, and what is fiction. Stone mixes actual news footage with staged images so effectively that viewers feel like they are watching an informative documentary on the assassination. In *Nixon*, Stone experiments differently, borrowing ideas for his structure from Orson Welles's *Citizen Kane*. Like Welles, Stone employs flashbacks to probe roots of character. And like Welles, he uses deep-focus photography and sharp camera angles to convey a dark and disturbing vision. Scenes showing Nixon's loneliness in the cavernous, shadowy White House resemble scenes at Xanadu, the huge estate of the troubled personality in *Citizen Kane*.

Stone also strives for authenticity in his films. Through research in the preproduction phases, he attempts to gather information that makes his presentation appear realistic. In creating *The Doors,* for example, he interviewed more than a hundred people who knew rock star Jim Morrison or attended his concerts. Preparation for *Wall Street* involved discussions with individuals who knew the social and physical environment of the subject. Stone talked with dozens of investment brokers, assigned an ex–investment partner as a key adviser to his project, and visited the trading room of the stock exchange as well as the offices of leading brokerage houses such as Salomon Brothers. He put the principal actors through a sort of business "boot camp," requiring them to spend time shadowing brokers in the financial district. In preparing for *Platoon*, Stone required his actors to experience a much more painful sort of training. He made them work with former marine captain Dale Dye, who, under Stone's direction, ordered several days of arduous military exercises. Later, Stone employed Dye as a trainer for actors in *Born on the Fourth of July*. He also sought help from Ron Kovic, the real-life Vietnam veteran who wrote an autobiographical book of the same title. Kovic guided Stone on the details of his personal experiences, providing, for example, information about conditions at the veterans' hospital where Kovic recuperated from the wound he received in Vietnam.

THE CONTROVERSIAL NATURE OF STONE'S FILMS

While Stone's movies contain numerous authentic elements, they also include many fictional flourishes, and critics have been quick to complain about these inventions. In some cases, Stone grossly simplifies characterizations to advance his plot. A good example of this form of manipulation can be seen in his portrayal of Jim Garrison in *JFK*. Garrison was the New Orleans district attorney who tried to prove in court that the Kennedy assassination involved a broader conspiracy. Through much of *JFK*, Garrison sounds like Jimmy Stewart in *Mr. Smith Goes to Washington*. He is an honest, decent man of the people who battles alone for truth against rich, powerful, and evil forces. But critics familiar with the real Garrison's investigation pointed out that he had been accused of bullying witnesses and suppressing evidence from a polygraph test. They also accused Garrison of maintaining long-term associations with Mafia figures (Stone responds to both of these assertions in these pages). Stone admits that he made Garrison more heroic than he was in real life, but Stone denies that any flaws in Garrison prevented him from acting correctly in the case. To advance his movie's case for a conspiracy, it was important to make the messenger of the news attractive and believable. Similarly, Stone portrayed President John F. Kennedy in heroic fashion. His brief documentary-style coverage of Kennedy's presidency in *JFK* suggested the Camelot image in order to help viewers sense the tragedy of Kennedy's death.

Of course, the most controversial aspects of *JFK* involve the movie's suggestions that the Warren Commission was wrong in concluding that Lee Harvey

Oswald alone killed Kennedy (President Lyndon B. Johnson created the Warren Commission to investigate the circumstances surrounding Kennedy's death and to report the conclusions to the nation). Stone's movie drops numerous hints about the possibility of an assassination conspiracy involving several individuals. The most important foundation for this argument is 8mm film footage photographed at the scene by Abraham Zapruder, who watched the motorcade pass by in Dallas and directed his camera at the presidential limousine during the fateful moments when gunshots hit the president. Dramatizing arguments made by many critics of the Warren Commission, JFK claimed that a frame-by-frame examination of the Zapruder film reveals that Kennedy's head bounced back from the force of the shot. This movement suggests that the shot came from a different direction than where Oswald supposedly was situated. Stone's movie leaves the impression that shots could have come from a grassy knoll near the murder site, and it asks how Oswald could have fired three shots at Kennedy in just 5.6 seconds. JFK also refers mockingly to a "magic bullet," observing that a projectile could not have penetrated the bodies of Kennedy and John Connally, the Texas governor seated beside him, in the strange manner identified in the Warren Commission report. Furthermore, JFK hints that high-level figures probably played a role in an assassination plot, including figures from the FBI, the CIA, and the military-industrial complex.

Many people were suspicious of the Warren Commission's claims before the appearance of Stone's movie, and they challenged them more vigorously after JFK excited an enthusiastic response from millions of moviegoers. A number of notable figures lined up to attack Stone's cinematic interpretation, including Richard Nixon; John Connally; Jack Valenti, adviser to President Johnson and later head of the Motion Picture Academy of Arts and Sciences; journalists Tom Wicker and Anthony Lewis of the *New York Times;* George Lardner, Jr., of the *Washington Post;* and CBS television news anchorman Dan Rather. These critics and others questioned the movie's assumptions about the Zapruder film, ballistics evidence, and the information suggesting a larger conspiracy. They observed that nineteen of twenty medical experts who had served over the years on four independent panels that examined X rays and autopsy photos concluded that the president had been shot from the rear. They noted, too, that Lee Harvey Oswald had not needed to fire three shots within 5.6 seconds to match the claims of the Warren Commission. A possible third shot, which missed the president, could have been fired before or after those 5.6 seconds. Expert panels also concluded that when Connally heard the first shot, he rotated his shoulders slightly, bringing his body into an alignment that made him vulnerable to the five wounds he received. There was nothing "magic" about the bullet. Furthermore, it seemed impossible that several high-level figures in the government would cooperate in an assassination conspiracy and succeed in hiding evidence of it completely. Governor Connally summarized the impressions of a number of the movie's critics when he concluded that *JFK* was "a powerful propaganda piece. . . . It's fiction. . . . It's for sure not a documentary." To all these charges, Stone responds within.

The movie also came under assault for its manipulation of evidence. Stone filmed enacted scenes in grainy black-and-white footage, giving these dramatizations the appearance of actual documentary information. He then mixed this material with real imagery created in 1963. This mixture of fact and fiction flashed by so quickly on the screen that viewers could not intelligently distinguish true evidence from staged evidence. Many historians and journalists were troubled by the blend. They thought Stone's technique aimed to mislead unsophisticated audiences, moviegoers who were not familiar enough with the visual details to question Stone's sources.

The debate over manipulation of evidence applies not only to big issues, such as the suggestion of an assassination conspiracy, but also to the staging of specific actions in Stone's movies. Critics frequently complain that Stone does not get the facts right; Stone defends himself by maintaining that his presentations aim not to replicate every detail but to speak to larger truths. Several good examples of these points of disagreement appear in Jack E. Davis's discussion about *Born on the Fourth of July*. There is a memorable scene in the movie showing police breaking up demonstrators at a peace rally at Syracuse University. The portrayal angered the city's police officers, who argued correctly that the incident had never occurred. Furthermore, Ron Kovic was never gassed and beaten in Miami, as seen in the movie, but he was gassed and beaten in that manner in a political protest by veterans in Los Angeles. Also, Kovic never went to Georgia (as he does in the movie) to confess to the parents of a dead soldier that he had accidentally killed their son. The portrayal of Kovic apologizing to the dead soldier's parents in Georgia acted out an inner sense of Catholic guilt and confession that formed the central theme of Kovic's book. For Stone (and his defenders), these inventions served a purpose. They represented larger realities, not the specific details of Kovic's personal experiences. Police beatings of students did take place on many college campuses at the time. Major rioting by Vietnam veterans and others occurred in Miami at the Republican National Convention in 1972, and Kovic, loudly protesting Nixon's speech, was evicted from the convention hall. For Stone, these were legitimate exercises of artistic license. They dramatized broader truths.

As Robert Rosenstone observes in this book, Oliver Stone did not design a complete fabrication "but, rather, a cunning mixture of diverse elements — fact, near fact, displaced fact, invention." His movie "refers to the past" and "prods the memory." To Stone's critics, however, these are examples of the movie's loose relationship with historical evidence. In changing the details of Kovic's life, the filmmaker deceives audiences and leaves them with an inaccurate report. And if we are to tolerate this fudging of small details, ask the critics, how can we be sure that a filmmaker like Stone will not fudge larger ones as well?

A much more intense point of disagreement relates to Stone's suggestion of a conspiracy in the murder of President John F. Kennedy. The idea of a conspiracy was central to the thesis of *JFK*, and it appeared in briefer and somewhat different form in *Nixon*. *JFK* suggested that a cabal of powerful figures in politics, the intelligence community, and the military-industrial complex may have plotted the president's death in order to prevent a withdrawal of U.S. troops from Vietnam. *Nixon* showed the president meeting with a nasty-looking group of big businessmen from Texas (Larry Hagman plays their leader) and facing pressures to pursue specific policies. The film connects Nixon to plans for the Bay of Pigs invasion and plots to assassinate Fidel Castro, and the movie vaguely relates these activities to the Kennedy assassination. It also connects the Watergate cover-up to Nixon's desire to keep one of the Watergate burglars, E. Howard Hunt, quiet because of Hunt's supposed understanding of Nixon's indirect association with the Kennedy assassination.

Arthur M. Schlesinger, Jr., sharply criticizes Stone's attention to conspiracy in his essay in this volume. He argues that *JFK* and *Nixon* give too much support to the notion that cabals of highly placed individuals make the decisions that broadly affect American life. Schlesinger likens this outlook to the "paranoid" explanation of events described by historian Richard Hofstadter years ago. Hofstadter observed that notions of conspiracy had been popular in America for a long time — from the ideas about the Masons and the Papists in the nineteenth century to the claims about the Elders of Zion and the Communist Party in the twentieth. Hofstadter claimed that such visions of conspiracy were not very realistic or perceptive. Stephen E. Ambrose also expresses discomfort with the conspiracy thesis in his essay in this book. He concludes that "Stone's Bay of Pigs–assassination business is all fantasy." Ambrose insists that Nixon, when vice president, never headed any CIA project and did not mastermind the Bay of Pigs invasion or attempts to kill Castro. Ambrose also is uncomfortable with *Nixon*'s reference to the "Beast," which Stone's cowriter, Christopher Wilkinson, interprets as "a metaphor for the darkest organic forces in American cold war politics: the anticommunist crusade, secret intelligence, the defense industry, organized crime, big business, plus the CIA." Stone's references to the Beast are a "gross simplification of how and by whom the United States is run," says Ambrose.

Stone has defended his references to conspiracies by suggesting that his dramatic intent is to interpret a mixture of fact and fiction, based on a wide body of "facts" on which people do not agree. On the matter of Kennedy's murder, for instance, he says that *JFK* does not advance a single and certain explanation for the president's assassination. Rather, Stone claims that the film "explains one of the ways in which a murder plot could have developed as directed from high-level sources in our government." He also says, "In hindsight, the film is about more than the murder of a president. It asks the audience to think for itself and begin the process of deconstructing the meaning of its own history." Stone claims that the "implications are enormous. They have been driven home to me through the years by young people who sense that the very foundation of government, not only in America but elsewhere, is being corrupted."

The principal goal in making the movie, Stone says, was to follow Garrison "in his labyrinth of deconstructing reality" and, in the process, to poke holes in the Warren Commission's report. It was not to substitute a specific and certain set of conclusions about how the assassination took place. But for Schlesinger, Ambrose, and others, these hints about dark plots are based on unsubstantiated claims. The suggestions about conspiracy can create much mischief, for they give millions of gullible movie viewers an illusory perspective on the past.

THE DEFENSE OF STONE'S ARTISTRY

When considering this debate about conspiracy, we confront some interesting questions about history-oriented cinema: To what degree should we excuse a filmmaker's efforts to incorporate symbolism that communicates his personal vision? Should we tolerate some of these liberties? Should we view the inventions as appropriate flourishes in a medium that gives individual artists considerable freedom to dramatize their own viewpoints? Should we consider Stone's attention to conspiracies a legitimate form of artistic expression?

Some defend Stone by noting that his movies contain much of value. They insist that our discomfort with the director's hunches about conspiracies should not prevent us from recognizing his films' intelligent handling of important historical topics. For instance, *JFK* advances ideas about Kennedy's planned withdrawal from Vietnam, which many writers believe are probably true (we can never know for sure, as Kennedy died before he had a chance to implement proposals he had discussed). Robert S. MacNamara, secretary of defense under Presidents Kennedy and Johnson, supported some of the main elements of Stone's thesis in his important book *In Retrospect: The Tragedy and Lessons of*

Vietnam (1995). MacNamara believes that Kennedy would have moved away from U.S. military commitments to Vietnam had he lived. Schlesinger endorses this idea, too, in his essay in this book (Schlesinger was an adviser to Kennedy). In contrast, Randy Roberts and David Welky's essay in this collection articulates doubts that have been expressed by a number of historians. They support an interpretation advanced by distinguished scholars of the Vietnam conflict such as George Herring. Roberts and Welky note that Kennedy made public promises about staying the course in Vietnam, and they place little credence in the claims about Kennedy's plans for a substantial troop withdrawal.

JFK, then, provoked our thinking about an important controversy. It aroused the public's thinking about the origins of America's commitment to war in Vietnam. We fail to do Stone's movie justice if we concentrate only on the director's provocative suggestions about a conspiracy to assassinate the president.

Arguing for a sense of balance may seem even more appropriate in an evaluation of *Nixon*. In that movie, the suggestions about a conspiracy occupy much less time than in *JFK* (just a few minutes in a production that runs more than three hours). Stone's defenders argue that *Nixon*'s brief and highly speculative references to a conspiracy behind Kennedy's death should not sour our appreciation of the entire film.

There is certainly much to commend in *Nixon*. The film brilliantly employs flashbacks to engage the audience in a search for the origins of a self-destructive personality that resembles the style of *Citizen Kane*. The story examines Nixon's relationships with his brothers, his mother and father, his wife, and others in an effort to understand why he appeared insecure despite his notable political climb from California politics to leadership in the White House. Stone's script draws on insights from respected historians of the Watergate scandal, such as Stanley I. Kutler; from the controversial descriptions of journalists, such as Carl Bernstein and Bob Woodward (whose sources for many claims about Nixon remain secret); and from the work of even more controversial biographers, such as Fawn Brodie, who published a provocative psychohistory of Nixon that traced the sources of much of his adult behavior to hang-ups developed in childhood. Stone employs information and theories from these authors and others to fashion an interpretation of Nixon's motivation and behavior. At the end of the movie, he shows Nixon (played by Anthony Hopkins) delivering an awkward farewell speech to staff at the White House. When Americans heard that address in 1974, it seemed confusing and disjointed. Against the background of Stone's cinematic psychoportrait, however, Nixon's scattered references to his childhood, his parents, and the disappointments of his life make sense. The final speech in the film serves to summarize a thesis about the impact of life experiences on character that Stone advanced throughout his movie. Of course, Stone's interpretation is just one of many possible explanations that we can consider in trying to understand Nixon's personality. It is, nevertheless, a persuasive suggestion in view of his clever integration of fact and personal theorizing.

Perhaps we are too wedded to the expectations of print-oriented history when we blast Stone (and other filmmakers) for incorporating personal theories in their movies. We scan the treatment of evidence, expecting an accurate and authentic representation of the facts at every turn — just as we would expect from a work of nonfiction that deals with the past. But we are talking here about history delivered through the popular cinema — an important distinction. Cinematic history is often fictional, poetic, representative. Its stories communicate messages through metaphor and allegory. Hollywood cinema informs not by rendering events with factual exactitude but by creating compelling dramatic images that engage our senses, excite our emotions, and stimulate our thinking. Stone's attention to conspiracy, then, may serve as a vague, broad, and symbolic statement that communicates distrust of government. His suggestions about conspiracies warn us that appalling political behavior often occurs behind the scenes. Lobbyists delivering favors away from the public eye have wielded tremendous influence over the votes of politicians (serious questions about such activities involving Chinese and Indonesian interests emerged during the presidency of Bill Clinton, and concerns arose over the tobacco lobby's expensive and quietly delivered contributions to members of Congress). Presidents have deceived the people, as Lyndon B. Johnson did in a largely contrived crisis in the Gulf of Tonkin. Some historians consider that deception a type of conspiracy. And there have been conventional conspiracies at high levels (Watergate and the Iran-contra scandal are among the most prominent ones of recent years). Stone's characterizations of the seamy side of politics arouse our thinking about the way power may be wielded beneath the surface of politics. His allusions to conspiracy suggest a variety of troubling activities at high levels that deserve our attention.

Perhaps, too, we should recognize that creative artistry is inherent in the motion picture business. Moviemaking today is often an intensely personal endeavor. Directors wield much more influence over their productions than in the 1930s and 1940s, when executives from the major studios forced them to conform to the industry's cookie-cutter plans for scripting, production, and acting. Today, a successful director like Oliver Stone enjoys the right to inject large elements of personal philosophy and personal politics into his scripts. His motion pictures are not just moneymaking enterprises. They work as personal instruments for expressing Stone's perspective on modern times. *The Doors* gave Stone a chance to recall the images and music that fascinated him in the 1960s. *JFK* enabled him to speak to the disillusionment he felt after the assassination of John F. Kennedy. *Platoon* expressed his troubled memories of combat in Vietnam. In related ways, Stone's attention to conspiracies communicates his objection to the way power is wielded in modern America. As a cinematic artist, Stone enjoys splendid opportunities to dramatize this concern.

The provocative emphasis on conspiracies in Stone's films may diminish as the director continues to mature as a filmmaker. Stone is tremendously sensitive to criticism, and often he attempts to respond to it energetically both in his moviemaking and in his public comments. When critics complained that he seemed obsessed with the Vietnam War, Stone insisted that his vision was not limited, and he began to create movies that did not put concerns about Vietnam at the center of the stories. Then women argued that his films were primarily about men and communicated a male point of view. Women also pointed out that the few female characters in his scripts were typically passive figures, such as Sissy Spacek's role as the deferential wife of Jim Garrison (Kevin Costner) in *JFK*. Stone responded with *Heaven and Earth* (1993), a story about a Vietnamese woman who suffered greatly during the war. This was Stone's first film with a woman as the central character. Perhaps Stone will respond to the abundant criticisms of his conspiracy theories in a similar way. He may give less screen time to this dramatic device that has become a popular target for historians and journalists.

DO STONE'S INTERPRETATIONS MAKE AN IMPACT?

Stone may adjust to some attacks, but he is not likely to compromise in reaction to criticisms of *Natural Born Killers,* because the complaints against that movie touch sensitive questions about legal liability and censorship. Stone's 1994 picture excited heated debates in the press because some critics charged that its bloody story inspired copycat crimes by savage individuals. According to some claims, at least fourteen people in the United States and Europe were killed by attackers who emulated behavior they saw in the film. *Natural Born Killers* shows Mickey Knox (Woody Harrelson) and Mallory Knox (Juliette Lewis) going off on a joyful killing spree that results in the death of more than fifty people. Mickey and Mallory begin their bloody activities by drowning Mallory's father in a fish tank and burning her mother alive in her bed.

The most notable claims about the movie's impact involved the real-life actions of an Oklahoma couple. After watching *Natural Born Killers* several times and consuming LSD, the young man and woman gunned down an individual working at a cotton gin and shot and paralyzed a clerk in a convenience store. The gin worker was an acquaintance of novelist John Grisham. Grisham claimed that Stone's movie "is saying that murder is cool and fun," and he supported a lawsuit against the film. Stone retorted, "John Grisham predictably draws upon the superstition about the magical power of pictures to conjure up the undead specter of censorship." Stone's defenders claimed that Grisham's books (usually made into movies), such as *A Time to Kill*, also portrayed antisocial behavior that might be imitated by viewers. Movies, they claimed, should not be held accountable under product liability law. To Grisham's supporters, though, *A Time to Kill* and *Natural Born Killers* were strikingly different. *Natural Born Killers* featured far more violent action and placed questions about violence in American culture much closer to its core.

Natural Born Killers was primarily about the publicity-crazed media's tendency to idolize and glamorize venal killers, but that message got lost in the more dramatic public controversy over the movie's possible impact on criminal behavior. Stone's film became the focus of attention for debates about movie violence and censorship, much as *Bonnie and Clyde* served as the focus for such debates in the 1960s and *A Clockwork Orange* caused similar controversies in the 1970s. As David T. Courtwright observes in his essay in this book, a study of reactions to *Natural Born Killers* gives us an opportunity to examine the issue of violence on several levels. The movie arouses our thinking about the wave of violent crime that surged from the 1960s to the 1980s, excites discussions about the impact of popular entertainment on criminal behavior, and provokes our consideration of the mass media's abundant attention to criminal violence.

There is greater agreement about the *positive* impact of other films by Oliver Stone. In several cases, Stone appears to have sparked very useful discussions about America's recent past. For instance, Stone's movies dealing with the Vietnam War made worthwhile contributions to the public's thinking about that historical experience. In the months when *Platoon* and *Born on the Fourth of July* appeared in the theaters, newspapers, magazines, and television programs devoted a great deal of discussion to these films' emotionally gripping images and the controversial nature of Stone's messages about war. The movies helped to advance public discussions about the lessons Americans could draw from their country's troublesome engagement in Vietnam.

Walter LaFeber finds much of value in Stone's treatment of another foreign policy issue — revolution in Latin America. Although LaFeber objects to some of the specific portrayals in *Salvador* (1986) in his essay in this volume, he argues that Stone "caught much of the political debate accurately." *Salvador* effectively shows that resolution of the political problems in El Salvador was extremely difficult in the 1980s because politics had become polarized and militarized. There was no viable middle ground for compromise, notes LaFeber. As the movie demonstrates, U.S. foreign policy makers supported the Salvadoran military, a form of interference that complicated the Salvadorans' efforts to work out a settlement of their civil war. LaFeber praises Stone for raising intelligent and relevant questions about the impact of U.S. meddling in El Salvador's tragic conflict.

Another interesting example of the tremendous impact of Stone's films can be seen in the way the mass media have invoked images from *Wall Street* to communicate a symbol for America's business culture in the 1980s. The movie serves as a popular point of reference when Americans contrast the benefits of the go-go economy of the 1980s with a darker picture of developments in the decade. *Wall Street* reminds us that not everyone benefited from the spiral of stock market gains and corporate profits during the boom times. Some, like the union leader of the airline mechanics (played by Martin Sheen), saw their jobs threatened by mergers, buyouts, downsizing, and corporate scheming. When Americans speak about the underside of the business surge in the 1980s, they often quote the movie's detestable mogul Gordon Gekko (Michael Douglas): "The point is greed is good . . . greed is right . . . greed works." For instance, when a CNN reporter summarized the spirit of recent decades in a 1998 commentary, he used Gekko's comment as the single representative image for America in the 1980s.

Martin S. Fridson questions this influential message. His essay points out that American businesspeople (including securities brokers) were not *unusually* greedy in the 1980s. Their commercial activities in the period were not much different from the aggressive business practices their counterparts demonstrated in the 1920s or the 1950s or any other decade of the twentieth century. "Opportunities to surrender to greed abounded in every era," Fridson observes, "even if the specific outlet of hostile takeovers did not." But Stone's powerful imagery and the Academy Award–winning performance by Michael Douglas as an avaricious Wall Street broker helped to strengthen the popular view that the 1980s was a uniquely depraved period in which American big businesspeople exhibited selfishness and greed as never before. The stereotype Stone put on the screen found a respected place in the nation's legends and myths.

Oliver Stone disputes this interpretation, claiming that he never attempted to market *Wall Street* as a broad statement about American society in the 1980s. The media seized that opportunity, he says, and made the most of it. In a fascinating discussion of the public debates about the movie, Stone ties the film's story to the memory of his father, a Wall Street broker, and to his judgments about America's effervescent economy in the age of Reagan.

The case of *JFK* represents the most notable example of Stone's impact on politics. As Michael L. Kurtz explains in this volume, Stone's powerful challenge to the Warren Commission's findings in *JFK* led Congress to press successfully for the release of thousands of pages of documents related to the assassination. Very few Hollywood filmmakers can claim that their productions helped to nudge Congress into legislative action. Furthermore, as mentioned before, *JFK* made waves through its suggestion that Kennedy would not have led the country into the nightmare of combat in Vietnam. Debates about that issue amplified impressively in the years after Stone's provocative movie appeared in the theaters.

Oliver Stone, in short, has made a significant impact on his society (and on many people living outside the country as well, for today's Hollywood movies often attract larger audiences abroad than at home). Far more than the works of most other movie directors, Stone's films have packed a substantial political and social punch.

THE QUESTION OF STONE'S POLITICAL PERSPECTIVE

Some observers have tried to identify the direction of that punch, but it is interesting to note that their conclusions have landed all over the political spectrum. They have not been able to establish a clear consensus about Stone's ideology or about his politics. Early in his career, when Stone wrote scripts for brutal, violent stories such as *Midnight Express, Conan the Barbarian, Scarface,* and *Year of the Dragon,* he established a reputation as a designer of aggressive, macho, "right-wing" movies. With pictures such as *Salvador, Platoon, Wall Street,* and *Born on the Fourth of July,* a number of critics considered him a flaming liberal, and others insisted on calling him a spokesman for the radical Left. *JFK* added to the confusion. Was Stone on the Left, taking aim at the military-industrial complex? Or was he on the Right, in league with the paramilitary types who intensely distrusted their government? With the release of *Nixon,* a somewhat sympathetic and ambiguous portrait, Stone received praise for recognizing the humanity of a rather conservative president, and some applauded him for displaying a greater degree of political balance than was evident in his previous films.

Where does Oliver Stone really stand politically? If Stone has spoken through his film productions, the answer is not simple. He is a complex artist with multidimensional and changing thoughts. It is difficult to box him into an ideological corner. Furthermore, Stone demonstrates tremendous breadth of interest in historical subjects; for instance, he coproduced *The People vs. Larry Flynt* (1996), which dealt with the court battles over obscenity led by the publisher of *Hustler,* and he cowrote the movie script for *Evita* (1997), which examined Eva Peron's controversial role in Argentine politics in the 1940s and early 1950s. The task of codifying Stone's political beliefs becomes more challenging as his historical works expand across diverse topics.

The job of drawing conclusions about Stone's social commentaries is also becoming more difficult as his movie themes proliferate. Motion pictures he released in the 1990s carried more ambiguous messages than his cinema of the 1980s. *The Doors,* for example, told a disturbing tale of the rise and fall of rock music star Jim Morrison. In the first hour, the obscure artist surges to fame and seems to reach a large measure of success with a national appearance on the *Ed Sullivan Show.* He goes downhill quickly, though, by indulging in a decadent, nihilistic, and abusive lifestyle. Morrison becomes an aimless womanizer and drug addict. His emptiness and depravity lead to an early death. What is the intended message of this emotionally taxing tragedy set in the late 1960s and early 1970s? To show us how success can ruin an individual? To make us lament the loss of a talented musician? Or is Stone's goal simply to help us recall the extraordinary times of sexual, cultural, musical, and political rebellion? Oliver Stone remains somewhat mysterious about the point of his disturbing portrait.

Perhaps the mystery is a natural reflection of Stone's own complex association with the subject. As James R. Farr explains in his essay in this book, Oliver Stone was intensely enthusiastic about Morrison when he was a young man. The Doors' music thrilled him during his days in Vietnam. Later, says Farr, Stone became fascinated with the "Dionysian" impulses exhibited by Morrison — artistic insights achieved through emotion and feeling. "Jim was Dionysus personified," says Stone, and he tried to communicate the power of the Dionysian spirit through his high-energy story and cinematography. The result gives us a view of the past that is rather different from the kind we find in books. Farr asks, "What kind of history is this?" Is it a true picture of the 1960s? Is it a real portrayal of Morrison? Is it a legitimate representation of the past? Does the movie's blending of myth and history undermine its achievement or strengthen it?

Natural Born Killers raises interesting questions, too, about Stone's purposes and achievements. Does Stone show us the despicable behavior of Mickey and Mallory to make us wake up to American culture's love affair with violent entertainment? Is he urging us to question the media's romanticizing of criminal violence and the public's apparent fascination with it? Or do we strain too hard when we claim that the movie carries important social messages? Was Stone simply attempting to entertain audiences with a shocking and stylish film that resembled *Bonnie and Clyde,* the 1967 hit about a criminal couple's strangely violent adventures?

It is, of course, helpful to know about Stone's background when attempting to interpret his perspective on American society. Stone is emotionally and personally connected to many of the themes that appear in his movies. He draws on his own past when crafting stories for the cinema. Randy Roberts and David Welky argue that Oliver Stone's experiences in Vietnam had a tremendous impact on his thinking and artistry. Stone went from presenting an autobiographical view of the war in *Platoon* to creating a sociological analysis of the American culture that supported the war in *Born on the Fourth of July* to an exploration of the political nature of the war in *JFK* and *Nixon*. Roberts and Welky also note Stone's interest in delivering a personal message about Vietnam in *Heaven and Earth*. That movie, say the authors, introduced audiences to the Vietnamese victims whose lives and culture had been ripped apart by U.S. military intervention. Roberts and Welky recognize many of the problems created by Stone's angry fascination with America's tragic history in Vietnam. Stone's polemics sometimes distorted evidence and produced simplistic explanations for complex causes. Yet Roberts and Welky also see some good coming from the emotion-laden portrayals of war issues. Stone shook our consciousness, presenting us with painful questions about the past that are difficult to answer. In boldly confronting audiences with the ghosts of Vietnam, Stone became "the most successful and controversial historian of the war," say the authors.

Le Ly Hayslip also throws light on the filmmaker's interest in Vietnam by giving us an insider's view of Stone's work in *Heaven and Earth*. Oliver Stone based the drama on her experiences growing up in Vietnam and later living in the United States. Hayslip describes the conditions that led her to write down her recollections about Vietnam (notes that later became sources for two books she published). When she moved to the United States in the early 1970s, Hayslip found that many Americans had a dark view of her country and her people. Americans she encountered in the San Diego area described Vietnam as a hellhole and referred to "gooks" in the war as if they were subhuman monsters. Hayslip believes that many Americans could not see the Vietnamese for who they were — people who wanted freedom from dominance by foreigners. U.S. intervention in Vietnam's civil war made a bad situation much worse, she observes. It led to the death of about 2 million people in her country (far more than the 58,000 Americans killed in the Vietnam War), destroyed much of the beautiful natural environment, and tore apart a traditional, village-based society.

Hayslip praises Oliver Stone's work in *Heaven and Earth* for attempting to show the beauty of the people and the land before the war destroyed so much.

The Vietnamese characters in *Heaven and Earth* were not simply enemies to be "wasted" by gun-toting American soldiers, she says. Nor were they nameless foreign figures serving as background for a story about U.S. heroes. Instead, *Heaven and Earth* put the Vietnamese people at the center of the drama, making them the protagonists who deserved audience sympathy.

Le Ly Hayslip recalls her first introduction to Oliver Stone and the way Stone drew her into his movie project. She describes her role as counselor in crafting a script, choosing sites, designing sets, and training Hiep Thi Le, the actress who played Hayslip in the movie. Hayslip offers a few personal criticisms of the production, noting its limited attention to social conditions in Vietnam and its understated portrayal of wartime atrocities. Overall, though, Hayslip gives a rather positive assessment of Stone's portrayal of her life, claiming that the filmmaker "stirred the souls of the American people, challenging their sense of morality and fairness."

THE CONTRIBUTORS' ASSESSMENT OF STONE AS A HISTORIAN

Several contributors to this volume applaud Stone for his emotionally riveting forays into history, but they also raise some serious questions about his handling of cinematic history. This is as it should be. From the beginning of this project, I hoped to find a team of contributors that would offer both strong praise and strong criticism, and I have not been disappointed. This volume includes energetic attacks on Stone's films, such as those offered by Ambrose and Schlesinger, and considerable praise, as in the essays by McGovern and Hayslip. Interestingly, a number of the authors offer both compliments and criticisms when assessing Stone's cinematic spins on history.

I commissioned all of the essays in this volume, but some of the writing began to take shape before the project evolved into a book. In my capacity as editor of film reviews for the *Journal of American History,* I secured Ambrose's essay on *Nixon.* The chapters from McGovern and Schlesinger represent expansions of remarks these individuals made in a meeting of the American Historical Association that I organized and chaired. Courtwright and Davis originally prepared their essays for a special issue on Stone's films that I edited for the journal *Film & History.* They, too, have revised and expanded their observations.

Le Ly Hayslip asked me to assist her in putting her thoughts about *Heaven and Earth* on paper. She wrote a very detailed initial draft herself. Then we held several lengthy telephone conversations, completed three revisions, and finally got the document that she wanted.

Oliver Stone agreed to comment after having an opportunity to read all the contributors' essays. (In several cases, the authors revised their drafts substantially and Stone read both versions.) Given his very demanding schedule, our original plan called for me to conduct only one interview for a few hours. Much to my surprise and delight, Stone offered much more than that.

Obviously engaged with what the contributors had written and passionately committed to setting the record straight, Stone allowed me to interview him seven times over several weeks in conversations that totaled more than twenty-one hours. He commented with great candor and considerable reflection on the contributors' views of his work. Whether he agreed or disagreed with any particular author, he consistently and patiently explained the underlying rationale for his position and used these opportunities to comment on a wide array of historical and political topics.

Needless to say, the interviews produced a mound of transcriptions, which I proceeded to pare down to a workable length. By eliminating the inevitable overlap and repetition that occur in such interviews, I condensed everything down to the most essential points. I also removed my questions to make for a much smoother reading experience — leaving only the distinctive voice of the artist. I then sent this material to Stone for his revision and clarification. Subsequent exchanges further refined the material.

Although careful readers will note some unavoidable stylistic variation in Stone's writings, ghost traces from the interview format, they are sure to be impressed with the provocative insights Stone provides into his own work and its relation to history. Readers may not always agree with Stone but will surely respect his effort to communicate with all of us. Few other American filmmakers have done as much.

Oliver Stone As Historian

For anyone who lived through the 1960s on a campus, there has to be a shock of recognition on seeing the antiwar demonstration in *Born on the Fourth of July* — a feeling that you were present at this very scene, saw these very students on the steps of a university hall with their long hair, Afros, beards, Levis, bandannas; witnessed these very gestures, the clenched fists, heard this speechifying by blacks and whites, the denunciations of war, the shouted words. Even that middle-aged figure on the steps wearing a dashiki and calling for a march on Washington looks strangely familiar — but at the same time, somehow too old and out of place. Before the tear gas bombs explode and the cops descend with swinging clubs, you may realize that this is Abbie Hoffman, King of the Yippies, saying precisely the kind of things he said at such demonstrations thirty-five years before.

The sequence is based on a real event. The film has let us know that this is Syracuse University shortly after the Cambodia "incursion" and the killings at Kent State, that moment in early May 1970 when tens of thousands of college and high school campuses went on strike. Syracuse was among them, but the demonstration there was far different from the one we see on the screen. At Syracuse, the words might have been violent, but the afternoon was peaceful; the police did not shoot off tear gas, and they did not wade into the crowd with clubs. Nor was the demonstration there attended by Ron Kovic, the hero of the film and author of the book on which it is based. Nor was it attended by his girlfriend, for he did not have a girlfriend. Nor was it addressed by Abbie Hoffman.

A creation of director Oliver Stone, this sequence is not a complete fabrication but, rather, a cunning mixture of diverse visual elements — fact, near fact, displaced fact, invention. It refers to the past, it prods the memory, but can we call it history? Surely not history as we usually use the word, not history that attempts to accurately reproduce a specific, documentable moment of the past. Yet we might see it as a generic historical moment, a moment that claims its truth by standing in for many such moments — the truth that such demonstrations were common in the late 1960s; the truth of the chaos, confusion, and violence of many such encounters between students and police; the truth of the historical questions the sequence forces viewers to confront: Why are these students gathered here? What are they protesting? Why are they so critical of our national leaders? Why do the police break up the rally with such gusto? What is at stake on the screen for our understanding of the 1960s? Of recent America? Of the United States today?

This is an essay about Oliver Stone as Historian. About how filmmakers in general and this filmmaker in particular can and do create a meaningful sense of the past. Obviously it is possible to find hundreds of films made in the last thirty years that contain images of American social, political, and cultural life, but such images do not tell us anything important unless they are pulled together into a vision or interpretation of the American past. This is where Stone comes in. He has been the contemporary American filmmaker most committed to charting the recent American past and has done so with a strong thesis about the meaning of that past. What's more, his problems both in making dramatic historical features and in thinking about what he has made are the same problems faced by every filmmaker who attempts to do history by means of dramatic historical films. The sequence from *Born on the Fourth of July* set at Syracuse University is a typical example of how the historical film creates the past, creates images of a world that is at once fiction (in the sense of being "made") and history. But it is a special kind of history that, like all forms of history across the ages, has its own particular rules of engagement with the traces of the past.

Given the way everyone has been taught history in school, the idea of history on film is not an easy one for us to accept. It is also not easy for Oliver Stone. To judge by many interviews, Stone is — or has become — as confused by the historical status of his work as everyone else. It is clear that once upon a time, he thought that what he was doing on the screen was history. At times he even had the temerity to proclaim himself a historian. Then came the years of criticism from historians and members of the press denouncing him, often viciously, for alleged inaccuracies, misrepresentations, and even lies in his films. In angry responses he first defended himself and then decried the whole notion of history, claiming that nobody really knows or can know the past. Yet at the same time he retreated toward the rules of the academic game and apparently accepted the notion (as a marketing strategy?) that the dramatic past is different from the academic one. Why else the disclaimer preceding *Nixon,* one of his later historical films, which in part reads, "Events and characters have been condensed, and some scenes among protagonists have been conjectured"?

Stone's problems with the reception of his films speak to a larger issue: is it possible to put history on film? Here I answer yes, but only by giving a particular meaning to the word "history." This meaning long predates our idea, which dates from the late nineteenth century, that history is a matter of telling the past as it really was — or, in the case of film, showing us the past as it really was. In a deeper sense, history is no more (and no less) than the attempt to recount, explain, and interpret the past, to give meaning to events, moments, movements, people, periods of time that have vanished. There is no doubt that Oliver Stone has been involved in such a process. Over the years, he has directed a body of work — *Salvador, Platoon, Born on the Fourth of July, JFK,* and *Nixon* — that consciously confronts some of the major historical issues of our time. As much as any historian who works in words, Stone has wrestled with the recent history of the United States: the 1960s, the war in Vietnam, the Kennedy assassination and what followed, the presidency of Nixon, the Watergate scandal, repeated intervention in Latin America. Doing so, he has created a powerful interpretation of contemporary American history.

To accept Stone as a historian, it is necessary to understand that the theory and practice of history today are not what they were when you went to school or when I received my Ph.D. three decades ago. For at least the last half century (and more in some quarters), the practice and truth claims of history have been under major attack from philosophers, literary and cultural theorists, postmodern critics, and historians themselves. The literature on this is too huge to deal with here, so let me only suggest that the cumulative weight of the arguments adds up to the following: Written history, academic history, is not something solid and unproblematic, and certainly not a "reflection" of a past reality, but the construction of a moral story about the past out of traces that remain. History (as we practice it) is an ideological and cultural product of the Western world at a particular time in its development when the notion of "scientific" truth, based on replicable experiments, has been carried into the social sciences, including history (where no such experimentation is possible). History is actually no more than a series of conventions for thinking about the past, and these conventions have shifted over time — from the stories of Herodotus to the scientism of von Ranke — and will obviously shift in the future. The "truth" of history resides not in the verifiability of individual pieces of data but in the overall narrative of the past and in how well that narrative engages the discourse of history — the already existing body of data and arguments on a topic.

To think about a filmmaker as a historian is to raise the larger issue of history on the screen and to move toward an investigation of the possibilities and practices of the medium. The useful questions to ask here are not the ones that every journalist seems to put to a film: Does the screen literally represent the world of the past? Does the historical film convey facts or make arguments as well as written history does? Instead, one must go to a more fundamental level and ask the following: What sort of historical world does film construct? How does it construct that world? How can we make judgments about that construction? What does that historical construction mean to us? Perhaps only after these are answered should we ask, How does the historical world on the screen relate to written history?

As a way of beginning to answer such questions, let me point to six elements that mark the historical practice of mainstream films:

1. The dramatic film tells history as a story — a tale with a beginning, a middle, and an end. A tale that leaves you with a moral message and (usually) a feeling of uplift. A tale embedded in a larger view of history that is always progressive. No matter what the historical film, be the subject matter slavery, the Holocaust, the Khmer Rouge, or the horrors of Vietnam, the message delivered on the screen is that things are getting better or have gotten better. Even a film about the Holocaust (such as *Schindler's List*) may be structured to leave us feeling, Aren't we lucky that certain people kept the flag of hope flying?

Oliver Stone's films work this way, with just enough hints at counterexamples to underline the point. At the end of *Born on the Fourth of July,* Ron Kovic remains paralyzed and in a wheelchair, and the problems stemming from the Vietnam War have hardly been solved. But as Kovic gets ready to deliver a speech to the 1972 Democratic National Convention and the music swells up, he tells a reporter, "I have the feeling we have come home," leaving the audience with the feeling that after the trauma of Vietnam, everything is okay in American once again. Even *JFK,* Stone's blackest work, with its pervasive fears about the future of American democracy, pulls the sting from its condemnations by having district attorney Jim Garrison played by Kevin Costner, a big, conservative star whose very presence tends to reassure us that the problems of the nation will soon be solved.

2. Film insists on history as the story of individuals — either men or women (but usually men) who are already renowned, or men or women who are made to seem important because they have been singled out by the camera. Those who are not already famous are common people who have done heroic or admirable things or have suffered unusually bad situations of exploitation and oppression. Putting individuals in the forefront of the historical process means that the solution of their personal problems tends to substitute for the solution of historical problems. In *Platoon* and *Born on the Fourth of July,* the experience of a single company or a single soldier is made to stand for America's Vietnam experience; in *Salvador,* the education of an American journalist becomes our education into the United States' complicity with Central American militarists.

3. Film offers us history as the story of a closed, completed, and simple past. It provides no alternative possibilities to what we see happening on the screen, admits of no doubts, and promotes each historical assertion with the same degree of confidence. Works like *Salvador, Born on the Fourth of July,* and *Nixon* do not give us time or space to think about situations or characters in any other way than what is shown. *JFK* gets away from this convention to some extent as Stone tells multiple stories and creates many interpretations of the assassination, including some that contradict each other. In a sense, a paradox lies at the heart of this work: Stone creates a certainty that there was a conspiracy but insists that it was so complex that we will never be able to understand it. (Interestingly, this anomalous feature of multiple interpretations, suggestions, or plausible alternatives was a chief source of media criticism of Stone — as if journalists and historians fear ambiguity more than misinformation.)

4. Film brings us history as experience. It emotionalizes and dramatizes the past, gives us history as triumph, anguish, joy, despair, adventure, suffering, and heroism. Doing so, it collapses the measured distance of the traditional historian's stance and suggests that emotion is an important part of our historical legacy, that somehow we can gain historical knowledge through empathy. For Stone, the issue might be too much emotion. Both *Born on the Fourth of July* and *Salvador* are harrowing in their depiction of assassination, war, social turmoil, and the treatment of veterans, harrowing too in their portrayal of the violence of intrafamilial relationships. For us, assessing this sort of experiential knowledge is difficult because emotion lies so far outside the normal historical vocabulary. But scenes like those in the veterans' hospitals certainly tell the audience something it did not know before, and tell it in a powerful and unforgettable way.

5. Film shows history as process. The world on the screen brings together things that, for analytic or structural purposes, written history often has to split apart. Economics, politics, race, class, and gender all come together in the lives and moments of individuals, groups, and nations. This characteristic of film throws into relief a certain convention — one might call it a "fiction" — of written history: the analytic strategy that fractures the past into distinct chapters, topics, and categories. Written history may treat gender in one chapter, race in another, economy in a third. It compartmentalizes the study of politics, family life, or social mobility. History in film becomes more like real life: a process of changing social relationships in which political, personal, and social questions and categories are interwoven. Ron Kovic in *Born on the Fourth of July* is at once a man, a son, a wrestler, an Anglo-American, a resident of Long Island, a Catholic, a marine, a gung-ho patriot, and an antiwar activist.

6. Film so obviously gives us the "look" of the past — of buildings, landscapes, and artifacts — that we may not see what this does to our sense of history. Certainly film provides a sense of how common objects were used. In film, period clothing confines, emphasizes, and expresses the moving body; tools, utensils, and weapons are objects that people use and misuse, and such objects can help define their livelihoods, identities, lives, and destinies. Stone is particularly good at recreating this tangible feeling of reality — the confusion of trucks and guns surrounding the assassination in *JFK*, the sight and sound of the antiwar demonstrators in *Born on the Fourth;* the shocking realism of battles in that film and in *Platoon* that led veterans to say, "That's the way it was in my Vietnam."

These six conventions are inextricably involved in the world of the past as it appears on the screen in a dramatic film. In a real sense, they both enable film to do history and impose the limits to the history that film can do. Whatever the shape of the past or the particular historical lessons brought to us on the screen, they will be shaped by the closed story, the notion of progress, the emphasis on individuals, the single interpretation, the heightening of emotional states, and the focus on the surfaces of the world.

If these conventions were not enough to ensure that history on film must be different from history on the page, there is another, even more controversial element of history on the screen: historical film invents facts. We all feel uneasy about this, including Stone, hence the disclaimers preceding his recent films. Yet it is important to remember that written history itself is not devoid of invention. The underlying convention of history is an invention, a convention, and a fiction: this is the notion that individuals, social and political movements, decades, and nations occurred in linear stories that have a beginning, a middle, and an end and are moral in their implications. Daily life and past life are, in truth, an ongoing flow of stuff. (We like to call this stuff "events," but even that word partakes of fiction, for the beginnings and endings of such events are always arbitrarily demarcated. And besides, can we really call something as complex as, say, the American Revolution an "event"?) Such stuff is so incredibly complex that we can describe only the tiniest portion of it. The notion that one can actually and truthfully tell the story of the United States or the history of the Western world or the biography of Ron Kovic is itself a fiction. What history gives us is no more than an arbitrary set of data pulled together by an ideology, a teleology, and a moral that, in the case of the story of a country or a civilization, always ends up by telling us how wonderful we are.

Fiction, invention, and creation mark all attempts to describe the past and make it meaningful. The point is not to decry them but to understand how such elements help to make history. As the antiwar demonstration sequence in *Born on the Fourth of July* suggests, the past on the screen is shot through with invention from the smallest details to the largest events. And this would be so even if Stone were attempting to recreate a specific, historically documented demonstration as accurately as possible. Consider, for example, a room in Kovic's family home on Long Island in 1965 or the battle in which he commits atrocities or the firefight in which he suffers his wound. The room and the battles have to be, at best, approximate representations that say, this is more or less the way a room might have looked in 1965; this is more or less the way the battles took place. People wore these kinds of uniforms, carried these kinds of weapons, yelled these sorts of epithets. But this is not and cannot be a precise copy of what occurred, because we can never know precisely what occurred.

The motion picture camera is greedy. It demands more particularity about the past than any historian can ever know. Invention is always necessary to fill out the specifics of a particular historical scene. It is also necessary to create a coherent (and moving) visual sequence or to create historical characters. Think of it. The very use of an actor to "be" someone is already a fiction. In giving us a historical character, the film says what cannot truly be said: that this is how this person looked, moved, and sounded. And certainly looks, movement, and sound help to create the meaning of the past. Actor Tom Cruise can be made up to resemble Ron Kovic, but at some level, viewers always know he is Tom Cruise, which means that the figure of Kovic on the screen carries a host of extra meanings (meanings we call "intertextual"). With Cruise playing Kovic, we have to know at some level that before us — at least for an audience in the United States — we have an all-American hero.

If historical settings and people on the screen necessarily involve fictional or invented elements, so do the events depicted. Incidents inevitably have to be invented by the filmmaker for a variety of reasons — to keep the story moving, to maintain intensity, to create a dramatic structure, and, above all, to allow the history to fit within time constraints (a life, a war, or a revolution, all within two hours). For historical films, different kinds of techniques are involved in this invention, techniques that we can label *Compression* (bringing together actual events that occurred in different times and places), *Alteration* (changing events slightly to highlight their underlying meaning), and *Metaphor* (using an invented image to stand for or sum up events too complex, lengthy, or difficult to depict).

As an example of *Compression,* we can consider the assassination of Archbishop Romero in *Salvador.* The film sequence brings together three historical events that took place at different times: a speech by Romero in the cathedral denouncing right-wing death squads, his assassination while giving the Eucharist in a small rural church a week later, and a gathering of the archbishop's followers at his funeral that was brutally broken up by the military. By compressing them into one sequence, the film works for the viewers and for history. It allows the hero, American journalist Richard Boyle, and thus the audience to witness these events, and it makes clear the connections between Romero's views and his assassination, as well as the complicity between the right-wing death squads and the military in El Salvador.

Alteration and *Metaphor* come together in the sequence from *Born on the Fourth of July* when Kovic, paralyzed and back home, participates as a local hero in his hometown's Fourth of July parade and then later becomes mute at a public gathering while attempting to speak to the crowd about Vietnam, his mind filled with flashbacks from the war. In truth, Kovic was one of two marines riding in the parade and sitting on the podium that day, but director Stone is obviously emphasizing the larger theme of the film — the difficulty of conveying to those who were not there the horrific experience of Vietnam and the physical and mental toll it took not just on our hero but also on Kovic as a symbol of patriotic America or, if you will, on all of us in the audience.

Another key scene in this same film works as a *Metaphor* for a psychic state that the filmmaker could express in no other way. Besides being haunted by the memory of the atrocities he committed in Vietnam, Kovic is disturbed even more by the fact that during a firefight he inadvertently killed one of his own men. One way to read his entire autobiography is as a confession of this crime (brushed aside by his military commander), an act of expiation, and a plea for forgiveness. To create images for this internal process, for the guilt that prompts Kovic to write, and for authorship itself, with its confession that works as a kind of self-forgiveness, Stone invents an entire sequence. He has Kovic visit the family of the man he shot, confess his crime to them, and, from the victim's mother, receive a tepid but real kind of forgiveness. That is what, by writing his book, Kovic received from the public at large.

Normally we think of the difference between fiction and history as this: both tell stories, but the latter is a true story. The question is, What kind of truth? A "literal" truth, an exact copy of what took place in the past? Hardly. On the printed page, a description of a battle or a revolution is not a literal rendering of that series of events. In our writing of the past, some sort of "fiction" (call it a "convention," if you will) is always involved, one that allows a sampling of reports to represent the collective experience of thousands or millions.

In part, this happens because the word works differently from the image. The word can refer to vast amounts of data in a small space. The word can generalize; talk of abstractions such as *revolution, evolution,* and *progress;* and make us believe that these things exist. But they do not exist, of course, except on the page. Such words are shorthand markers for incredibly complex processes — so complex that once the designation is given, we continue to argue over what the word actually signifies. (Witness the scholarly debates over the French Revolution, with certain major scholars essentially saying that the Revolution never took place, that it was no more than the Terror. The same debate has more recently begun over the Russian Revolution.) To talk of such things is not to talk literally but to talk in a metaphoric way about the past. Film, with its need for a specific image, cannot make general statements about revolution or progress. Film must summarize, synthesize, generalize, symbolize — in images.

Let me underline what has to be a counterintuitive point: Film, the most literal of media, does not open a window onto the past. What happens on screen is at best a distant approximation of what was said and done in the past, a series of visual metaphors that do not depict but rather point to the events of the past. A historical film always includes images that are at once invented and, at best, true — true in that they symbolize, condense, or summarize large amounts of data; true in that they impart an overall meaning of the past. Film always mixes things that did happen with things that could have happened; filmmakers compress a lot of what happened (data) to make it fit within the visual and time constraints of the medium and the form. Here is a paradox: This apparently most literal of media never delivers a literal representation of the past. It speaks about the past, it comments on it, it raises the issues of the past and tells us what those issues (can) mean. But it cannot show the past to us.

Yet history on film does not entirely cut loose from data — not if it is a serious historical film rather than a costume drama. Indeed, there are ways of judging historical films, but one cannot use the same standards that we have for written history. *Historical film must be judged not on the level of detail but at the level of argument, metaphor, symbol.* It must be judged against what we know that can be verified, documented, or reasonably argued. In other words, we must judge it against the ongoing discourse of history, the existing body of historical texts, and their data and arguments.

Any historical film, like any work of written, graphic, or oral history, enters a body of preexisting knowledge and debate. To be considered "historical" rather than simply a costume drama, a film must engage the issues, ideas, data, and arguments of that field of knowledge. A historical film does not indulge in capricious invention and does not ignore the findings and assertions of what we already know. Like any work of history, it must be evaluated in light of the knowledge of the past that we possess. Like any work of history, it situates itself within the ongoing debate over the meaning of the past.

To label Oliver Stone a historian is to say that his films engage the discourse of history and add something to that discourse. They make the past meaningful in three different ways: Stone's films, like the best works of history, *Vision*, *Contest*, and *Revision* history. These labels are hardly meant to be exclusive. Each film probably does all three to some extent, but for purposes of underlining the categories, let me deal with one of his films under each label.

To *Vision* history is to put flesh and blood on the past; to show us individuals in lifelike situations, dramatize events, give us people to identify with, make us feel to some extent as if we have lived moments and issues long gone. To vision is to give us the experience of the past, and in this film is very different from the distancing and analyzing of a written text. In *Born on the Fourth of July*, we see a small community both before and during the war; we undergo the harrowing experience of battle with its atrocities, suffer the degradations of a handicapped veteran's life, and confront the gap between the rhetoric of justification and patriotism and the reality of events in and after the war itself.

Along with *vision*, the film provides elements that are very much a part of traditional history: (1) *Born on the Fourth of July* recounts, explains, and interprets a single life and, by extension, a whole period — the American experience of Vietnam. (2) In depicting the actions and attitudes of Americans in Vietnam and afterward, the film engages and adds to the body of evidence we have about the war from other books, essays, films, and works of history. (3) It provides an original and interesting interpretation of American involvement in Vietnam by linking the high cost of blind patriotism to a certain kind of American masculinity — what might be called the John Wayne syndrome. (4) It generalizes the experiences of one man to be those of a nation, showing the way war touched not only other veterans but also civilians who lived outside the circle of experience of the war. By giving us images of a painful split in the Kovic family, the film suggests a split in the family of the nation itself.

To *Contest* history is to provide interpretations that run against traditional wisdom or generally accepted views. *Salvador* provides a good example. This is the story of a once famous photographic journalist who is now a drunk and a deadbeat. Wanting to redeem his reputation in a country he already knows and loves, he convinces a friend to go with him to El Salvador. Their stories run on parallel tracks: The journalist uncovers evidence about death squads and American complicity with the reactionary elements of the nation. His friend gradually learns how different this Central American world is from the picture provided in the press back home. They and we witness the rise of the Right, the death squad assassinations of Archbishop Romero and some American nuns, and the crushing of a leftist revolution by the military with the aid and complicity of the U.S. government.

In a sense, the story of the two men becomes symbolic not just for what happened in El Salvador in the early 1980s but also for the whole thrust of American anticommunist foreign policy, with its history of covert actions. By telling the story obliquely, through the eyes of these two Americans, Stone engages the debates about American foreign policy since World War II. The critique made by the film is rarely expressed outside history books written by leftists or published by the small radical press: that anticommunism is a cover for American corporate profits and for U.S. military and secret intelligence power; that in the name of this anticommunism the United States has joyfully played a basically antidemocratic role throughout the Western Hemisphere, supporting killers and thugs who masquerade their own self-interest behind anticommunism. Agree or disagree, this is at once a legitimate and an exceedingly contestable interpretation of history rendered for the general public.

To *Revision* history is to show us the past in new and unexpected ways, to utilize an aesthetic that violates the traditional, realistic ways of telling the past, that does not follow a normal dramatic structure, or that mixes genres and modes. Stone's best example is *JFK,* a film that re-visions history through both its form and its message — which are inextricably linked. (The violent objections to the work have had to do with both.) The film does not, of course, tell the story of JFK in office but of the assassination and its aftermath. Rejecting the Warren Commission findings that Lee Harvey Oswald was the lone assassin, the film explores the question of who was really responsible for the president's death. To do so, it recounts the events — real, possible, and imagined — that lie behind the assassination; explains them as part of a major conspiracy at the highest levels of the U.S. government; and interprets this conspiracy as one set in motion by various people, groups, agencies, and companies that had much to gain economically from the continuation of the cold war and the hot war (in Vietnam) against communism. The driving force in the film is New Orleans district attorney Jim Garrison, a stand-in for all people of goodwill who believe in democracy and want the truth to be uncovered.

To put a label on it, *JFK* may be seen as a work of modernist or postmodernist history. It presents events from competing perspectives; it mixes film stocks (black and white, color, and video), idioms, genres, and period styles (documentary, Soviet montage, Hollywood naturalism, domestic melodrama) to represent the variety of contexts in which the event occurs. It suggests competing possibilities for what happened, thereby emphasizing the artificial and provisional reconstruction of any historical reality. In a sense, *JFK* both questions history as a mode of knowledge and asserts our need for it. Garrison questions witnesses, ferrets out documents, and tries out theories, seeking the truth and at the same time showing that truth is impossible to find. History in the film thus becomes an unstable mix of fact, fiction, truth, and illusion, a fragmentation of contexts, motives, beliefs, and rumor. *JFK* leaves us with the feeling that we live in a dangerous national security state that is out of the people's control, a state of hidden powers that control national and international events — including the assassination.

The engagement of Oliver Stone with the discourse of history cannot be accidental. His works have a conscious thesis about the past, almost always stated at the outset in a montage or a speech or some image that lets us know that great public issues are at stake. *JFK* opens with President Eisenhower's farewell address, with its warning about the dangers of the growing military-industrial complex. *Salvador* begins with a montage of slaughter and terror that comes to symbolize the betrayal of democratic elements in that country. Early in *Born on the Fourth of July*, Ron Kovic's family gathers to hear President Kennedy's inaugural address, with its call for Americans to bear the burden, to pay any price to defend democracy. In all these works, the following dramatized history plays out this early thesis.

In Stone, you also find a larger, cumulative body of meaning. Taken together, his films create a kind of collective historical argument about contemporary America. Central to his historical vision is the assassination of his hero, JFK. (Like any historian, Stone can be contradictory, for *Born on the Fourth of July* seems to point to Kennedy's rhetoric and stance as the cause of the Vietnam War.) He goes on to suggest that the U.S. government is out of control or in the hands of secret agencies, that lots of things being done in the name of the American people are criminal, that our democratic heritage and institutions serve as a kind of ideology to cover the activities of greedy men and scoundrels. One may ask, Is this a true picture of America? Nobody can answer such a question for anyone else, but certainly enough evidence has become available since Vietnam — of assassinations, secret wars, Watergate, Iran-contra, the recent allegations concerning CIA involvement in crack cocaine — to say that this portrait is at least a historically plausible interpretation.

To what extent does Stone himself believe this interpretation? In truth, there is a kind of running contradiction in his historical work. In interviews and in his films, he sometimes insists on the chaotic, multiple, relativist nature of history — in essence, on the impossibility of telling the truth of the past. But this does not prevent him from going ahead and telling us stories that carry the force of truth. Indeed, more than simply storytelling, Stone uses the past for the purpose of delivering certain kinds of truths about our national life. In his insistence on the moral lessons of history, he is exceedingly traditional.

Stone's dilemma springs from a simple human problem: he wants to have it both ways without having to reconcile the differences. He wants to get the history right, yet he knows that such a task is essentially impossible. Perhaps this is why, in a film such as *JFK,* form seems to be at war with content — the razzle-dazzle multiple realities of the montage at odds with the limp realism of the domestic drama. Stone's sense that history is not a single story also can run against his notion that it is important to tell the truth of the past. This dilemma may be why he appears to be angry in so many interviews about whether his works should be labeled history or fiction. Often he tacks back and forth, claiming at one moment that he is a historian, then saying that he is only an entertainer. It is as if he dimly recognizes the dilemma and, stymied by the contradiction, occasionally bursts into verbal violence, saying things like, "Who knows what history is? It's just a bunch of stories people tell each other around the campfire."

My suggestion is that history also resides in the kinds of works Stone has created for the screen. Given a society in which reading, particularly serious reading about the past, is increasingly an elitist endeavor, it is possible that such history on the screen is the history of the future. Perhaps in a visual culture, the truth of the individual fact is less important than the overall truth of the metaphors we create to help us understand the past. Fact has not always been the primary tool for telling the past. The truth of facts was never very important to griots in Africa or to history makers in other oral cultures. Maybe Oliver Stone is a kind of griot for a new visual age. He is, in a sense, making history by making myths, making myths by wanting to tell truths, wanting the myths he recounts to have a truth value. And they do, but not the literal truths of the history of a scientific age as expressed in print. The problem Stone and other filmmakers face is real: How do you make the past serious to a large audience? How do you communicate lessons from the past to a public in a postliterate age? Surely public history in the future is less likely to be propagated by scholarly monographs than by stories presented on the large and small screens.

However we think of it, we must admit that film gives us a new sort of history, what we might call history as vision. Its earliest predecessor, oral history, tended to create a poetic relationship to the world. Then, over a 2000-year period, written history created an increasingly linear, scientific relationship. Film changes the rules of the game and creates its own sort of truth, creates a multilevel past that has so little to do with language that it is difficult to describe adequately in words. Certainly the historical world created by film is potentially much more complex than written text. On the screen, several things occur simultaneously — image, sound, language, even text — elements that support and work against one another to create a realm of meaning as different from written history as it was from oral history. So different that it allows us to speculate that the visual media may represent a major shift in consciousness about how we think about our past. If this is true, then it may well be that a historian like Oliver Stone is doing much more than showing us images of recent America. He is also probing the possibilities for the future of our past.

Stone on Stone's Image

(As Presented by Some Historians)

"CINEMATIC HISTORIAN"

Over the years, numerous articles have asserted that I think of myself as a "cinematic historian." That assertion has been carelessly picked up by several authors in the present volume. So, let me make this as plain as I possibly can: *I do not think of myself as a cinematic historian now or ever and, to the best of my knowledge, have not made that claim.*

My staff and I conducted an exhaustive search through my existing files dating back to *Salvador* (1985–1986) and found no direct quote describing myself as a "cinematic historian." The only such description we can trace comes from a 1991 interview with Stephen Talbot in *Mother Jones* that assigns me that description in a sentence reading, "Oliver Stone readily describes himself as a 'cinematic historian,' but insists: 'I don't believe in official history. I don't accept the scenario of the JFK assassination we've been given, or the version of Vietnam foisted upon us.'"[1]

Without context, it is not clear whether I volunteered this description of myself in a playful moment or whether the writer used it to describe me and the quotation marks are meant to define the category to which I belong — for example, "bowling expert," "butterfly collector," "self-professed radical," and the like. The real point is that in repeated interviews and quotes, from *Salvador* and *Platoon* in 1986 through *JFK* in 1991 and *Nixon* in 1995, my files continually refer to my work and to me in terms of my being a dramatist, *mixing fact and fiction* — the fiction, I emphasized, based on a combination of research, intuition, and my private conscience — in the tradition of historical dramatists before me, admitting that no one can get behind the closed doors of history and hear the actual dialogue of its participants. I remember once, when describing for the nth time what I tried to do, saying that it was something akin to what Shakespeare and the Greek dramatists had done. The *New York Times* correspondent wrote, in an article on *Nixon* in December 1995, that my hubris was such that I would *compare* myself with Shakespeare. This was hardly the case at all, but sometime there's just no way you can get your point across in this critical age except by a false modesty that is hypocritical at best but seems to serve the leveling demands of our media.

I again went far out of my way to describe the actual liberties taken by the screenwriters for *JFK* and *Nixon* by cowriting two long, mostly unreviewed, books.[2] Few filmmakers have taken the time and energy to do this, but it is precisely because of the many misquotes and misinterpretations of my work that I revealed the context of my speculations as a dramatist.

In any case, this dubious quote — "cinematic historian" — in the well-meaning *Mother Jones* interview was quickly picked up the same month by George Lardner, the national security reporter for the *Washington Post* and long a defender of the Warren Commission. He used this description as a bludgeon to discredit and ridicule the film in a long Sunday front-page cultural essay. This first story about *JFK* was quickly picked up and reinterpreted by other publications, blindly damning our enterprise some nine months before the film's release. Lardner was, without inquiring, working from a copyrighted and illegally obtained first draft of the script, while we were shooting draft six or seven at the time. Thereafter, "cinematic historian" was repeated ad nauseam and is found in several essays in this book. Thus history is made, and thus my frustration at ever trying to set the record somewhat straighter. Forgive me — and I am being falsely modest — *if I try*. It is my right, because at stake is the meaning of my life, my name, and ultimately my integrity as a man, not only to myself and my children but also to those who might still be interested in my work in the future. There is little I value higher.

"DEFINING SPIRIT"

Let me also put to rest another myth regarding how I view myself and my work. I have never explicitly designed any of my films to "represent the defining spirit of an age." Yet a number of commentators, including authors Martin Fridson *(Wall Street)* and James Farr *(The Doors)* in this volume, have perpetuated that erroneous assumption.

Jim Farr repeatedly cites my claim that the Doors was the quintessential rock band of the 1960s. We have, however, found no such quote in my research files. Perhaps he is taking his lead from press accounts of the film, which have a tendency to exaggerate the intentions of my films far more, I think, than any of the supposed inaccuracies in my work. Regardless, Farr should check his facts more carefully. Time and again I said that the Doors was a dark-side band, on the edge, and that the far-ranging Beatles was without doubt the mainstream band of the 1960s. I likened the Doors to an Americanized version of the Rolling Stones. Farr does, however, say some very interesting things about Dionysian history with which I agree.

Concerning *Wall Street,* once again there is no statement to the effect that I thought the movie represented "the defining spirit of the 1980s." To me, it was about the quantum leap American society took in that decade. I first noticed the phenomenon as I was writing and researching *Scarface* in 1981–1982 in Miami — that Wall Street was acquiring the same get-rich-quick characteristics of the young drug profiteers in Miami. Kids fresh out of business school were making hundreds of thousands of dollars in their twenties, showing off expensive lifestyles, and buying into ridiculous, material extensions of themselves. The computer age was indeed beginning, and the movie was about that wild shot of upward mobility that came to be identified, I believe, with the spirit of Reaganism in America — "Joy in the morning!" The brokers I came to know were perhaps more educated than their dope-dealing counterparts in Miami, yet they reflected a similar lack of ethos, not thinking beyond the present, hedonistic moment of money, money, and more money.

My father, who had been a stockbroker since the 1930s and wrote a respected, internationally translated economic newsletter, would have been astounded, had he lived past 1985, at the volume of shares traded each day. Contrary to Fridson's beliefs about my knowledge, my father told me many stories of various crooks throughout his decades on the Street, particularly the infamous Jimmy Ling of the 1960s. It was well known to me that people had been embezzling fortunes for years, but in the 1980s, I believe the get-rich-quick concept was extended on a far broader scale to young people. The MBA became the chosen Holy Grail of the college graduate, as entertainment and Internet companies would be in the 1990s.

My father often complained to me that Hollywood movies dealt unrealistically with Wall Street, that capitalists were misunderstood and too easily pictured as "bad guys." Utilizing newfound capacities after the success of *Platoon,* I quickly plunged into making what I hoped would be a business movie my father would be proud of. I paid homage in interviews to Robert Wise's *Executive Suite* (1954) and saw myself as continuing in that tradition of making a movie that would be honest to contemporary business. But again, I made no special claims as to the movie's authenticity when it was released, as it was very clear to me from the large amounts of research my cowriter, Stanley Weiser, and I did that the facts were, as usual, elusive in questions of money and how it is made and lost. And the more people we interviewed, the more we heard stories that were not necessarily unified in their depiction of Wall Street. Thus, I find some of Fridson's monopolizing interpretations a little pretentious.

Some media certainly exalted *Wall Street* into this category of "the 1980s movie" and suggested that Gordon Gekko's speech about greed was a defining emblem of the "decade of greed." But the media, as we all know by now, like situations that are dramatic, often hyperbolic, and as I have come to learn, they often put or distort words in my mouth, setting me up in a sense as a "straw man" to be easily promoted or attacked in the name of selling papers. I often found phrases like "the self-announced," "self-anointed," or "self-proclaimed interpreter of the 1960s, 1980s, Vietnam," and so forth used to describe me, claims I have not made, much less thought. I wonder where they come up with that horrid, entrapping word — "self-proclaimed." By its very nature, it makes the person described sound smug and unsympathetic. I often see that word employed, not just about me. As far as I know, I never proclaimed anything. I offered my interpretations, sometimes in strong words — but proclamations, according to my history, are made by kings.

"JUST A MOVIE"

Another example of this fraudulence lies in the work of columnists such as Maureen Dowd on the revamped *New York Times* editorial page under Howell Raines. Dowd claimed that I was unwilling to accept responsibility for my work by saying that it was, after all, "just a movie." She never directly stated this as coming from my mouth but implied that this was my true feeling. Perhaps Dowd was confused by *Newsweek*'s December 23, 1991, article on *JFK*, wherein the critic counters Alfred Hitchcock's famous dictum "it's only a movie" with the statement "no movie is just a movie" in referring to my film. Dowd used this method again in her attack on *Nixon.*

The truth is, I have always taken responsibility for my movies and have never said anything as irresponsible and pathetic as "it's just a movie." The editorial page of the *New York Times* has refused to print any column or letter of rebuttal that I have written since 1991, thereby allowing me to be easily misunderstood and set up as a straw man with a conspiratorial mind-set. Howell Raines and Brent Staples have written that I point to a vast conspiracy in *JFK*, and then, along with other "interpreters" of the film, they claim my film represents Lyndon Johnson as one of the killers of John Kennedy — *which the film does not state* (see page 283 in my essay on *JFK*).

If anything, I see myself as somewhat of a passionate blunderer who puts his foot in the proverbial dog shit now and then because the contemporary subjects I've dealt with are complicated and the central facts generally unagreed upon. But until someone else comes along and is willing to have his reputation ripped apart by those who have inherited the vulture's nature, I fear these shadows will continue to circle me. And even if an "Oliver Stone type" were not around, I think these modern creatures of an old venom, disguised as protectors of our history, would find one. Seriously, when was the last time you read an impartial review of a serious book attacking the Warren Commission's conclusions in the *New York Times?*

The American media have also praised my efforts. Some have understood and empathized deeply; but the shadow of acceptance is still a long way away. Some just don't see the world the way I see it or, as the Indians say, have not walked in my moccasins. Some never went to Vietnam, some didn't grow up like I grew up, and some don't in any way share my subjective views or interpretations of history. Some simply have not liked me because they've already formed an impression of me from other media. For instance, I'm a war veteran, stand six-feet tall, have very black hair, eyes, and brows, and some think I can be very intimidating looking. I try to play this down on TV, as I realize I have that effect on people. If I were five foot five and looked like Woody Allen, I don't think people would think me such a threat. At first, when I jumped up into the ranks of directors in 1986 after fifteen tough years of rejection, I may well have said some things and made some decisions that were brash and easily misunderstood, which I now regret. It took me years to truly understand and negotiate the treacherous byways of this modern media state with its endless capacity for echo, but by that time, it seemed it was too late. The simplicity with which people are characterized in a fast-food, fast-think culture is amazing and, I think, detrimental to the public good. Gradually I came to feel that I was carrying several miles of historic chains on neo-Promethean shoulders, when in fact, the person that I am — who wakes up each day, the person I *know* — travels a lot more lightly, on moccasins mostly, as did the Indian spirits of old — that is, on my best days.

ROSENSTONE AND OTHER CRITICS

While I appreciate Robert Rosenstone's examination of my work, in a few important places he damns me thoroughly when he denigrates my integrity as an individual, saying things like, "Stone tacks back and forth, claiming at one moment he is a historian, and another saying he is only an entertainer." In his introduction, Robert Toplin sums up my critics' view of changing the details of Ron Kovic's life in *Born on the Fourth of July* by claiming that "[Stone] deceives audiences." Deceives? Is it not clear by this alone that the power of words is akin to that of the camera in its ability to "deceive" the reader? (see my specific responses to these accusations about *Born on the Fourth of July* on pages 236–37).

Illusion is what they once called it, the magic eye, when filmmakers stared at the first projectors. If you can create an illusion of 10,000 troops by using 1,000 troops, is that a deception, or is it an artful recreation, or both? Yet the association of the word "deceive" sets up the idea that somehow the artist is morally evil. I find this to be a reckless accusation. The profession of drama is a legitimate profession, or art form, by any standard. From the day I first wrote a screenplay, I knew I was employing attractive actors, makeup, hair, set design, and so forth — that I could create more from little, making something from nothing. I'm proud of that. I see it not as deception but as mastery of an art form. In a film you can create the illusion of having been in Vietnam, or at Dealey Plaza, or inside the White House with Nixon. In a film, you can take a Welsh actor like Anthony Hopkins, build a false nose on him, change his hair and brows, and create the illusion of Nixon — not the real Nixon, but a Nixon that will be believed by your audience. You trust in the imagination of the audience.

Toplin addresses the critics' point with a question: "And if we are to tolerate this fudging of small details, ask the critics, how can we be sure that a filmmaker like Stone will not fudge larger ones as well?" All dramatists, by necessity, fudge the details. The previously mentioned books on the making of *JFK* and *Nixon* explained in depth what we combined, condensed, and collapsed. But did I ever claim that it was my right or intention to "fudge" the larger details, the things that matter? No, I never did, nor even thought in this manner. To do so would have stunk of dishonesty and ideology. Especially now, having been through so many accusations about my integrity these past thirteen-some years, I'm perhaps overcareful, too much so to strike with the necessary lightning fist of the dramatist, now spent in "the slough of information."

Anyone who knows history knows that one must deconstruct who the author is and from where he comes. I think of Charles Dickens and his view of the French Revolution in *A Tale of Two Cities,* the aristocratic Leo Tolstoy and his perception of Russian history, his disdain for Napoleon, and his willingness to put words in the mouths of his real and unreal characters alike. Frank Capra was, I believe, closer to the truth in his films of the 1930s than any other director. They shared with the audience the frightening sense that fascism could easily come into being in this country. And it almost did when a cabal of oligarchs on Wall Street, with some military backing, sought to overthrow President Franklin Roosevelt in 1933–1934 (for details of this astounding intended coup, see pages 289–90). I think of William Shakespeare and Julius Caesar. I think of Sergei Eisenstein and his lens on the Russian Revolution. I think of Oskar Schindler: was he really similar to the actor who portrayed him, Liam Neeson —a strong, conflicted human being, empathetic to a humanity that included the Jews — or was he, as some claim, a typically greedy Nazi businessman making money off the war and trying to survive? I think of David Lean and Robert Bolt and their *Lawrence of Arabia* and that I didn't necessarily believe their movie after seeing it. Only the literal-minded do so. I knew that it was a movie, but it inspired me to go out and read T. E. Lawrence's *The Seven Pillars of Wisdom,* which charts the enigmatic soul of the man. I learned, among other things, the obvious differences between life and art. Peter O'Toole is about six foot three, while T. E. Lawrence was about five foot four. It is true that he was not at the Turkish massacre dramatized in the film, but the facts do bear out that Lawrence, by his own perception, was becoming the creature of bloodlust Bolt depicted. But ultimately it is *you,* the student of history, who should read for yourself and discover what is true. Never base your views on one movie, one historian, one dramatist, one ideology, or one perception, no matter how seductive or convincing the messenger. Life is far too ambiguous. Allow your natural sense of judgment, generosity, and empathy to prevail. You could certainly say that *Born on the Fourth of July* presented a "debatable biography" of Ron Kovic's life. But Ron cries when he sees it. Why? I think because he recognizes that "thing" in the movie that may not be his exact life but is something he is very close to.

Rosenstone says: "He [Stone] even had the temerity to proclaim himself a historian." I've dealt with this faux criterion in the preceding pages, but, as in bogus history become nightmare, this misrepresentation has led to years of criticism from historians and the media. Some of these critics go further and accuse me of lying.

Lies imply intent to conceal. My understanding is that a dramatist is working to achieve what he perceives to be the truth. To imagine myself as a dramatist lying with an ideological or financial purpose in mind, as Stephen Ambrose paints me in his short and harsh essay, is revolting. First of all, I have no overriding ideology beyond that of, let's say, "common sense." Second, I have limited ability in financial affairs, beyond its survivalist qualities, and in starting up many of my own risky movies have turned down many far more lucrative "for-hire" offers. And last, I would not know *how* to motivate a convincing drama from an ideology. My method of working has generally been the same. After finding a protagonist, be it Jim Garrison, Ron Kovic, Le Ly Hayslip, Jim Morrison, or Richard Nixon, I seek to create a believable, empathetic (if not sympathetic) central character who dominates the foreground and takes us into the background of his or her time. That background, which involves social history, grows on us as the result of the inductive behavior of the protagonist — that is to say, it is the protagonist's choices that guide us through the maze of the history of that time, but those choices do not necessarily *define* the time. You follow Garrison through his version of the JFK murder, realizing that his actions were an aberration against the conformity of the time. You follow Kovic through *his* Vietnam and *his* return to the United States. You follow Le Ly Hayslip through *her* Vietnam in *Heaven and Earth,* and you follow my own journey in *Platoon.*

Contrary to Rosenstone's claim of my excusing myself by saying I'm "only an entertainer," I have never said that in such a context or as an excuse, because I have never thought that way. I believe there is more to my films than their entertainment value. I have written and directed with the purpose of seeking out the truth as best I can, using the tools of the dramatist. In that regard, Rosenstone might allow me the amplitude of context in quotes on such matters. I guarantee that you can take anybody out of context — *anybody* — including Rosenstone and Toplin, quote them, and make a fool of them.

Rosenstone, in another instance, paraphrases me, and while still out of context, here's the actual quote: "What is history? Some people say it's a bunch of gossip made up by soldiers who passed it around a campfire. . . . The nature of human beings is that they exaggerate. So, what is history? Who the f____ knows?"[3] I was speaking to a reporter who printed that sentence as a snappy sound bite. It certainly makes me look like I disdain historians, which I do not, and that is one of the reasons I accepted Toplin's invitation to speak at the American Historical Association meeting in New York in January 1997 — I wanted to address these misunderstandings.

When you hear my response in context, you might understand that my intention was to illustrate the ambiguity of history as passed down from generation to generation. I have come to believe that much of what we hear of history is the elitist "official version," provided by men of wealth and power with money to afford the costs of widespread communication and, thus, the dissemination of their point of view. But what of the little men of history, the foot soldier, the Good Soldier Schweik? In recent French deconstructivist schools of thought, we have read of the worlds of the village plowman and farmer and worker, the man who experiences history in a totally different way from the owner, student, or historian for that matter. I know from my own personal experiences as a foot soldier, merchant marine sailor, assistant cocoa salesman, taxi driver, messenger boy, New York City temp worker, and high school teacher in Vietnam that there are many things unknown to the ordinary citizen outside the professions I've worked in. I also know that many events that do not fit the pattern the historian is seeking to superimpose *are omitted.* I also know that whenever two people get together in a room and talk about an old battle they fought in, there is a natural human tendency to exaggerate the pathos and the pain. It's human — people like to feel good about themselves. Thus I am skeptical of the memoirs of famous men such as Henry Kissinger, because at the end of the day, he is justifying himself; or of the supposed World War II histories of Stephen Ambrose, the most popular deductivist historian of the moment, who has not seen a nanosecond of actual combat and writes of it with great conviction. But how in the world could he ever be sure in differentiating the true from the false in these accounts?

It is ego that drives the world more than money, and ego is what destroyed Kissinger's political life. I, too, am justifying myself in my own way here. Therefore, be skeptical, but be open to my argument as well.

Rosenstone suggests that I've devised a fraudulent marketing strategy for my films. Stone has "apparently accepted the notion (as a marketing strategy?) that the dramatic past is different from the academic one. Why else the disclaimer preceding *Nixon,* one of his later historical films, which in part reads, 'Events and characters have been condensed, and some scenes among protagonists have been conjectured'?"

Well, for one, I put a disclaimer at the front of *Nixon* — and only *Nixon* — because there had been so much wasted energy and misunderstanding over *JFK.* But Rosenstone need look no further than studio policy for the real answer. At some studios it is the company's policy — or the insurance company's — to have a disclaimer. Warner Brothers, where *JFK* was made, does not, in general, use disclaimers. This is its legal right, and I felt no hesitation about it, given that, in numerous interviews at the time and in the press materials attached to the film when it was first shown at media screenings, I made it clear that the film was a blend of speculative fiction and facts, many of which were unagreed upon. The catchphrase of *JFK* was "the story that won't go away"; the copy at times also stated: "He's a District Attorney. He will risk his life, the lives of his family, everything he holds dear for the one thing he holds sacred . . . the truth." The advertising never said this *was* the truth, and I *never* endorsed the notion that we were presenting the solution to this crime; *searching* for the truth was the right phrase.

What, in the end, is a dramatist to do to satisfy all naysayers? Include extensive footnotes discerning fact from fiction, to be read in the dark during or at the end of the film; or denote the fiction parts with little smears or smudges over the heads of the actors? I put out the highly annotated (and largely unreviewed) books I previously mentioned on *JFK* and *Nixon,* with numerous pro and con essays. But in the latter case, many sloppy historians and journalists indicated to their audiences that this was the first instance of my doing so — as an example, I suppose, of my remorse — entirely ignoring the existence of the previous book on *JFK*. And by the way, Rosenstone's comment almost makes me laugh, as I am probably one of the worst amateurs at marketing, which I don't really understand and have failed at more than I have succeeded. Several ridiculous critics in mainstream publications have even suggested that I deliberately manufactured the *JFK* controversy to sell the film, or have hinted at some dark scheme on Disney's part to refurbish the Nixon image through my film. That's almost as ludicrous as Martin Fridson faulting me for knowing there was going to be a stock market crash in October 1987 and thus taking advantage of it (see my response on page 232). In any event, most of the top directors can legally "consult" the financing entity, but, truly, most of us have no powers of approval over marketing. It's considered too important a job to be left to "the talent."

Yet the Maureen Dowds of the world will say things like, "But when asked about some blatant twisting of facts, he argues that it's just a movie."[4] That's cleverly put. The quote is not in my mouth, thus she cannot be sued for defamation, but this (along with adjectives such as "blatant") is an excellent example of how journalism has debased itself these last twenty years. I see this verbal assassination going on quite a lot now, and I truly think these people are shortsighted and miss the most important point of all, the point that has kept me going for some fifteen years of moderate fame through thick and thin and allowed me, in spite of a truly horrible press, to feel good about myself. That moment comes when kids come up to me with an innocent respect and mutter embarrassed things like, "Your movie is the most important movie I ever saw! It really hit me in the gut. It made me want to go back and read more about everything that happened back then. I even went to the library (or bought books) and I learned a lot." Or with rushed, adolescent wonder say things such as: "I don't think it was so much the Kennedy thing, I don't really know what happened, but the movie opened up something in me. We don't really get the truth, there's another reality underneath." Sometimes it's simply a wave and a passing shout of encouragement: "Don't let the bastards get you down, Mr. Stone! You're doing a great job!" Or in Ireland once: "Keep on rockin', you rollin' Stone!" Things like this, little miracles, have happened to me over and over through the years and give me a true feeling that I have done some right, not this great wrong the media assign me.

In any case, I will try to continue as an inductive thinker, as difficult as it may be. When we were discovered to be working on a Martin Luther King, Jr., project (rarely have we given out a press statement), I was immediately criticized in major media for *even contemplating making the film*. Many know-it-alls remarked in belittling terms that King was my next "conspiracy opus"; yet few of these high-level reporters bothered to call and ask what kind of movie it might actually be. Separate sets of writers, who worked with me for almost two years, went down to talk to those who were involved with King. The last solo writer, Kario Salem, returned sure that there was *no* conspiracy. He sat with me over time and gave me many details, and as I had never researched the subject in depth, I listened and gave him the benefit of the doubt. His final script was entirely *without a conspiracy*, except for a minor one among the Ray brothers.

Here's a typical example of my being led to a conclusion by a young, intelligent screenwriter. I had no ax to grind with those who may have murdered King, unless I was sure in my gut. But the point I'm trying to make is how outrageous *Time, USA Today*, and the other publications were when they started going on about how Stone was making another conspiracy film for profit. Soon thereafter, partly because of this extensive and negative prejudgment in the media, the project was rejected by the studios. We still hope to find the right home for it and make it.

Why, if I were the deductive thinker Rosenstone paints, would I be empathetic to Richard Nixon as a figure of tragedy? One day I hope to make a film about Martin Luther King, Jr., because he is a great and worthy subject for a film. And if I do, I will then deepen my own knowledge through my own research and go as far as I can in pursuit of the truth, as seen through my eyes.

A similar prejudgment occurred at a major television network when it was found out that we were working on TWA 800 as part of a larger news concept. Most media reported our project once again as a "conspiracy show" dealing only with TWA 800 (which was incorrect). James Kallstrom, chief investigator for the FBI in the case, was quoted as saying that I was "a bottom-dweller profiting off the tragedies of others," without a clue as to what we were up to — which, unlike Kallstrom's comments, was actually something inductive in nature, interviewing numerous people who actually *saw* the crash and whose testimony was ignored by Kallstrom's FBI. Within a few days of Kallstrom's widely published and despicable comments, our show was abruptly canceled after six months in development. I didn't abandon it because it lacked a conspiracy. Not at all.

To me, finally, the King project was a great story about *a man under pressure.* There were many problems with King's life story besides the lack of a conspiracy (if in fact there wasn't one). There were problems of his nature and the demands of duty and sacrifice, which I thoroughly respect. He was no saint, and I am told that many African Americans would be offended by this portrait. They are not ready to accept the humanization of a martyr, especially coming from a white director. That may be true for some, but somehow in my gut I feel that the American people are diminished and underestimated by saying such things. Even if we were to go into King's woman-loving nature, it is far more exaggerated now because of Hoover's deceitfulness than it ever really was. But there was certainly some semblance of a serious relationship. And in these types of things people get hurt, and no doubt it would've been very painful for the widow and the children. But, as in the Kennedy case, I believe the public arena is better served by the revelation of the true, but realistic, greatness of Martin Luther King, Jr.

HISTORY, HISTORIANS, FILM, AND POLITICS

Let's face it — any historian knows that jealousy plays a huge factor in human affairs. We're especially vulnerable here in Hollywood in a public fantasy business that is fodder for the media. The outside world thinks of us all as rich and irresponsible. But the truth is, many of us work long hours (sixty- to eighty-hour weeks for some directors) and are harried by the pressure to make films pleasing to large audiences within an expensive financial structure. I think many historians, whether they know it or not, are equally subject to this jealousy, and, thinking that history is their territory only, they come at filmmakers with an attitude of hostility. To them we pervert the paradigm with emotion, sentimentality, and so on. But historians exhibit much pomposity when they think that they alone are in custody of the "facts," and they take it upon themselves to guard "the truth" as zealously as the chief priests of ancient Egypt; the prophecies must belong to them and them alone. I don't think anyone who knows of the jealousies extant in any cerebral profession, be it history or filmmaking, will question the petty infighting that results each year for prizes, awards, and tenure — all at the expense of true investigation or creation.

In the matter of journalism as well, we must wonder how a young journalist in this day and age can advance up the corporate ladder by further investigating the long-ago Kennedy assassination, now a home for the "nuts" and other "cranks and conspiracy theorists" so easily lampooned by the mainstream media. When was the last time you heard anyone come at the Kennedy assassination without a preconceived opinion, often shaped more by attitude than any real knowledge of the facts? The opinion of an event has now become more important than the event itself. The evidence comes last.

It amazes me that young people coming out of journalism schools, without much life experience, are so easily handed the power of the pen to injure, harm, or destroy the reputations of people older than themselves, often with concoctions of rumor, lies, and some truth. If the First Amendment is so precious — and it is — so is the right to be "expressed" or represented correctly, which may require a little more thought before we write or speak. Why does a medical student, a lawyer, a broker, or a pilot struggle hard to win a license to operate, and not a journalist? A journalist's license, like one for driving a car without killing anybody, should *at least* show that the student has the mental capacity to write the same story from several different viewpoints, displaying an awareness of the prismatic aspects of our human reality; he should display an ability to sustain the contradictions of life. The journalist's "license," in reality, can be as deadly to the life and soul of his target as any similar mistake of the mind coming from the scalpel of the surgeon, the judgment call of a lawyer, pilot, or broker. The media in this country, with profit driving them, have become so viciously competitive that now even fact-checking is often *not* done to save money. In this decade of trivia, I've noticed the growing practice in mainstream publications of *not even consulting* the written-about parties for their point of view on the alleged rumors involving them. Thus, a very lazy, sensationalistic sort of journalism — printing the lie when the truth is not as colorful — has slipped into the capitalist system, violating all tenets of the Jeffersonian creed that proclaimed, without any obfuscation, that we had an inalienable right to *the privacy of our own conscience,* which, I believe, is linked to the inalienable right to have our private conscience truly and fairly *expressed* if publicized or attacked. This should be a *credo* for the twenty-first century: if intelligence is to win out over ignorance in the culture war now raging, the journalist on the front lines must begin to act responsibly.

I have learned from my own personal travels to Europe and Russia, Vietnam and the rest of Asia, that much of our journalistic reportage is ambivalent at best. It is certainly self-interested and largely pro-American — often ignoring the points of view of our sister nations. On the domestic side, I will go to a ball game, see it with my own eyes, and read a different version of it the next morning in the sports page (e.g., the turning point was different, player X did great, player Y was a bum). Movies about history are similarly disputed. I mentioned *Lawrence of Arabia* earlier, which was unfavorably reviewed by many, one of whom called it a "camel opera." They said that many of the events never happened — that Lawrence was never at the massacre of the Turks. And it's true, he wasn't. But the film's power encouraged me to read T. E. Lawrence's *The Seven Pillars of Wisdom,* thereby increasing my awareness of the man and his time.

Thus the movies can serve as a first draft of knowledge for those who are seriously interested. But are we supposed to diminish our entire culture so the nonserious and the literal among us can receive their PG-13 version of history? Do we make films for adults or children? Do we simplify our society's varied cultures and standards to the mind of the child or the lowest common denominator of society? Are films supposed to be for everyone? Can't they be for those who understand them?

Some people say that Hollywood brainwashes young minds. Not really. Movies, if they're any good, raise questions and inspire students to find out more. Stephen Ambrose criticized *Nixon* from this perspective. His books show a historian who I would say is "proper" but loathes to dwell in the darker shadows that were woven through Nixon's life. Ambrose gives us a sanitized Nixon, and in so doing, I think he misses a very important point (see my response to Ambrose on pages 249–50).

American historians want respectability. They want prizes. Many simply don't want to rock the academic boat. And some fear that if they take a chance, they will be assassinated in the *New York Review of Books* by another trophy-hunting historian. It seems that the only people left who take chances are dramatists and a few progressive historians who are willing to undertake a deconstruction of history and question given realities.

The style of my films is ambivalent and shifting. I make people aware that they are watching a movie. I make them aware that reality itself is in question. That's why *JFK* is personally important; it represents the beginning of a new era in terms of my filmmaking. The movie is not only about a conspiracy to kill President Kennedy but also about the way we look at our recent history. That movie — and *Nixon* also — calls attention to itself as a means of looking at history — shifting styles, such as the use of black and white and color, and viewing people from offbeat angles. You might see Nixon saying something in a shot that doesn't match. His lips are out of sync, and his facial expression implies something completely different from what is being heard. Or we might throw out five staccato images that add up to a contradictory portrait of the man. In such ways, we make you aware that you are watching a movie. We don't pretend that this is reality as in a conventional historical drama.

As far as facts go, I used them as best I could, but the truth is, *you can't use them all.* You are forced to omit some. And any honest historian will tell you that he does that, too. At three hours, *Nixon* may have been too much for some moviegoers anyway. We created dialogue because there is no record of most of the discussions that took place behind closed doors. The Richard and Pat Nixon marriage that we dramatized was based on several reports of its coldness, originating from their domestic staff, Woodward and Bernstein's *The Final Days,* Fawn Brodie's *Richard Nixon: The Shaping of His Character,* and Robert Scheer, a journalist and one of our consultants who had interviewed the Nixons and developed that opinion.[5]

You cannot string together a movie from a series of random and interesting facts. As a dramatist, you seek a pattern, a theme. But you begin, of course, with: what are the known facts? In cases such as Watergate and the Warren Commission, many facts are still so clouded in mystery that you cannot even *begin* the humbling process of knowing the "facts" until you've interviewed some ten to twenty people, each of whom will tell you something different about Richard Nixon, Jim Morrison, Ron Kovic, or Jim Garrison. The truth is never easy to grasp, because life — as we all know, if we've lived one — is ambiguous. So is the truth. Often the larger historical truths that the best dramatists go after involve the *absence* of a pattern in the historical record. You have to look for the "in-betweens." If you study Nixon, every one of the president's major decisions is awash in 46 meetings and 400 phone calls. This man would make phone calls all night long to canvass reactions, his own form of poll-taking. Every decision was the result of a lot of hesitation, doubt, and back-and-forth discussions. We thus clearly simplified, for instance, his decision-making process on the bombing and invasion of Cambodia, a choice plagued by much doubt on Nixon's part. In a movie that is not a documentary (but there, too, omissions are made), you don't have the time or the interest to show all these meetings and phone calls. Thus you collapse time and go for the greater truth, using not the chronological time in which we live out our lives but that interworld of texture, circumstance, and meaning.

Dramatic License

The concept of being a historian really, I think, began with oral storytellers — dramatists — who acknowledged the concept in the human mind that memories are a form of godhead or sacredness. The original Western historians were Homer, Aeschylus, Sophocles, Euripides, and the many others who wandered the sealanes of the world, passing on the mythologies of their tribes around banquets and campfires at night, encoding them by day in ancient libraries such as at Alexandria in Egypt. Our known Western historians came into being during Greek and Roman times, and because of their intense politicking and subjectivity, it is conceivable to me that the subject of history was not considered as significant as philosophy, drama, poetry, mathematics, or even physical sport. In defining the various Greek schools of thought, we find their historians viewed highly subjectively, depending on what their outlook of life was, what school they'd been to, what philosophy they adhered to. There was nothing like the trend toward consensus and tenure today. The historian must sing for his supper, too, and as in almost every profession in the late twentieth century, he has created around himself barricades of specialization and thickets of prizes, money, and fame.

Subjectivity rules, even achieving some degree of objectivity in the end. They've been tearing apart Plutarch for years, but almost every fifth-grade history teacher will tell you there's still a degree of truth in Plutarch. In fact, there's some "truth" everywhere in everything, but you've got to dig for it and sew it together from the contradictions. As a historian or a dramatist, what you really need is an intellect that's capable of absorbing contrary points of view, perhaps as many as half a dozen versions of this thing called "the truth."

I think of dramatic license as a restaging of any recorded action. It uses actors and costumes and makeup and is *not* necessarily factual. The moment you employ that license, you are no longer literally a "historian." But Hayden White made the point in "Tropics of Discourse" that the narrative interpretation provided by historians *is also definitely subjective,* insofar as research brings out *too many facts* to include in any historical work. He concludes that facts have to be deleted in order to present an interpretation.

I have come to believe that the concept of dramatic license should be placed in a broader context. For example, it is clearly something politicians use to start a war. The Gulf of Tonkin incident in 1964 has been revealed to be a mostly fabricated hostility (as was the burning of the *Maine* before the Spanish-American War) to incite Congress to support President Lyndon Johnson's unofficial "war" against the sovereign nation of North Vietnam. The president, whether he knew it or not, was employing a highly egregious form of dramatic license.

But how about the numerous *Time* and other magazine covers demonizing Saddam Hussein during the Gulf War? That is certainly dramatic license, as not all the facts about the Gulf War were revealed. Who owned the oil? What did these business cartels mean? Who really owned Kuwait? What was President Bush's past involvement in Kuwait, Iraq, Lebanon, and Syria? These questions were not dealt with in any depth by our establishment media, because whenever the United States goes to war, the coverage, especially in its earliest stages, involves a great deal of conscious and unconscious dramatic license.

As we know from Henry Kissinger's memoirs and those of so many other prominent people, if you have five men in the room when an important decision is made, no two of them will agree later on what exactly happened, unless perhaps there is a conspiracy to agree. They might agree, for example, on what time of day it was.

I had the experience of working on a Manuel Noriega script several years ago, and I came across an old Mike Wallace interview of Noriega on *Sixty Minutes.* It was truly unbelievable to watch. Wallace certainly seemed to be substituting his judgments — call it "dramatic license" — for any sort of neutral fact. I knew a little about the case, involving drugs and the CIA, through my research, and I had interviewed Noriega in jail. It seemed to me that Wallace had a large and sharp ax to grind against a man he didn't like at all. Most, of course, would defend Wallace's work, as he's become a trusted icon of the talking-head generation, much like Walter Cronkite and his dolorous establishment voice. Such men emanate an air of great authority, although in reality they are mostly actor-puppets *reading,* not interpreting, material.

Given the huge conglomeration of entertainment, publishing, and news, I don't think anyone would disagree that the formerly somber nature of news has reached out for new levels of frenzy at any cost. As Mark Twain reportedly said of his day and its first tabloids, "the truth is still putting on its socks while the lie is flying around the world." But I doubt he'd seen anything like the twentieth century.

I am certainly not qualified as a "scholar" or as a "historian," and I may be dead wrong in some of the details and themes I present — certainly many neocontemporary details are elusive to begin with — but I do pay attention to the details and, contrary to what some think, I *do* a great deal of research, which comes from the discipline of going to tough schools and being especially interested in history and current affairs. But, stylistically, the weave and bob of fact and nonfact, for which I am much criticized, blur the line of what is "reality" and raise, I think, the deepest question of all: what is reality? Is there a reality that we all share? Is there such a thing as a collective unconsciousness or an archetypal dream state as described by Jung — a sort of collective campfire tale passed down from generation to generation?

The historian Howard Zinn, in reading a portion of this manuscript, commented:

> I've never accepted the haughty claims of orthodox historians to "objectivity," and never believed in a clear line between "fact" and fiction. . . . I believe there are "larger truths" than the supposedly "factual" accounts of events given in orthodox histories. In my teachings I always assigned *The Grapes of Wrath* rather than a sober recitation of the facts of the Depression, and used *Johnny Got His Gun* to give a larger truth about The Great War — indeed about any war.
>
> Those who are shocked by the invention of characters and scenes, and worried about the effect of taking such liberties *show no such concern about the disastrous effect of generation after generation getting a history which reinforces traditional, dangerous beliefs about the world. They talk as if viewers come to movies as blank slates, when in reality these viewers have already been inundated with images and facts, many of them harmful — so that whatever startling new idea is presented must push against a mountain of lies offered as "history."*
>
> To me, the role of art (film, music, fiction, poetry) is to make up for the overwhelming power of the Establishment by using emotion to intensify and magnify suppressed truths. You have done that in your films.[6]

Inductive Thinking and Politics

Rosenstone, in calling me a deductive thinker, claims that "Oliver Stone wants the details to fit his thesis." Yet I consider myself, above all, an inductive thinker whose ideas have evolved from the experience of living as fully as I can. When I first read *On the Trail of the Assassins,* Jim Marrs's *Crossfire,* and the many other books on the JFK case, I thought this scenario increasingly incredible. I read portions of the Warren Commission report. I read the apologists' books, but I could feel that the thinking behind them was defensive and rigid. In fact, I absorbed more information on the assassination than I ever put in the movie. And I was approached by many strange and eccentric individuals with striking visual and dramatic theories that I omitted from the film because they did not come across as reasonable.

Thus, while people claim to know my politics, jumping to facile conclusions that I am "leftist" or, according to others, a "macho right-winger," I am only comfortable with the thought that my politics, like my films, are inductive. If a conservative says things that make sense to me, I'll go along with him. If a progressive says things that make sense to me, I'll go along with him. If anything, I think of myself as someone of the "radical center." I want change, but commonsense change. I believe in Edmund Burke's standards that change must be examined. But sometimes we don't have that luxury. Change erupts. Often it has the look of an eruption because we have not been paying attention. The pundit and historian classes are now so out of touch, living in Washington, D.C., New York City, and their ivory towers, reinforcing each other's opinions in easy communication at ceaseless dinner parties and social events, that all establishment thinking has tended to the centripetal, seeking consensus rather than serious dissent. Hollywood is also such a tower. Those in Hollywood are not necessarily hearing the people. And all of a sudden, one day the lights go out and the people march. Change happens that way, abruptly.

Burke was reportedly shocked by the French Revolution and acted negatively, rigidifying his thought. Classic conservatism also resists attempts to change its tradition, yet there has always been the mind-set of those who set themselves up as judges of social and ideological behavior, some who try to inject religion into the concept of politics, which is *not* religious in essence (it is, after all, "the art of compromise," not the love of the Lord). Fanatics of any order pervert the real meaning of conservatism for me. And there are *idiotes* (Greek for "private person, a person having no involvement in public life") on the other side of the political spectrum who want the world to change without strife or the burdens of office; they, too, damage the progressive cause. But it's amazing how we still kowtow to a warped conservatism in this country. Although those on the Right are a minority, they are certainly well financed and, like the Religious Right, operate more as a force to fear than a force for life. They have helped create a climate resembling, as President Franklin Roosevelt described it, "the fear of fear." We've given far too much credence to the likes of Oliver North, Pat Buchanan, Pat Robertson, Jesse Helms, Rush Limbaugh, and the many other crackpots indulged by the media. Must we be held hostage to them, as President Clinton has been throughout his presidency, with no hope for redemption? I believe that a man can dramatically redeem himself. I believe in this hard-earned, progressive, humanitarian liberal doctrine, which tells us redemption is possible *now* (why, if you are truly spiritual, can you not accept this doctrine?). You don't have to go to jail to become a better person; you can be rehabilitated outside the concrete walls of profit and hate. Perhaps the strongest theme I remember from studying Burke is the meaning of change — and *the fear of change.* Those given to progressive mind-sets tend to accept change more readily than those who are not. Yet I sometimes despair and feel that God (or whatever spiritual force we communicate through) lacks any power to heal this ongoing, brutal, spiritual civil war in every country of the world through every century between those who want change and those who fear it.

Meanwhile, we have a government to run, not a system of personal morality and "family values"; that's not the government's business, although many times the media, in the endless search for some "responsibility" (itself, it is nothing but a ghost), have assigned it that task. Such intervention is in every sense of the word a violation of Jefferson's creed of a private conscience apart from the public duty. We *can* have contradictory impulses as people; it is human — sometimes admirable, sometimes not.

But the last thing we need, as a free people, are hypocrites wearing political disguises to waste everyone's time with vague, impossible-to-win wars on "values," drugs, other ideologies, and, in its final onslaught, our private minds.

Let's get back to business.

ON CONSPIRACY

We are all victims of counterfeit history. In my lifetime I have learned this lesson by head and heart. Through the cauldron of Vietnam and the message of a morphing, modern life, with the increasingly vast control given to media, it has been burned onto the template of my brain: *never underestimate the power of corruption to rewrite history.* We catch the tip of the iceberg on a couple of things here and there, like Watergate and the Iran-contra affair, and some of us feel reassured. But we continually underestimate the power of individuals and systems to get things done and get them done quietly.

Having written a screenplay about Alexander the Great, I was intrigued to discover that his famous father, King Philip of Macedon, had been assassinated under mysterious circumstances. Alexander, not far from his father's side that day, was immediately suspect, as was his mother, Olympia. The assassin himself was quickly slain, and the murder to this day remains an enigma. What did Alexander really know of the supposed homosexual feud at the root of the revenge taken that day?

In Alexander's own untimely death at age thirty-three in 332 B.C. we again have strong speculation of a conspiracy of Macedonian family clans. They may well have come together to terminate a young ruler who had no pure Macedonian heirs but was dangerous in his desire to radically globalize the known world by, among other things, intermixing Macedonian and Oriental bloodlines. Did a battle-weary Alexander die of fever or from poisoned wine? After my research, I intuit the latter.

I think of Julius Caesar, stabbed repeatedly by respectable senators in Rome itself, at the heart of the empire. I think of Archbishop Thomas à Becket of Canterbury and his historic feud with King Henry II delimiting the power of the state over religion, where we find perhaps the first use of "plausible deniability" in that disarming rhetorical question attributed to Henry: "Who would rid me of this man?"

I think of the serene Pope John Paul I dying of a supposed heart attack in his sleep after thirty-three days of papal rule in 1978. From day one, rumors of murder have persisted despite a powerful, suspected cover-up. Was this innocent pope sniffing out the massive fraud perpetrated in the name of God by the Vatican Bank, or was he aware of its ties to the shadowy neofascist undergrounds in Europe and Latin America?

Could the Russians handle a movie that implied that Stalin had poisoned Lenin before Lenin could change his mind about who was going to run the place? The French have long insisted that Napoleon was poisoned by arsenic and that DNA revelations from his hair point to this. Was this ugly deed done to him by the British, or was it a traitor in Napoleon's own circle? More recently, the handprints of Pol Pot's friends and enemies were seen everywhere in his death and rapid cremation.

I remember the doomed reformer Luis Donaldo Colosio, shot down campaigning for the presidency in the turbulent Mexico of 1994. The lone-gunman theory does not hold up to serious investigation. Was Colosio the target of drug lords (the equivalent of our Mafia in the assassination of President Kennedy), or was he the victim of bitter political rivalries within his own PRI Party (akin to our own intelligence services murdering the president)? The powerful Tijuana police chief, who was investigating the case, was himself brutally murdered in an ambush that many believe was staged by drug dealers (could there have been a parallel here to Jack Ruby's death?). For those who follow these things, the Mexican government's investigation resembled the Warren Commission's in its bumbling dishonesty, cloaked by establishment prestige.

In our country, if we search, we find that a coup d'état planned against President Roosevelt in 1933–1934 has amazingly disappeared from the history books. You don't have to wonder why when you understand the power of the conspirators — J. P. Morgan, Jr., Bernard Baruch, Thomas Lamont, General Douglas MacArthur, and others — or the incredible ability of the media, which were then as now basically controlled by the establishment of this country, to vaporize the incident into the black hole of ridicule. Henry Luce's magazines (*Time, Life,* and *Fortune*) trivialized the various testimonies at the time, including that of two-time Medal of Honor winner General Smedley Butler, and the incident was buried largely because Roosevelt himself was weathering a major storm and feared a revolution if these events were revealed. Thank God for the memory of the few men still around who do not so conveniently forget (for further details, see pages 289–91).

The awkwardness of conspiracy theories still prevails in American politics, as we pride ourselves on being a country where political change occurs without violence through peaceful democratic process. People, rather than the shadowy motives of the State, guide the future. The deaths of our leaders are tragic acts of faith, accidents, the work of unbalanced madmen who, once destroyed, can no longer harm us. In such a view, tragedy becomes a random event, an act of God that could not have been prevented. Only in empires long since turned to dust do honorable men actually conspire to kill for the cold motive of power. Those who would suggest that it happens here, as it does in European or Asian history, are frowned upon, painted as eccentric by our society's leaders and its media. Yet any thorough examination of history reveals a consistent thread of convenient tragedy linked to the turning points of the fates of nations. And, in the smoke of the funeral pyre, not all the faces are crying.

Following the disastrous Bay of Pigs invasion of 1961, President John Kennedy forewarned of his own death after he read Fletcher Knebel's novel *Seven Days in May,* about military men taking over the office from a "liberal" president. When he was asked by a friend of his, "Could it happen here?" Kennedy replied, "It's possible. But the conditions would have to be just right. If the country had a young President, and he had a Bay of Pigs, there would be a certain uneasiness. Maybe the military would do a little criticizing behind his back. Then if there were another Bay of Pigs, the reaction of the country would be, 'Is he too young and inexperienced?' The military would almost feel that it was their patriotic obligation to stand ready to preserve the integrity of the nation and only God knows just what segment of Democracy they would be defending. . . . Then if there were a third Bay of Pigs it could happen."[7] Perhaps Kennedy, in allowing himself three miscues, underestimated the power of his opposition. The president's biographer acknowledged that Kennedy distrusted the military and handed a copy of Knebel's book to his secretary of the army, mandating that every army officer read it. As a student, you have to go back to the mentality of the 1950s and 1960s to understand how familiar we were with war, crisis, and fear during the Cuban missile crisis and just how treacherous those times were.

Kennedy in 1963, like Alexander the Great long before him, was increasingly calling for radical change on several fronts — the USSR, Cuba, Vietnam, and our internal policies on civil rights, oil tax depletions, even the federal currency. *Nothing* was off-limits. Looming ahead was his certain victory in 1964, with the specter of a Kennedy dynasty lasting well into the 1970s. If nothing else, history has taught us that politics is power and people do kill each other if they want to *acquire* that power or, equally important, *prevent* that power from being exerted. In John F. Kennedy's nascent radicalism, a motive for murder is clear (see further comments in my response to *JFK* on pages 288–89).

In our present-day life, it is ironic that the media, like the Greek Furies of old, have inherited the malevolent power to drive any one of us who would question state power mad. In essence, the echoing power of modern communications has replaced the assassin's bullet as the means of political destruction. The media's capacity for malice has been phenomenally effective in ending the presumptions of thousands of outspoken iconoclasts by simplifying and marginalizing them — Gary Hart, Ross Perot, Jim Garrison, Jane Fonda, Dick Gregory, Jerry Brown, Louis Farrakhan, Abbie Hoffman, the Berrigans, Pierre Salinger, anyone who has questioned TWA 800, and the list goes on into the thousands and is far too saddening. But note how little success they've had, as hard as they've tried, with foreign tough guys Saddam Hussein, Fidel Castro, and Hafiz al-Assad of Syria.

At the same time, there is a devastating irony to the fact that my own generation grew up under the biggest conspiracy theory of them all — "The Mother of All Conspiracies." Yet few recognized this conspiracy because it was so ingrained in our schoolroom consciousness. My father and mother and their peers, in a sense enslaved by Orwellian imagery, fear, and thought, thoroughly convinced us that there was a monolithic communist conspiracy at work to destroy the United States involving all Russia, China, and Eastern Europe — two-thirds of the world map. Not only were they going to invade America militarily, but they had already started the moral and spiritual destruction of our values in our schools, our arts, and, most prominently, our State Department. No wonder so many in our generation *are* paranoid, and that's not such a bad thing, either. No one, by the way, has ever apologized to our supposedly spoiled generation for the brazen dishonesty of this belief system and the enormous damage it caused us.

Most recently, the Assassination Records Review Board, which was appointed in 1992 as a result of the outcry over *JFK,* revealed, among other things, that ex-president Gerald Ford, also a member of the Warren Commission, raised Kennedy's bullet entry wound by two to three inches, from an area in his upper back to an area in his lower neck. He apparently made this adjustment, in his own words, "to clarify meaning, not alter history," whatever that means.[8] To any impartial and intelligent observer, the phrase "to distort meaning" is more applicable here. It's sort of like getting caught with your hand in the cookie jar and saying you're just checking inventory. By raising the bullet wound a crucial two to three inches, Ford was perhaps thinking that this would limit the protest over the viability of the "magic bullet" itself when it became public. If the wound had been two to three inches lower — where it really was, according to the drawings of J. Lee Rankin, chief general counsel to the Warren Commission — the bullet (nicknamed the "magic bullet") would have been even more improbable than it is now. Ford defended himself by turning on people like me, saying, "My changes had nothing to do with a conspiracy theory. My changes were only an attempt to be more precise." In other words, Ford had no defense and, using an old public relations tactic, attacked rather than defended. When people these days use Salem-witch-hunt-like words such as "conspiracy theorist," they are heroically made to sound as if they are speaking about a child pornographer. In no civilized country in the world would an ex-president, in a crucial role as a public servant, be let off the hook so lightly in the back pages of most major newspapers.

Thus I find it so condescending that Richard Hofstadter, author of the 1963 essay "The Paranoid Style in American Politics," is trotted out each time by the self-righteous media to attack those who investigate conspiracy in our culture.[9] It's condescending simply because we've had so many *provable* conspiracies in our history — from the first gathering of conspirators against the Stamp Act, kicking off the Revolutionary War, to the conspiracy that murdered President Lincoln, and recently to the Watergate and the Iran-contra conspiracies. Investigations into the later conspiracies have barely scratched the surface, as they had such significant implications for our military-industrial-communications empire.

Our reporters, time and again, are backing off stories because of their editors, who seem to become more conservative with their accretion of power.

These editors and their moneyed bosses, entrenched in the status quo, are telling the kids to back off — not directly, as in "Don't undertake this story," but in contexts such as "Who cares? It's boring! No ratings. Been there before, done that," or "If you go there, it'll be controversial, which basically will not help your career at this organization." All this need not even be spoken. All of us understand in some way; we all collude in the emperor's game of no clothes. In a controversy these days, we all know; everybody gets soiled. And who really wants to be a troublemaker in a society of silent consent? Don't we all want to join in, be part of something, be loved and approved of? No one seriously sets out to rock the boat except the occasional intellectual loner, the historian long after the fact when the flame does not burn so hot, and occasionally, if he can take the heat, the dramatist. Think of Euripides in a cave in Thrace, in exile from his beloved Greece.

All this is not to deny the role of accident and individual choice in history. Kings *do* fall off horses and break their necks. Individual men and women sometimes single-handedly change the course of their nation's fate. Floods, storms, bad harvests, and the global greenhouse are causations as well. In fact, accident, individual choice, and conspiracy have lived comfortably side by side for centuries, but in the simplistic anticonspiracy ranting of the media, the historians, and the joke-tellers on late-night TV, there seems to be an inability to allow for more than one cause and one effect. The opposite seems true to me. History *is* ambiguous. Cause and effect are also ambiguous.

That's why I started *JFK* with President Dwight Eisenhower, that most conservative of presidents, because in his farewell address he made a significant point. He saw something with major consequences coming, and in an otherwise ordinary speech, he shifted tonality and, almost as a non sequitur, warned of a new phenomenon he called the "military-industrial complex." In the way that men sometimes change and reveal inner emotions and perhaps fears as the specter of old age and death creeps across their intellects, Eisenhower, I believe, foresaw the enormous power that money would have over government — the power of the multinational corporation, thriving for the most part on state money to build better weapons and stronger airplanes. If fascism is defined as corporations owning the state, and communism is defined as the state owning the corporations (we must sometimes wonder: what is the difference?), then that is what he saw — a benign, almost bland hybrid of American values (i.e., money and optimism) combined with a European form of fascism (i.e., fear of disintegration), rendered popular by the Germans and Italians of the 1920s and 1930s — in short, a pure and simple American fascism. Interestingly, the idea of it is all over our best dramatists' work in that era, from Sinclair Lewis and John Dos Passos and John Steinbeck to Frank Capra.

Not without calculation did we begin "World War III" (i.e., the cold war) in 1944 against the Soviet Union, using what we could of the experienced Nazi intelligence apparatus against the property-destroying communists. And through the later years of the twentieth century, the power that Eisenhower foresaw has only grown and grown, like Jack's beanstalk. What president now could stop it? Jesse Ventura? It would certainly take great courage. The war in Vietnam cost, depending on who you believe, between $100 billion and $200 billion, perhaps more. When the cold war was finally declared "over" in the late 1980s, where did the promised "peace dividend" our political puppets talked about actually go? The military-industrial complex, with $100 billion secret research projects, has indeed become an octopus, a "beast" without super-vision that drives the individual to the knees of his meaninglessness. Ultimately, it's a "system" (a very twentieth-century word, evoking Kafka) of checks and balances driven, I believe, by (1) the power of money and markets, (2) state and government power, (3) corporate power, (4) a political process that has been wholly corrupted by the money required to win office, and (5) the media, which for the most part protect the status quo and their ownership interests.

I don't even believe assassination would play a significant role today. If any president were to seek to change the Federal Reserve Board in any significant way, there would be no need to assassinate him. The stock and bond markets would simply tremble worldwide, and that eruption would be felt through the media (so much bigger now than in Kennedy's time), which would echo such a loud message of distrust that it would force the president to back down. In this era, the power of money and of the media is enough to prohibit any presi-dent from making any significant change in the way the system works.

Ultimately, all this has more to do with the fear of change than anything. I truly believe that the thing that terrifies men in society the most *is* change. Often it is just Roosevelt's "fear of fear," but it becomes far more subversive and dan-gerous when that fear crystallizes into hatred and terror and destroys other people's lives in the name of an ideology of stasis, of conservatism, of seeking refuge in the past for fear of an unknown future — in fact as we all do each night when we sleep and dream. Boldness, that reaching into the unknown future to make things better for oneself *and perhaps for all,* is not a motivation or a trait often shared by society, with the exception of enterprises such as war or space travel, and even then not often. I believe that in five years, between 1963 and 1968, three men ran on a platform of change and suffered enormously for it. They were John Kennedy, Martin Luther King, Jr., and Robert Kennedy.

Nations, I think, plunge further into the abyss by silencing the voices that cry for independent inquiry at a time of change and crisis. Where is the imme-diate dissent when politicians scream for tougher civil and criminal laws at the first sign of some new terrorist outrage or criminal horror? Where is the dissent against the vengeful drug sentencing of the last ten years? Or against the many "mini-wars" we've fought since Vietnam — in the name of what? Revenge, anger, getting ratings, getting votes? It always seems that the loudest voices win these days — the bully's way. Yet the lessons of history *repeatedly* point out the virtue of independent thinking — the need to Question, Disbelieve, Defy.

Allow then, in our million-dollar-a-minute TV culture, a little space and time for the contrarian in you, and allow that paranoia in moderation, like red wine, is healthy precisely because conspiracy does not sleep. Our failure of perception is the reason we rarely see it. Why? "Treason doth never prosper," an English poet once wrote. "What's the reason? For if it prosper, none dare call it treason."

A Sacred Mission

Oliver Stone and Vietnam

To me the '60s were very hard — my parents got divorced, I went to Vietnam.

If it's a movie worth making, you should make it. If you can convey that passion, it should all be open. Anything is permitted.

Vietnam is not over, although some people say it is. Vietnam is a state of mind that continues all over the world — as long as m[a]n in his quest for power interferes in the affairs of other men.

Part of me is scared, and wants to say, let's pull back, let's make a film that is understandable to everyone, that's sweeter, that the whole country can believe in, like Forrest Gump.

— *Oliver Stone*[1]

In September 1967, Oliver Stone departed the United States on a transport bound for Vietnam. Behind him he left his life — an unhappy childhood; frustrating, lonely years at Hill School and Yale; a long, rejected novel manuscript. He might have been Ernest Hemingway heading for Italy, or Joseph Conrad bound for the sea. Perhaps his mind was already tracking film images, imagining what might have been and what would be. Perhaps Vietnam was more of an escape than a mission. Whatever the case, the country would soon take hold of him, and it would occupy his thoughts and his creativity for much of the next thirty years. Few artists would delve so completely into the nature, texture, and causes of the Vietnam War. Fewer still would produce such a dazzling body of work. And at the heart of it all would be biography — Stone's and America's.

For Oliver Stone, exploring Vietnam would become a sacred mission. As a young man, he served two tours in the country — one as a civilian, the other as a soldier. These experiences changed him and set his artistic agenda. For the next twenty-five years he would return repeatedly to Vietnam for inspiration. The conflict became his touchstone; it provided him with both an avenue for personal exploration and a tool for understanding larger historical questions.

In a series of brilliant films about America and Vietnam, Stone moved from autobiographical observations about the nature of war, to a sociological analysis of the American culture that led to the war, to historical investigation of the political causes and course of the war. In the process, Stone became the most influential historian of America's role in Vietnam. But to understand Stone's position, one has to come to terms with Stone himself.

Considering his career as a writer and director of powerful films that deal with war, it is perhaps not surprising that, had it not been for World War II, Oliver Stone's parents would never have met. Louis Stone, Oliver's father, was a Wall Street stockbroker and the scion of a wealthy family. He met Jacqueline Goddet, a poor nineteen-year-old beauty, shortly after V-E Day, while he was serving as a financial officer for General Eisenhower in Paris. After some initial hesitation, Jacqueline wed Louis in November 1945. By the time the couple returned to New York City, Jacqueline was pregnant with what would be their only child. William Oliver Stone was born on September 15, 1946.[2]

The future critic of the establishment grew up within its comfortable embrace. Despite being prone to making poor financial decisions, his father generally proved to be a good provider, enabling Oliver to lead, by his own admission, "a sheltered existence." Oliver lived in a large townhouse complete with a nanny and a butler, dressed stylishly, studied piano, and listened to classical music and Broadway show tunes. After finishing eighth grade at Manhattan's Trinity School, his parents shipped him to the exclusive Hill School, an all-boys academy in Pottstown, Pennsylvania. Oliver knew that Hill was the first step that would probably lead to Yale and Wall Street, the path his father had taken.[3]

Oliver's childhood was pampered, but hardly happy. Both his parents were distant. His mother seemed more interested in New York's party scene than in him, and his father was a "dark and pessimistic" man who had a hard time expressing his emotions. Oliver's closest family may have been his grandparents in France. As a youth, he spent his summers in Europe, raptly listening to his grandfather tell stories about the Great War and happily playing army with his cousins on the battlefields where millions of men had lost their lives. He passed summer days writing plays, many about war, that willing locals performed.[4]

But the carefree summers ended, and he faced the unappealing prospect of returning to the States and school. Although he was intellectually curious and fascinated with American and European history, he was uncomfortable at Hill. A self-proclaimed "outsider," he made few friends, chafed under the strict discipline of the boarding school, and resented its efforts to impose a rigid "orthodoxy" upon him. Like many adolescents, Oliver was extremely "self-conscious," living in constant fear of being ridiculed by fellow students. Burdened with feelings of isolation, he pursued his interest in writing, primarily as a means of "retreat[ing] from reality."[5]

His family life got even lonelier. In 1962, when he was fifteen, the headmaster of Hill called him to his office to inform him that his parents were separating. The news shocked him; he had failed or refused to see any signs of discord in his parents' relationship. In fact, the split surprised few others. Louis had had a string of affairs, and Jacqueline, fully aware of her husband's philandering, coped by partying, popping uppers, and, finally, taking lovers of her own. By the early 1960s, the Stones' marriage existed solely on paper. Now, when Oliver most needed attention, his parents reinforced his sense of isolation by refusing to visit him. Oliver wanted to take a leave from school, but his father would not hear of it, claiming that he was too busy at work to attend to anyone else. Jacqueline was even more remote — she left for Europe, expressing no interest in seeing her son. Oliver received another shock when he learned that Jacqueline's free-spending habits had driven the family into debt. Louis moved, with Oliver's possessions, from their spacious town house to a cramped hotel room. Oliver was devastated. His parents' actions taught him that "adults were dangerous" and "not to be trusted."[6]

Abandoned by his parents, he accepted the grind at Hill. Unsure of his future, he struggled through his last tedious years of high school. World events seemed remote. Certainly, he did not see his destiny in the assassination of President Kennedy. Raised a staunch Republican by his conservative father (Oliver voted for Barry Goldwater in 1964), he has only vague memories of being "on a lunch break or something" when he heard of the president's death. Although he was never a "Kennedy lover when he was alive," Stone was shocked by the crime, but no more than others. He was not burdened with concerns for America's future, only "stunned" that "a young, handsome president could be killed like that." He fully accepted the Warren Commission's finding that Kennedy had been killed by Lee Harvey Oswald alone.[7]

Personal concerns were more pressing. In accordance with his father's wishes, in 1964 he enrolled at Yale. He quickly realized that college would be more of "the same crap" that Hill had been. Even more than before, he desperately searched for meaning in his life, longing to break out of the constricting East Coast conservative mold that his father had crammed him into. Books provided a means of escape. He devoured Joseph Conrad's writings and was especially drawn to *Lord Jim,* with Conrad's dark view of human nature and his lush depictions of the exotic Orient. The idea of living in a primitive land, unsullied by civilization, consumed him, and he began inquiring about possibilities for overseas employment. After several rejections, he was finally accepted by the Free Pacific Institute in Taiwan, a church-based organization that operated a number of schools. The Institute offered him a position as an English teacher at a school in Cholon, the Chinese suburb of Saigon. In 1965, he dropped out of Yale and headed for Vietnam.[8]

Saigon, with its gambling, drugs, and prostitution, was no Yale. It "was like Dodge City." Hookers stalked busy street corners, drunks spilled out from numerous bars, and guns and violence were common. The hot sun and the nearby ocean lent a sense of romance to the chaotic scene. Stone felt alive. After the suffocating depths of Hill School and Yale, Saigon was like coming up for air. He plunged into his new job, working hard and living a spartan life, but loving it all.[9]

But an immediate, itchy restlessness persisted. Travel had gotten into his blood, and he wanted to see more of the world. He quit his teaching position after two semesters and joined the merchant marine, where he passed his days cleaning toilets and engine rooms. After a long voyage from Vietnam to Oregon, the nineteen-year-old Stone drifted south to Mexico to write a novel. The manuscript, which he called "A Child's Night Dream," grew into a 1,400-page stream-of-consciousness look at the psyche of a bright, troubled youth. The largely autobiographical story followed the protagonist through his experiences in Asia and the merchant marine. Stone worked furiously through much of 1966 at what he thought was a literary masterpiece, eventually feeling confident enough to return to New York City and the harsh judgment of his father, who desperately wanted his son to return to Yale and a buttoned-down life. Stone finally gave in and reenrolled, but unenthusiastically. "Night Dream" continued to occupy his thoughts and his energy. He worked on his novel at a punishing pace, skipping classes and writing about ten hours every day. Not surprisingly, his return to Yale was brief and inglorious. He was expelled but, undaunted, returned to New York to finish his book. The incredible effort he poured into the novel only made it more painful when publishers panned the manuscript. Frustrated, he threw hundreds of pages into the East River and decided to take a drastic step. He would visit Vietnam again, this time as a soldier.[10]

Because he was a well-educated white male, the army offered Stone a position at Officer Candidate School. He refused and requested infantry duty. His decision to go to war appears rash but actually stemmed from a number of factors. To be sure, he had been hurt by the series of personal and literary rejections. But he was equally upset by the grand literary pretensions he had harbored. In a sense, his decision to enlist was an act of atonement for his perceived character flaws; he yearned to "obliterate" the ego he had created and, after a long bout with individualism, become an "anonymous" grunt. Though he often considered suicide, he could not bring himself to "pull the trigger." Instead, he resolved to let someone else pull it for him on a battlefield.[11]

But perhaps more than anything else, Stone went to Vietnam simply because he believed in the war. Like many other Americans who grew up during the 1950s, he had learned to "fear Russians and hate Communism." He fully believed that communism needed to be stopped in order to preserve American democracy, and he felt it was his duty to fight. His father had served during World War II, his grandfather during World War I. Now it was his turn to serve his country and, by doing so, to announce that he was "a man." Imbued with both pathos and patriotism, Private Bill Stone (he opted to enlist using his first name, fearing that "Oliver" was too effeminate) left for Vietnam on September 14, 1967, and was assigned to the second platoon of Bravo Company, Third Battalion, 25th Infantry, stationed near the Cambodian border.[12]

Naive optimism and idealism soon crumbled under the weight of reality. Vietnam was not the same place it had been in 1965. By 1967, many Vietnamese had gone from loving to loathing the occupying Americans. Corruption ran rampant as noncombatants lived high, far behind the lines, and unscrupulous sergeants stole supplies to sell on the black market. Stone quickly discovered that Vietnam was not a people's conflict but a politicians' war fought by the poorest Vietnamese and Americans. Just as disconcerting for him were the unexpected attitudes of his new comrades in arms, who made it clear to him that he was as "expendable" as a piece of "raw meat." Very quickly he realized that enlisting had been "a terrible mistake" and that he was "in deep." One of his only pleasures was writing long, introspective letters to his grandmother, Adele Goddet, in France.[13]

Stone was given little time to adjust to his new surroundings. After only a week, he found himself on point in a night ambush. He struggled through nearly a week of field duty without confronting the enemy. His greatest adversaries were the incessant swarms of mosquitoes that kept him awake at night, the spiders that crawled in his shirt, and the fifty pounds of equipment on his back that nearly overwhelmed him as he humped through the jungle. One night he fell asleep during his watch, waking to discover that the Vietcong (VC) were practically on top of the platoon. "Scared shitless" and numbed with fear, he forgot his training and silently stared. A comrade opened fire on the oncoming troops, jolting Stone out of his stupor. He pulled the trigger, but had forgotten to take the safety off his M-16. Eventually, he regained his bearings and the platoon beat back the VC approach, but not before at least one American was severely wounded. Stone received a flesh wound in the neck during the melee and was briefly out of action.[14]

His first taste of battle improved his combat sense. It also, despite his mistake during the ambush, put him more at ease with the other members of the platoon. He could not, however, completely fit in. The differences in background between him and the other grunts were obvious. He enjoyed classical music and serious literature, while they favored Hank Williams and Motown, hard liquor and serious drugs. One of Stone's comrades later recalled that he was "a quiet person who kept to himself." At first, he did not drink, spending his leisure hours writing stories of his experiences. Slowly, however, the war changed him. As his tour dragged on, he felt himself becoming disconnected from his civilized roots and becoming a "jungle animal," operating less on reason than "instinct." Increasingly, he sided with the progressive element of the platoon, who preferred Motown and drugs to the country music and alcohol that fueled the platoon's other faction. Stone's association with this group, composed mostly of lower-class blacks and whites from small towns, expanded his horizons and exposed him to the social injustice and prejudice of American life.[15]

Then came 1968. There was nothing happy about Stone's new year. On January 1, he and 700 other U.S. soldiers were attacked by some 2,000 VC troops at Firebase Burt. The enemy lobbed mortars into the American entrenchment before beginning a ground assault at one in the morning. The American perimeter collapsed, and Stone's platoon was thrown into the counterattack. The VC inched forward, taking bunker after bunker, and the battle quickly devolved into brutal hand-to-hand combat. But the fighting came to an abrupt close when American planes dropped bombs directly on the American position, killing friend and foe without discrimination. The incident embittered Stone. As he watched bulldozers push lifeless Vietnamese bodies into a mass grave, he wondered if the American force had been no more than bait, a dab of honey designed to lure the antlike VC army into the open.[16]

But Stone had little time to ponder. Just two weeks later, Bravo Company was hit again, this time while on patrol a few miles from Firebase Burt. Bravo's third platoon stumbled into a VC bunker complex and got pinned down. The first platoon faced a similar predicament. It was up to Stone and the second platoon to extricate the men from the morass. But Stone's jungle instincts let him down; he got caught in a trip-wire explosion and received shrapnel in his leg and his rear. Medics shot him full of morphine, packed him on a stretcher, and loaded him on a helicopter. Bravo Company took about thirty casualties without inflicting any. Stone's rehabilitation kept him off the field during the Tet Offensive, which further devastated Bravo. By the time he returned to duty, he barely recognized anyone in his largely reconstructed platoon.[17]

After another brief stint on combat duty, he was transferred to a military police auxiliary battalion in Saigon, where he guarded barracks and trolled for miscreants. The new duty bored Stone, and he numbed the tedium with drugs. The jungle beckoned. He wanted to get back into the heat of battle and got his wish after brawling with a rear-duty sergeant. In order to avoid having his tour extended as punishment, Stone opted in April 1968 to volunteer for the First Cavalry Division's reconnaissance and minesweeping detail.[18]

The transfer proved portentous for his later career. While in the First Cavalry, Stone met a large black man from a small town in Tennessee who would later become the basis for "King" in *Platoon.* He also met a half-Spanish, half-Apache sergeant named Juan Angel Elias, who fascinated him. Elias, recalls Stone, "was like a rock star in the body of a soldier." Rather than terrify, the compassionate Elias inspired his men. He was a heavy drug user who was loathed by the lifers and juicers. Stone stayed close to Elias, learning how to rely on his senses, not his intellect, during combat. For the first time, Stone believed that it was possible to be both a good soldier and a good person.[19]

By now, Stone had become a veteran, a fact he demonstrated in August 1968 when the platoon got pinned down by a North Vietnamese Army (NVA) soldier with a machine gun in a foxhole. With his fellow soldiers trapped under a hail of bullets, Stone lost contact with reality and functioned on pure instinct. With reckless abandon, he charged the bunker and, while on the run, lobbed a grenade directly into the hole, thus buying time for the platoon to be rescued. He is still at a loss to explain what happened to him. "Something went crazy in my head," he explains. "I flipped out." He received the Bronze Star for his heroism/confusion.[20]

As the war dragged on, Stone sensed a loss of basic humanity. Yet another transfer brought him under the influence of Platoon Sergeant Barnes. Barnes had become something of an army legend. He had been wounded six or seven times, and one shot over the eye had left a large, sickle-shaped scar down the left side of his face. A passionate soldier, he volunteered to return to combat after every wound. In contrast to Elias, Barnes was "a very frightening man" with a "cold stare" that grunts felt "all the way down to [their] balls." Stone and the other awestruck soldiers were terrified yet intrigued by the grizzled warrior. From Barnes, Stone learned how to suppress his emotions, kill, and become a disciplined, mechanized soldier. Death came to concern him no more than life, and his sense of right and wrong eroded. He burned villages on "a steady basis." He watched uncaringly as frustrated U.S. troops sprayed mosquito repellent on their feet to make them sore so they could avoid marching and as they committed random acts of violence against Vietnamese civilians. He coolly stood by as one soldier, who would become "Bunny" in *Platoon,* bashed an old woman's head in with his rifle butt. In one village, Stone lost control and began shooting at an old man's feet because "he wouldn't stop smiling" at him. He could not, however, bring himself to kill the old man. Finally, he was shaken out of his complacency when he witnessed two U.S. soldiers raping a young village girl. He broke up the incident and decided that it was time to reassert his humanity. Looking at the world around him, he noticed the natural beauty of Vietnam. He purchased a 35mm Pentax and took the first of hundreds of snapshots of the country. For the first time, he thought of the war in visual terms.[21]

Stone received his discharge orders in late November 1968. In fifteen months, he had earned a Bronze Star and a Purple Heart with an Oak Leaf Cluster for his multiple wounds. Yet even now there was sadness. Just before he was shipped home, he learned that Sergeant Elias had been killed, possibly by an errant American grenade. Stone was eager to leave the heat, insects, fatigue, jungle rot, and frustration behind, but he was still uncertain about his future. He thought that the war was "rotten and corrupt" and lacked "moral purpose" and integrity, but he did not feel that he could challenge the system. Burned out and drugged up, the twenty-two-year-old private returned to the United States with no immediate plans.[22]

He was not prepared to return to New York — his father's New York, a city of commerce, commitment, and respectability. So, without even letting his parents know that he had come back from the war, he fled to Mexico. He found the experience unsatisfying and headed north after only a few days. But his homecoming would not be a happy one. American authorities busted Stone at the border for carrying two ounces of Vietnamese marijuana and threw him into a federal jail in San Diego. He faced the unpleasant prospect of five to twenty years behind bars. It was two weeks before prison officials allowed him to call his dad, but once Louis put up $2,500 for his son's defense, the public attorney suddenly took an interest in Stone's case, and he was soon released. The experience convinced him that nobody in America cared about Vietnam veterans and served to further radicalize him. Having seen injustice abroad, conditions in the prison alerted him to injustice at home. The jail was as horrible as those in Saigon. Inmates were stuffed "in every fucking nook and cranny," and 5,000 prisoners, mostly young blacks and Hispanics, had to sleep on the floor.[23]

Life outside of prison was not much better. Stone returned to New York and life with his father. Louis, however, complained about Oliver's drug use and ghetto speech. Further, Oliver felt estranged from his old acquaintances. His friends had avoided the war, and most of his Vietnam buddies went back to the small, southern towns they came from. Americans' lack of interest in the war, their "mass indifference," stung him. Nobody wanted to hear his stories of Vietnam's horrors; they were much more interested in "the business of making money." Even the antiwar movement troubled and disgusted him. He felt that it was not really serious about becoming "militarized and politicized" in order to force a peace and served only as a means for pampered college students to blow off steam.[24]

Deciding that he would never be at peace with himself until he had written about Vietnam, Stone began writing a screenplay called *Break,* a story that moved on a symbolic level but contained characters that would later become Rhah, King, Bunny, Lehner, Barnes, and Elias in *Platoon.* After working slavishly on the script, he sent it to Jim Morrison of the Doors, whom he envisioned as the star. Though he never heard back from the singer, the experience convinced him that he could be a filmmaker. He was accepted at New York University's film school and studied under Martin Scorsese, who believed that, despite his penchant for cinematic excess, Stone showed potential as a filmmaker. He was particularly impressed with his student's first film, *Last Year in Vietnam,* a touching appraisal of the trials and tribulations of a Vietnam vet coming home. But Stone did not blend well with the other students. He was older than most and a loner by nature, leading many to believe that he was arrogant. Similarly, he found himself unable to participate in NYU's political scene. While other students marched, Stone advocated "a fucking revolution." He wanted to push beyond "bullshit meetings and conferences" and called for an armed march on Washington.[25]

Stone's marriage in 1971 to Najwa Sarkis, a Lebanese woman who worked for the Moroccan Mission to the United Nations, seemed to calm him a bit. She made enough to support them both and encouraged him to work on writing screenplays. He completed his degree in September 1971 and began to bounce from job to job. While he wrote screenplays, he earned money as a Xerox boy for a copy pool, a messenger, and a cabdriver. By mid-1976, he had written eleven scripts and even directed one, *Seizure,* on a shoestring budget in Canada but failed to attract much critical or popular attention. It seemed he was going nowhere at a frantic pace. His marriage fell apart, he quit one job after another, and success continued to elude him. As America celebrated its bicentennial, Oliver Stone was a marginally employed twenty-five-year-old living in a cheap apartment in New York City.[26]

Had Stone been a movie character, he would have been *Taxi Driver*'s Travis Bickle. He had lost all faith in the government, largely due to the trauma of Watergate. Oddly, he admired Nixon, whose toughness, conservatism, and emotionlessness reminded him of his father, but the scandal destroyed any respect he may have had for the president. Watergate also convinced him that the government was "a lie" and "hammered home the point" that it had "lied to us about Ho Chi Minh and it lied to us about the Vietnam War." His depression was magnified when his grandmother died in 1976. Instead of adding to his rootlessness, however, her death inspired Stone to rededicate himself to making something of his life. Armed with this newfound conviction, he turned once again to Vietnam — the real Vietnam this time, not a symbolic one. In a few weeks of furious typing he produced the screenplay for *Platoon*.[27]

Stone started shopping *Platoon* around Hollywood and attracted the attention of Stan Kamen of the William Morris Agency. Encouraged, he moved to Los Angeles, but no studio expressed interest in the film. The writing, however, was powerful enough that Columbia Pictures hired him to write a treatment of Billy Hayes's autobiography, *Midnight Express*. His screenplay won an Academy Award for best adapted screenplay of 1978 and brought more opportunities his way, including an offer from producer Marty Bergman *(Serpico, Dog Day Afternoon)* to write a screenplay for Ron Kovic's book, *Born on the Fourth of July*. Al Pacino was set to star, and William Friedkin was to direct. The releases of *The Deer Hunter* and *Coming Home*, however, threatened to overload the market for Vietnam films, and *Born*'s funding fell through three days before shooting was to begin.[28]

But work was now easier to find. Stone wrote and directed *The Hand* (1981), a low-budget thriller starring Michael Caine, and produced an early version of the script for *Conan the Barbarian* (1982). In Hollywood, he was earning a reputation for writing violent, right-wing screenplays, a charge that gained strength from his scripts for *Scarface* (1983), *Year of the Dragon* (1985), and *8 Million Ways to Die* (1986). He resented the stereotype and found inspiration in Warren Beatty's *Reds*, a film that proved to him that a Hollywood movie could be both big-budget and leftist. Then, in 1984, Dino DeLaurentis agreed to finance *Platoon*. Once again, however, funding fell through at the last moment. It was not until after the surprise success of *Salvador* (1986), which did well on video despite being underpromoted, that he received solid backing for *Platoon*, and then only by Hemdale, a British-based operation.[29]

Part of Stone's problem with getting the funding for *Platoon* had to do with Hollywood's suspicion that Vietnam War films were both too controversial and too economically risky. This notion began to take form while Stone himself was still serving in Vietnam. In 1967, John Wayne filmed *The Green Berets* at Fort Benning, Georgia. Released in 1968 after the Tet Offensive, the hawkish, pro-American film provoked a violent left-wing critical response. "Unspeakable . . . stupid, . . . rotten, . . . false, . . . vile and insane," commented Renata Adler in the *New York Times.* "Immoral . . . racist," agreed Michael Korda in *Glamour.* "Childishly sleazy," added Frank Mararella in *Cinema Magazine.* Although the film found its audience and made money, Hollywood producers who did not have Wayne's clout with moviegoers decided that the war was simply too hot.[30]

For the next decade, filmmakers treated the war as little more than a reference or a source of inspiration. The WAR — that bloody, passionate creature sitting in America's living room — was not mentioned. Then came the first tentative steps. In 1978, *Coming Home* and *The Deer Hunter* explored the mentality of soldiers returning from the war, with mixed critical and financial results. The same year, *Go Tell the Spartans,* a fine film, was all but ignored. In 1979, Francis Ford Coppola released *Apocalypse Now,* a film buried beneath so much myth and symbol that critics read it as both hawkish and dovish. Its profound ambivalence — or perhaps its psychological complexity — may have penetrated to the heart of war's darkness, but it failed to say much about the everyday nature of combat.

During the Reagan era, Hollywood retrieved, dusted off, and modestly updated stock war-film materials. Once again, combat became a heroic enterprise, corrupted only by politicians. The *Rambo* films and the *Missing in Action* series captured the big bucks. Americans wanted to watch winners, not agonize over what happened or why it happened. They desired action, not introspection; results, not meaning. They wanted heroes for their next wars, not victims of lost crusades.

But Oliver Stone had his own agenda, which smacked against the political currents of Hollywood and Washington. Much of *Platoon* is an echo, not only to the themes of *Apocalypse Now* but also to the antiwar literature of World War I. Sergeant Barnes, the scarred figure from both Stone's own tour in Vietnam and *Platoon,* recalls Hemingway's injured hero Jake Barnes in *The Sun Also Rises.* And the use of Charlie Sheen as not only the protagonist but also the narrative guide serves the same purpose as Martin Sheen did in *Apocalypse Now.* The twin references announced that *Platoon* would explore both coming of age and the futility of modern war.

The strength of *Platoon* emerged from Stone's passion for and his palpable understanding of the subject. Like Hemingway, war was the defining experience in his life. He enlisted, he fought, he killed, he was injured; he believed, he questioned, he lost faith. He suffered the full range of emotions, entertained the gamut of thoughts. And when he turned to the subject, it was not like Francis Ford Coppola, Sylvester Stallone, or Chuck Norris, filmmakers and actors who embraced the war as a commercial vehicle rather than a biographical necessity. Stone, unlike others who depicted Vietnam on-screen, viewed the war as the central event not only in his life but also in the "soul" of America "and the world."[31]

From the beginning of the *Platoon* project, he insisted on absolute realism. Anything less than fidelity would have betrayed his memory and experiences — although the U.S. Department of Defense refused to cooperate on the film because it believed that it was a "totally unrealistic" depiction of the war. Stone maintained that the film was not about larger issues; it was about "boys in the field." To ensure that his actors were as knowledgeable and competent as the real men of Bravo Company, he imposed a rigorous, two-week-long boot camp in the Philippine jungles under the dictatorial supervision of Captain Dale Dye, a twenty-year marine and a Vietnam veteran. Captain Dye subjected the cast to long marches with sixty-pound packs, cold army rations, and uncomfortable nights in foxholes, punctuated by sudden bursts of explosions to guarantee that no one would sleep. By the time filming began, the actors had the "tired, don't-give-a-damn attitude" that Stone had hoped to achieve. In a short time, Stone and Dye had made soldiers out of actors.[32]

To maintain faith with his past, Stone set *Platoon* in a real time and a real place — his time, his place. The film details the activities of 25th Bravo Company, operating near the Cambodian border, in 1967. The film's central character, Chris Taylor (Charlie Sheen), views the war from a perspective similar to Stone's. Like Stone, Taylor is a white, upper-middle-class kid who went to Vietnam to escape from the boredom and rigors of civilized life. His experiences in Vietnam mirror Stone's — one reason why the film is so realistic and personal.

The film's initial impression of Vietnam focuses on the landscape, perhaps the overriding presence in the film. It is, in the fullest sense, a world without vision, a land of eight-foot elephant grass, overgrown virginal forests, and lush jungles. It is a landscape that one needs a machete to hack through. Much of the tension of the film originates in its confining setting; danger always seems to threaten from behind the next tree.

Daily discomforts add to the tension. Stone's Vietnam is a place where a grunt cannot relax. Mosquitoes swarm, ants bite, and leeches cling. Insects maintain a perpetual hum in the background, constantly reminding the viewer and the soldier of their presence. The product of a wealthy family, Chris finds it difficult to adjust to Vietnam's fatal environment; he staggers under the weight of his pack, gags at the sight of a dead body, and attracts the ants and leeches like a magnet. Making matters worse, night seems to conspire with the harsh environment to deny rest to the weary Americans. Bombs explode, flares light up the sky, ambushers lurk everywhere. "You never really sleep," observes Chris in a voice-over, as his year-long tour of Vietnam assumes the dimensions of an 8,760-hour day.

The language in *Platoon* is similarly authentic. Fresh soldiers are "cherries" and "newbies"; Vietnam is "the Nam," and America is "the world"; pot smokers are "heads" that meet in the "underworld." The film is also littered with obscenities, as Stone refused to pull any verbal punches. The music the soldiers listen to and the words they use reflect Stone's own experiences. The use of Motown hits like "Tracks of My Tears" alongside country classics like "Okie from Muskogee" adds to the realistic aura and helps to divide the platoon into two hostile camps — the "heads" and the "juicers" — just as it was in Stone's platoon. They are his people, "guys nobody really cares about" from small towns and villages, "the bottom of the barrel," the undereducated and the uneducated.

It is in the realistic portrayal of the platoon itself that the film departs most radically from the traditional war genre. The classic World War II film upholds the ideal of the melting pot: out of many, one. Multiethnic, multireligious, and multiregional, the platoon is a smorgasbord of Italians, Poles, and Irish; Protestants, Jews, and Catholics; Brooklyn sharpies, southern Rebs, and midwestern rubes. Yet they all pull together toward a common goal. No such comfortable — and comforting — arrangement is present in *Platoon*. Stone observed a clear "moral division" in his platoon when he served in Vietnam, and Bravo's cinematic counterpart is faithful to Stone's memory. On a symbolic level, the film centers on the two sergeants, Elias and Barnes. For Barnes, all civilians are potential Vietcong and are liable to ruthless treatment. Elias, however, takes a more compassionate "hearts and minds" approach to the war. He wants to save Vietnam; Barnes merely wants to destroy the country.[33]

But the platoon is split over more than war aims. Unlike traditional war films, Stone shows how race divided soldiers in Vietnam. In the base camp, African Americans are usually by themselves, shunted off to one side. Black soldiers are aware that they are being treated unfairly. One complains that they have to take extra turns on ambush patrol because of racial "politics," and another objects to "always being fucked by the rich." They are not, however, passive victims. Junior, a black grunt, for example, is not afraid to order Chris around. "Hey, white boy!" he shouts, before encouraging him to dig a foxhole with a little more enthusiasm. The only place blacks and whites can comfortably coexist is in the underworld, where, supervised by Sergeant Elias, they dance together in a drug-induced haze to the sounds of Smokey Robinson. In 1967, a year that saw vicious race riots in Detroit and other cities and heard former Student Nonviolent Coordinating Committee chairman Stokely Carmichael call for a black revolution, race was as much of an issue in Vietnam as it was in America. Stone, unlike other filmmakers, brought this reality to the screen. By doing so, he added a deeper, more nuanced understanding of America.

Despite their divisions, soldiers have to pull together when they are in combat. It is in these sequences that Stone achieves the greatest sense of realism in the film. Stone's war is the grunt's war, a war without maps, red and blue arrows, or a grand design. Men fight because they are attacked, not for any lofty goal or territorial objective, and battles often end as inconclusively as they begin. In such contests, "winning" loses any elevated meaning; soldiers fight to survive. Period.

The mise-en-scène of the battle sequences underscores Stone's idea of combat. His camera work captures Karl von Clausewitz's notion of the "fog of war." The camera becomes Chris's eyes — jerking back and forth, seeing nothing distinctly, and blindly reacting to threats both perceived and real. Violence erupts suddenly and brutally, often without warning or meaning. Death and injury are neither noble nor ignoble, they just are. The best answer to the suffering and violence is given early in the film by Barnes. In true Hemingway fashion, he clamps his hand over a screaming, dying man and demands that he "take the pain."

Premiering in New York and Los Angeles in December 1986, *Platoon* created an international sensation and propelled Stone into the forefront of American directors. *Time* proclaimed that Stone's effort portrayed "Viet Nam as It Really Was," and the *New York Times*'s Vincent Canby called the film "a succession of found moments" — that is, it had rediscovered the lost reality of the war. More importantly for Hollywood and Oliver Stone, *Platoon* was a massive commercial success as well. Made for a paltry $6.5 million, the film grossed $136 million in U.S. box office receipts. Video sales pushed the total gross to a staggering $250 million. For now, Stone believed that he had exorcised the demons of Vietnam, and he looked forward to new projects. Having suddenly become a famous director, he planned to move to a lighter subject for his next film. In 1987, he remarked that he "would love to do a comedy."[34]

Had Oliver Stone been Francis Ford Coppola or even Sylvester Stallone, perhaps he could have jumped genres and made a quick transition to another project. But the whole point of *Platoon* was that it was not just a film project; it was Stone — his biography, his vision, his nightmare. He could no more set Vietnam aside than Hemingway could forget his war or Ahab abandon his whale. *Platoon* had not ended his dialogue with America about the war; it had only started it.

After *Platoon*, Stone made two movies, *Wall Street* and *Talk Radio*, before returning to Vietnam with a version of Ron Kovic's autobiography, *Born on the Fourth of July*. He had been interested in the project since 1980, but there was no money in Hollywood for a film about a paraplegic Vietnam veteran who discovers that all his country's cherished ideals are false and that the war in Vietnam was a sham. In a Hollywood marked by escape and fantasy, and a Washington following in lockstep, Kovic and Stone were as warmly embraced as repo men. They were pounding on the door, trying to get inside to claim their America, but nobody was at home. The financial success of *Platoon*, however, gave Stone the sledge he needed to break down the door.

Born on the Fourth of July centers on America's fatal flaw, the culture that conditions and indoctrinates young men to go to war. It is a brutal culture, life-hating, joy-denying, pleasure-destroying. In the film, Stone labors to subvert that culture, and by casting Tom Cruise in the lead, he moved far in that direction. By the mid-1980s, Cruise had become America's smile, the charming good-bad boy of *Top Gun* and *Risky Business*. Stone took Cruise's chiseled good looks and spit-shined image and caked them with mud. "Tom had the classical facial structure of an athlete," noted Stone. "He's the kid off a Wheaties box. I wanted to yank the kid off that box and mess with his image — take him to the dark side."[35]

Seldom in the American cinema has the dark side initially seemed so benign. The opening sequences of the film are infused with a soft, golden light, and falling autumn leaves create a snow-globe effect. Everything about Kovic's Massapequa has a Norman Rockwell familiarity — small town and safe streets, boys playing war in the woods and men mouthing platitudes about the need to serve, rippling flags and firecrackers on the Fourth of July, baseball games and Yankee caps, wrestling matches and first loves. Kovic is his mother's "little Yankee Doodle Boy," born on the Fourth of July and raised with loving care. Yet something is out of whack in his comfortable, middle-class America. A parading World War II veteran flinches at the sound of an exploding firecracker, a coach's quest for victory borders on obsession, a mother's religious faith merges into zealotry. Kovic is taught not only to be upright, courteous, reverent, and clean but also that winning is everything, God hates quitters, communists are banging on our doors, and Uncle Sam needs you. As America's perfect son, he moves naturally from the Boy Scouts to the marines.

For Kovic and Stone, the culture of winning, violence, and unquestioning loyalty was America's dark side. It was a culture that despised softness and sensitivity and created a god out of John Wayne — in the book, Kovic writes that he resented having to give his "dead dick for John Wayne." These forces — family, community, school — imbued Kovic and Stone with a cold war mentality and the idea that manliness could be found only on a battlefield. The power of the culture makes Kovic's disillusionment all the more wrenching. After being wounded and returning home, he blames his country for making him go to Vietnam. "They told us to go," he cries, implicating the faceless establishment for perpetrating an immoral war.[36]

Kovic's story also shows how easily this dark side can be foisted onto the next generation. As he rides through a crowd during a Fourth of July parade, his eyes come to rest on a boy who looks much as he once did. The child's

Yankees cap and his toy gun suggest that little has changed since his own youth. By exposing America's dark side, Stone pushes his analysis of Vietnam beyond that presented in *Platoon*. Unlike *Platoon,* which made no effort to explain the larger issues behind the war, *Born on the Fourth of July* suggests that Vietnam, and war in general, are a product of America's own moral deficiencies, a theme that he would further explore in later films.

Kovic's and Stone's disillusionment is fueled by outrage, because they believed that they had been duped by their country's martial culture. The film implies that only the true believers, boys like Kovic born on the Fourth of July, evinced a willingness to fight and die for their country. Most of Kovic's high school classmates cannot understand why he wants to enlist; they do not feel particularly threatened by communists, and they are not moved by any overwhelming impulse to be "part of history." They seek only normal lives and a chance to prosper financially. When Kovic returns from Vietnam in a wheelchair, his friends have moved on with their lives. They are husbands, fathers, budding entrepreneurs, as distant as people can be from what he experienced on the other side of the world. Perhaps even more than his injuries, his friends' apathy gnaws at him. While he is consumed with the war, they could not care less. A hospital orderly tells him, "You can take your Vietnam and shove it up your ass." "They don't give a shit about the war," his friend Stevie adds. Even his mother switches the television station to *Laugh In* when a story about a Vietnam War protest comes on the news.

Stone shared Kovic's attitude toward America and his desire to shake his sleeping countrymen. The messages of *Born on the Fourth of July* are don't forget and get involved. America fought and lost the wrong war in the wrong place at the wrong time. It was a needless, senseless war, the product of a military culture and blind ideological faith. And unless Americans begin to question that culture and that faith, it will happen again. On this point, Stone and Kovic are products of the late 1960s and early 1970s political radicalization. Conservatives argue that protest movements had no effect. Stone disagreed. "That's why making *Born* was a particular thrill, 'cause it was flying in the face of that shit," he said. "People were outraged, I'd get letters saying . . . there was no protest, no hatred, why are you bringing up all this divisiveness? But I remember the late '60s as a very rough time. . . . A lot of people can't face their past, you know."[37]

Stone felt so strongly about the message of the film that he allowed it to interrupt the narrative flow. Most of the film deals with Kovic's coming to terms with the forces that shaped him, a struggle that is largely internal and intellectual. The film ends, however, with sketchy scenes of Kovic's political activism, and the manipulation of historical footage to put Cruise/Kovic at the 1972

Republican Convention contrasts sharply with the camera work of the rest of the film. But the transition from internal search to external activism — personal to political — is the message of *Born on the Fourth of July*.

Stone's concern for America's involvement in the war runs even deeper, however. It was not enough for the director just to show the impact of the war on an individual — on Ron Kovic, Chris Taylor, or Oliver Stone. It was not enough just to be the cinematic Hemingway of the Vietnam War. Stone wanted to be the war's historian as well. As a historian of the war, Stone moves on two levels: personal and political. *Platoon* and *Born on the Fourth of July* are primarily personal statements, though the political lurks beneath the surface. Both films were huge critical and commercial successes (*Born on the Fourth of July* was nominated for eight Academy Awards and won four, including an Oscar for Stone for best director).

Heaven and Earth (1994) is also largely a personal film of self-discovery, although it too has a historical and political message. The war, Stone says, was not only, or even mostly, about the United States. The overwhelming majority of people who were killed in the war were Vietnamese, and most of them were civilians. It was their land that was destroyed, their economy that was shattered, and their culture that was threatened with ruin. Stone commented that he made the film for two reasons — first, to explore the themes of Buddhist spirituality, reverence for ancestors, and respect for the land, and second,

> to respond to, in part, the blind militarism and mindless revisionism of the Vietnam War as typified by a certain odious brand of thinking that has snaked its way into our culture over the past decade or so, in which the conflict is refought in comic-book style by American superheroes, with a brand new ending . . . we win! Within the moronic context of these ideas, hundreds of nameless, faceless, Vietnamese are blithely and casually shot, stabbed, and blown to smithereens, utterly without the benefit of human consideration. Entire villages are triumphantly laid to waste, with not one microsecond of thought or care given to those inside the little bamboo hamlets being napalmed. Who were they?[38]

In his attempt to give "the reverse angle" of the war, Stone succeeds. He depicts Phang Thy Le Ly Hayslip's world in loving detail, from the agricultural cycle to the serene beauty of the land to the peaceful stability of village and religious life. Seldom has a commercial filmmaker devoted so much attention to the undramatic nature of a third-world culture. When Stone finally turns his attention to Americans, he portrays them as rich, barbaric invaders. They intrude into the Vietnamese civil war, overlay it with an alien ideological meaning, then take it over, destroying or corrupting everything they touch. They disrupt nature by destroying entire villages, defoliating forests, and severing the rice cycle. American forces turn Le Ly's "most beautiful village on earth" into a scene from Dante's *Inferno*. Culturally, American capitalism corrupts the country, sending villagers to cities and bases where they become pimps, prostitutes, and black marketeers. Drawing not only on Le Ly's memoirs but also on his own experiences as an MP, Stone is at his best when showing American GIs at their worst.[39]

Stone even contends that Americans are at their worst when they are trying to be at their best. In one scene, South Vietnamese soldiers — American allies — use honey donated by the United States and angry ants to torture Le Ly. On a metaphoric level, Stone uses Steve Jones (Tommy Lee Jones) as the representative American. A twisted, misguided killer, Steve attempts to atone for his own sins by showering Le Ly with gifts and by taking her out of her natural environment and dropping her in the United States. But just as the relationship between the United States and the Republic of South Vietnam rotted, so the unnatural union of Steve and Le Ly turns exploitive and violent. Steve's suicide reinforces Stone's view of the results of the American mission in Vietnam.

Heaven and Earth differed from *Platoon* and *Born on the Fourth of July* in its public reception. Expensive to make, it failed miserably at the box office. Production costs exceeded the combined costs of *Platoon* and *Born on the Fourth of July,* but *Heaven and Earth* grossed only $6 million in the United States. Although it was critically applauded — one reviewer called it "Stone's ultimate war film" — it failed to reach the audience the director intended it for. It had a message for all Rambo-cheering, Reagan-voting Americans, but few people paid it even passing attention.[40]

After the success of *Born on the Fourth of July* and before the debacle of *Heaven and Earth,* Stone moved on to new topics. Instead of fulfilling his dream of making a comedy, he decided to catalogue the life of his musical hero, Jim Morrison. But even before *The Doors* was completed, he had laid the foundations for a bold return to the Vietnam genre. By the late 1970s, he had decided that the assassination of John F. Kennedy had drastically altered the course of the war and America's future, but it was not until 1988, when book publisher Ellen Ray gave him a copy of Jim Garrison's *On the Trail of the Assassins* in an elevator in Havana, that he became convinced that Lee Harvey Oswald had not acted alone. Stone devoured Garrison's work, buying the rights to the book with his own money. He then immersed himself in the "serious research" required of any historian. He read every book on JFK and the assassination that he could lay his hands on and, along with screenwriter Zachary Sklar and coproducer A. Kitman Ho, conducted over 200 interviews with conspiracy theorists and other people with knowledge of the case.[41]

Stone's conception of the film soon outgrew the mere circumstances of the assassination. "The central historical question" that courses through the movie centers on neither Jim Garrison nor the identity of the president's killers. Instead, Stone used the murder as a means of exploring the event that was central to both his and, he believed, his nation's life — Vietnam. In this way, he was building on issues he had explored in his previous films. *Platoon* was an autobiographical study that showed how the everyday horrors of the war affected a young man. *Born on the Fourth of July* carried the war home by examining how indifference, misunderstanding, and the perverted nature of American life affected Ron Kovic's life. But now, Stone cast an even wider net. *JFK* is a biography of America since World War II, with Vietnam serving as the defining event for the period.[42]

Stone begins *JFK* by rehabilitating the slain president's image. A narrator informs the viewer that Kennedy represented "change and upheaval" in American government. We see Kennedy as he wanted to be seen, making conciliatory speeches toward the Soviets and frolicking with his family. Most importantly, we learn that Kennedy, through no fault of his own, found himself "embroiled" in a war in Southeast Asia. After the assassination, a stricken black maid, perhaps the mother of a grunt, sobs as she tells a reporter what "a fine man" Kennedy was. Meanwhile, Guy Banister (Ed Asner) cheers the killing, ripping Kennedy for letting the "niggers vote." Those who supported and those who objected to Kennedy are neatly delineated. Stone seems intent on transforming Kennedy into the stained-glass hero that the Vietnam War never had.

Vietnam barely ripples the surface of the first half of the film. As New Orleans district attorney Jim Garrison (Kevin Costner) initially becomes obsessed with the assassination, there is little indication that the war plays a pivotal role in anything. Instead, the war appears, as it did in the mid-1960s, as background noise — always present, but rarely commented on. A brief clip shows Lyndon Johnson declaring his intent to vigorously prosecute the war. Another quick mention informs us that Johnson is asking for more money and more men to fight the war.

As Garrison unearths more information, however, Vietnam becomes increasingly central to the story. The pivotal scene comes when Garrison travels to Washington, D.C., to meet "Mr. X" (Donald Sutherland). Mr. X gives him the broader perspective that the DA could never have unearthed on his own. Mr. X cannot tell Garrison who killed Kennedy, although he suggests that top government officials were involved — when he refers to "the perpetrators" and calls the killing a "coup d' état," Stone flashes images of LBJ. He can, however, give Garrison information on the more important issue — *why* "they" killed Kennedy. Kennedy had irritated powerful militarists with his refusal to invade Cuba and his decision to eliminate the CIA's power to conduct covert activities during peacetime. The central issue, however, was Vietnam. Kennedy wanted to pull out of Vietnam by 1965, a decision clearly unacceptable to the military and the big arms dealers, who stood to make a killing if the killing continued. Somehow, these forces colluded, perhaps in combination with others, to remove the offending executive and replace him with the more hawkish Johnson, who was "personally committed" to Vietnam. Once Kennedy was out of the way, the war could start "for real." Kennedy's murder and the continuation of the war marked the final triumph of the military-industrial complex, a powerful junta that could run roughshod over any elected official. The personalized war Stone presented in *Platoon* had thus grown into a critical event that marked a decisive shift in the power structure of the United States.

JFK was a mortar lobbed at the establishment, and it set off a firestorm of controversy. Many critics ignored Stone's central thesis, seizing instead on the idea that he had proposed a "grand conspiracy" involving the CIA, FBI, elements of the military, anti-Castro Cubans, New Orleans homosexuals, the Dallas police department, and God only knows who else. Others blasted Stone for lionizing Garrison, who had, in real life, used some questionable methods (including truth serum and questioning hypnotized subjects) to gather his evidence, and for presenting speculation and composite figures as factual. Indeed, *JFK* attains the highest level of realism in any of Stone's films. As in *Platoon*, the camera acts as an eye, as fallible as any human's. The camera jerks as we see something out of the corner of our eye. Did we really see what we thought was there? Stone never provides an answer. Further, Stone has mastered the technique (first seen in the 1972 Republican Convention scene in *Born on the Fourth of July*) of combining documentary and new footage into a seamless unity. His realistic approach went too far for many of his detractors, one of whom referred to *JFK* as "the cinematic equivalent of rape."[43]

Stone responded to the furor surrounding his film. He was willing to give way on most issues. He freely admitted that *JFK* was intended as "entertainment" and that he had taken "dramatic license" with the facts. *JFK* was not supposed to tell the truth about the assassination; Stone simply wanted to present a "paradigm of possibilities" that would point out the shortcomings of the Warren Commission's report. He noted where he had fictionalized or created composite characters and agreed that he had made his Garrison "better" than the real person. He was even willing to negotiate his portrayal of Kennedy. Stone was aware of Kennedy's faults — the pattern of "sex" and "drug use" that marked his life, his "stealing the election in '60," and his penchant for saying "one thing to the public" and doing "another thing behind their backs." In his defense, Stone correctly maintained that three hours was insufficient time to fully develop Kennedy's character and that, in any case, there was "a larger issue at stake."[44]

On the "larger issue," however, Stone would not budge. He continued to insist that, had Kennedy lived, he would have ended the Vietnam War. Stone firmly believed that Kennedy had been reevaluating Vietnam and the cold war throughout 1963. Citing national security memoranda and statements made by Robert McNamara, Kennedy's secretary of defense, Stone claimed that Kennedy was only waiting to be reelected before withdrawing from Southeast Asia. Instead, he was murdered, thus putting "an abrupt end to a period of innocence and great idealism."[45]

Though passionately and eloquently argued, Stone's position, however ardently held, does not stand up to scrutiny. There was, in fact, little to suggest that Kennedy wanted to end either Vietnam or the cold war, unless it was on America's terms. The conciliatory speeches that Stone quotes were anomalous. Even the speech he was to give in Dallas on November 22, 1963, took a hard-line stance on communism. McNamara may have believed that Kennedy would have pulled out of Vietnam (even though he wrote to Kennedy in October 1963 that the "security of South Vietnam" was "vital to United States security"), but Kennedy advisers McGeorge Bundy and Robert Kennedy did not. Only three weeks before he was killed, Kennedy approved the overthrow of South Vietnam's president, Ngo Dinh Diem, on the grounds that a new government was needed to save South Vietnam from communism. Kennedy's National Security Memorandum (NSAM) 263, which Stone cites, did call for the withdrawal of 1,000 U.S. troops, but this was merely giving notice to Diem that the United States was not pleased with his corrupt regime. At no point did Kennedy plan to abandon Vietnam. Lyndon Johnson's NSAM 273, which Stone claimed was a radical departure from Kennedy's position, was nothing of the sort. In fact, the document appears in *The Pentagon Papers* as an "Order by Johnson Reaffirming Kennedy's Policy on Vietnam" and stated that the United States' "objectives" remained identical to those stated by Kennedy.[46]

If Stone has been flexible on other issues, why does he remain so steadfast in his assertion that Kennedy would have ended the Vietnam War? To do otherwise would be to undermine all that he has done in the last twenty years. In his films, he has constructed an explanation for an unexplainable war, reducing a complex swirl of ideology and global politics to a simple cause-and-effect relationship. Further, his theory supports his contention that the war had "no moral purpose." In *JFK*, Vietnam resulted from the cowardly murder by a group of vicious, power-hungry warmongers of a benevolent "king" who was trying to bring peace to the world. A more despicable beginning could hardly be imagined, tainting the war with evil before it even began in earnest. Finally, placing Kennedy's death within the context of Vietnam gives Stone and other veterans a hero in a war without acknowledged heroes. Kennedy represents the only hope that America could escape from the clutches of "the Beast" that has held the reins of power since 1963. If Kennedy did not offer hope in the 1960s, what chance is there that any future leader would be inclined to give power back to the people?[47]

In showing how a corrupted American society created Vietnam, Stone returned to the theme of *Born on the Fourth of July.* In earlier films, he showed how a culture of violence, manifested in both public and private institutions, caused one young man to go to war. *JFK* maintains the same image of America but makes a quantum leap in interpretation. Instead of exploring the effects of this culture on one person, he demonstrates how one manifestation of violence affected the course of the entire nation. Whereas Chris Taylor and Ron Kovic may have been naive individuals with no direct relation to viewers, the events in *JFK*, with Vietnam as its centerpiece, implicate all Americans who remain complacent and refuse to challenge the system.

Having, for the first time, explored the origins of the Vietnam War and situated it within a particular view of how American history operates, Stone was prepared to show how the war ended. Although it is impossible to say what he will do in the future, it may be that *Nixon* will mark Stone's final cinematic statement on the war. Although *Nixon* lacks some of the stridency of his earlier films, it reinforces the themes posited by Stone's other Vietnam War films. Instead of merely discussing the end of the war, he continues his bold explorations of the conflict's impact on both American and global history.

Even while he was president, Richard Nixon had intrigued Stone. Stone saw his father in the blunt and withdrawn executive, and the shame of Watergate helped turn Stone into a critic of America. Nixon, along with Kennedy, "shaped the era in which [he] grew up," and Stone eagerly plunged into the task of bringing the story of "the dominant figure in the latter part of this century" to the screen. Again, as with *JFK*, he engaged in the basic research required of any historian. He read "everything there was" on the ex-president and spoke with many of the people who would be portrayed on-screen. Stone also listened to some of Nixon's presidential tapes that had not yet been released to the public. Still smarting from critics' accusations that he had created characters and evidence for *JFK*, Stone released an advance copy of the script for *Nixon*, complete with hundreds of footnotes listing books, interviews, tapes, and oral histories.[48]

At over three hours, *Nixon* is a lengthy yet compelling portrait of a complex politician. Stone's Nixon (Anthony Hopkins) is a master of detail, yet prone to confusion; a caring yet cold person; a man with a bold vision of the future who is haunted by the past. Nixon's greatest demon is the memory of JFK. Nixon resents Kennedy as only a hardscrabble, self-made man can resent a person who has been handed everything. At the same time, he maintains that he and the man from Massachusetts were like "brothers." Not content to merely expose this contradiction, Stone digs deep to explore the roots of Nixon's guilt, suggesting that he was indirectly responsible for Kennedy's death. Nixon, he says, was in charge of a program called "Track Two," a covert program to assassinate Fidel Castro, and may also have been involved in the Bay of Pigs in some way. By participating in this effort, Nixon unwittingly helped create the culture of violence that, as detailed in *JFK,* led to Kennedy's death and, as seen in *Born on the Fourth of July,* inspired Ron Kovic and others to go to war.

Although there is no evidence that Nixon knew of the plot to kill Kennedy, Stone shows him near the scene of the crime and explicitly links Kennedy's death to the Vietnam War. In the film, we see Nixon in Dallas in November 1963, meeting with a group of far-right businessmen headed by Jack Jones (Larry Hagman). As Nixon uncomfortably banters with high-class prostitutes, Jones and others urge Nixon to run for president in 1964. The wealthy businessmen are displeased with how Kennedy is handling Vietnam and promise Nixon "a shit-pot" of money and a victory in the South in exchange for a more militant foreign policy. Nixon demurs, claiming that Kennedy is unbeatable. But what if, one of the extremists asks, Kennedy does not run in 1964? Nixon is unnerved by the implications of this statement and beats a hasty retreat. Although he was clearly not responsible for Kennedy's death, Nixon's association with the forces that killed the president haunted him. Stone beautifully captures this mood by drenching the White House in a stormy, almost gothic atmosphere. In a very real sense, *Nixon* assumed the quality of a horror film.

Besides deepening his explanation of the causes of the war, Stone continues to expand his vision of how the war affected the world. *JFK* treats Vietnam as an event of national importance. *Nixon,* however, goes beyond this, and shows how the war played a critical role in the development of the global cold war. At times, Nixon seems to prosecute the war solely to salve his own bruised masculinity; he refuses to be pushed around by a smaller country. But, for the first time, we also see how Vietnam was but one aspect of a larger scene; Nixon refuses to back down in the face of a communist alliance. When he is in control of events, Nixon realizes that he has to continue to vigorously prosecute the war in order to gain concessions from the Soviets and the Chinese. He is successful in this endeavor. Stone shows Nixon's success in his meetings with

Mao Zedong and Leonid Brezhnev. But, he argues, simply demonstrating Vietnam's importance in international politics does not make it a worthwhile war. Instead, Vietnam is reduced to a mere pawn in a global game. In January 1968, Private Stone's platoon acted as human bait to draw out a larger Vietnamese force. Other Vietnam veterans served the same purpose, only their job was to lure the world's major communist countries into negotiations with the United States. In Stone's view, the war was a chess game with one king and many pawns.

Finally, the Vietnam War comes to a close. It does not, however, reach either a glorious end or a satisfying resolution. After learning that the North Vietnamese are prepared to sign a treaty, an exhilarated Nixon calls a press conference to announce the conclusion of a successful war. He believes that he has finally negotiated a "peace with honor" and is prepared to join the country in celebration. But the press conference quickly turns hostile. One reporter challenges the president, claiming that the last several years of the war accomplished nothing, that the terms Nixon got were little different from those offered in 1968. As the president stammers, reporters bombard him with questions. Much to his surprise, they are less interested in the end of the war than in the breaking Watergate scandal. Vietnam has become a footnote in the history of the cold war. For Nixon and America, the war did not end so much as just fade away. There were no parades, no celebrations, and, for Stone and others, no closure. This stands as the final insult for a generation of soldiers and forced at least one to begin writing about his experiences. The lack of closure in 1973 led Stone to follow a twenty-year-long path to find redemption. In ending the war on-screen, Stone has taken us to the beginning of his own life as a filmmaker.

In a 1991 *Rolling Stone* interview, journalist David Breskin asked Oliver Stone if he felt like a great artist. "I never doubted it, from day one," Stone replied. "When I was eighteen, I just felt like I had a call. . . . And living up to that call has been the hardest part." From the first, Vietnam was an integral part of that calling. As a nineteen-year-old, he began a long, sprawling manuscript entitled "A Child's Night Dream." As a twenty-three-year-old film student at NYU, his first picture was entitled *Last Year in Vietnam*. At the age of forty, his first great commercial success as a director was *Platoon*. The circle closed eleven years later when *A Child's Night Dream*, heavily edited and slimmed down, was published by St. Martin's Press. The link between the nineteen-year-old would-be Hemingway and the fifty-one-year-old established artist was a passion for America's involvement in Vietnam — why we went, how we fought, what were the results and the implications.[49]

In the process of becoming an artist, Stone also became the most successful and controversial historian of the war. For him, the past had an irresistible pattern, one woven with lost opportunities, conspiracies, fallen heroes, personal biographies, and impersonal forces. "I'm looking for a very difficult pattern in our history," he said. "What I see in 1963, with Kennedy's murder at high noon in Dallas, to 1974, with Nixon's removal, is a pattern." It is a pattern of promise and betrayal, vision and death, from John and Robert Kennedy to Martin Luther King, Jr., and Richard Nixon. "These four men came from different political perspectives, but they were pushing the envelope, trying to lead America to new levels. We posit that, in some way, they pissed off what we call 'the Beast,' the Beast being a force (or forces) greater than the presidency."[50]

Stone's burden is to be history's witness. For him, the past is a very real, painful, and unresolved phenomenon. Like William Faulkner, he believes that "the past is never dead." In fact, "it's not even past." But Stone's view of history contains inherent problems. It indicts an entire culture but suggests that members of that culture can make a lasting difference. For example, in *Born on the Fourth of July*, Stone contends that a martial culture packed Ron Kovic off to Vietnam, but in *JFK* he argues that Kennedy would have ended the war and that his promise died with him. But on a higher level, Stone realizes that the duty of the historian is to keep the past alive. It is the tension between his desire to teach and entertain and his desire to be taken seriously as an arbiter of the past that makes Stone such a controversial figure. Always reluctant to accept the work of popular historians (which Stone certainly is), academics have resisted embracing his vision of the past. And yet, his Vietnam films seem to have touched a nerve in the American public. To his credit, as his fame has grown, he has consistently adopted more sophisticated methods of exploring the past. Beginning in 1986 with an insulated, autobiographical view of history, Stone has expanded his analysis to incorporate the broader themes and movements that lay behind his own experience in Vietnam. In doing this, he uses the methods of a professional historian, going so far as to issue footnotes to accompany his work. Still, Stone remains true to his vision above all else; the details must be subservient to the big picture, the facts must support the conclusion. As Stone wrote, "Elie Wiesel reminds us that survivors are all charged with a sacred mission: to serve as witnesses and teachers of what they suffered, thereby preventing such catastrophes from occurring again."[51] It is this goal, this quest for relevance, that drives Oliver Stone's pursuit of the past, separates his work from that of academic historians, and forces Americans to decide which is more important: a truthful rendition of the facts, or facts rendered in such a way as to illustrate the truth.

*James Woods as photojournalist
Richard Boyle in* Salvador *(Photofest)*

*Elpedia Carrillo, James Woods, and
James Belushi take cover during rebel
uprising in* Salvador *(Photofest)*

James Belushi, James Woods, and John Savage in a scene from Salvador *(Photofest)*

Charlie Sheen as a new arrival to Vietnam in Platoon *(Museum of Modern Art Film Archive)*

*Charlie Sheen,
Chris Pedersen,
and Francesco
Quinn in* Platoon
*(Museum of Modern
Art Film Archive)*

*Tom Berenger as
Barnes in* Platoon
*(Museum of Modern
Art Film Archive)*

*Left to right:
Charlie Sheen,
Corey Glover,
Chris Pedersen,
Willem Dafoe,
Forrest Whittaker,
and Keith David
in* Platoon
*(Museum of
Modern Art
Film Archive)*

*Michael Douglas
as corporate raider
Gordon Gekko
in* Wall Street
*(Museum of Modern
Art Film Archive)*

*Gekko and young
trader Bud Fox
(Charlie Sheen)
confer in* Wall Street
*(Museum of Modern
Art Film Archive)*

*Something catches
Charlie Sheen's eye
in* Wall Street
*(Museum of Modern
Art Film Archive)*

Tom Cruise as Ron Kovic in Born on the Fourth of July *(Museum of Modern Art Film Archive)*

Willem Dafoe and Tom Cruise in Born on the Fourth of July
(Museum of Modern Art Film Archive)

Tom Cruise as Ron in Born on the Fourth of July *(Museum of Modern Art Film Archive)*

Val Kilmer as rock singer Jim Morrison leaps wildly during one of his concerts in The Doors *(Museum of Modern Art Film Archive)*

Val Kilmer as Jim Morrison in The Doors *(Museum of Modern Art Film Archive)*

The motorcade just moments after the assassination in JFK
(Photofest)

Gary Oldman as alleged assailant Lee Harvey Oswald in JFK
(Photofest)

Kevin Costner as New Orleans district attorney Jim Garrison in JFK
(Photofest)

Garrison secretly meets with Colonel X (Donald Sutherland)
in JFK *(Museum of Modern Art Film Archive)*

Hiep Thi Le as Le Ly Hayslip in Heaven and Earth *(Photofest)*

Le Ly and her sons are evacuated by Sergeant Steve Butler played by Tommy Lee Jones in Heaven and Earth *(Museum of Modern Art Film Archive)*

Le Ly tries to sell black-market goods to an American GI in Heaven and Earth *(Museum of Modern Art Film Archive)*

Woody Harrelson as Mickey Knox in Natural Born Killers
(Museum of Modern Art Film Archive)

Juliette Lewis as Mallory Knox with Mickey in Natural Born Killers *(Museum of Modern Art Film Archive)*

Mickey and Mallory get violent in Natural Born Killers *(Photofest)*

Robert Downey, Jr. (center) as tabloid TV star Wayne Gale interviews Mickey in prison in Natural Born Killers *(Photofest)*

Anthony Hopkins as Republican presidental nominee Richard Nixon in Nixon
(Museum of Modern Art Film Archive)

Joan Allen as Pat Nixon dances with her husband the president in Nixon
(Museum of Modern Art Film Archive)

*In the Oval Office, President Nixon rebukes his Secretary of State Henry Kissinger
(Paul Sorvino) in Nixon as his aides look on (Museum of Modern Art Film Archive)*

Under the immediate threat of impeachment, President Nixon contemplates resignation (Museum of Modern Art Film Archive)

PART II
THE
FILMS

Salvador

The 1986 film *Salvador,* resembling the actual U.S. policy in El Salvador between 1979 and 1991, resulted when the historical memories and corrupted idealism of the 1960s confronted the Central American revolutions of the 1980s. Above all, those memories revolved around the tragedy of the U.S. war in Vietnam. That war became the specter that haunted both Oliver Stone, as he made his breakthrough film, and the advisers of Presidents Jimmy Carter and Ronald Reagan, as they channeled into El Salvador nearly $5 billion in aid — making that country the largest per capita recipient of U.S. foreign aid in the world, as Stone noted at the end of *Salvador* — so that the dominant right-wing military and its brutal "death squads" could eliminate the revolutionaries of the Farabundo Martí National Liberation Front (FMLN).

The film, ironically like the war effort it condemned, was a nearly no-holds-barred effort to exorcise various forms of the Vietnam specter. Stone had grown up in a conservative household that simply assumed anticommunist cold war ideology. A short stay at Yale did nothing to shake those assumptions, nor did a volunteer trip to Vietnam in 1965 to teach English. Mainly to prove to his father that he was not a "bum," Stone returned to the United States and enlisted in the army. Sent to Vietnam, he was wounded twice in battle and returned not only with a Purple Heart but also with a Bronze Star for bravery. Not knowing what better to do, he enrolled in the New York University film school, where he learned the rudiments of screenwriting. He also experienced major antiwar protests at NYU.[1] After making several small, unsuccessful horror films, Stone gained his professional reputation in Hollywood by cowriting *Year of the Dragon, Conan the Barbarian,* and *Scarface.* His screenplay for *Midnight Express* won the Academy Award in 1978. *Midnight Express* tells of the horrors encountered by a young American in a Turkish prison after he was accused of possessing drugs. In this film, as in the final scenes of *Salvador,* Stone could draw on his own experience of being arrested on the U.S.-Mexican border and thrown in jail after being charged with smuggling drugs.

Stone's arrest occurred immediately after he returned from Vietnam as a hero. The horrors and disillusionment he experienced in Vietnam, along with the drug arrest and then the antiwar protests around New York City, destroyed his cold war orthodoxies but left a political vacuum in his thinking, not an alternative ideology. Such an ideology took on a more discernible shape in the late 1970s when Stone struck up a friendship with Richard Boyle, an unpredictable, unorthodox, freelance newspaper and television reporter. Having gone to Central America seven times between 1979 and 1982 (largely because of severe marital and financial problems back home in California), Boyle was one of the first reporters who understood both the growing Salvadoran revolutionary movement and the U.S. involvement with the right-wing military that aimed to destroy the FMLN. He had a more personal reason for the trips: Maria, a beautiful Salvadoran woman with whom he had fallen in love, and her brother, Carlos, who was murdered by the right-wing death squads. Boyle was one of the first to inform the world of the martyrdom of Salvadoran Archbishop Oscar Romero, who was shot by a death squad on March 24, 1980, after he had excoriated the military and its allies in the rich, selfish oligarchy for exploiting and killing thousands of peasants.[2]

Boyle had earlier covered the wars in Vietnam and Cambodia, experiences that made him a soul mate of Stone's. It seemed to be the reporter's persona, not his politics, that the screenwriter found most interesting. Boyle "was always broke," Stone recalled, "always needing to be bailed out of jail, always on drunken driving charges. He was a womanizer and a drinker, yet he would always be popping off to these small places, like Ireland or Lebanon, and doing these stories."[3] In December 1984, Boyle gave Stone a rough manuscript of his experiences in El Salvador, which led to a trip by the two men to the ravaged Central American country.

Stone was horrified by the brutalities of the war and the U.S. involvement in it. He quickly linked the conflict to the Vietnam War. "There's going to be another Vietnam," he told the *Los Angeles Times* in late 1985 as he was preparing *Salvador* for release, "and it's going to be in our own backyard. . . . When you look at Central America, it's obvious that it's going to be the next war zone unless the American public wakes up and finds a way to change our foreign policy."[4]

He was partly correct. The United States was regularly holding war games in the region, and its military was deeply involved in fighting the revolutions in the "backyards," especially El Salvador and Nicaragua. The mass of Americans had little interest in or knowledge about the region, but this was not new. Until they faced a major crisis, most Americans had little or no knowledge about or interest in foreign policy. The Central American story in the 1980s, however, turned out to be somewhat different because of the existence of elite, informed, and politically influential antiwar groups that were determined to stop U.S. officials from replaying Vietnam in Central America. Many of these critics were not the usual anti–cold war groups, but instead emerged out of the Roman Catholic Church and such mainstream Protestant denominations as Baptists, Presbyterians, and Methodists — that is, the churches that provided many of the missionary and medical efforts in Central America. These antiwar groups sometimes knew El Salvador or Nicaragua firsthand, even more intimately than did the State Department officials sent to American communities to defend U.S. policies.[5] *Salvador,* contrary to Stone's hope, did little to further enlighten the growing antiwar voices in the United States. It did — to the extent a virtual box-office failure could — reinforce these voices and perhaps make a few others aware of (if not necessarily active about) the tragedies unfolding with massive U.S. help in Central America.

As far as Stone personally was concerned, *Salvador* resulted from the collision of his and Boyle's 1960s idealism, and its consequent dissipation, with the blood-soaked realities in El Salvador. Stone discovered the country as its military was at the midpoint of a decade in which it killed 70,000 Salvadorans. On a proportional population basis, this was the equivalent of murdering over 3 million people in the United States. Stone emphasized that U.S. personnel were deeply implicated in the training and supplying of the Salvadoran death squads: "One clear thesis of the film is that the death squads are the brainchild of the CIA. It goes all the way back to the '60s when we actually trained the original members of the Salvadoran death squads in Vietnam."[6] That statement exaggerated. The death squads were the "brainchild" of the Salvadoran military and oligarchy, and nearly all the U.S. training of that military was done by uniformed officers either in the United States or at the U.S.-operated School of the Americas in Panama. Stone understood, moreover, that the revolutionaries also resorted to brutalities, though not nearly to the degree indulged in by the right wing. "I'm not naive," Stone remarked in late 1985. "I know that if the guerrillas take over, it'll be a bloody revolution."[7]

Stripped of whatever idealism the 1960s had given him, unable to find steady work as a correspondent, Boyle, played brilliantly by James Woods, makes a final return to El Salvador in 1980 — partly to experience the rush of war to prove to himself that he is still alive, partly to file some stories for a little money, and mostly, it seems, to find Maria. Boyle's own marriage has ended in squalor and poverty in San Francisco, that supposed mecca of the 1960s counterculture. He cons an unemployed disk jockey friend, Dr. Rock (James Belushi), to travel with him to El Salvador. In real life, Dr. Rock never went to Central America. The Dr. Rock character was attacked by some critics for being irrelevant and unattractive. But the character is essential to the film. He is a sounding board for Boyle's and Stone's hatred of the 1980s, especially its "yuppie" phenomenon ("this town [San Francisco] is full of god-damned yuppies"). This hatred is notably expressed when Boyle is driving his old Mustang. "Yuppie" was an unknown term in 1980, when this action occurs, but it was known when Stone shot the scenes in 1985. In Stone's hands, Dr. Rock is notably ignorant about the American "backyard."[8] The character becomes virtually irrational when he meets Salvadoran reality headon. As the two men drive into El Salvador, they see a body burning. Dr. Rock screams, "They kill people here." "Relax, man," the world-weary Boyle responds, "it's just some guy."

This is not another Hollywood "buddy" movie. Dr. Rock is bitter about being maneuvered into going to El Salvador (he thought Boyle was driving to Guatemala), and he no sooner arrives and witnesses the ongoing horror than he tries to escape from the country.[9] Dr. Rock, however, like many Americans who went to Central America in the 1980s, becomes enamored with the people and virtually hypnotized by the daily catastrophes that threaten to pull everyone over the edge of civilization. He is soon living with a Salvadoran woman and, near the end of the film, makes a dangerous call to the U.S. embassy that saves Boyle from a death-squad execution. If Boyle is the scarred, warped, lost innocence of the 1960s, Dr. Rock is the ignorant-American-turned-involved-American who might offer some hope in a world of Salvadoran murderers and their U.S. accomplices.

Critics admired *Salvador*'s depiction of those bloody realities. For American audiences, even those inured to images of Vietnam on television screens, some of the realities shocked. When Dr. Rock watches a Salvadoran military officer shoot in cold blood a student simply because he has no identity papers, the American goes nearly berserk. But the film also understated and avoided some of the realities. Stone admitted this when he noted, "I've edited some of the violence."[10] To reach a larger U.S. audience, he felt it necessary, apparently, to pull punches. An example of avoidance occurs early in the film when Boyle and his photographer friend John Cassady (John Savage) visit El Playon, the garbage pile outside the capital city of San Salvador where the death squads daily dump their victims. Buzzards are seen. Bodies are strewn around the hillsides. But they appear to be movie extras. The bodies are not bloated or decomposed. The smells are so tolerable that Boyle and Cassady carry on a philosophical discussion as they walk among the victims. It is not the first time in American film that the process of killing has been shown graphically and in bloody detail but the results have been greatly sanitized for the viewers' comfort. For a supposed antiwar film, however, the sanitizing makes for bad history and confused politics.

Boyle begins to succeed in his main mission. That is, he finds Maria and asks her to marry him. He conveniently lies about the fact that he is already married, although his wife and daughter have left him to return to family in Italy. Maria requires that Boyle rediscover his religious roots, repent his many sins, and become a good Roman Catholic. As a first step, he confesses a few of his sins to a priest in San Salvador's main cathedral. Thus, for reasons of personal penance as well as for professional pay, Boyle is in the cathedral when Archbishop Romero delivers his attack on the Salvadoran military and their oligarchic allies.

Romero's appearance and assassination form the pivot of the film. His character allows Stone to personify both murderers and murdered; provides, in Romero's homily to his congregation, the historical background of the revolution; and gives Boyle the opportunity to forget his personal problems long enough to take sides in the conflict. Stone sets up Romero's killing with a scene depicting Major Max (Tony Plana), the leader and most psychotic and charismatic of the death-squad members, haranguing his advisers about "these fucking priests who are poisoning minds of our Salvadoran youth." Major Max hates any idea of compromise. U.S. Ambassador Thomas Kelly (Michael Murphy) and middle-of-the-road Salvadoran presidential candidate José Napoleon Duarte are, in Max's view, "shitfaces" who sell out to communists. In a moment from *Beckett,* Major Max asks which one of his followers will relieve him of this archbishop.[11]

Stone begins *Salvador* with the notice that "This film is based on events that occurred in 1980–1981. Characters have been fictionalized." The "fiction" about Major Max or Ambassador Kelly, however, is paper thin, and for Duarte and Romero, it disappears completely. Major Max is based on the right-wing military terrorist Roberto D'Aubuisson — constantly identified in real-life classified U.S. diplomatic cables as "Major Bob." In March 1981, the CIA told U.S. Vice President George Bush that D'Aubuisson was the "principal henchman for wealthy landlords" as he coordinated "the right-wing death squads that have murdered several thousand suspected leftists and leftist sympathizers during the past year." This CIA briefing included the top-secret U.S. embassy telegram of November 19, 1980, describing how D'Aubuisson had his followers draw lots to see who would "win" the chance to kill Archbishop Romero.[12]

After Romero's murder in March 1980, U.S. officials grew so concerned that D'Aubuisson would try to kill the new U.S. ambassador, Thomas Pickering, that they sent a secret military emissary, General Vernon Walters, to warn him not to attempt it. "Bloodthirsty, insane, and a pathological murderer" was how U.S. embassy cables quoted left-wing Salvadorans describing D'Aubuisson. Major Bob enjoyed important U.S. support, however, especially from some in the executive branch and from Senator Jesse Helms in Congress. Despite, or because of, his brutality, D'Aubuisson was growing increasingly powerful as

Stone made his film in 1985. By 1990, U.S. Ambassador William Walker reported that "Roberto D'Aubuisson runs El Salvador." Any hope that the murders of Romero, other Salvadoran leaders, or even U.S. citizens would be resolved was impossible as long as Major Bob could kill off informants and intimidate Salvadoran courts.

When the revolutionaries launched an all-out offensive in late 1980, President Jimmy Carter and then, after January 1981, the Reagan administration accelerated military and economic aid to the Salvadoran government. Stone accurately depicts that policy in a scene showing presidential candidate Reagan warning on television that the communists aim not "just . . . at Salvador" but at "North America" itself. Major Max interprets Reagan's words as a "green light" for his death squads. Dr. Rock represents for Stone the increasingly knowledgeable but still naive American public when he asks incredulously, "A straight man to a chimpanzee will be the next president of the United States?" But Major Max had it right: D'Aubuisson's power grew throughout the Reagan presidency until he finally exited in 1992 not from U.S. pressure but from fatal throat cancer.

Stone was harshly criticized for not showing that between D'Aubuisson's death squads and the FMLN stood an acceptable middle position led by Duarte.[13] In the revolutions they have confronted since the late nineteenth century, U.S. leaders have invariably searched for such a middle ground. They have usually failed to find it because none existed. Stone did not fall into that trap. As a relative moderate, Duarte is not "fictionalized" in the film, only marginalized. Major Max, in a scene that D'Aubuisson regularly played out during Salvadoran presidential campaigns, uses his bayonet to slice open a watermelon, then tells cheering onlookers it resembles Duarte's Christian Democratic Party: green on the outside, red on the inside. Duarte had been a highly popular and effective politician in the 1960s and 1970s, but the post-1979 revolution made his moderation more irrelevant. With the United States spending millions of dollars, mostly covertly, to back his candidacy, he finally won the presidency in 1984. But Stone was correct; the real struggle was between Archbishop Romero's principles and D'Aubuisson's brutality. Duarte, even with U.S. support and his own considerable bravery, could find no useful middle way between those poles. By the late 1980s, he was rendered tragically ineffective by both his nation's political fissures and his own stomach cancer.

Archbishop Romero's appearance allows Stone to explain all too succinctly how El Salvador reached the point where a relative moderate like Duarte was irrelevant. Romero gives a brief explanation of the revolution's causes in his homily. Stone surprisingly received less criticism from conservatives about this explanation than from liberals and other antiwar voices, who accused him of ignoring El Salvador's horrible economic and social inequalities, which were the causes of the revolution, and focusing instead on only the symptoms: military brutality, senseless killing, Major Max.[14] The criticism has merit. Only in a fleeting scene in a restaurant does an old Salvadoran woman (never to be seen again on-screen) refer to the 1932 revolution, the eruption whose causes and results were both a preview and an important root of the 1980s upheaval. Stone drops in but never explains the reference to the 1932 events.

He instead has Archbishop Romero provide historical background in the sermon that leads to his death. The army is an "obstacle" to peace, he tells his people, and the government (that is, the Duarte types) cannot control the "paramilitary" death squads. Romero then, if briefly, identifies the reasons for the revolution: land reform is necessary for justice, political power, and even survival for a large majority of Salvadorans because they are landless while the oligarchy — the famous Forty Families — controls much of the land. But the reform is doomed because the army defends "the interests of the rich oligarchy." This is the film's only important, explicit reference to the Forty Families that had exploited and ruled El Salvador since the mid-nineteenth century by any means necessary.

Romero declares that he and others have "repeatedly" asked the United States to cut off aid to the army and help find the tens of thousands of "disappeared," but Washington makes little response. "When this happens," Romero continues ominously, "the Church speaks of the legitimate right of insurrectional violence." So, "my children, you must look to yourselves in this sad time for El Salvador." If he has not crossed the line already, he does so by urging the military to stop killing "your own peasant brothers and sisters." "Violence on all sides is wrong," Romero announces. "I order you in the name of God: stop this oppression!"

If Stone committed any error in giving the historical background of the revolution, it was in limiting the delineation of that background to Romero's homily. The film never adequately shows in other contexts the oligarchy, its uncivilized greed, and the horrible poverty that engulfed a country whose resources, especially those of its hardworking people, could have made it one of the most prosperous and peaceful in the region. But in explaining the causes as Romero saw them, Stone and Boyle were accurate. Fundamental reforms, especially land redistribution, were the prerequisites for political and economic justice, not to mention for the removal of support for the FMLN. U.S. policy makers realized the need for these reforms as early as the 1960s, when they tried to convince the oligarchy to accept such change. The oligarchy, supported by its longtime ally the military, refused. The United States did nothing more. Revolution accelerated. So did the army's brutality. The "violence" and "oppression," as Romero identified them, began a deadly self-generating cycle.[15]

The archbishop pays for confronting this history when, as he is giving communion to supplicants who include Boyle and Maria, Major Max's henchman murders him from inches away. Chaos ensues as the panicked congregation flees into the city square. Machine guns are heard. People fall. The military quickly accuses a human rights advocate (and friend of Boyle's) as Romero's murderer. In a public speech, Major Max declares, "In my book it was the subversives that killed him."

Romero actually did give his sermon in San Salvador's main cathedral. Several of D'Aubuisson's followers, as well as military officers, heard him on March 23 urge the army to stop the oppression — that is, to stop protecting the oligarchy by killing suspected leftists. His actual speech was close to Stone's version, but tougher: "You ought to reflect on the law of God which says: do not kill. No soldier is obliged to obey an order that is contrary to the law of God. . . . I beg, I ask, I order you in the name of God: stop the repression."[16]

Romero had been developing this message over the previous eight months, a period in which at least another thousand people had been massacred and opposition radio stations destroyed. The day after the sermon, the archbishop said mass in the small chapel of a cancer hospital, where he had chosen to live. As he performed the ritual, four men entered the chapel. One fired a shot that cut through an artery to Romero's heart, killing him instantly. Worldwide protests erupted, protests that led the priests, nuns, and others who worked among the poor to condemn the military publicly and to hold the United States responsible for its support of the military. Many of these persons had good reason for their passion; they, like Romero, were on the death squads' lists of potential victims. On March 30, the Plaza Burrios by the cathedral was packed with people who had journeyed to San Salvador for the funeral. As the service began, the square was shaken by an explosion. Shots were fired. The 100,000 people panicked. Some were shot; others were trampled to death. At least fifty people died.[17]

In telescoping the seven days of March 1980 into less than an hour, Stone heightened the dramatic effect but understated the political effects. He understated Romero's actual message, understated the cold blood with which the murder was committed a full day after the incendiary sermon, and understated the time the military took to prepare the massacre on the Plaza Burrios. His filming of the scene on the plaza is superb; critics noted that Stone's handheld camera brought a sense of panic, even suffocation, to the viewer that had rarely if ever been caught on film. For all its power and horror, however, Stone's camera understated what Salvadorans endured in 1980.

The horror, of course, had only begun. The two events that shook even U.S. government officials in 1980 were Romero's murder in March and then the rape and killing of three nuns and a lay churchwoman in December. The churchwoman, Jean Donovan, is Cathy Moore (played by Cynthia Gibb) in the film. She demonstrates her goodness by being a friend and even protector to Boyle, while somehow maintaining both a worldliness and a purity. When Moore (as did Donovan) brings three newly arrived nuns from the airport into San Salvador, they are stopped, raped, shot, and buried in a shallow grave by a death-squad "paramilitary," as Romero had termed such groups.

Stone's 1985–1986 account of the atrocity was substantiated by the evidence that later became available, some of it only in the 1990s. Less substantiated is the encounter at the shallow grave between Ambassador Kelly and his military adviser, Colonel Hyde (Will MacMillan). Kelly accuses Hyde of not informing him about the colonel's collaboration with a transition team sent from Washington by the newly elected Reagan that wanted a bloody, all-out military solution. Kelly, whom Stone later characterized as "a sort of liberal muddlehead," has been a good soldier in carrying out U.S. policies, but he now accuses Hyde of giving a "clear signal" to the death squads — and the result "was this."[18] Although the scene at the grave site probably did not occur, it is true that Ambassador Robert White, on whom Kelly's character is based, was terribly conflicted about U.S. support of the Salvadoran military. After Reagan removed him as ambassador in 1981, White devoted himself to publicly condemning U.S. policy in the region.

But Stone accurately caught another, highly important aspect of the killings. Valerie Wildman (played by Pauline Axelrod) is a U.S. television newswoman whose main purposes in life seem to be defending U.S. policy, regardless of what it is, and leaving behind a trail of sexual exploits that draw comments from her highly cynical colleagues, especially Boyle. Wildman declares on television that "rumor has it they [the four murdered women] ran a roadblock and there was an exchange of gunfire." As Wildman knows by personal observation, not a shred of evidence has surfaced to support such an accusation, but overwhelming evidence does point to death-squad brutality. In reality, Reagan's first secretary of state, Alexander Haig, told a congressional committee that "perhaps the vehicle the nuns were riding in may have tried to run a roadblock." Haig even ignorantly called them "pistol-packing nuns." Reagan's ambassador to the United Nations, Jeane J. Kirkpatrick, declared with total inaccuracy, "The nuns were not just nuns" but FMLN "political activists."[19]

By putting these views in the mouth of a television newswoman whose character has already been questioned, rather than attributing them to two of the highest and supposedly most responsible U.S. officials, Stone again understates the corruption and effect of Washington's policy. He understates another death-squad atrocity when he has the head of El Salvador's land reform killed by the military. The reformer was killed in 1981, but two U.S. AFL-CIO labor organizers were slaughtered with him, and in full view of onlookers in San Salvador's Sheraton Hotel. Stone does nothing with this killing. Nor does he touch on the war's most horrible death-squad acts: the massacre of 767 persons, including 358 babies and children under 13 years of age, at El Mozote in the days following December 11, 1981.[20]

U.S. officials did little to find and bring to justice the killers at El Mozote. Ambassador Dean Hinton, like Ambassador White, had been traumatized by other atrocities, especially the killing of the nuns and Jean Donovan. Washington officials even helped the death squads cover up the El Mozote massacre. One U.S. embassy official, who did investigate and knew the truth, recalled that "people like Enders" (Thomas Enders, who was in charge of the State Department's Latin American desk) had "priorities" that were "definitely not necessarily about getting at exactly what happened."[21]

That Stone did not exploit the massacre is especially puzzling, because while writing the screenplay he relied heavily on Raymond Bonner's *Weakness and Deceit: United States Policy and El Salvador*.[22] Bonner was the *New York Times* correspondent who revealed the massacre in January 1982. For his honesty and accuracy, Reagan administration newspapers, led by the *Wall Street Journal,* attacked Bonner, while U.S. embassy officials in San Salvador ominously announced that the correspondent was "going to get himself killed." Caving in, the *New York Times* called Bonner back to the United States.[23] Bonner, like Boyle, was from California and was fearless about revealing the Salvadoran horrors, but he was unlike Boyle in nearly every other way. The *New York Times* correspondent was a sophisticated law school graduate, a Vietnam veteran. But Stone saw Bonner and Boyle as being alike on crucial points: both arrived in El Salvador understanding little about the revolution; both learned firsthand about its causes and the death-squad atrocities; and both were essentially repudiated by the society they tried to educate, at risk to their own lives, about that society's closest Salvadoran friends.

Stone used yet a third journalist to tell his story. Photographer John Cassady (played by John Savage) was based on the real-life John Hoagland of *Newsweek,* who was killed in El Salvador. Cassady, whose discipline and commitment are considerably closer to Bonner's than Boyle's, utters the most quoted lines from the film when he and Boyle are snapping pictures of the victims on El Playon's human trash heap: "You know what made photographers great, Rich? They weren't after money — they captured the nobility of human suffering. That's what [Robert] Capa caught, he caught that moment of death. You got to get close, Rich, to get the truth. You get too close, you die."[24] Cassady and Boyle decide to "get the truth" by going into the mountains to see the revolutionaries firsthand. Boyle has other reasons for taking this risk. He not only needs the money such a scoop might bring, but he is willing to trade information he gleans from the rebels with the U.S. embassy's hard-line military adviser, Colonel Hyde, in return for papers that will allow Maria to return with Boyle to the United States.

Some critics blasted Stone's handling of the revolutionaries. Walter Goodman wrote in the *New York Times:* "One look at the youthful, idealistic guerrillas, accompanied everywhere by folk music, and you know where Mr. Stone's heart lies. . . . For a movie with pretensions to laying out the political realities, the colorful 'Salvador' is black and white."[25] The "political realities," however, were that of the 70,000 Salvadoran civilians slaughtered in the 1980s, the overwhelming majority were killed by the guerrillas' opponents. The "political realities" in 1980–1981 were also the murder of Romero, the rape and shooting of the nuns and Jean Donovan, the El Mozote atrocities, and the killing of the three reformers in the Sheraton Hotel. No guerrilla activities even faintly approached those horrors. As Goodman acknowledges, Stone shows the guerrillas executing captured enemy soldiers, an act that leads Boyle to cry out, "You'll become just like them." (Stone apparently did not share Boyle's concern; he said he'd understand if, once in power, the guerrillas executed the entire Salvadoran high command.[26]) Boyle, moreover, is no romantic about the revolutionaries' chances. Commandante Martí (Miguel Ehrenberg) declares that their offensive will conquer El Salvador before the new Reagan administration can act. Boyle responds, "The Pentagon won't let that happen."

And it did not. When the FMLN launched its major offensive in late 1980, outgoing President Jimmy Carter, acting in part on Ambassador Robert White's advice, turned his eyes away from the Romero and nuns-Donovan murders that had led him to cut off military aid to El Salvador. He resumed sending the aid, then watched as the Salvadoran military, advised by U.S. officers, smashed the offensive. Stone attempts to show vividly the rebels' spirit and the military's overwhelming, U.S.-supplied firepower. Perhaps he tries to do so too vividly: he has the revolutionaries attacking on horseback. Such a cavalry charge never occurred in the conflict (a point most critics of the film seemed to miss). Stone granted the overdramatization: "We knew the horseback scene wasn't accurate, but we went with it because essentially we were romantics and we just wanted to have a charge on horseback."[27]

There is little romanticism in the scenes, but when horse met American-made military machines, the scenes did underline the heavy U.S. involvement with the Salvadoran military. The involvement was already becoming sensitive. Even as Congress worked with the Reagan administration to pump $1.5 million of military aid per *day* into El Salvador, the House and Senate later tried to appease the growing number of antiwar critics by limiting U.S. military personnel in the country to fifty-five and prohibiting them from combat zones. Stone notes this point when the television newswoman encounters a group of U.S. soldiers entering the country. Their colonel assures her it is not a troop buildup, but only the advisers authorized by Washington. In reality, the fifty-five limit was easily and regularly flaunted. At least twenty-one U.S. military personnel, moreover, died in El Salvador. The complete list has never been made public by the U.S. government. Some died, the Pentagon later acknowledged, while advising troops in the field or flying helicopters in combat zones. Most of the known involvement occurred after 1982, but given the extent of the support in 1980–1981, Stone did not exaggerate in showing the U.S. involvement in stopping the rebels' offensive. Even as he made the film, and indeed throughout the late 1980s and early 1990s, U.S. officials denied that the Pentagon had violated the congressional restrictions. Then in 1995, President Bill Clinton signed legislation that allowed those U.S. servicemen who had operated in Salvador's combat zones to be given medals. Their service was by some weird reasoning to be rewarded rather than condemned as illegal.[28]

Cassady gets "too close to the truth" in the offensive. He dies when he moves into an open space to get a clear photograph of a U.S.-supplied plane strafing the rebels. The professionals, the idealists — Cathy Moore and John Cassady — are tragically killed while Boyle survives. Before the offensive, Boyle tries to exchange the information he obtained from the rebels with the U.S. military adviser and an embassy (no doubt CIA) official; in return, he wants Maria's emigration papers. But Boyle, having experienced the deaths of Romero, Moore, and Maria's brother, grows reluctant to give U.S. officials much information. The officials, whose distaste for Boyle and what news reporters stand for is unbounded ("I hate the species you belong to," Colonel Hyde says bluntly), refuse to provide the papers. Stone uses their conversation as he used Romero's homily, that is, to delineate some historical background (above all, the ghost of Vietnam) and especially the ideologies that supposedly pragmatic, non-ideological Americans prefer to think they do not have even as they express their ideology in the strongest terms. It is also a conversation that one analyst said helped make "*Salvador* the most politically outspoken and also the most raw-edged of any of Stone's films."[29]

When the colonel declares flatly that powerful U.S. technological surveillance and intelligence have proved "10,000 percent that this ain't no civil war, but outright commie aggression," Boyle responds, "You guys have been lying about it from the beginning. You have not presented one shred of proof to the

American public that this is anything other than a legitimate peasant revolution." In quite different ways, Hyde and Boyle are both right: the United States had incredibly powerful surveillance instruments working in El Salvador, but Washington officials could never come up with legitimate evidence to convince the American public that the revolution was instigated and kept going by outside communist forces. Thus trapped, much as they were in Vietnam by a similar dilemma, the officials, Boyle charges, have been trying to escape by lying about the extent of U.S. involvement and "lying saying that this war can be won militarily, which it can't." (And it never was. A military stalemate led to a United Nations–brokered peace in 1991.) By allowing the CIA to help build the military and its death squads in the name of "bullshit anticommunism," Boyle adds, "you've created a major Frankenstein." Colonel Hyde replies, "It was that kind of crap thinking that got us into Vietnam — this guilt shit." Boyle exclaims, "Is that why you guys are here? Some kind of post-Vietnam experience, like you need a rerun or something?"[30]

Boyle's reference to "Frankenstein" was accurate. Either the U.S. military could not control the Salvadoran terror or it was an accomplice in it. The former, not the latter, was the case, even though Pentagon and State Department officials showed too little enthusiasm for discovering the truth about how Frankenstein had murdered the nuns and Jean Donovan or committed the massacre at El Mozote. The Vietnam analogy was more complex. President Reagan was determined to neutralize the bad memories of Vietnam so that he could use military force or threats of force more liberally. Some of his team, most notably Lieutenant Colonel Oliver North, were Vietnam veterans who believed that their nightmares of the 1960s and early 1970s could be exorcised in Central America by pouring in U.S. aid and advisers until the revolutionaries surrendered.[31]

Other U.S. military officers, unlike Colonel Hyde or Oliver North, were wary of turning El Salvador into a rerun of Vietnam with a happier ending. They knew that they could march into the battle on the orders of ardent civilian and military policy makers only to discover — as they had to their great cost in the early 1970s — that as their casualties rose and antiwar sentiment increased in the United States, their political leaders would leave them without the necessary support. Because of this reasoning, by 1984–1985, when Stone was making the film, the Pentagon had become strongly opposed to further U.S. military commitments in El Salvador unless Reagan and Congress would provide a foolproof pledge that they would support such a commitment to the bitter end, if necessary. No such commitment could be made.[32]

There remained the Colonel Hydes, whose memories and anticommunism took them deeper into El Salvador. But there were others, especially in the higher reaches of the Pentagon, who feared that a rabid determination to kill the white whale of Vietnam would fatally expose them to public antiwar pressures shaped by the Boyles, Cassadys, and Bonners. U.S. officials consequently did all they could to fight the revolutionaries in El Salvador (and Nicaragua) during the 1980s, but to fight as quietly as possible. One form this effort took, as Stone had Boyle point out, was lying about the extent of Washington's involvement. Another form was the Reagan administration's immigration policy, which Stone noted at the end of *Salvador,* without exploring its larger meaning.

In the film's final scenes, Boyle has barely missed being murdered by a death squad as he tries to leave the country with Maria. As they ride northward in a bus, discussing their future life and believing that they have finally escaped the war, black-suited U.S. immigration agents wearing sunglasses board the bus. They demand papers from Maria. When she admits she has none, they put her in an automobile and take her back toward El Salvador. Boyle screams, "They'll rape her, they'll kill her" if she is sent back. In captions at the film's end, Stone notes that Maria was last seen in Guatemala, where she had escaped, and Boyle continues to look for her.

These final scenes were personal for Stone because of his own brief imprisonment in San Diego by U.S. border agents immediately after he returned from Vietnam. Until his father found a lawyer who could pull political strings, Stone faced a five- to twenty-year prison term for attempting to smuggle drugs. "That was my homecoming," he told *Time* magazine in early 1987. "I got a true picture of the states. I hated America. I would have joined the Black Panthers if they'd asked me. I was a radical, ready to kill."[33]

That personal episode helped dramatize a larger historical truth. The U.S. Immigration and Naturalization Service's treatment of Maria was not unusual. During the 1980s, some 500,000 Salvadorans tried to flee the fighting and death-squad horrors by seeking refuge in the United Sates. Most did not find refuge. In fiscal year 1984, for example, when Stone was becoming committed to his project, U.S. immigration officials allowed only 328 Salvadorans to remain and turned back 13,045 on the grounds that they only sought jobs in the United States — and they no longer faced danger if they returned to El Salvador.[34] Notably, Nicaraguan refugees received asylum from the Reagan administration in nearly the reverse ratio. But Washington officials were trying to discredit and weaken the revolutionary Nicaraguan government, while supporting the military rule in El Salvador.

Not surprisingly, Stone had difficulty finding money to get such messages on film. "*Salvador* was just too anti-American for the American money people," he recalled. Moreover, "the track record on Central American films was real poor." *Missing* and *Under Fire* were critical successes and box-office disappointments. "Certain people," Stone noted, "hated the script because of its portrayal of Americans." He finally found the necessary $4 to $5 million from Hemdale, a British company that, Stone believed, saw irony in the film and viewed the Boyle and Dr. Rock characters "as funny, almost in Monty Pythonesque terms. I sold it as 'Laurel and Hardy go to Salvador.' I wanted the movie to start that way and then twist."[35]

He hoped to film in El Salvador, because of both the authentic settings and how inexpensive it would be. D'Aubuisson and his henchmen actually welcomed Stone at first. They admired his screenplay of *Scarface,* especially its macho treatment of criminals. But when Richard Cienfuegos, Stone's main contact with D'Aubuisson and the government, was killed by the FMLN in March 1985, the plan fell apart. Filming was done largely in Mexico. Hemdale approached major U.S. studios for distribution, but they refused unless they controlled video rights, where they estimated (correctly) the profits would be. Hemdale then tried to distribute the film. It impressed filmgoers in several major cities, especially Los Angeles, but was not seen or failed elsewhere.[36]

Critical praise, however, made Stone a more bankable director. *Salvador* thus helped him realize his long-held dream of making *Platoon,* which appeared to acclaim weeks after the first film. In truth, the critical praise for *Salvador* was far from unanimous. Nearly every reviewer admired what Paul Attanasio called its "irresistible brassiness, a swing-at-the-moon quality — it's big and loud and bold . . . and has more energy than any 10 films this year." Attanasio added: "But if Stone's metier is a brand of left-wing machismo that's nearly extinct, it's also a style you wish were around more these days, especially when it results in movies like 'Salvador.' "[37] Charles Champlain, in contrast, saw "a kind of painful balance in the film that in effect says 'A pity on both [the military's and the rebels'] households.' Its message . . . is not that we're betting on the wrong team but that we shouldn't be in the game at all."[38]

Gene Siskel did not directly attack the political message but condemned Stone's apparent put-down of rational and sober, as well as courageous, foreign correspondents and television reporters. Siskel termed "absurd" the "concluding scene in which the U.S. border patrol is equated with the right-wing monsters in El Salvador."[39] Pauline Kael and Walter Goodman were among the few who directly attacked what they saw as the film's political message. Of all the major films about "third-world repression" *(State of Siege, Missing, Under Fire, The Killing Fields),* Kael considered *Salvador* "perhaps the most visceral. It's also possibly the most politically simplistic. It shapes the issues so that we're seeing the primal battle of good and evil." Stone's film, she charged, "is a right-wing macho vision joined to a left-leaning polemic."[40] Goodman criticized

Stone for "no acknowledgment here of any political position between the murders on the right and the Marxist-led young agrarian reformers on horseback."[41]

That *Salvador* did so little to intensify the debate raging over Reagan's Central American policy in 1986–1987 was due in part to its box-office failure. It was also due, however, to attacks from the Left, especially some political activists, as well as from the Right. Novelist Robert Stone dismissed the film as a "true descendant" of *Arise My Love,* whose "lovely phony international sophistication makes it as much an artifact of its time as *Salvador* is of the eighties." Robert Stone and others on the Left especially disliked Oliver Stone's failure to trace the socioeconomic condition that finally exploded into revolution.[42]

As an attempt to show the realities of the Salvadoran upheaval, the film's refusal to delineate those socioeconomic conditions is a major weakness. Too often Stone lapses into using stereotypes of Latin America, notably in portraying peasants and especially peasant women like Maria, rather than showing the variations and rapid evolution of that culture in revolutionary conditions.[43] Nor do the comparisons continually made with Vietnam turn out to be entirely accurate, in part because the two wars were so dissimilar (for example, Vietnam was much more of an anticolonial conflict, whereas El Salvador was an internal revolution), and in part, perhaps, because voices such as Stone's helped limit the direct U.S. military involvement in Central America. Another major weakness is that *Salvador* softens the horror of the atrocities and how U.S. officials ignored or, at certain moments (as in the deaths of the churchwomen), condoned the brutalities.

To a remarkable degree, however, Stone caught much of the political debate accurately. Neither side was without sin, although one was certainly much more sinned against than the other. The conflict was bloody, horrible, confused, and, notably, unresolved — not at all resembling the conflicts in such box-office winners of the 1980s as *Rambo* and *Top Gun*. There could be no political resolution in El Salvador because, as Stone correctly argued, during the 1980s there was no viable middle ground. As he also noted, the United States continued its all-out support of the Salvadoran military even as Washington officials hoped that in some miraculous way the more moderate Duarte could control the politics. This contradiction made a political resolution in the 1980s impossible. It would take strong initiatives from other Central American leaders (especially Costa Rica's Oscar Arias), a long military stalemate, and pressure and mediation by United Nations officials before a truce and then elections finally came about between 1991 and 1996. Even with the peace, however, political control remained with only a slightly more benign version of D'Aubuisson's political party, Arena. U.S. as well as Salvadoran officials, moreover, had little luck in bringing to justice the killers actually responsible for the deaths of Romero, the three nuns, Jean Donovan, and the victims at the Sheraton Hotel and El Mozote, not to mention much less famous victims such as Maria's brother.[44]

In *Salvador,* Stone realized his ambition of becoming, as he termed it, a "cinematic historian."[45] He did so because he understood, as Simon Schama later phrased it, that "memory is not always identical with consolation."[46] For many Americans, such a view is un-American. But then for many Americans, including Oliver Stone, so was the U.S. involvement in the tragedies of El Salvador.

Platoon

I remember with great clarity the day I saw *Platoon* for the first time. A call had come in from the producers at *Nightline* asking me to go on the show that night to talk about an unusually gritty new movie about Vietnam, and I, knowing nothing about the movie, had immediately accepted and then scurried around to find out where it was playing. My only shot was to go to an afternoon showing in one of those giant Times Square theaters, places that are usually two-thirds empty in the afternoon during the middle of the week.

Until the call from *Nightline*, I had heard nothing about the movie — nothing from my old colleagues who had covered the war (we sometimes, it seems to me, form our own small VFW Post), no word of mouth from the movie cognoscenti, no printed teaser in the local media about it, no publicity agent tipping me off that this was a movie I ought to see. I was therefore stunned when I got to the theater and found a huge line already waiting outside. That was the first tip-off: a long line at a huge downtown theater in Times Square in midafternoon for a movie no one had heard about with no recognizable stars in it. The second clue was that the line was composed entirely of men, and they were all in their early to mid-forties. Clearly the word had gotten out, and even more clearly, it had gotten out among Vietnam veterans.

What I remember clearly about the afternoon, in addition to the excellence of the movie, was the audience. The men who saw the movie that day were the men who had fought the war, and almost all of them were there by themselves. They, less clued in to what the cognoscenti knew, had somehow picked up word of mouth on it already. They looked like they were blue-collar workers, construction men, and outdoor men for the electric company, and they had come right from work without changing. Nor was this in any sense a social occasion, for they had not brought dates or wives or buddies. There was a certain apartness or aloneness to the men in that line, one that would match the aloneness showing on the screen. It was a very quiet group; there was no joking, no instant camaraderie of men with common experiences establishing their connections. This was serious business to the men in that line. I do not want to be melodramatic, but certainly some of them wore their interior wounds on their faces.

If it was quiet in the line, it was even more quiet in the theater once the movie started. I remember two things about that showing — first, how good the movie was, tough and unsparing and filled with all the little truths about the war that filmgoers had so long been denied; and second, the silence in the audience. One could feel the cumulative tension of men watching a terrible but important part of their lives flash in front of them again. It was a special kind of quiet in the theater, a tense, almost fearful quiet, as if they had been transported back to the worst moments of their lives with this special two-hour visa courtesy of Oliver Stone.

There is a scene early in the movie when the freshly minted grunt and the film's essential narrator, played by Charlie Sheen, is part of an ambush deep in heavy foliage in the mountainous part of the central highlands. We see him and his buddies half asleep, paralyzed, as North Vietamese Army (NVA) troops deftly and quietly move up on them, ready to whack their would-be ambushers. There is an eerie truth to the scene: the terrain itself is lush and therefore terrifying, the NVA soliders move with a lethal professionalism on soil far more familiar to them than to the Americans. The Americans seem utterly immobilized even as the North Vietnamese are right on top of them. It is the moment that anyone who ever went to Vietnam feared the most, and it seems unlikely that anyone will get out of this moment alive, including, because of the power of Stone's direction, those of us in the theater. Rarely have I seen an audience so completely trans ported into the world of the cinematic image in front of them: at that moment it was truly airless in the theater, as if we were all about to be hammered by the NVA while trying to set — ineptly — our own ambush.

Platoon is a great movie — a great American movie and a great war movie. It ranks with one of my other favorite war movies, Stanley Kubrick's *Paths of Glory*. More, it was the movie I had been hoping to see for a long time, for more than twenty years. Those of us who had written critically or pessimistically about the war had waited for Hollywood to match our efforts. My first book on Vietnam, *The Making of Quagmire*, which was quite pessimistic, had come out some twenty-two years earlier with a strong portrait of John Vann, a leg-endary dissident adviser. There had been much talk at the time of a movie about him and the war. Nothing, of course, happened in terms of a movie sale, not for me nor for the countless others who came along right after me and had written with some degree of realism about what was happening there. We all received quick, flattering phone calls from people in Hollywood allegedly eager to turn our books into movies; Hollywood, we were all to learn, was a place for the large of ego and the faint of heart.

To say that its inhabitants were schizophrenic about the war seems an under-statement. As the antiwar movement grew (and became systematically more legitimate), no industry seemed so committed to the war's end. No industry's leading citizens gave and attended more fund-raisers or signed more petitions. Old-time lefties, who had been blacklisted during the McCarthy period, were now rehabilitated in a show of solidarity and a stand against the war. Hollywood did everything to show its dissent from the war except make movies about it. In terms of Vietnam, Hollywood gave at the fund-raiser but not at the office.

Significantly, the one important movie made early on was pro-war, made by the odd man out politically, John Wayne. Whatever else can be said about Wayne, on this occasion he put his money where his mouth was. Naturally, his movie could readily have been made by the Pentagon itself. It accepts all the official (highly dubious and very different from the unofficial) rationales for American intervention and departs completely from any thoughtful understanding of modern Vietnamese history; it is Vietnamese history as the Americans wished it had been, not, regrettably, history as the Vietnamese lived it. It is more cartoon than anything else, but in order to understand the true historical validity of what Stone did — to break with the American cinematic propaganda of an earlier and more conventional incarnation — it remains important. It might have been a terrible movie, but it got made.

The Green Berets, which came out in 1968, the year of Tet, can be generously described as the last World War II movie, regrettably produced for a war that was diametrically different. It is childishly simplistic: we are the good guys, the other side the bad guys. The Duke is the Duke, the leader that the other good guys can always turn to. In real life, he was apparently too ambitious to take a three- or four-year sabbatical to serve his country during World War II, back when patriotism truly mattered, but he obviously decided to make up for that little gap in personal heroism — the fact that he had never heard a shot fired in anger — by talking and acting, both off and on camera for the rest of his life, as if he were the distilled essence of American patriotism. In this movie he replays all the old Duke roles. He is gruff but humane, tough enough to get the job done but sensitive enough to let the men around him know he cares, a man's man who uses his considerable muscle only when it is time to teach the local bully a lesson or two. Wayne, by 1967 when *The Green Berets* was made, was a little long in the tooth and heavy in the gut, as befits someone who had been making comparable movies for nearly thirty years and had starred cinematically as far back as Iwo Jima. He plays Mike Kirby, a Special Forces colonel who is supposed to command all the Special Forces troops in Vietnam but ends up leading a thirteen-man A team near the Cambodian border. We know that the Duke is something of a hero to all the other Special Forces people he meets, because they all tell him how good it is to have him aboard and how they've heard so much about him and always admired him. It's that kind of screenplay.

Almost everything about the movie is derivative of Wayne's movie past, but in this particular case, it was going into uncharted territory. The American forces were not fighting the Germans and Japanese or even the North Koreans in an old-fashioned border-crossing war. Instead, we were plunking young men down in the middle of a revolutionary war, and we were fighting because of the nature of Vietnamese history, nothing less than the birthright of the nation. We were going against the most powerful historical force imaginable, the force of indigenous nationalism, which had always worked for the other side. As such, *The Green Berets* is almost uniquely simplistic and wrongheaded. It is quite possible that much of the historiography of the early Wayne westerns, the John Ford movies on the cavalry, is equally wrong, but that particular history has long ago blended into myth, so whatever liberties the storytellers took is not so jarring. Not so with *The Green Berets.* It's contemporary, it's dishonest, it's wrong, and it's the kind of movie, with its uniquely American arrogance, that encourages politicians and policy makers to make horrendous decisions because of an almost unconscious racism. Almost everything in the movie is in one way or another wrong, and it's the kind of dopey movie that gets kids killed.

It is full of speeches and agitprop and bluster. Any sense of the war — that is, the history of the war that produced this melancholy outcome — is nonexistent. So we have a group of American soldiers posted in difficult, godforsaken terrain leading primitive local tribesmen or montagnards against hated ethnic Vietnamese. It is important to understand that the Special Forces worked primarily with montagnards, and the montagnards, simple tribal people who had been abused for centuries by the Vietnamese, hated *all* Vietnamese, both the ARVN (Army of the Republic of Vietnam) and the VC (Vietcong). To understand these tribal differences and ethnic hatreds, I suggest we reverse the optic and then try to imagine that we can, historically, jiggle the time frame of history and blend the history of the westward movement with that of the cold war. In a comparable modern-day scenario, the Americans are trying to wipe out a powerful Native American presence in the West while the cold war is at its height, and the Russians are sending weapons and advisers to the Sioux and the Apache. The Duke in that scenario would be a Russian adviser to the Apache, but he would be advising a renegade group of American soldiers who, for various reasons, were fighting alongside the Russians.

The complexity of that historical fact seems not to have dawned on the makers of the movie. Indeed, in the movie, the A team seems to be married to Vietnamese regular units. In real life, the American A teams worked with the montagnards, and they — montagnards and American sneaky Petes alike — despised the South Vietnamese regular units. Journalists like me based in Saigon only had to go and spend some time with our friends in the Special Forces A teams to be updated on, among other things, how poorly the ARVN troops were behaving and how corrupt many of the local officials were. One of my great sources in those days was a Special Forces captain named George Gaspard who ran an A team in a place called Dak Pek. He and others like him were a fountain of information about ARVN inadequacies.

In *The Green Berets,* the true enemy is not just the VC but also, inevitably, the American press. Reporters are represented cinematically by David Jansen, normally a gifted actor, in an unusually robotic performance. Jansen plays a cynical, contrarian reporter who will, in the end, be swayed by the sinister deeds of the other side and come over to the Duke's view of things. There was a very good reason why, for the first time in this century, a giant chasm existed between what the military command in Saigon was reporting and what American officers in the field (and thus American reporters in the field) were reporting. This explanation would have been at the heart of a movie about my friend Lieutenant Colonel John Vann, which is one reason it was never made. Not only would it have gone against the grain in terms of taking on a war that was not yet unpopular, but it would have meant showing that the American government was systematically lying, something that Hollywood of the mid-1960s was not prepared to do. But Wayne does not seek complexity: he comes to history and to war armed with certitudes, so he does not try to explain why there were two distinct and separate channels of reporting — the unofficial one, which was accurate, and the official one, which was not. He seeks only to diminish the credibility of the journalists. Late in the movie, after the Jansen character switches sides and becomes something of a hawk, the Duke asks him what he's going to write "in that newspaper of yours." "If I say what I feel, I may be out of a job," he answers.

Perhaps the most egregious sin of the movie is its characterization of the strength, will, and talent of the other side (which is a critical reason it is hard on the journalists, who were, unlike the Saigon command, constantly factoring American field advisers' respect for the enemy into their dispatches). But the Vietcong and the NVA (and the Vietminh before them) were formidable fighting forces, the former generally fighting in smaller units (occasionally reaching regimental strength) and the latter in traditional large units that moved in-country once American combat units arrived in mid-1965. Both forces were very good, very well led, and very brave, and both were fighting what was by then roughly their twentieth year of a revolutionary war in which they had always been pitted against either a Western army or a Western-sponsored army that had far greater technological advantages. Yet the Vietminh/VC/NVA had always managed to succeed. Known as the Vietminh in the first part of this ongoing war, they had defeated the ARVN (which had American advisers down to the battalion level as well as helicopters, fighter-bombers, and armored vehicles) from 1960 to 1964. When the movie was made in 1967, they, now as the NVA and the VC, were in the process of first stalemating and then defeating a powerful American army composed of half a million extremely well armed men. (It should be noted that the decision to turn the forces of the other side into ludicrous cartoon figures is something that Wayne shares with Sylvester Stallone in the latter's equally ugly Rambo movies, which were the lineal descendants of *The Green Berets* some fifteen years later. The main difference is the powerful new aroma of paranoia that marks Rambo — after all, in the early 1980s it was obvious we had lost in Vietnam. And if we lost to a bunch of goofy little Asians, Stallone [who sat out much of the war teaching in a girls' school in Switzerland] seems to be saying, it must have been because we were betrayed by our *politicians.*)

In *The Green Berets* the NVA and the VC are deprived of their historical cause and thus their historical legitimacy. That, of course, was always the key to their battlefield victories and their ability to keep recruiting, keep coming, and thus withstand the awesome technological advantage of their Western opponents, a use of firepower that might have destroyed the will of a lesser people. Wayne (and Stallone after him) was not alone in separating the other side from its cause, from the source of its valor and strength. The American architects of the war did the same thing in 1965 when they made their decision to intervene; in their discussions of whether to send troops, the architects — with the exception of George Ball, who argued against intervention — never mentioned the eight-year French Indochina war that had preceded what would be our Vietnam War, nor how and why the Vietminh had defeated the mighty French.

If there is one large historical truth to Wayne's movie, it is an involuntary one: the history of Vietnam, as far as the Duke is concerned, begins only when he arrives in-country, which is a *very* American outlook. More importantly, he sees Vietnamese history and thus Vietnamese politics through what are completely American eyes, not deigning to know or to understand why a people who have been colonized for so long by a Caucasian nation might be fighting so bravely to rid their soil of all foreign influences. The Duke is fighting communism, but what is working for the other side in this case is nationalism. The idea that the Duke might be fighting on the wrong side — a side that the rest of the world sees as a bully — is not permissible.

Inevitably, the men who fight against him become cartoon figures, untrustworthy and treacherous little men. The climax to the movie comes when the

Duke, aided by a seductive Vietnamese beauty, leads a team of commandos deep into VC territory and they successfully kidnap a VC general. If you think anything like that happened in real life, you have surely got the wrong war.

At the very end, after the VC general is captured, there is the requisite was-this-worth-fighting-for scene. It shows the Duke and the mandatory young war orphan (playing the role of the person we're there fighting to protect) walking toward the South China Sea. The orphan, Ham Chung, has just lost his best pal, an American soldier named Peterson.

"You always knew it [Peterson's death] could happen, didn't you?" says the Duke.

"But I didn't want it to," the orphan says.

"None of us did," comforts the Duke.

"Was my Peterson brave?" the boy asks.

"He was very brave. Are you going to be brave?"

"I'll try," the boy says.

"I know you will. And I'm sure your Peterson would want you to have this." He thereupon gives the orphan Peterson's own green beret. "You're what this is all about," he tells him. The kid dons the beret. Then they keep walking toward the South China Sea as the sun continues to set in front of them, marking the first time, my colleague Charley Mohr once noted, that the sun has set in the east.

That is the least of its historical inaccuracies. The war was never about Ham Chung. It was about many things. In the minds of the Democratic Party architects who took us past the Rubicon, more than anything else it was probably about the fear of losing Saigon to the communists and a repeat performance of Red-baiting by the Republicans in Congress. Because of the virulence of the attacks on Harry Truman after China went communist some fifteen years earlier, Lyndon Johnson feared that he would lose Washington if he lost Saigon. And so, quite wary and unhappy with his direction, far from optimistic about the outcome but unable to turn back, he made the fateful and tragic decisions that brought us to a combat commitment in an unwinnable war.

It is that fateful misreading of history by an American president and his arrogant set of advisers that Stone deals with. *Platoon* begins with the bastardized product of a terribly flawed reading of history and thus a terribly flawed policy: we see shrewd, hip, skeptical, almost cynical grunts caught up in events far beyond their making that have placed them in the central highlands in the early fall of 1967. It would be hard to think of territory more alien for men of a rich, comfortable, highly industrialized Western nation; whatever else, these men will never gain any kind of traction in this terrain. At this point in the war, draftees have already begun to replace career enlisted men. The somewhat edgy enthusiasm of the regular army that marked the first year of the war has long since disappeared. If back in Saigon and the Pentagon much of the military command is still misreading and thus underestimating the vitality and resilience of the other side, these young men know how tough the enemy is. It is increasingly clear that this is a meat-grinder war, that the other side's main-force units are very good, that they are willing to accept very high casualty rates to sustain the war, and that the only American advantage is its superior technology, its airpower and helicopters.

More than anything else, the historic miscalculations by the war's architects are made clear in *Platoon*. Not only has the other side chosen to reinforce the Vietcong by sending main-force units in, but the use of strategic airpower — that is, the ability to limit infiltration — is (predictably) a great deal less than the air force commanders implied. Here is another miscalculation: Vietnam on the map looks small, but it is not small at all, and it has the kind of terrain that can swallow up half a million men and limit their combat effectiveness because the historical forces at work control only the land they stand on. They can fight bravely in the central highlands and even win the occasional set-piece battle, but the next day they will be gone somewhere else and the terrain will belong once again to the other side. What emerges more clearly than anything else in this movie is the power of both the terrain itself and the richness of the foliage to diminish any technological advantages. The other side shrewdly learned to fight on terrain favorable to it, to use the night as an ally, and to close to within thirty meters to negate its opponents' greater material advantage. We have a small sense of one other miscalculation: because of the French Indochina war, Hanoi, unlike Saigon, has a dynamic that works and that allows its soldiers to take a terrible pounding and keep coming. Inevitably, although the kill ratio was probably ten to one in our favor, the fact that the war was part of a historic revolution to them and a war of luxury to us made that kill ratio acceptable to them.

I have a good deal of trouble with the history presented in some of Stone's subsequent films, which seems to be driven too much by what Vietnam did to him emotionally, by a need to find clear answers to justify what he witnessed and was a part of in Vietnam, when the real answers are in fact all too ambiguous. But I think he serves history well in *Platoon*, because his sense of what happened is so pure. When we are talking about his subsequent portrait of Lyndon Johnson, we are not talking about Stone's life, but when we are talking about Vietnam, we are. This movie is *of* him. The truth and pain of his own experience are there in scene after scene. He would not know how to get it wrong or to accommodate to the fantasy machinery of Hollywood.

What is palpable, for example, about Stone's grunts are their jarred nerves. Unlike in many movies, where the screenwriters seem to be giving us people they know about only from other movies, we are dealing here with Stone's contemporaries and comrades, the men with whom he shared that terrible experience, doomed as it was. Not surprisingly, the American soldiers he portrays tend to have a markedly different sensibility from those we have met before, a sensibility that is surely part generational and part environmental. That is, they have a certain wariness and skepticism that existed even before they arrived in-country, but it flowered into true cynicism because of the very nature of Vietnam itself and because of a shrewd capacity on the part of most grunts to calculate who had been sent to serve and who had not. In time they came to understand that the war was unwinnable and that their job would be to fight the war and prolong it until some kind of peace settlement could be worked out. If it was a meat-grinder war, they came to understand that they were the meat.

That knowledge greatly heightened the sense of alienation. In *The Green Berets,* the actors always seem like actors, albeit, because of the wooden nature of the screenplay, not very good ones. It is hard to imagine them as actual grunts, and they are given to patriotic speeches; they talk like almost no one I ever met in Vietnam, and the movie's screenplay seems to have been written in a secret windowless office of the Department of Defense, Division of Agitprop. By contrast, Stone's people, both white and black, know that they have drawn the short end of the stick; one thinks of them as grunts, not as actors. They know that they are part of the cruelest joke imaginable and that the joke is always on them. Unlike American soldiers in the past, they smoke dope. They do not talk agitprop; they think survival, how many days they have to go. To the degree that they esteem Sergeant Barnes, one of Stone's two authority figures, it's not because he is likable, which he most assuredly is not. It is because he is very good at what he does — killing and surviving — and he seems like the best (and perhaps only) ticket out of there alive.

In Stone's movie, the NVA soldiers are very good. They do not bunch up, as both sides seem to in *The Green Berets.* Instead, they move skillfully through the jungle, and they use the night extremely well. Anyone watching the film who never went to Vietnam will have an instantaneous sense of how good they were and why it was so hard to fight them. The terrain is clearly always on their side. Meanwhile, Stone's Americans always feel alien, as if they are visitors not just from another country but from another planet; they are never an organic part of the land. They are *always* surrounded — by the terrain, by the NVA; they exist in a constant shroud of vulnerability and fear. The next step may trigger a land mine. I think this is Stone's great triumph, for although the acting, cinematography, and writing are all very good, and the individual scenes are excellent, the whole greatly exceeds the sum of its parts. I find it inconceivable that someone who had not been to Vietnam could see this movie and not sense its authenticity and immediately understand why the war was unwinnable.

The grunts in this movie are always alone. They have each other and nothing more. They never belong there, not from the moment they first land at Tan Son Nhut, and not in the pathetic little huts they carve out in their base camp. Watching them move through the jungle, one is always aware of them coming from some distant place much against their will, sent there for a task that is hopeless.

When they eventually go through a village, murdering and raping the villagers, it is not because they are bad people. They behave this way because they are kids who have been scared to death for too long, sent to a place that should never have been their destiny, and finally because they are poorly led, or at least led by men who no longer care about the lives of anyone else in this country. What Stone has given us is the ability to see the reality of a bad and cowardly policy: this is what happens when you take a group of ordinary American kids and send them 12,000 miles away to a very bad war, where they are completely disconnected and scared to death every day and have lost not only their closest friends but also any inner compass they might have been raised with. The truly dysfunctional men are not the ones fighting there but the men who sent them there in the first place.

When *Platoon* first came out, a number of critics were bothered by the allegorical use of the two sergeants: Barnes, played by Tom Berenger, as the sergeant of darkness, and Elias, played by Willem Dafoe, as the sergeant of light. "I am reality," Barnes says at one point. And who, that deep in the jungle, is going to argue with him? At first, I was somewhat neutral on the debate. I liked the movie, and I was more than willing to grant Stone the liberty for a piece of work that I greatly admired and had so much else to commend it. Now, looking back, I am inclined to think that Stone got this right, too, even if it makes the movie a little more stylized. There is a reason for this. When *In Retrospect,* Robert McNamara's book on Vietnam came out, I was asked to go on Charley Rose's television show. My companions were writer Stanley Karnow and David Hackworth, a much-decorated combat officer. We were not allowed in the same green room with McNamara, nor were we part of the program on which he was interviewed. Our segment followed his. At one point, Rose asked why Vietnam still divided us so much, and I said — something I had not thought of before — that it was because it was not really us against the Vietnamese, it was us against ourselves. The second American Civil War, I said. And I think that is what Stone was saying with Elias and Barnes.

Wall Street

Whatever its aesthetic merits or historicity, the cultural impact of Oliver Stone's *Wall Street* (1987) is undeniable. Most famously, corporate raider Gordon Gekko's credo "Greed is good" has become proverbial for ethical failings in the business world. For example, no fewer than three contributors to a 1992 conference book on white-collar crime invoke the phrase.[1] A collection of the 100 most memorable movie lines, published in 1996,[2] includes the words that Michael Douglas actually intones in the film: "Greed, for the lack of a better word, is good." No other line from an Oliver Stone screenplay appears on the list.

Wall Street has had an enduring impact despite the mixed reviews and unspectacular ticket sales that greeted its theatrical release. Critics paid Stone and cowriter Stanley Weiser a backhanded compliment by acknowledging their meticulous fidelity to details of securities industry practices and language. This very verisimilitude was thought to make the film inaccessible to lay audiences. Reviewers also complained that *Wall Street* lacked emotional depth. Many pejoratively described it as a "morality tale."

As for the film's faithfulness to history, a proper assessment must address a difficulty invariably posed by works of historical fiction. The problem is that although nonfictional characters or incidents may serve as models for the scenarist, some measure of artistic license must be granted. In the specific case of *Wall Street,* offended investment bankers miss the point when they protest that the film portrays their business in a manner that, though not false, is unrepresentative. The average stockbroker's life is indeed much duller than Bud Fox's, but it would be naïve to suppose that a faithful depiction of the mundane reality could have obtained commercial backing.

Instead of faulting *Wall Street* for failing to present a perfectly balanced picture, this essay focuses on the film's central historical thesis. In essence, Stone ascribes the prevalence of hostile takeovers[3] and insider trading[4] during the 1980s to a flowering of greed (indeed, *Greed* was the original title).[5] Blaming the period's financial excesses on avarice, however, begs the question: what caused the sudden popularity of an age-old sin?

An alternative to Stone's moralistic interpretation can be found within the realm of finance. Money lust, after all, is a perennial element of human aspirations. Satisfying it by Gordon Gekko's patented methods, however, is feasible only under certain economic conditions. The conditions under which hostile takeovers and insider trading gained increased prominence included depressed stock prices and narrowly focused enforcement of the securities and antitrust laws. These factors are explored in detail following an examination of the film's reception upon its 1987 release.

CRITICAL RECEPTION

Wall Street reached the theaters just two months after a spectacular stock market crash. On "Black Monday," October 19, 1987, the Dow Jones Industrial Average shattered all previous records for one-day declines by plummeting 508 points. Some reviewers congratulated Stone on his lucky timing, implying that events had vindicated his denunciation of speculators' greed. *The Nation*'s James Lardner offered a minority opinion, however, suggesting that in the wake of money manager Ivan Boesky's November 1986 confession to insider trading charges, Stone had rushed the film's production to capitalize on the headlines. Lardner noted that whereas *Platoon* had been years in the writing, financing, and producing, scarcely a year had passed between its completion and the release of *Wall Street*. "With Black Monday so fresh in our memory and Ivan Boesky so recently dispatched to his new life, Stone has certainly struck while the iron is hot. But it's a crude blow."[6]

Crudeness was a charge that several other reviewers also leveled against the film. *National Review*'s John Simon wrote, "The crudeness of sensibility is right there in the nomenclature: Gordon Gekko = Gordon Getty lizard; Bud Fox = budding slyboots; Darien Taylor = upper-crust suburban version of Liz,[7] etc. They did these things better in Restoration comedy."[8] Hal Lipper of the *St. Petersburg Times* similarly complained that the "characters have no subtlety. They practically wear placards — 'GOOD,' 'BAD,' 'CORRUPTIVE,' 'REDEEMED' — tacked to their $2000 suits."[9]

New York Times reviewer Janet Maslin picked up the theme of heavy-handedness: "*Wall Street* eventually takes a dive as precipitous as anything the stock market has done, descending into the worst sort of black-and-white moralizing."[10] Chimed in Michael Kolbenschlag of the *Orange County Register,* "The main failing of this film is a lack of attention that would suggest meaningful depth. The characters are shallow and the basic plot of searching for a father figure is hackneyed."[11] Assessments by other reviewers included "simple-minded,"[12] "simplistic and often melodramatic,"[13] "a little too obvious for its own good,"[14] "sentimental, two-dimensional, the stuff of soap opera,"[15] and "a lush soap opera — *Dynasty* with a moral."[16] Concluded the *Village Voice*: "*Wall Street* is thrilling left-wing trash, and it's more or less disposable."[17]

Wall Street was not universally panned, however. Stone's cinematic technique, which one reviewer described as a "walloping visual style,"[18] won particular praise. "The picture may not be a work of art," commented *New York*'s David Denby, "but it's a great potboiler and the most enjoyable movie of the year."[19] At least one critic, Peter C. Newman of *Maclean's*, found the film's didactic style palatable: "Stone's portrait of moral decay within the upper reaches of U.S. capitalism suspends disbelief without ever becoming preachy, and it is this quality that makes it so compelling."[20]

If the film itself received mixed reviews, however, its lead actor's notices were mostly raves. "Michael Douglas is superb and delivers the finest acting performance of his career," was a typical comment.[21] One of the few dissenters was Stanley Kauffmann in the *New Republic:* "I felt he was just about keeping up with the part's demands. It's almost as if he was presenting the role for a stronger person to see and take over, like a model presenting a garment for someone else really to wear. This is certainly not to say that Douglas is ineffectual, only that he and the part are no more than evenly matched."[22] Other critics, however, hailed Douglas's "nice, greasy performance,"[23] called it "a superbly crafted portrait of Gekko that the Academy Awards should recognize,"[24] or praised the actor's "reptilian brio."[25]

Amplifying Michael Douglas's triumph was an echo of *Wall Street*'s father-son theme. The acclaim elevated the veteran actor to a stature akin to that of his famous parent, Kirk Douglas. In the *New York Times,* Helen Dudar called the Gordon Gekko character a breakthrough role for Douglas, eighteen years after his first screen appearance (in *Hail Hero*).[26] Derek Malcolm of the *Manchester Guardian Weekly* elaborated, "Michael Douglas, in a role fit for his father at last, proves himself a very worthy son."[27] Accepting an Academy Award for his performance in April 1988, Douglas thanked his father "for helping a son step out of the shadow."[28]

Wall Street's other principal actors generated less enthusiasm from reviewers. Unfortunately, from a box-office viewpoint, the romantic leads came in for particularly harsh criticism: "Charlie Sheen, as the neophyte broker supplying Douglas with insider information, lacks the emotional breadth to carry the film. His performance is further burdened by his affair with Daryl Hannah, or the cardboard facsimile passing for her on the screen. Hannah, playing a shallow, money-grubbing interior decorator, threatens to swallow entire personalities in her void."[29] "Sheen has all the verve and displays all the lineaments of desire of a supermarket manager," sneered another critic.[30] Newman of

Maclean's chimed in, "At 22, he lacks the face and body language to portray pathos, and his upward mobility is about as interesting as an elevator ride." He likewise gave Hannah poor grades for her effort "to turn herself into a sort of Hertz bimbo (for rent if not for sale)."[31] *Policy Review*'s John V. N. Philip called Hannah "disappointingly wooden, especially considering she has most of the movie's scarce humorous lines."[32] Lamented Vincent Canby of the *New York Times,* "Miss Hannah has the screen presence of a giant throw-pillow."[33] A bit more kindly, *The Nation*'s Lardner questioned whether any actress "could have brought the character of Darien Taylor to life."[34]

In at least Charlie Sheen's case, the problem with the portrayal may have resulted partly from a lack of application. One of the film's technical advisers chastised Sheen for failing to take full advantage of opportunities on the set to pick up details from real-life Wall Streeters. The technical adviser noted that even the extras profited from extensive coaching by the pros on how to dress, stand, and yell. "In contrast, Charlie Sheen, the focus of the trading-floor scenes, has had little contact with investment bankers or brokers, all of whom he calls 'yuppie.' He resists any suggestions about how to behave or deliver his lines."[35] To be fair, however, the screenplay at one point obliged Sheen to stare into the night sky and ask, "Who am I?" This leaden soliloquy nearly rivaled "Greed is good" and "Lunch is for wimps" in its frequency of mention (invariably in disparaging terms) by reviewers.

POPULAR RECEPTION

The broad moviegoing public did not buck the critics on *Wall Street.* Both Orion's *Throw Momma from the Train* and Disney's *Three Men and a Baby* heavily outgrossed the Twentieth Century Fox release in its initial weekend. Industry sources reported that although the film was "'extremely hot' in Manhattan and upscale pockets of Los Angeles, Washington, and other big cities," it was drawing disappointingly in suburbs of cities such as Detroit, Atlanta, and Houston.[36]

Some theater operators thought that *Wall Street* alienated mainstream filmgoers. "There isn't applause at the end of the movie," commented the representative of a Middle Atlantic chain. "The audience comes out, and I think many are annoyed, especially if they're in the [brokerage] business."[37] Ventured a Pacific Northwest film buyer, "Maybe there wasn't enough love in the picture."[38]

Fox tried to alter the latter perception by playing up the romantic angle in a second wave of advertising. The financial theme, acknowledged the studio, was a tough sell. One theater executive claimed that prior to *Wall Street*'s release, Fox asked exhibitors to guarantee at least as much revenue as *The Jewel of the Nile,* Michael Douglas's 1985 adventure-romance hit, had generated. Thomas Sherak, Fox's chief of marketing and distribution, declined to confirm or deny that the studio backed down when theater owners raised serious doubts about *Wall Street*'s box-office potential.[39]

STONE'S QUEST FOR VERISIMILITUDE

To some extent, Stone probably narrowed the appeal of *Wall Street* by his insistence on accurate dialogue. "While thoroughly researched and seemingly authentic in its portrayal of trading and arbitrage," noted one regional critic who panned the film, "it often threatens to leave viewers in a tangle of market jargon and ticker tape."[40] Stone defended his artistic decision, noting that *Platoon,* too, contained jargon ("grunt-talk") that was indecipherable to most moviegoers. "We would have been dead in the water if we had more exposition," he argued. "We would have driven them out of the theaters in droves because it is b-o-r-i-n-g."[41]

Even financial experts who thought that Stone had grossly distorted the big picture acknowledged that he had gotten the details right. "Filmed at the New York Stock Exchange during trading hours, the movie captures the frantic energy of the floor in action," wrote the *American Banker*'s Susan Festa.[42] Before commencing construction of a $500,000 trading room, production crews spent several days photographing the layouts of actual examples. Technical advisers ensured the accuracy of "the level of activity, noise, and garbage for each scene, depending on the time of day."[43] Stone followed the experts' advice on the brand of computers to portray on the trading floor (AT&T, mostly) and the correct proportion of women to cast for a business meeting (35 percent).[44]

Michael Douglas prepared for his role by meeting with prominent Wall Street executive Alan Greenberg and studying television footage of corporate raiders Ivan Boesky, T. Boone Pickens, and Carl Icahn. Oliver Stone and his staff also spent time with Icahn, as well as takeover artist Asher Edelman, Wall Street executive John Gutfreund, and Drexel Burnham "junk bond" chief Michael Milken. (Ironically, the last two men were subsequently forced out of the securities industry for, respectively, failing to report and actively participating in securities law violations. Their advice during the filming may have tempered Stone's condemnation of Wall Street ethics, but their subsequent actions vindicated it to some extent.)

The same technical adviser who chided Charlie Sheen for spurning bona fide traders and salespeople praised Stone for modifying his screenplay in response to the professionals' criticisms. For example, on the advice of experienced Wall Streeters, the director scratched depictions of salespeople mixing drinks at their desks. Stone also acceded to the New York Stock Exchange's wishes by converting Bud Fox from a retail stockbroker to an institutional salesman. (The Big Board reportedly objected to the screenplay's original depiction of an ordinary broker trading 50,000-share blocks of stock without immediately drawing suspicion.)[45]

Stone was adamant, however, about having Gekko send Fox a prostitute in appreciation of a profitable tip. Told by the adviser that the incident was anachronistic, the director replied that he had heard that the use of hookers was common on Wall Street. Indeed, plying clients with prostitutes was not entirely obsolete in 1985, according to investigative journalist Connie Bruck. A former corporate finance partner of Drexel told Bruck that the companionship of "girls" was a staple of the firm's lavish annual junk bond conference in Los Angeles. Bruck quoted the chairman of a major corporation as confirming that Drexel paid the women "varying amounts, depending on how pretty they are, and what they'll do."[46]

Much of the credit for *Wall Street*'s authenticity belonged to Kenneth Lipper. Stone invited the investment banker and one-time deputy mayor of New York City to become chief technical adviser after the brokerage industry initially stonewalled the film's production. By Stone's account, he turned to Lipper while under pressure from Twentieth Century Fox to abandon on-location shooting in New York in favor of a Hollywood set.[47] Lipper initially rejected Stone's offer. Along with his fellow Wall Streeters, he feared that the movie would portray his industry unfairly. Stone, however, prevailed on Lipper to read the script and write a critique.

In his recommended screenplay revisions, Lipper insisted on the necessity of portraying at least some Wall Streeters as honest. He particularly objected to a proposed scene in which Lou Manheim, the virtuous but financially strapped broker portrayed by Hal Holbrook, succumbed to the temptation of profiting from information provided by a possibly illegal source. Stone eventually agreed to keep Manheim honest, but only after first filming the scene both ways. The director also consented to give Wall Street more credit for policing itself than in the original draft.

Stone did not adopt all of Lipper's suggestions, however. He acknowledged, moreover, that part of his reason for asking the investment banker to write a novel based on *Wall Street* was to give the newly recruited technical adviser his own creative outlet, while keeping full control of the film for himself. "The movie is my vision and the book is your vision," the director told Lipper.[48] Stone sweetened his offer of the chief technical advisory post with a share of the profits and a cameo role.

Reasoning that the film's portrayal of the brokerage industry would be harsher without his participation, Lipper joined the production. Once the Wall Street insider was on board, Stone later recalled, "the dike began to break."[49] The New York Stock Exchange quickly warmed up to the project, allowing Stone's film crew onto its floor during trading hours. Lipper's door-opening services extended to persuading Le Cirque to let Stone shoot on location. The investment banker's hairstylist served as go-between with the upscale restaurant's maître d'hôtel.

Lipper contended that the final film, incorporating the concessions he had wrung from Stone, was essentially fair. "It's not Wall Street bashing," he told the New York Times. "It starts with the premise that Wall Street has a critical and necessary function and that it has an ability to heal itself."[50] Some of Lipper's industry colleagues vehemently disagreed, however. Takeover lawyer Arthur Fleischer, Jr., denounced the film as "a ludicrous portrayal and completely unbalanced."[51] Said investment banker Stephen Schwarzman after attending a private screening of Wall Street, "It was an accurate portrayal of a relatively small sliver of the Street. That .001 percentage is nuts."[52] Concurring with Schwarzman's characterization of Wall Street as unrepresentative was Steven Rattner. The journalist–turned–investment banker criticized the film for dwelling on the sensational aspects of corporate finance, to the neglect of humdrum realities. According to Rattner, Stone fulfilled Alfred Hitchcock's formula for a movie — "like life with the boring bits cut out."[53] La vie quotidienne on the stock exchange actually entailed neither pandemonium at the opening bell nor the purchase and sale of airlines in an afternoon. "And, sad to say," added Rattner, "not many investment bankers are attacked by blondes in stretch limos."[54]

Not only ex-newspaperman Rattner but also practicing journalists criticized Wall Street on grounds of both balance and realism. "Instead of presenting a real-life world of finance in which a few bad apples mingle among a mostly sane and healthy crop," wrote Nigel Andrews of the Financial Times, "Stone puts out a search-and-destroy order on the whole orchard."[55] In Policy Review, a somewhat more sympathetic John V. N. Philip credited Wall Street with depicting the market's many honest workings: "If Stone's story is unrealistic concerning the stock exchange it may be only in the degree to which it overemphasizes the ultimate impact of stock manipulators like Gekko."[56]

At a finer level of detail, Michael Cieply of the Los Angeles Times ridiculed the scene in which Bud Fox passes a coded tip to a reporter, who then announces that Anacott Steel is "in play" as a takeover target. Cieply said that when he covered the financial beat, material obtained in such a manner would have been rejected by his level-headed editor as obviously unusable.[57] The

Nation's James Lardner challenged the plausibility of Gekko choosing as his protégé a youngster with such a limited network of contacts that, in order to secure privileged information for Gekko, he must masquerade as a night maintenance man at a law firm specializing in takeovers.[58] Daniel Seligman found it unrealistic for Fox to gain access to Gekko by remembering the great man's birthday, a factoid culled from *Fortune*. After 37.524 years with that publication, wrote Seligman, he could not recall a single profile mentioning the subject's birthday. Seligman also pointed out that the 1971 recession, in which upright Lou Manheim supposedly lost everything, never happened.[59]

On balance, it seems a fair judgment that *Wall Street* presents a highly selective and, therefore, somewhat distorted picture of the securities business. It is standard operating procedure, however, for Hollywood to highlight the exceptional. The investment bankers who protested Stone's sensationalizing of their comparatively drab lives had a valid point, but no more so than lawyers, police officers, or private detectives in criticizing countless other films. (Members of these other professions, it is true, have the consolation of being depicted in many films, at least a few of which feature their more mundane activities.)

For historians, it matters little whether *Wall Street* paints the securities industry in excessively lurid colors. The key issue is whether the film portrays changes in the securities industry that were in fact observable in 1985. If the depicted changes prove genuine, a natural follow-up is to determine whether Stone explains the changes in a credible manner. These tests will now be applied to the two most important financial phenomena described in *Wall Street*, insider trading and hostile takeovers.

INSIDER TRADING IN THE 1980s

Consistent with the impression created by Stone, prosecutions for insider trading increased significantly in the early 1980s. During the first forty-seven years following its establishment in 1934, the Securities and Exchange Commission (SEC) brought an average of less than two insider trading cases a year. The number soared to twenty-five cases a year between 1982 and the conclusion of Reagan appointee John Shad's chairmanship in 1987. Upon taking the post in 1981, Shad had vowed to come down on insider trading "with hobnail boots."[60]

Although the rise in *prosecutions* for insider trading is documented, the trend in insider trading activity is highly disputable. Anticipating *Wall Street*'s take on the question, SEC commissioner Barbara Thomas in 1982 called insider trading "a proliferating problem . . . encouraged by greed."[61] In contrast, Stanley Foster Reed, founder of *Mergers & Acquisitions* magazine, pointed out that the pickup in prosecutions could be explained by either an increase in insider trading or increased detection by law enforcement agencies. "My vote is for detection," said Reed in a 1986 debate. "I believe that insider trading has been going on since public markets in securities were established more than 250 years ago."[62]

Even Oliver Stone acknowledged that the illicit use of nonpublic information was no innovation of the 1980s. "In the '50s and '60s, people always took tips. It was never a big deal," he told the press.[63] Stone, whose father was a stockbroker and investment newsletter writer and to whose memory he dedicated *Wall Street,* knew whereof he spoke. "My father would say there was more inside tipping in the old days than there is now," he ventured.[64]

The hypothesis that insider trading was more frequently detected in the 1980s rather than more frequent is supported by several developments that made perpetrators easier to catch and more worthwhile to prosecute. For one thing, SEC chairman Shad launched the enforcement effort in 1982 in a meeting with heads of the leading stock exchanges and the over-the-counter market. The purpose of the gathering was to speed up implementation of electronic surveillance and transaction audit trails, all with the goal of spotting questionable transactions. Also in 1982, the government of Switzerland agreed to measures that made it harder to use secret Swiss bank accounts to conceal illegal insider trading. Finally, in 1984, at the urging of the SEC, Congress passed the Insider Trading Sanctions Act (ITSA). The new legislation enabled the SEC to bring civil cases in insider trading actions, thereby substituting a less stringent standard of proof, namely, preponderance of evidence, for the criminal courts' standard of guilt beyond a reasonable doubt.[65]

If historical analysis, too, can be judged by the preponderance-of-evidence rule, Shad's stepped-up pursuit of insider trading cases represented a shift of emphasis by the SEC, rather than a response to a sudden outbreak of greed. During the late 1970s, chairman Harold M. Williams had sought to expand the commission's traditional mandate of protecting investors. Corporate governance became a central concern of the SEC, highlighted by enforcement chief Stanley Sporkin's crackdown on bribery and hidden perks for executives. Critics charged that by diverting enforcement staff to those areas, over which they claimed the SEC had no legislative authority, Sporkin had allowed insider traders and stock manipulators to run rampant. Critics of Williams's policies viewed Shad's 1981 appointment as an opportunity to return the SEC to its original mission, which included the prosecution of classic securities law violations.

If, contrary to the picture presented in *Wall Street,* insider trading was not necessarily more widespread in the 1980s than in earlier periods, the film nevertheless captured a genuine change in the nature of the crime. Previously, the nonpublic information that speculators hoped to pick up tended to involve corporate operating events, such as new product announcements by pharmaceutical companies. Advance notice of mergers and acquisitions (M&A) was not yet the bread and butter of illegal tipsters.

In contrast, risk arbitrageurs, the special breed of operators to which Gordon Gekko belonged,[66] had always focused on M&A. In the old days, however, they did not try to learn of takeovers in advance. Instead, the "arbs" handicapped the odds that already-announced merger proposals would be blocked by the antitrust authorities. (The Department of Justice's Antitrust Division and the Federal Trade Commission shared the responsibility of determining whether proposed transactions were anticompetitive.)

Because the probability of an antitrust objection was nontrivial, the shares of a company targeted for acquisition did not rise fully to the would-be acquirer's bid. Investors were unwilling to pay that premium price, knowing that a quashing of the deal would likely send the stock plummeting back to its lower, preannouncement level. As a result, shares of target companies invariably traded meaningfully below their takeover bid levels until the antitrust authorities completed their deliberations. Risk arbitrageurs profited from the market's discount for uncertainty, reacting swiftly to any new disclosure that suggested either an increased or a decreased likelihood that the merger would be consummated.

Risk arbitrage began to change in 1981 when the Reagan administration narrowed the focus of antitrust enforcement, which had focused on conglomerate mergers under Richard Nixon and on supposed "shared monopolies" under Jimmy Carter. This shift paralleled the SEC's abandonment of ambitious reforms of corporate behavior in favor of prosecuting clear violations of the securities laws. In *Time*'s estimation, Reagan's trustbusters were "the most permissive ever, approving virtually every large merger proposed."[67] Naturally, the stock market adjusted to the greatly reduced risk that M&A deals would be undone by the antitrust enforcers. Investors became less averse to buying the shares of targeted companies at prices very close to the bids that would-be acquirers put on the table. For the arbs, that meant smaller price swings from which to profit. Already-announced deals offered fewer opportunities for capital gains than under previous administrations.

Some risk arbitrageurs responded to the changed environment as Gordon Gekko did, shifting their attention to not-yet-announced transactions. This was clearly a departure, and it worried old-style practitioners who were accustomed to trading on nuances of the antitrust review process. How, they wondered, could arbs survive the wide swings inherent in speculating on whether a deal would occur at all, unless they obtained inside information illegally?

In short, unscrupulous stock market operators discovered a new outlet, courtesy of a revised antitrust policy and the consequently reduced profitability of traditional risk arbitrage. There is no need to posit, as *Wall Street* does, that greed was the novel element. Back in the 1920s, cupidity was gratified by the creation of stock pools, elaborate conspiracies to manipulate prices through sham transactions. Around the same time, Joseph Kennedy and Bernard "Sell 'em Ben" Smith developed another disreputable but not yet illegal technique, insider trading, into a fine art. Penny-stock scams, boiler-room operations, and financial reporting irregularities antedated *Wall Street* by decades. The appetite for ill-gotten gains is a constant; Gordon Gekko simply capitalized on new opportunities.

The vulnerable points in *Wall Street*'s treatment of insider trading do not end with the suggestion that the crime suddenly became epidemic in the 1980s through an unleashing of greed in American society. Daniel Seligman even questioned whether Stone understood the legal definition of insider trading. The *Fortune* columnist contended that when Bud Fox tailed corporate raider Larry Wildman (played by Terence Stamp) to learn what he was up to, he broke no law: "Were the [viewers of *Wall Street*] supposed not to have heard of the U.S. Supreme Court's ruling in *Dirks v. SEC,* in the wake of which people became free to trade on material nonpublic information provided that they owed no fiduciary duty to the companies involved?"[68] Fox and Gekko, in other words, had no connection to the company Wildman hoped to acquire. They therefore violated no duty of loyalty and, consequently, no statute by exploiting their knowledge of the flight plan of Wildman's private plane.

Seligman was correct on this point. The 1983 decision he cited had overturned the conviction of a securities analyst who, on the basis of material nonpublic information, had advised his clients to sell a company's stock. Because the analyst owed no duty to the corporation's shareholders, ruled the High Court, he had committed no crime.

In fairness to Stone, however, prosecutors probably could have made at least one charge stick against Fox and Gekko. In all likelihood, the duo's network of tippees legally constituted a group of investors acting in concert. If so, the consortium acted unlawfully each time it failed to disclose to the SEC that it had acquired a 5 percent interest in a company.

THE RISE OF HOSTILE TAKEOVERS

Just as Oliver Stone correctly depicted insider trading prosecutions as increasingly frequent occurrences in the 1980s, he was accurate in suggesting that hostile takeovers represented a rising tide in the United States. According to

Securities Data Company, unsolicited bids for corporate control numbered no more than five a year between 1978 and 1980. The count leaped to forty-seven in 1981, then trended upward to a peak of eighty-five in 1988. Moreover, hostile bids did not merely grow in parallel with a general rise in M&A activity. In 1988, by Mergerstat's calculation, M&A announcements of all types (net of cancellations and competing bids) totaled 2,258, up only 7 percent from 2,106 in 1978. Total M&A announcements crested in the interim at 3,336 in 1986, a level not exceeded until 1995, but unsolicited bids rose far more sharply. Clearly, hostile takeovers skyrocketed in the years leading up to *Wall Street*'s action.

It is far less clear that the impetus was a surge in get-rich-quick thinking, despite the rhetoric that *Wall Street* puts in the mouths of Lou Manheim and Bud Fox's father (portrayed by Charlie Sheen's real-life father, Martin). Once again, it makes sense to seek the explanation of economic phenomena first within the economic realm. A standard economic measure known as Tobin's Q ratio frees historians from the dubious technique of probing the zeitgeist.

The Q ratio, devised by Nobel economics laureate James Tobin, compares the stock market value of corporate assets with their replacement cost. A company's replacement cost is the amount of money that would be required to construct all its physical assets from scratch. To understand why this ratio matters to takeover specialists, suppose that a capitalist wishes to build a new widget factory. Further suppose that there is an established widget manufacturer trading on the stock exchange, with a market capitalization (share price times number of shares outstanding) substantially below the cost of replicating its sole factory. A shrewd market operator could profit by acquiring control of the widget manufacturer, dissolving it, and selling the factory to the capitalist at less than the cost of new construction. Whenever Tobin's Q ratio is unusually low as a result of depressed stock prices, many such hostile takeover opportunities are likely to exist.

Reflecting a bear stock market, Tobin's Q ratio for U.S. nonfinancial corporations plunged from a peak of over 1.0 in 1968 to less than 0.4 between 1974 and 1984, according to the Federal Reserve Board. No comparably low ratio of market value to replacement cost had been recorded since 1953. Historian Robert Sobel describes the financial market's response as the fourth great wave of U.S. industrial consolidation since the late nineteenth century:

> It began in the early 1980s as the country recovered from stagflation, and at first the glamour was generated by a technique, not a product, hostile takeovers. Inflation and a flat stock market meant that many established concerns — most of which had been created during the first three waves — were worth more dead than alive. Raiders, backed by bankers and then by junk

bonds, could bid 60 for a stock selling at 40 knowing the assets could be sold for 80 — thus buying the company with its own money and reaping a hefty profit.[69]

Like insider trading, hostile takeovers had precedents in earlier times. One dramatic example was the 1867–1868 battle over the Erie Railroad, fought by Cornelius Vanderbilt, Daniel Drew, Jim Fisk, and Jay Gould. Louis Wolfson's 1954–1955 proxy fight for control of Montgomery Ward likewise prefigured later raids by Gordon Gekko's real-life models. Both history and Tobin's Q ratio refute Oliver Stone's attribution of the hostile takeover wave to a breakdown of traditional moral standards.

If the causes of the takeover surge were primarily economic, it is worth commenting on the surge's economic consequences. Carl Fox's talk of the necessity of creating something, rather than living off the buying and selling of others, upholds a venerable populist tradition of regarding financiers as parasites. (Political commentator George Will's 1987 column on *Wall Street* derides the elder Fox/Sheen's lines as "economic baby-talk," while denouncing Stone's "agitprop" and "statistical rubbish about America's distribution of wealth.")[70] Gordon Gekko, it is true, presents takeovers in a more positive light, hailing their power to discipline inefficient and self-serving corporate managers. Viewers are unlikely to regard this villainous seducer's viewpoint as the movie's message. Rather, audiences will probably infer that battles for corporate control throw people out of work simply to enrich greedy speculators.

Curiously, Oliver Stone took a more sanguine view in a 1988 *Playboy* interview:

Personally, I think most corporate raids are good. Not always, but most times. . . . Management's become so weak in this country, so flaccid. These guys are into their salaries, their golf trips, their fishing trips; there's so much fat and waste in these companies. A lot of these corporate raiders are guys who want to make the money, but in doing so, they clean up these companies. So corporate raiding is a reformation of the system. It's a natural correction.[71]

Perhaps Stone suppressed his own views, reckoning that Carl Fox's populism would draw better at the box office. Be that as it may, there is credible evidence that the 1980s-vintage corporate raiders played a positive role by promoting economic efficiency. For one thing, the raiders helped dismantle unwieldy conglomerates. These hodgepodge companies, which vainly tried to compete in several unrelated businesses, arose during the 1960s wave of corporate consolidation, when prevailing antitrust policy largely blocked intra-industry mergers. A 1990 summary of economic studies of 1980s hostile take-overs[72] found that, contrary to popular impressions:

- Shareholder gains from takeovers were too large to be explained as transfers of wealth from empoyees, suggesting that other efficiencies resulted.
- Most takeovers were not premised on reductions in expenditures aimed at updating or expanding plant and equipment.
- Takeovers did not lead to damaging cuts in corporate research and development spending.

To the extent that corporate takeovers improved the economic competitiveness of the United States, their long-run impact presumably was to preserve rather than eliminate American jobs.

One related, albeit minor, point vindicates Stone as a historian. In his attempt to persuade Blue Star Airline's union representatives to support his takeover bid, Gordon Gekko argues that the incumbent management may file to reorganize in bankruptcy. That ploy would enable the company to cancel its labor contracts unilaterally and lower workers' pay. Gekko's argument would not have been as persuasive if *Wall Street*'s action were set in 1987, the year of the film's release, rather than in 1985. Section 1113 of the 1984 U.S. Bankruptcy Code amendments permitted a corporation reorganizing under Chapter 11 to terminate a labor contract, provided such a step was essential to the company's continuation in business. That is where the law stood when Gekko urged Blue Star's union leaders to accept voluntary concessions. For instance, in 1985, Wheeling-Pittsburgh Steel Corporation successfully invoked Section 1113 to end a United Steelworkers of America contract prior to expiration. One year later, however, the Third U.S. Circuit Court of Appeals reversed a federal district court's upholding of Wheeling-Pittsburgh's action. Henceforth, bankruptcy judges would have to apply a stricter standard in determining whether wage reductions were necessary to avoid liquidation. Stone was accurate in presenting the case as he did, set in 1985.

CONCLUSION

Oliver Stone could have set Bud Fox's story in any decade of the twentieth century and made it historically sound. Opportunities to surrender to greed abounded in every era, even if the specific outlet of hostile takeovers did not. Instead, Stone chose to present the 1980s as a uniquely depraved period. He depicted certain financial activities, which historians could readily explain as outgrowths of specific economic conditions, as consequences of moral decay.

However much historians might regret Stone's choice, it is understandable in financial terms. Cogent economic analysis probably would have had even less box-office appeal than a film about investment bankers with no crime or sex. In any case, a sound economic grounding would have been a stretch for a moviemaker who, by his own admission, was "confused by economics." Stone managed a grade of only seventy in the one economics course he took at Yale and confessed that he could never understand Paul Samuelson's introductory textbook on the subject.[73]

Speaking for himself, rather than through his film's characters, Stone acknowledged that insider trading was nothing new. He even conceded that Gordon Gekko's brand of greed was good, up to a point. Nevertheless, the director of *Wall Street* rejected a historically defensible account in favor of a morality tale that could have been expected to play better in Peoria. Ironically, the populist version failed to wow audiences outside of the nation's financial centers.

New Left, Revisionist, In-Your-Face History

Oliver Stone's *Born on the Fourth of July* Experience

Several years ago, I was reminiscing with a friend about our enlistments in the military. I was astonished to learn that the 1973 movie *Cinderella Liberty* had prompted him to join the navy. The film had inspired the same impulse in me. Childhoods saturated with box-office blockbusters like *The Great Escape* and a weekly barrage of television programs like *Combat,* not to mention the unrelenting Saturday-afternoon serials of war documentaries, had groomed us for military service. By the time I had reached enlistment age, *Cinderella Liberty*'s leading character, portrayed by James Caan, had eliminated any doubt about which branch of the armed forces to join. He plays a modern-day swash-buckler — strong, independent, self-assured, and sexy. I watched the redoubtable Caan and dreamed of foreign ports, tough-guy rumbles, respectability, and women. I dreamed of manhood. This, combined with the navy's dashing dress blues, complete with bell bottoms and Dixie-cup, was too much for a fresh-faced seventeen-year-old male to resist.

Then on the first day of boot camp, the real-life experience of military regimentation immediately shattered my celluloid dream world. The truth proved to be too strong a match for the myths that Hollywood and television projected. The navy dealt me five miserable years, most of them in the post-Vietnam era. I encountered an undisciplined culture of alcoholism, drug abuse, indolence, racism, misogyny, and indifference. As nearly ruinous to my experience and in gross betrayal of my image of the seafaring life, the navy had phased out the traditional crackerjack dress uniform and issued a terribly uninspired replacement. Caan, as my friend and I reflected, had lied to us in 1973.

Three years later, ex-marine and Vietnam veteran Ron Kovic published his scorching memoir about how the military had shattered his own dream world and also his body. Not since Dalton Trumbo's 1939 *Johnny Got His Gun* had there been written such a graphic and outspoken document against war.[1] As with many young males of his generation, the cinematic illusions of war had convinced Kovic that the military would bestow his manhood; instead, a crippling spinal cord injury sustained in battle stole it from him. Once a love-it-or-leave-it patriot, he chose the year of the nation's bicentennial to share his experiences with America. The outgrowth of his antiwar activities, Kovic's autobiography subverts the post–World War II popular cultural romance with war and replaces it with the grisly truth of human sacrifice in battle and the institutional indifference to Vietnam veterans.[2] Kovic's journey in pursuit of the American dream to the nightmarish discovery of Vietnam stirred the emotions of Oliver Stone, himself a veteran, who envisioned his own life and America's Vietnam experience as variations of the same journey.[3] Eventually, he and Kovic adapted the best-selling memoir to the screen.

What Stone produced in *Born on the Fourth of July* embodies elements of both illegitimate and legitimate history. He employs a methodology, medium, and rigor that differ from those of academic historians, and at times he resorts to sensationalism, composite images, and even fiction. Mythmaker, presentist, reductionist, and manipulator of facts all describe Stone as a film artist. Yet these are labels that also apply to academic historians. The professionals, David Hackett Fischer writes in his iconoclastic *Historians' Fallacies,* sometimes artfully and sometimes unwittingly "prune away the dead branches of the past, and preserve the green buds and twigs which have grown into the dark forest of our contemporary world."[4] The mere selection of truths, an unavoidable process of doing history, jeopardizes the objectivity of even the most conscientious historian. At the same time, some of his or her colleagues are no less innocent than Stone of engaging in iconoclasm, mythbreaking, and historical revisionism. Indeed, *Born* is more honest and forthcoming than the typical institutional history, and it rejects the ancestor worship pouring forth from public history. Stone's film can also be seen as an actual inquiry rather than a mere presentation. He frames the movie around a historical problem, addresses critical questions about the American experience, and offers an interpretation of the recent past that approaches that found in academic scholarship.

Perhaps Stone bears the least resemblance to the conventional historian not in his excesses but in his basis of knowledge. The historian's knowledge is generally cognitive, a knowing through logic and reason; Stone's comes from experience, which includes the cognitive as well as knowing through action and correlating feeling and emotion. In this regard, Kovic's odyssey — enlightenment through experience — and Stone make an ideal match. The task of the brash director of *Born* was to fit Kovic's journey to America's discovery of truth through the Vietnam experience.

Long before making his first Vietnam film, *Platoon,* Stone clearly wanted Kovic's story to have impact.[5] The two Vietnam veterans had originally hoped to bring it to the screen in 1978, when Stone was still an aspiring director and Kovic was still in the streets agitating for veterans' rights. Stone was to write the screenplay, Al Pacino to play Kovic, and Dan Petrie to direct.[6] A·few days before shooting the principal photography, the film's financing fell through, and the project was canceled. Kovic was crushed, but he was warmed by Stone's promise that "if I get the opportunity, if I'm ever able to break through as a director, I'll come back." Stone says of his special, almost messianic relationship with Kovic: "It was as if we had been linked by destiny. Chosen as God's instruments to get a message, a memory out about the war."[7]

Stone fulfilled his promise to Kovic twelve years later after establishing himself as a filmmaking force. Premiering December 20, 1989 (the day the United States invaded Panama), *Born* drew mostly luke-warm reviews from critics, but it enjoyed box-office success, grossing $70 million at American theaters alone. It collected eight nominations for Academy Awards and won two, including Stone's second for best director. Stone also won the Directors' Guild of America Award and a Golden Globe Award for best director.[8]

STONE'S REVISIONIST HISTORY

Like *Platoon, Born* represents the new genre of war films that emerged after Vietnam. From 1939 to 1992, over 600 films — shorts, features, television, and pilots — related to Vietnam were made. Prior to 1975 and the fall of Saigon, these films tended to follow the traditional superpatriotic World War II formula.[9] In other words, they glorified military conflict, giving value to war while extolling the twin virtues of personal sacrifice and group solidarity. It was, Kovic insisted in his book and Stone suggested in *Born,* a dangerously intoxicating formula for young male viewers.

After Vietnam, Hollywood learned that moviegoers no longer insisted on John Wayne or Audie Murphy interpretations. Film critics and scholars began to note in the post-Vietnam movies a new emphasis on personal revelation and individual survival. The real enemy was within — if not within oneself, then within one's government and misguided culture. At the same time, screenwriters and directors began turning the camera on the combat veteran, who had previously been subordinated to the warrior in action. Although out of the shadows, he was cast in unflattering light. The typical veteran was a flashback-burdened social recluse, habitually packing a knife or gun and lusting for bloodshed, if not mutilation, while in hot pursuit of innocent victims. The lengthy list of such films is perplexing.[10] One could guess that the Vietnam veteran was being made to carry the burden of the still-troubled American conscience. Struggling to reconcile loss with honor, Americans needed their scapegoat.

Ironically, Jane Fonda, who in her Hanoi Jane days had ridiculed American fighting men, helped restore popular respectability to Vietnam veterans with her 1978 movie *Coming Home.* In it, a paraplegic veteran, played by Jon Voight, is the victim of American foreign aggression. He is bright, compassionate, and reasonably stable emotionally. Despite *Coming Home* signaling a new direction in Vietnam films, moviemakers seemed to accept only the disabled, battle-wounded veteran as a sympathetic character. His story was not even new in Hollywood and, in fact, had appeared decades earlier in flag-waving World War II films.

Two poignant examples are *The Best Years of Our Lives* (1946) and *The Men* (1950). Both candidly illustrate the price of military conflict, and, for the times, they offered a bold treatment of their subject. But neither questions the wisdom of war, and both reveal a tension between history and a mythic ideal. Homer, played by Harold Russell in *Best,* and Ken, played by Marlon Brando in *Men,* are sustained by loving families and unwearyingly understanding fiancées. A competent staff of doctors and nurses provides Ken with expert medical care. Homer is openly prideful of the physicians and therapists who rehabilitated him after he lost his hands. "They took care of me fine," he says. (Russell, who had actually sacrificed his hands to the war, could not have given a more convincing performance. He won an Oscar for best supporting actor and a special award for "bringing hope and courage" to other veterans.) While Homer and Ken confront their own emotional demons, society readily accepts their disabilities. Consistent with the national mood of the time, the common underlying message of the two films is clear: war is at times an unfortunate necessity, as are the human costs that come with it; good Americans accept those costs without protest and with understanding.

From a post-Vietnam perspective, attaching such a message to a film paying tribute to war veterans can seem cruelly duplicitous. Stone and Kovic understood that the hawkish ideas coming out of Hollywood helped lead America and young men into Vietnam. Stone wanted to recast the message of the traditional war movie and inject it with historical honesty. His first effort came in 1986 with *Platoon.* From there he went on to tackle the domestic ideological and emotional conflict over Vietnam, which he believed Kovic's struggle with readjustment symbolized so profoundly. There was "a second war after we came back," Stone says. "People didn't care about Vietnam. Their attitude was: 'I'm sorry, that was a waste of your time.' It wasn't hostility. It was indifference."[11] *Born* imparts a more daring message than the World War II veteran films, and even *Coming Home,* by not only recognizing the sacrifices of the veteran but also protesting the war. One reviewer described *Born* as "perhaps the first I-was-there picture (including Stone's own *Platoon*) to vent fullblast the self-doubt and self-pity and justifiable rage so many veterans have felt."[12]

The point here is that Stone was more than a major player in the new genre of war films. He was responding to contemporary issues, sensitive ones that moviemakers — and historians — had traditionally swept under the rug of silence. *Born,* one reviewer wrote, renders "more political honesty than anyone could expect from Hollywood."[13] With his three major Vietnam films (including *Heaven and Earth*), Stone is much like the New Left historians of the 1960s and 1970s who recognized the need to fill gaps in the American story. He looks at events not from the point of view of the command post, a wooden-postured military officer, or a combat hero but from that of enlisted men who make mistakes — ordinary Americans. To put the point another way, Stone views history from the bottom up. Like blacks, women, workers, and others whom New Left historians rescued from the dungeon of passive victimhood, Stone's Kovic rises above the historical forces that crippled him to become an agent of historical change. As New Left historians had, and still have, Stone has an obvious political agenda — he wants to "fix" the real Vietnam experience in public memory.[14]

Born, then, is both revisionist Hollywood and revisionist history. Aided by the visual power of film, Stone's nontraditional theme carries an emotional force not enjoyed by the scholar historian, who typically has only the dubious aid of academic prose and sometimes a small selection of grainy photographs. Even the casting of Tom Cruise in the role of Kovic smacks of revisionism. Born July 3, 1962, Cruise belongs to a generation bearing a fresh, post-Vietnam innocence, betrayed in Cruise's American schoolboy looks. Stone saw the young star as "a kid off a Wheaties box. I wanted to yank the kid off the box and mess with his image — take him to the dark side."[15] Stone uses Cruise, the camera, and Kovic's tragedy to attack the official and cultural rationale for military confrontation. In keeping with Kovic's book, he exposes the mythic legacy of World War II, the culture of the cold war, and the icy bureaucratic treatment of Vietnam veterans.

Many of the revisionist themes Stone introduced in *Born* (and his ideas predate the film) academics have only recently begun to explore in earnest. In 1991, for instance, historian Stephen J. Whitfield eloquently described the infiltration of the nation's obsessive preoccupation with anticommunism into unimaginable areas of 1950s American culture, including television quiz shows, religion, and even the modern-equipped kitchen and the behavior of snitching.[16] In *Born,* viewers can find evidence of the anticommunist ethos in the backyard play of children, Massapequa's Fourth of July parade, the jingoistic public speeches of Veterans of Foreign Wars officials, Ron's boyhood friendships, his clumsy attempt at courtship, and his concept of manhood. Even his mother's pious condemnation of the godless Soviets seems to bring her closer to her Catholic savior. It was within this cultural milieu that Kovic's love-it-or-leave-it patriotism was spawned.[17]

To illuminate the formative pressures in Kovic's childhood, Stone relies less on dialogue than on emotion-evoking images. The film opens in 1956 with young Ron and his pals playing war in the woods of their Massapequa neighborhood. Stone deploys a steady-cam to sweep through the trees, over ridges, and into gullies to evoke the drama of real military conflict. Elevated strings in John Williams's music warn of imminent danger before Ronnie is clobbered by a dirtball hand grenade. It is as if Stone is saying to the audience, "Pay attention; there's more going on here than children at play." What the audience witnesses in Ronnie's backyard rangers is learned behavior in action, an animated rehearsal of good-old American sensibilities about warfare.

The film's opening credits continue as the scene changes to Ronnie's tenth birthday and the Massapequa Fourth of July parade. Within its ranks marches a motley procession of veterans of foreign wars. The intended standouts are the limbless and wheelchair bound (including the real-life Ron Kovic in character, flinching at the sound of firecrackers). Stone has shifted to slow motion at this point, and again the audience is encouraged to contemplate the significance of the scene. The disabled veterans are a foreshadowing of what is to come for Ronnie. They are living symbols of war's painful price. Although Ronnie fixes his eyes on one particular armless veteran, a different message clicks for the young patriot, much as it did for most other Americans of the time. It is the same message conveyed in *The Best Years of Our Lives* and *The Men:* sacrifice in combat is honorable.

Critics complained that in such scenes of Kovic's childhood, Stone oversimplified complex events and ideas, that he reduced history to "imaginatively static . . . push-button images."[18] (Has anyone read a survey history textbook lately?) One might wonder whether film can deal with complexities as effectively as written history without obscuring basic messages. Stone strays beyond the latitudes of historical fact in part because of the budget and time limitations filmmaking puts on the storyteller.[19] By the same token, he is a storyteller who tries to gauge his audience. Stone's father, who privately longed to be a poet, taught him early in life to reject obscurity for clarity. Stone collapses multiple events and personalities into one so that an otherwise complicated story will make sense to average moviegoers — many of whom are too young to have known the Vietnam experience or are unaware of the cold war culture. The usual moviegoer does not relish a rendition of complex historical events. Yet the provocative and the controversial can carry subtextual messages of historical importance.

As Stone understands, popular film is less suited as an "intellectual medium," like a history book, than as an emotional one.[20] Unlike the historian, Stone's task as a filmmaker is to convert critical ideas into engaging visual moments.[21] In *Born,* Stone's paintbrush images of Americana, the herky-jerky camera that he regards as "another actor,"[22] the amplified sound effects, and the orchestral music score encourage a multisensory experience. Stone excites the visual, auditory, and even tactile senses, knowing that viewers by and large go to movies to escape, not to ponder. He wants viewers not to simply witness or contemplate his film's images. *Born* prods the audience to *feel* the trauma of Ron Kovic and of Vietnam rather than imagine or identify with it. Stone encourages viewers to experience history not on an intellectual level but on an emotional one, as he and Kovic experienced the Vietnam era. The idea here is that the emotional will have a more lasting impact than the intellectual. Even Stone's harshest critics acknowledged the emotional power of *Born* while objecting to Stone's in-your-face style.

Many panned the red-white-and-blue cacophony of the Independence Day celebration as too obtrusive. This, though, is Stone's intent and point: American patriotism and conformity in those days were so overbearing and their propagation so far-reaching that they were impossible to escape. During Kovic's childhood, everyday experiences nourished the attitudes that elevated war to a rite of passage. For instance, as the opening credits continue to run, Stone introduces two more historically significant scenes. In them he brings together the ideas of cultural fidelity and virility in Ronnie's religious-like devotion to baseball — America's game — and wrestling — a manly sport; indeed, both are proving grounds for the United States Marine Corps. Ronnie will not even risk his dreams of gallantry and valor to the distraction of young love, and in *Playboy* the marine wanna-be finds the solitary soldier's substitute for the real thing. But Ronnie loves his country if not his teenage girlfriend. He is willing, if need be, to rise to President Kennedy's challenge, made on the black-and-white television in the Kovics' living room, to "do for your country."

By suggesting that Ron's patriotic response has been preprogrammed, Stone offers a new interpretation of one of Kennedy's most famous lines. Just as Stone had done, Kovic answers the call to help roll back the Red tide of communism in Vietnam. Stone devotes only seventeen minutes to Vietnam scenes, but in that time he accomplishes what consumed two hours in *Platoon:* he exposes the audience to the heightened fear and tension, the confusion and chaos — not to mention the bloodshed, slaughter, and evisceration by automatic weapon — of the battlefield. Stone wants to draw the audience into the accelerated pace of the firefight. He accomplishes this with swish pans, hyperkinetic shooting, glare shots, and an aural track of deafening, clashing sounds. No revisionist history book can so completely and graphically demolish the cultural image of war as glamorous and exciting.

HISTORICAL MYTHMAKING AND THE NEW GENERATION

Whether written by veteran or academic, most World War II histories did just the opposite and glamorized war. As we know now after Vietnam, the lessons that come with victory differ from those that come with defeat. The Vietnam story has been a corrective of its predecessor, which held up World War II as a "good" war. Americans knew that war as a confirmation of their "superior" values and democratic ideals, which have historically helped justify military conflict. Those who participated in Vietnam and World War II have largely controlled the collective memory of their respective wars. During World War II, for example, Winston Churchill assured his fellow Tories in Parliament that history would be kind to them because he planned to write it.[23] But "great" statesmen and generals have lost oversight of the history of the Vietnam War to the "lowly" grunts like Kovic and Stone.[24] One of their chief lessons is that the history of World War II is distorted by the myth of boundless possibilities for America.

Probably the depiction of home-front activities accounts for the greatest contrast between the World War II and Vietnam histories. The domestic scene in the 1940s was a showcase of national unity, sacrifice, patriotism, volunteerism, and government efficiency. Everything, from manufactured products to family life, was supposedly better then.[25] In *The Best Years of Our Lives,* even Fred Derry (Dana Andrews's hapless character), who comes from the impoverished side of the railroad tracks, can turn to his pitiful but caring father and a woman who is presumably his stepmother when he needs support. Granted, the air corps captain sadly discovers that his military honors count for nothing as a promise for a decent job. But he is spared the widespread "indifference" — if not hostility — that later shadowed returning Vietnam veterans.

For Ron Kovic, rehabilitation and reintegration after Vietnam represent the worst years of his life. His experience in the Bronx Veterans Hospital makes finding peace with the permanence of his "half-dead" body more difficult. The rat-infested, filth-ridden facility, the uncaring orderlies, and the uncertain physicians are a chilling opposite to the efficient, antiseptic VA hospital depicted in Brando's *The Men.* Stone's "choking close-ups" of Kovic struggling to recuperate under the horrid conditions heighten the audience's own sense of agony. The gruesome, unfortunate realism of the hospital scenes in *Born,* in fact, forced merits from Stone's toughest critics, and other veterans have testified to the atrocities of the Bronx facility.[26] While its extreme inhuman conditions were not representative of most VA hospitals, they were the product of a government system that, according to Paul Starr in *The Discarded Army,* was long on bureaucracy and short on supplies and sympathy.[27] Many unsuspecting veterans returning home to their beloved country clashed with a new enemy in an unexpected place.

Like Kovic, some combat soldiers turned into war protesters. On that subject, Stone ventures into new territory. *Born* was the first popular film to deal seriously with the antiwar movement. In the last part of the movie, viewers can find in the Vietnam veterans on parade another departure from the World War II image. With Kovic as flag bearer, the paraders are no longer the paunchy but proud veterans of foreign wars but long-haired, foul-mouthed Vietnam Veterans Against the War (VVAW). In actuality, only 7,000 or so of the 2.5 million men and women who served in Vietnam joined the protest group.[28] Nonetheless, its activities represented a historical precedent (of which most viewers may not be aware). In *Born,* the collective effort of the veterans turned protesters is presented as a vehicle of historical change, as it was in real life.

Although he was never an active antiwar demonstrator, Stone was a survivor of the same war. He could identify with the frustration of the VVAW and use that identity to communicate his message in film. His own status as a decorated combat veteran lends a quality of credibility to his Vietnam movies. Perhaps of all his films, *Born* limited Stone's tendencies toward fiction most. Unlike in *Platoon,* Stone had to deal with real-life figures in collaboration with the central historical participant, Kovic, who served as co-screenwriter and technical adviser. Both men understood that the tragic truth of Kovic's story did not require embellishment. Kovic has been philosophical about truth telling, insisting that movies and literature have "the responsibility to instruct, to teach, to portray truth so effectively that those who read it or watch it on the screen are not the same again and are so deeply moved that when choices are to be made, correct choices are made, and when decisions are to be made, correct decisions are made."[29]

Kovic and Stone, however, are not necessarily seeking literal truth in historical fact so much as universal truth in the broader experience and in circumstance. With *Born,* Stone says that he strove to "show the quintessential American experience," and to him, Kovic's crippling is a symbol of a larger American tragedy.[30] *Born* is based on Kovic's life, but it is a life caught up in the national political struggle that eventually consumed the war. One reviewer wrote that "the film probably tells us more about American society and politics than all previous Vietnam movies combined, with *Easy Rider* thrown in for good measure."[31] *Born*'s Kovic is the death messenger delivering the unbearable news about the Vietnam experience to the American public. Movies such as Stone's Vietnam pictures, according to film historian Jeanine Basinger, are "an example of using history in an atmosphere the audience understands to make a story about a modern contemporary issue."[32]

With that history, *Born* employs new myths to debunk old ones about the valor of war. The Vietnam experience alone challenged traditional attitudes about war and shattered many cultural myths on which the country was founded, the myths of Manifest Destiny and American superiority in particular. Since all cultures depend on myths to explain their existence, define their past, and chart their future, new and amended myths have replaced the old myths swept away in the stormy currents of Vietnam.[33] Recognizing this fact adds to the historical significance of *Born*, for embodied in the post-Vietnam myths are the values and beliefs of the generation of Stone and Kovic. Stone himself has implicitly confessed his role in mythmaking by admitting that he was not as interested in a faithful rendition of Kovic's life as he was at getting "to the truth of Vietnam" to help advance the healing of those who had fought and to enlighten those who one day may be drafted to fight.[34]

The academic historian typically does not, as Stone freely acknowledges doing, take "dramatic license" with historical facts.[35] In *Born*, for instance, the peasant village Kovic's platoon destroys in the film bore no association with a real enemy firefight; Kovic actually broke his leg not while in the Bronx Veterans Hospital but after he returned from Mexico and was living alone in a New York apartment; he never went to Syracuse University with his girlfriend, who does not exist in the book, and — according to those who were there — the police were civil, not hostile, toward students protesting the Kent State incident; in his memoir, Kovic never seeks out the family of the Georgia marine who fell to his friendly fire; and a Republican goon squad never physically assaulted the antiwar protesters at the 1972 National Convention.[36]

Equally problematic to Stone's tendencies toward fiction is his reductionist interpretation of the past. In Stone's history, Richard Nixon is the bad guy of military aggression, while Lyndon Johnson escapes complicity in the Vietnam War, even though he, more than any president, was responsible for escalating U.S. military action. The suggestion of Kovic as the archetypal grunt is also debatable. Just as most veterans refrained from protesting the war, most were not gung-ho volunteers like Kovic itching for combat. In a 1990 review of *Born*, historian Christian Appy pointed out that the majority of those who went to Vietnam came from poor and working-class backgrounds, as did Kovic. But *Born* only hints at Vietnam's blue-collar soldiery. There is Mr. Kovic's career at the local A&P grocery; the littered, rural environment of the dead

Georgia marine's family; Ron Kovic's lament to his boyhood friend and combat comrade, Timmie, that the war devastated their (working-class) town; his complaint to another boyhood friend — hamburger entrepreneur Stevie — that Stevie was saved from the war by college, recognized as a deferment of the privileged. Appy also makes the argument that most enlistees were either drafted or volunteered in anticipation of being drafted. Unlike the spirited Kovic, they "simply regarded [the military] as an unavoidable duty."[37]

But Appy's argument does not undermine the idea that American culture shaped young people with beliefs similar to those of Kovic. They perhaps only acted on their beliefs differently, less fanatically. In the post–World War II era, there existed a cultural reference to war — in film, literature, and attitudes — of an extent not found in previous eras.[38] Testimony to this effect is readily available. "We'd all seen too many war movies," remembers Michael Herr, who chronicled the war with the eye of a journalist.[39] Even Audie Murphy questioned the Vietnam War in his later years and worried about his own flesh-and-blood response to the manly lure of combat: "I don't want them to try to be what I was. I don't want dead heroes for sons."[40] Appy, who has published a book about American soldiers in Vietnam, acknowledges that although they preferred to avoid war, they liked John Wayne, trusted John Kennedy, and loved their country.[41] Finally, one should not forget that the power complex driving the war embraced and perpetuated the myth that sired Kovic's gung-ho attitude.

Some critics missed this point, maintaining instead that Stone went overboard with his depictions of blind patriotism. To one reviewer, *Born* represented "anti-American propaganda."[42] Noted film critic and Stone basher Pauline Kael complained that *Born*'s Kovic is an unbelievable character, inconceivably naive and zealous. Sometime, somewhere, she argued, someone or something must have informed young Ron Kovic "about the ugliness of war."[43] Kael was perhaps trying to caution against exalting a new myth about the Vietnam warrior being duped by a chauvinistic American culture. But her remarks ignore historical data consistent with Stone's interpretation, and they come at the expense of Kovic's experiences, essentially denying them.

Others with firsthand knowledge of war would also take exception to Kovic's experiences. A 1980 VA survey found that the majority of those Vietnam veterans polled reflected on their own experiences with pride in servitude and country.[44] Certainly, World War II veterans — like George Bush, for instance — tend to perceive the years between their war and Kovic's war differently. To many of Bush's generation, Vietnam carries a shameful and unbearable legacy of defeat and dishonor. For Kovic and Stone, there is virtue in that legacy's challenge to dangerous ideals born or affirmed in World

War II[45] — in spite of Bush acting out of experience and launching a redemptive war in the Persian Gulf. At the very least, Stone makes an important contribution to history by presenting a valid alternative viewpoint to those who would seek to revitalize the mythic legacy of World War II.

Yet Stone's own concept of the past has been informed by images imparted by experience as well. He sees his and Kovic's lives as having followed a like course, from innocence to loss to enlightenment. Kovic's took a more tragic path, of course, but post–World War II society had shaped their formative years in similar ways, and Vietnam had altered their destinies. Innocence corrupted by American arrogance is the central myth in Stone's history.[46] Before making *Born,* he had been working on a script about his experiences as a patriot and a veteran, his own fall from grace, but he remembered Kovic's story as more compelling and returned to it. As he did with *Platoon,* Stone taps into his own life story and projects it into *Born.* "In a way," he says, "I merged Ron's story with that of other veterans, including me." Stone, for example, "believed in the domino theory for a lot longer than Ron." On that, he says, "the movie is closer to my experience."[47]

PERSONAL EXPERIENCE AS HISTORY

Stone had once bought into the promise of post–World War II America. He and Kovic were both cold war babies; just as Kovic's mother feared Satan's Red menace, Stone's father "was an apologist — a defender of the Cold War."[48] Stone, too, succumbed to the Kennedy myth of youthful vigor and humanity and found himself volunteering for service in the Free Pacific Institute to teach Southeast Asian children. He was no counterculturist, though, and a year or so later he joined the army, announcing to his father that he was a man. "I had a serious dose of patriotism," Stone says. "I believed in the country, believed in the ideals, believed that the communists were undermining us everywhere." America was invincible, and Vietnam was supposed to be the war of his generation. "It was glorious," Stone remembers.[49]

Even so, he left Vietnam in 1968 doubting victory. It was the year of Nixon's election, and Stone trusted the new president to fulfill his pledge to end the war. Despite his conservatism, Stone had begun to question the world of his stockbroker father. *Born's* opening scenes in idyllic Massapequa are Stone's cinematic satire of that world — its duplicity, self-righteousness, political consensus, and suburban smugness. Stone's Kovic hungers to "be a part of history" like his father, who fought in "W-W-Two"; Stone in real life sought to carry on his own father's World War II legacy. As a Vietnam veteran enrolled in New York University's film school, Stone felt somewhat estranged from the other students, not unlike *Born*'s Kovic feeling ill at ease among the Syracuse protesters. Stone also had the experience of being caught in the middle of a construction-worker attack on student protesters while he was shooting a project for film class. Ultimately, enlightenment came for Stone with Watergate and Nixon's failure to end the war during his first term.[50]

Born can actually be seen as an extension of the antiwar movement, as Stone's way of keeping its meaning alive. Consequently, Stone seems to regard the historian's professed principles of detachment and objectivity as counterproductive to the film's political purpose. This naturally raises questions about *Born*'s historical validity and Stone's commitment to historical accuracy. But a little self-examination might be in order for the academics, for historians have introduced a new narrative style that smacks, one might say, of Stonism.

In recent years, a cadre of respected scholars has been nudging written history away from the formulaic expectations of the social sciences and back toward storytelling. At the risk of historical objectivity, the new direction has often brought with it a touch of personal impression and conjecture braided with historical fact. Natalie Davis's *The Return of Martin Guerre* (1983), which as book and movie ultimately enjoyed an audience wider than its comparatively narrow subject, was the pilot of the new model. A decade later, Yale historian John Demos yielded to a haunting inner impulse to storytelling when he wrote *The Unredeemed Captive*, in which he deploys speculative prose to flesh out the human drama in history.[51] When historical evidence runs short in *Celia, A Slave*, widely used in undergraduate history classes, author Melton McLaurin imagines for his readers what a desperate slave woman and others around her might have done.[52] The historian closest to Stone in approach is Simon Schama, who inserts himself as a subject in his *Landscape and Memory*; this followed a book whose content challenges the distinction between historical scholarship and historical novel.[53] Although sometimes scorned, the radicalization of the history narrative has also generated kudos from colleagues. Winthrop Jordan won the 1993 Bancroft Prize, one of the profession's most prestigious, for writing about a slave conspiracy that he can only guess happened.[54]

CONCLUSION

Ironically, as the outcry against Stone's brand of history grows louder and more haughty, many of the profession's leading scholars are expanding the role of the observer. For some years now, film historians have been discussing the occasional need "to cement the pieces of evidence with mortar of [the researcher's] own construction," to quote Robert Brent Toplin. Talk has also turned to the possibilities of enriching narrative history with the power of literary imagination, to paraphrase Robert A. Rosenstone.[55] Has Simon Schama perhaps warmed to the philosophy of Stone? "I don't believe in the collective version of history," Stone says, "but in the higher dialogues of Socrates: know thyself."[56] Maybe history does happen to historians more than we care to concede. Perhaps we should not simply intellectualize history, know it only as something that happened, but understand it as an experience — that of the historical actor, the historian, and the student. Are there not the likes of James Caan in the closets of us all?

But no matter how much historians fiddle with the narrative or how in-your-face they make classroom lectures, they will never command the reach and resonance of a Stone film. As popular culture, *Born on the Fourth of July* is part of the American experience and the Vietnam legacy; for good or bad, Oliver Stone is one of the public's chosen historians. "I think one day," says Stone's agent, "his movies will be viewed to understand what the world was like in the middle of the twentieth century."[57] On the subject of Vietnam and in light of ideologies and interpretations currently afoot in academe, Stone's history should give scholars little reason to fret. Then, too, no history is definitive; it is simply part of a collective work in progress. The related subjects of war and America's first acknowledged military defeat will always represent embattled terrain, and on the front line — if not in the crossfire — will stand Ron Kovic and Oliver Stone.

The Lizard King or Fake Hero?

Oliver Stone, Jim Morrison, and History

Let's just say I was testing the bounds of reality, that I was curious. . . . Me, they see exactly what they want to see. Some say Lizard King, whatever that means, or some black-clad leather demon, whatever that means. But really, I think of myself as a sensitive, intelligent human being with the soul of a clown that always forces me to blow it at the most crucial moment — a fake hero — a joke the gods played on me.

— Jim Morrison[1]

In his brash, oversized, daring, and loud movie *The Doors* (1991), Oliver Stone takes us on a kaleidoscopic journey back to the late 1960s and, along the way, offers tantalizing and controversial pronouncements about what the 1960s were really about and just what kind of a historian he is. Like the subject of this film, Jim Morrison, the lead singer of the rock band the Doors, Stone can be alternately abruptly frontal in his opinions and visions and frustratingly vague and even contradictory. Critics have repeatedly asked about the film (and a question Morrison asked himself), Is Morrison's life enough to base a movie on? Historians might also wonder the same thing, if for different reasons. Is this a "fake hero"? Do Morrison and the Doors represent the essential characteristics of that tumultuous decade? Is Morrison a worthy subject of a serious cinematic history? Is this film history at all, or is it myth and mythmaking? And if it is history, what kind of history is it?

There is no question that Stone's screen biography of Morrison is deeply sympathetic to its subject, something that has outraged more than one critic. Roy Anker, to take an especially hostile example, blasts Stone for pushing "a puerile romanticism of drug-induced . . . anarchism" and stands agape "that a half-sensible adult citizen can entertain such rubbish."[2] Whereas Stone wants us to view Morrison as a kind of cultural hero for dedicating his life to "breaking through to the other side," Anker sees an "everyday junkie who has less cultural or spiritual authority than the Easter rabbit . . . a runaway train of narcissistic abandonment," not the shaman-priest or tortured yet visionary latter-day Romantic poet we see through Stone's camera.[3] Other critics, such as Paul Baumann for *Commonweal*, sniff at Morrison's "pathetic artistic pretensions" (dismissing his poetry as trite, his musical talent as minimal) and, not surprisingly, write off Stone's film about such an individual as "obtuse, even silly."[4]

Whatever one may think of the pronouncements of critics, however, one can hardly deny that Morrison and the Doors were one of the biggest bands of the late 1960s or that Stone is one of the hottest filmmakers of the last two decades. The Doors and the director revel in the rejection of authority and have captured the imagination of many a rock fan and moviegoer from different generations. Morrison, the essence of lawlessness embodied in a rock musician (he was arrested ten times), and Stone were and are also good if scandalous copy when they choose to be. Listen to Morrison: "Sex is full of lies. The body tries to tell the truth, but it's usually too battered with rules to be heard. We cripple ourselves with lies. Most people have no idea what they're missing, our society places supreme value on control, on hiding what you feel. It mocks primitive culture and prides itself on the suppression of natural instincts and impulses."[5] And hear Stone: "'I believe in Morrison's incantations. Break on through. Kill the pigs. Destroy. Loot. Fuck your mother. All that shit. Anything goes. Anything.'"[6]

To be sure, as just about anyone who has viewed this almost frantic film will agree, almost anything does go in Stone's version of the life of Jim Morrison, played by Val Kilmer. It begins with a Morrison/Kilmer voiceover reciting words from Morrison's "An American Prayer," then, with the words "the ceremony is about to begin," the haunting first bars of "Riders on the Storm" waft through the theater and we see the Morrison family — with a twelve-year-old Jim asleep in the back seat — driving across a desert. They come upon an automobile accident where several native Americans lie dying in the road. Later in the movie, Morrison says that the soul of one of those killed passed into his. This scene sets the theme of death and transcendence that will mark the film continuously to its very end.

The story jumps quickly to a twenty-two-year-old Morrison arriving in Venice, California, in the summer of 1966, and again, as will be the case throughout the film, every scene is backed by music. Here Morrison meets Pam Courson, played by Meg Ryan, who will remain his girlfriend until his death in 1971, despite a tempestuous relationship. He briefly attends UCLA film school and then forms a rock band with keyboardist Ray Manzarek (he impresses upon Manzarek the depth of his lyrics by singing a verse from "Moonlight Drive"), guitarist Robbie Krieger (who wrote "Light My Fire"), and drummer John Densmore. This was, of course, the Doors. The California segment of the movie concludes with the Doors' initial success, first at the legendary Whiskey à Go-Go on Sunset Boulevard, then out of the nightclub scene and into the heady glare of the concert performance in San Francisco during the "summer of love," 1967.

Fame from "Light My Fire" won an appearance on the *Ed Sullivan Show* in New York in 1967 and then, in 1968, launched an East Coast tour. In this second section of the film, Morrison's inner torment really begins to surface, as do his self-destructive tendencies. At his New Haven concert he is arrested for inciting riot. Stone then recreates an explosive Thanksgiving dinner party at Morrison's and Courson's house in Topanga Canyon. Before the guests arrive, Jim induces Pam to eat a tab of LSD, and with guests assembled, Jim and Pam get into a fight, during which Jim flings Pam's turkey to the floor and stomps it to pieces and then chases Pam around the house with a knife, which he then hands to her and, on his knees, tells her to kill him. The guests file out, one muttering that the party had become distinctly "low rent."

Morrison's self-destructive slide toward death continues in the third segment of the film, capped by the infamous concert in Miami, Florida, in March 1969. In this segment, the sense of doom envelopes Morrison. We sense as viewers that Morrison is plummeting rapidly toward his end. Just before we see the frames that reconstruct the concert, Stone gives us a glimpse of a man in a bathtub, only the back of his head visible. For those who know that this was the position in which Morrison was found dead in a Paris apartment in 1971, the implication is obvious. We then jump-cut to the Miami concert and Morrison singing "Five to One," with the lyrics that tell us that Morrison is inescapably trapped in his own destruction: "Five to one, One in five, No one here gets out alive!" Of course, it was during this concert that Morrison was arrested and booked on four counts of lewd behavior, including allegedly exposing himself.

The fourth clearly defined section of the film begins with Morrison's trial in the Dade County courthouse in 1970. Then Stone flashes frenetic images of a world in turmoil across the screen: from speeches by Martin Luther King, Jr., and the assassination of Robert Kennedy to firefights in Vietnam, all these images backed powerfully by one of Morrison's most philosophic songs, "When the Music's Over." Free while his case is appealed, Morrison returns to LA, says goodbye to the other Doors, and flies to Paris with Pam. Within a year, Morrison is found dead in the bathtub. Then, backed by "LA Woman" and the verse that begins with "Mr. MoJo Risin'," Stone's camera escorts us through Père Lachaise cemetery where Morrison is buried, along the way panning gravestones of some of the most celebrated artists in European history, among them Honoré de Balzac, Molière, and Oscar Wilde. We then jump-cut to "a city at night," the camera soaring over Los Angeles while "LA Woman" can still be heard, and then, fading to black and rolling the credits, we hear one of the Doors' timeless, hard-driving rock 'n' roll songs, "Roadhouse Blues." Death, and transcendence.

Morrison's and the Doors' popularity endures (Stone's movie, with the aid of video sales, made money), the Lizard King's premature death at twenty-seven contributing mightily toward launching him to mythical status. Stone's film may convince fans that Morrison was a great artist, the Doors a great band, but for those of us interested in understanding whether the man and the band were the pulse of the 1960s or how history can be represented in film, that is really beside the point. What fascinates — and troubles — many of us is the blending of legend and a historical individual in a movie that the director assures us is a cinematic history.

FACTS AND FICTION

In this movie, Stone was a stickler for exact historical duplication of scenic elements of the various sets. The cigarette packs from which characters casually tap out their smokes are scrupulously historical. So is the costly reproduction of Sunset Boulevard in Los Angeles, where we see Morrison career drunkenly amid late-1960s automobiles, proclaiming from the hood of one, "I am the Lizard King, I can do anything!" The legendary Whiskey à Go-Go, the venue of the Doors' first success and Morrison's first outrageous extemporization of lyrics (when, while singing "The End," he wandered off into an oedipal nightmare of murdering his father and fornicating with his mother), was reconstructed exactly as it was in 1967. The same could be said for the notorious Miami concert (where Morrison was arrested for allegedly exposing himself). Here thousands of extras were gathered before eight simultaneously running cameras, everyone with dress (flowered shirts or no shirts at all, even for some women) and hair (long, often head-banded) again true to period. Even the New York apartment of Morrison's girlfriend Patricia Kenneally was painstakingly reconstructed, down to some letters bearing the correct address scattered across a desk.

Stone also stays faithful to the time by interviewing hundreds of people who knew Morrison and the other Doors. Period detail and historical investigation (including interviews with contemporaries) have been techniques of cinematic history long practiced by many Hollywood directors, and in this regard, Stone's approach appears little different from that tradition in the making of *The Doors*. He was confident, as he pointedly put it in an interview with Stephen Talbot of *Mother Jones*, that "'my movie is an accurate depiction of those times.'"[7]

But is it? Despite the rigor for certain scenic detail, factual inaccuracies also abound in this movie. True, almost every film biography alters facts or compresses episodes to fit the story, all the while seeking the "larger truth." In fact, as film historian Robert Rosenstone has written, "cinematic histories" are different by nature from "written histories" in the fact that they must compress the past dramatically and must invent elements of the past (most notably dialogue) that no longer exist amid the evidence left to us. He points out, however, that the difference between good film history and bad turns upon the difference between "true invention" and "false invention," the litmus test distinguishing between the two being whether the spirit of a filmmaker's inventions squares with the evidence available to historical researchers.[8] Because Stone claims to be a cinematic historian, we may fairly ask of Stone and his movies not whether there is invention (in all cinematic histories there must be) but rather whether Stone invents "truly."

This may seem like a simple question easily answered, but with Stone, nothing turns out to be simple. When asked how he had made his decisions about representing Morrison on screen, Stone responded at first directly, then elusively: "You have to stay true to the spirit of it. And I think I did. Literal facts? . . . Out of 40 witnesses, they'll all give you a different version of events in Jim's life. He was everything to everybody, and no one will quite agree on all the events."[9] Certainly Bill Siddons, the Doors' former manager, did not agree with the accuracy of Stone's rendition. He was so troubled that "so much of [the film] was inaccurate that [he] wanted to know if [Stone] had any interest in the facts or if it was just a fictional account." Stone told him, perhaps surprisingly in light of his claims for historicity, that "it was fictional."[10] The term "fictional" crops up again in Stone's own words when he says that critics won't "understand it will not be the real Jim on film — it will be my poem to Jim. It's my vision, my fictional poem."[11]

MYTHS AND HEROES

How can fiction and history coexist in such seemingly noncontradictory ways? The answer, at least with Stone, is that this filmmaker believes that fiction and cinematic history have a common meeting ground, and the former can be true to the latter if the filmmaker remains "true to the spirit of the times."[12] In other words, historical reality for Stone can be altered for film so long as the "spirit of the times" is respected. Thus far, this sounds like Rosenstone's "true invention," but for Stone, the spirit of the times is grasped through myth, and it is far from clear how myth and history can be made to tell the same story. What were the 1960s *really* like? Were Morrison and the Doors *really* like the men in the movie?

Most viewers of the film *The Doors* will agree that the portrayal of Morrison is larger than life, and one is easily led to the conclusion, intended by Stone, that Morrison and the Doors embodied in essential ways "the spirit" of the 1960s. To make this point through film, Stone (as in all his movies) casts his main character as an archetype, even an icon on which he paints what he believes were the fundamental traits of a culture. Was Morrison really like that? Yes and no, Stone seems to say, but — and this may surprise those of us who think that history is about real people as they really were — for Stone, such a question is not the one to ask. Thus he has little patience with critics who bash him for supposedly reducing his characters to two dimensions. The Morrison we see in the film, say some who knew him, was too serious. Where is the ironic Jim, the man who often joked about the "act" he put on to create the sexual persona that so excited his fans?[13]

Viewers of this film are likely to conclude that the filmmaker does not romanticize the man or the times. Instead, he portrays an excessive Morrison as a sometimes cruel, humorless drunk who is intoxicated with booze and at times arrogant self-importance. According to Morrison's biographer Jerry Hopkins, however, this was only part of the man, and to omit the sensitive, ironic, and compassionate other half was a betrayal of the Doors' singer, an "ugly, narrow picture" in which Morrison was "thoroughly . . . trashed."[14]

Critics have said that Stone trashed not only Morrison but also the 1960s as a whole. Wrote one critic in the *New Yorker*, "In *The Doors* Oliver Stone reduces the richly contradictory experience of the 1960s to the myth of Morrison, and, in the process, reduces Morrison and The Doors as well: the movie restricts the viewer's freedom to imagine the 1960s culture as anything but a movement with a single voice, or to imagine The Doors as anything but a metaphor."[15] Even less charitably, another critic rips Stone for "mangling or shrinking the issues to fit the faceless, mythic demands of his own sensibility."[16] As a result, according to this critic, a gifted actor like Val Kilmer, who played Morrison in Stone's movie, was forced to "play the icon, not the man."[17]

Regardless of the criticism of his portrait, clearly Stone believes that Morrison represents the essence of the 1960s, more than any other rock musician. When one considers the astounding variety of rock and roll in that remarkably innovative decade, such a claim is staggering in its sweep and difficult to accept, even for Doors fans. What about the Beatles, surely the popular choice for the representative band of the decade? When the Doors were turning out *Strange Days*, John, Paul, George, and Ringo were remaking themselves and rock music with *Magical Mystery Tour* and *Sergeant Pepper's Lonely Hearts Club Band*. Certainly a strong argument could be made that the English Beatles were the epitome of the 1960s. Many of their songs intoned the mantra of the decade — sex, drugs, and rock 'n' roll — every bit as much as those of the self-consciously West Coast band the Doors.

Others might point to psychedelic rock as the true sound of that decade and Led Zeppelin or the incomparable Jimi Hendrix as its ultimate expression. The year the Doors released their first album, *The Doors,* Hendrix asked, "Are you experienced?" in the legendary album of that name. And can we ever forget Hendrix at Woodstock in the summer of 1969 (the Doors were not there) — perhaps the defining moment within the defining event of the whole decade — playing an acid, antiwar version of the "Star Spangled Banner," complete with amplifier feedback that uncannily reproduced the sound of warfare precisely at the point when the words, had they been sung, would have intoned "and the rocket's red glare, the bombs bursting in air"? And lest we miss the connection between antiwar politics and drugs, Hendrix finished the national anthem and broke into "Purple Haze" (a popular form of LSD at the time) without missing a beat.

Vietnam hung over the 1960s like a funeral pall, and with sex, drugs, and rock 'n' roll, one would have to consider the antiwar movement an essential characteristic of the time. Does the Doors' music embody this sentiment? True, Morrison brazenly challenged authority in a general sense, but amazingly, given what was happening in Vietnam and at home at the time the Doors burst on the scene, only one of the Doors' songs is overtly political and antiwar, "The Unknown Soldier." Just as astoundingly, and in my opinion unfortunately, the deeply political Stone, whose very being as an adult was forged in the crucible of Vietnam, leaves this powerful song out of his movie and off the soundtrack of it.

Perhaps, then, it is futile to try to present a particular band as the essence of a musical decade that was so profoundly innovative. Let's not forget that this was also the time of Motown and, though we may be tempted to wipe this from our memory, bubblegum rock. Songs from the Temptations, Smokey Robinson and the Miracles, Diana Ross and the Supremes, the Archies, the 1910 Fruit Gum Company, and the Ohio Express all challenged the Beatles, Janis Joplin, Bob Dylan, Zeppelin, Hendrix, and the Doors for airtime and competed effectively with them in the marketplace, as evidenced by a look at the charts of top hits at the time. So, is there an essential band, and an essential sound, of the 1960s? Probably not.

Still, the Doors undoubtedly touched a pulse — even several pulses — of the decade, for they could play hard-driving, dance-inducing rock 'n' roll with the best of them (think of "Roadhouse Blues" or "Back Door Man"), while on the same album appeal to the more philosophical listener. Many of us welcomed songs that said something of importance, and the Doors provided many of them: tunes like the fatalistic and pessimistic "Riders on the Storm," with its haunting melody floating deliriously on the notes of Manzarek's keyboard; or "People Are Strange," with the troubling words that spoke of pointlessness and dislocation (what teenager hasn't felt that?); or "The End," with its brooding over sex and death; or the precociously environmentalist "When the Music's Over" ("What have they done to the earth? What have they done to our fair sister?"); or "LA Woman," which metaphorically bemoans the decline of Los Angeles from a free-spirited city to a tawdry, commercialized shell of its former self.

We may be inclined to view the Doors as an important and popular voice of the 1960s, but only one, however loud, among many. But even granting Stone the artistic license to make a case for the Doors as *the* band of the 1960s, we are still left with an iconic representation of a man and an era. The reason for Stone's choice of Morrison and his portrayal of him is deeply personal rather than historical, for he is clearly sympathetic to his subject and certainly wants us to believe that Morrison and the Doors were the life pulse of the era like no other band of musicians.

APOLLO OR DIONYSUS?

Stone defends his cinematic portraits as true, but Stone's truth results from the intertwining of myth and history. Such a breezy combination has prompted many a professional historian as well as many a moviegoer to simply dismiss Stone's claim that he is a historian (when I asked one viewer what he thought of Stone as a cinematic historian, he said: "Pfffft. He's no historian. He just makes it up!"). Unfazed by such criticism, Stone deliberately makes "historical" films that, in his words, unleash "the pure wash of emotion across the mind to let you see the inner myth, the spirit of the thing. Then, when the cold light of reason hits you as you walk out of the theater, the sense of truth will remain lodged beyond reason in the depths of your being."[18] This contrasting of the emotional and mythical with the rational is defining in Stone's films, and certainly in *The Doors*. "As a filmmaker," Stone tells us, "I do believe in what might be called 'Dionysian politics.'" Moreover, he felt that his film *The Doors* "was my chance to explore the Dionysian."[19]

Just what does Stone mean by Dionysian? And what does it have to do with Stone's understanding of what history is? Here Stone, like Morrison, is deeply influenced by the nineteenth-century German philosopher Friedrich Nietzsche, who suggested that Western civilization is basically driven by two contradictory impulses, the "Apollonian" and the "Dionysian." Stone and Morrison interpret Nietzsche as saying that the former is characterized by "the cold light of reason" — analysis, or, in a word, rationality — while the latter is marked by emotion, impulse, and feeling. Whether this is true to Nietzsche is beside the point (in *The Birth of Tragedy*, the German philosopher does not directly equate Apollo with reason but rather with the imaginative illusion of art forms that create repressive order from the chaos of existence). What does matter is that Stone and Morrison see the contemporary age as locked in an endless war between the contradictory drives of rational analysis and ecstatic feeling.

Moreover, they believe that in some individuals — usually artists and poets — these impulses can be *dramatically* opposed, and it is no accident that these individuals are Stone's and Morrison's heroes. Arthur Rimbaud, a nineteenth-century French poet, was one, and Stone lets us know this in a scene with Morrison and Courson lying on the beach. Stone pans his camera slowly across some books that Morrison has with him, and the first we see are Rimbaud's *A Season in Hell* and *The Drunken Boat*. And the sentiments Rimbaud once expressed in a letter to a friend could be mistaken for Morrison's or Stone's own. Wrote Rimbaud: "A poet makes himself a visionary through a long, boundless, and systematized disorganization of all the senses. . . . Unspeakable torment, where he will need the greatest faith, a superhuman strength, where he becomes among all men the great invalid, the great accursed . . . he attains the unknown! So what if he is destroyed in his ecstatic flight through things unheard of, unnamable."[20] In the script for the movie, Stone has Kilmer virtually paraphrase Rimbaud. Says Kilmer/Morrison: "I believe in a long, prolonged derangement of the senses to attain the unknown. I live in the subconscious. Our pale reason hides the infinite from us."

In Morrison, Stone certainly found his latter-day Rimbaud, but even more so, his Dionysus. Manzarek said of Morrison (again, a bit off the mark on Nietzsche): he was Dionysus, "a Greek god reincarnate. Whereas Apollo was the god of light, clear thought, logical thinking, Dionysus was the god of feeling, spontaneity, the dance, music. . . . Jim was Dionysus personified. The man onstage was an absolute genius, a human theatricon. . . . It was as if it wasn't Jim performing."[21] In the movie, right after Morrison and Manzarek decide to form a band, Manzarek says, "Morrison, we gotta make the myths!" after which Morrison tellingly launches into talk about the Greek god Dionysus, who drove women mad in a sexual frenzy.

Stone himself has said that he thought of Morrison as "a Dionysian figure. Remember, Dionysus was a god who came to earth to play and tease, to seduce and drive the women mad. Many of Morrison's performances resemble the [Dionysian] bacchanals."[22] All of the Doors concerts that Stone recreates are bacchanalian, but none more than the one in San Francisco in 1967. To "Light My Fire," Morrison swings across the stage clutching a rope like some swashbuckling pirate, clearly reveling in the adoration heaped on him by his frenzied fans. He then swan dives into a sea of people who hold him aloft, a sacrificed god, as the camera shoots the scene from directly overhead.

In Stone's hands, the Morrison story becomes something more than a screen biography of a lead singer of a popular band; it is, in Stone's words, "more a mythic story that belongs to any era. . . . I'm trying to show how Jim Morrison represented the desire for Dionysus, which is something we all want in our fundamental soul."[23] It remains puzzling, then, why Stone, so interested in the Dionysian and therefore theatrical aspect of Morrison, did not reproduce the most dramatically theatrical (and political) performance by Morrison and the Doors that I am aware of, that of "The Unknown Soldier." Preserved on film by the Doors themselves, Morrison is sacrificed to the nonsensical war, shot dead on stage by Krieger holding his guitar like a rifle, pulling the trigger/ string just as Densmore pounds his drum.

Let's return to our central, related concerns in this essay: Do Morrison and the Doors represent the essential traits of the 1960s? And does Stone's kind of history allow us to answer that question? We simply cannot deny that there was a powerful current of the "Dionysian," as Stone defines it, during that time, and Morrison was as Dionysian as they come. But history as most of us understand it is mostly an "Apollonian" venture, with rational analysis and criticism rooted in its very definition at least since the eighteenth century. How can history still be history when it abandons its essential characteristics? In fact, this is perhaps the fundamental question that professional historians over the past ten years have asked themselves, and the ever-daring Stone fearlessly wanders into this debate with a notion of what his answer is. History, or at least cinematic history, should be more "Dionysian" than "Apollonian"; it should appeal more to the emotions, not directly to the intellect.

So it is no accident that Stone's filmic heroes, Morrison included, "perennially slay the monsters of modern rationality,"[24] and his notion of heroism is such that a Jim Morrison could find a place within Stone's pantheon. Thus says Stone: "I think that the meaning of heroism has a lot to do with evolving into a higher human being. . . . Heroism is tied to an evolution of consciousness. . . . The ability to change is what sets apart the hero."[25] Following almost textbook Jungian psychology, Stone melds his notion of heroism with archetype and myth. According to Jung (and apparently Stone), the collective unconscious, or what Stone would call the "spirit of the times," expresses itself in individuals who become archetypes, or, as Stone would have it, a culture's heroes. These individuals, for whatever reason, feel compelled to push the boundaries of human consciousness, "to act as philosophical test pilots for an entire culture."[26] These kinds of heroes, and many of Stone's protagonists, fit the profile precisely; they "transcend self and death in the belief in something more."[27] Can it be surprising, then, that the defining song of the entire Doors repertoire for Stone's movie and for his portrait of their lead singer was "Break on Through to the Other Side," or that the image of death haunts the movie as completely as it did Morrison from first frame to final cut?

A DIFFERENT FILM TECHNIQUE FOR A DIFFERENT KIND OF HISTORY

As we will see shortly, Stone closely identifies with Morrison, and in the conceiving and making of the movie, the filmmaker became, as a biographer of both Stone and Morrison has written, "more and more engrossed with the idea that a film about Jim Morrison should have some of the same qualities that dominated Morrison as an artist and a man. That would mean pushing the envelope cinematically, taking risks with the structure and the dialogue. . . . If Morrison was anything he was extemporaneous, improvising not only his art but his life. A film about his life should also break tradition."[28]

What this meant for Stone was that he was going to have to structure his film around Morrison's poetry and song lyrics. This is a different cinematic history, with a vengeance. Says Stone: "The concept was that the movie was all in Jim's lyrics. I picked the songs I wanted and wrote each piece of the movie as a mood to fit that song. So it was sort of a new technique. . . . I trusted to his lyrics to tell his tale."[29] What results is, according to Stone, "a tone poem." The film "will be my poem to Jim. It's my vision, my fictional poem with the Doors' music threaded through it."[30] Stone tells us that he "let the music basically dictate the mood of each movement. The first part of the movie is the more innocent songs, the second part is 'The End,' more towards the psychedelic. Then we go to the New York section, which I saw as darker and more twisted, 'Strange Days,' 'People are Strange,' culminating in the decadence of 'Soft Parade.' Then coming back to 'Five to One' in defiance in Miami, and this coming to a whole softer thing in 'L.A. Woman' and framing the whole thing with 'American Prayer.' That was generally the movement of the film."[31]

Everything about the film reaches for the emotions more than reason, and the filmmaker availed himself of camera technique, color, and lighting that deliberately tried to reach the Dionysian side of his viewers. David Breskin once remarked to Stone that "some people feel that your camera is pushy, that they almost need to wear a seatbelt watching your films." To which Stone characteristically retorted, "That's their problem. The world is spinning much faster than my camera and myself. . . . I think movies have to break through the three dimensions, as close as you can get. . . . We're into new technology. Use everything you can. Make it breathe, make it coil, make it live."[32]

Stone's director of photography, Robert Richardson, said this about the film's camera work: "We tried to mirror both the time and the mind of Jim. In the earlier stages of his life, the camera moved very little. We used simple masters, over-the-shoulder shots and closeups. It was motivated by the action of the actor. As the band formed and the music started to flow, the camera again moved in the same way. It progressed that way, until the music became finer and the band grew into a strong mesh of steel, the camera was rolling even more fluidly, much more gracefully. As Jim started to deteriorate, we deteriorated."[33]

The use of color and light aimed at the same emotional — and historical — objectives. Again Richardson explains the overall plan: "Early on, the film is almost Technicolor, with strong reds, greens, and blues. . . . The color shifts when the band goes to New York, as both Morrison's life and the film become darker. It moved toward more blacks until at Miami, black is the only tone, with shafts of white and periodic washes of red. The film finishes with a very light tone."[34]

CRITICAL DISTANCE?

Can such a philosophical and technical approach to the past be good history? Most historians assume that a certain critical distance between the historian and his or her subject must be maintained to minimize bias and preserve objectivity. Stone, in contrast, deliberately shrinks, even obliterates, that distance. Take his well-honed and characteristic technique of rapid-splice editing (which he learned from the New Wave filmmakers), which disrupts narrative flow, fragments story lines, and hammers images directly through the senses into the brain. One critic, who wrote the appropriately titled interview with Stone "Splinters to the Brain," astutely observed that such a technique, so typical of Stone, "constitute[s] a kind of cerebral bypass in which surface appearances are transported directly into the depths — the subconscious realm of myths and symbols." This technique, which ideally matches Stone's Dionysian philosophy and a psychology wedded to archetypes, heroes, and myths, challenges the "critical pause for reflection . . . the reasoning mind that allows us to distinguish fact from fiction, truth from falsity."[35] In other words, it is not history as most of us know it.

How can a filmmaker who intentionally utilizes such a jackhammer technique to deny us a critical pause for reflection, to blur the distinction between fact and fiction, still consider himself a cinematic historian? Unrepentant, Stone fires questions at us that throw us doubters on the defensive: "Who owns reality? Who owns your mind? Isn't history a distorted hall of mirrors that depends on the kind of surface that reflects its essence and its events? . . . What form of representation best grasps reality . . . [?] Do you pile fact upon fact and call it history? Or . . . do you look at the vision of a man's life? A life, you see, is not based on the accumulation of facts, but on flashes of insight, on moments of the spirit. . . . In this sense, I like the MTV-style flashes of imagery because they have circumvented conventional narrative . . . in creating a form that represented the multiple perspectives of reality."[36]

For Stone, then, historical truth is plural and depends on perspective, on points of view. In other words, the vantage point of the observer determines the "reality" of what he or she sees, and therefore there are as many realities as there are vantage points. Stone offers no help to those of us who want to assemble such an endlessly fragmented vision into a reality that groups of individuals can agree on, but with its emphasis on points of view, it is a historical vision readily adapted to the filmmaker's craft. After all, films are almost always radically shortened presentations of events (fictional or real) that took longer than two or three hours to happen. This means that filmmakers decide what to include and what to leave out. In the case of a screen biography, only a tiny fraction of what happened in a person's life can be selected and presented. The conventional historian writing books, of course, must also do this, but the filmmaker has many more tools in his or her bag to manipulate the subject and the audience's reaction to it. For example, audience response is dramatically affected by placement or movement of the camera (different kinds of shots elicit sharply different reactions in the viewer), choice of lenses or filters, coloration of the film itself, the type of music accompanying the images, and so forth. The filmmaker decides how these tools are used, and if he or she also claims to be a historian, as Stone does, then we can see how subjective and relative filmmaking as history can be. What past is being represented here? For what purpose? And how are we the viewers to know whether it is true?

Once a historian assumes this kind of extreme relativistic position on truth, the necessary distance between historian and subject is likely to melt away, and this certainly characterizes Stone's cinematic history. Stone plunges himself into his main characters and identifies so completely with them in some cases that they become his alter egos. And one cannot escape the conclusion that Stone does this intentionally. Morrison is a classic example of this. Stone's crew could not help but notice that during the making of *The Doors* their director increasingly resembled Morrison, or at least what Stone construed to be the essence of this complex and enigmatic man. Just as Morrison was known to be wild and excessive, so Stone became. Like Morrison, during the shooting of the film, Stone drank heavily, even did peyote. Stone's cinematographer Richardson observed that Stone "went as deep and as dark as you can go."[37]

Excess is a term that well describes the filmmaker and his subject. Stone's script calls for Kilmer/Morrison to say at one point, "I believe in excess," and no one disputes that the historical Jim Morrison, for all the differences of opinion on other aspects of the singer, believed this. As fond of poet William Blake as he was of Rimbaud, Morrison was deeply moved by Blake's line that "the road to excess leads to the palace of wisdom." And so is Stone. Says the filmmaker: "I believe in the power of excess because through excess I live a larger life. I inflate my life and by inflating my life I live more of the world. I die a more experienced man."[38]

If Stone had in mind a movie that embodied this philosophy, once again he had the perfect subject in the Lizard King. There are countless reasons why Stone identified so closely, so immediately, with Morrison, and if Stone's films are essentially about himself, as more than one critic has observed, then it can hardly be surprising that a movie on Morrison would eventually be produced. Stone candidly remarks that he heard the Doors' first album "on acid in Vietnam," adding that "in Vietnam, the Doors spoke to me in a way that other groups didn't. . . . I was attracted by Jim Morrison's rebelliousness, his recklessness."[39] Later, when he was making the movie, Stone pointed out in a *New York Times* interview that Morrison was "the bad boy" of the 1960s and that in his film he felt that he could "shed some light on that [because] . . . there's a lot of the bad boy in me. There was a lot of the rebel: I really wanted to find the bottom of the barrel. . . . I identified with Morrison. . . . He was a shaman. He was a god. For me, a Dionysian figure, a poet, a philosopher. I'd like to bring his life out into the light."[40]

As with perhaps all of Stone's movies, the creative crucible that forged their essential backdrop was Vietnam, although with *The Doors,* the war in Southeast Asia is only implicit. Morrison, says Stone, "was singing about stuff that people like me in Vietnam could relate to: sex, death, and the meaning of life. . . . 'The End,' 'When the Music's Over,' they're epic stories, Homeric ballads, in a sense."[41] And when he heard of Morrison's death, he was devastated. "When he died in 1971," Stone recalls, "it was like the day JFK died for me. It was that shattering. I worshipped him."[42]

Even before Vietnam and Morrison's death, Stone was living a life that was conditioning his eventual identification with Morrison. And this would continue even after Morrison's death and the fall of Saigon. Both Stone and Morrison spent childhoods in moderately affluent middle-class families. Both were voracious readers and were influenced by some of the same philosophers (above all, Nietzsche). They were moved by many of the same authors (notably Rimbaud, Blake, Jack Kerouac, and the Beats). Both became interested in film and shared a view of this form of art that was surprisingly similar. Judging from the movies he has made, and especially *The Doors,* Stone certainly would agree with Morrison's observation about film as "the closest approximation in art form that we have to the actual flow of consciousness."[43] Both exiled themselves from their families (Stone to Vietnam, Morrison to Los Angeles and eventually the rock world), and both were fearless in their drive to experiment with life, to explore its horizons with unflinching passion. In fact, like Morrison and even Rimbaud, whom Stone liked immensely even before turning on to the Doors (Stone's long-unpublished novel was, in fact, according to him, "symbolist poetry, it was Rimbaud-like"), Stone lived a life of extremes. Each felt deeply alienated from the world around him, and each plumbed the suicidal depths of depression. Prone to violence and recklessness, each also eventually experienced huge success.

Stone and Morrison share yet another deeply felt preoccupation, and that is about death. As David Breskin pointed out in an interview after the release of *The Doors,* "Clearly, in some very fundamental way, it's a moving force in what you do." To which Stone impassionedly replied, "'Death shall have no dominion' . . . God, it was a great poem by Dylan Thomas. . . . He was a man wracked with death, as was Jim Morrison. I admire both of them as giant men who lived in the shadow of death. [Although] I feel much less enamored of death than they did . . . I think it's a strong force in my life. I've used it. It's there. I've thought of death, often. At the age of eighteen, I went to Vietnam as a form of death. I was ready to accept death. I saw much of it in Vietnam. . . . Death is a framing experience of life and birth. Everything is seen in that light to me. . . . [Life] quickly, obscenely, being cut off."[44]

Morrison was as preoccupied with death as Stone, perhaps more so, and this comes through clearly in the movie. The Native Americans dying on the highway in the Southwest desert open the movie, and the graves in Père Lachaise close it. Along the way, even the most casually attentive viewer cannot miss the constant references to death. When Jim is first courting Pam, lying on the beach at night he talks of death, saying, "I feel most alive confronting death." Pam then asks, "Does death turn you on?" Morrison doesn't answer the question, but the rest of the movie will. The answer was apparently yes, as many scenes confirm. Consider the one in which Jim demands that Pam kill him during that raucous Thanksgiving party, or when Morrison hangs from the ledge of the Chateau Marmont Hotel in Los Angeles shouting at Pam, "Will you die for me?" or on stage in Miami when Stone has Morrison freeze and the music stop (an arresting moment as silence replaces the almost constant music that backs the rest of the film) when Jim sees the dead Native American shaman whose soul had passed into his and understands this vision as a premonition of his own death.

CONCLUSION

So what are we to make of Stone's history? Do Morrison and the Doors represent the essential characteristics of the 1960s? Is Stone what he claims to be, a cinematic historian? And if he is, what kind of history is this? I think that Stone's argument that Morrison and the Doors were *the* band that represented the essential traits of the 1960s is difficult to sustain. There were just too many currents flowing through that decade, and too many different bands — from the wildly popular top-forty band the Association to the deeply influential Velvet Underground or Cream — tapped them in different ways.

But as a historian, Stone cannot easily be dismissed because, like many practicing historians, he clearly ponders the fundamental characteristics of historical study, and his collapsing of traditional distinctions between fact and fiction has already been done by historians such as Hayden White, historians who have reopened questions about what history really is. What Stone has done is push this rethinking onto the medium from which most people get their history nowadays — the cinema. And because Stone is an immensely successful Hollywood writer-director-producer, we must decide whether this form of history is a legitimate representation of the past.

There is no question that period accuracy matters to Stone, and many of his flights of invention can be found to square with evidence available through traditional methods of historical investigation. So far, Stone's cinematic history is typical of many other screen biographies. Where he departs from tradition, however, comes with his blending of myth and history, a mixture that rests on clear philosophic (Dionysian) and psychological (Jungian) foundations.

Yet Dionysian, archetypal heroic films like *The Doors* drive Stone's history in directions that challenge some of the traditional essential traits of what most of us think of as history. By emphasizing the emotional approach to the past more than the analytical or rational, he leaves behind the kind of history that most of us are familiar with. Even more nontraditional, Stone's filmmaking techniques fire "splinters to the brain" (camera movement, color, lighting, editing) that bypass analysis and deliberately assault our ability to pause for reflection, another of the defining characteristics of historical analysis or criticism. And his close identification with his lead characters obliterates what most historians think is necessary for good, bias-free history writing — a critical distance between the historian and his or her subject.

Still, if there is one lesson that historians have learned as the twenty-first century dawns, it must be that there is no single, shared vision of what historical study is, or of what history itself is. Perhaps there never was and never will be. Stone's artistic ramblings, his vague, sometimes contradictory pronounce-ments about cinematic history, frustrate as much as enlighten, and most people — professional historians as well as everyday moviegoers — will find troubling his claims to historical truth while he blurs almost beyond distinc-tion fact and fiction, historian and subject. Yet regardless of whether we em-brace Stone's vision, and I suspect few historians will, to dismiss it out of hand would hinder our attempt to come to grips with the ever-changing meaning of cinematic history. When commenting on the name of his band, Jim Morrison, forever invoking the spirit of Blake and Rimbaud, said, "There's the known. And there's the unknown. And what separates the two is the door. And that's what I want to be . . . the door." Oliver Stone could easily have spoken these words. The question remains, however, the door to what?

Oliver Stone, *JFK*, and History

When Oliver Stone released his film *JFK* in late 1991, he certainly knew that it would generate considerable controversy. Long before its public release, the movie had already drawn heated criticism for its use of New Orleans district attorney Jim Garrison as the central character to promote Stone's thesis that the assassination of President John F. Kennedy resulted from a conspiracy. As the film's producer and director, Stone continued his cinematic tradition of making movies based on factual events and inserting into them his deeply held viewpoints. In doing so, Oliver Stone crossed the line between artist and scholar by combining film with history, by projecting onto the silver screen his highly subjective version of actual persons and events and enlivening them with colorful imagery, concocted dialogue, and imaginary people. In *JFK*, Stone clearly had a message to convey to his audience: that the Kennedy assassination had resulted from a conspiracy and that certain individuals heading key federal government agencies had conspired to suppress the truth about it.[1]

In typical fashion, Stone produced a movie that had an almost hypnotic effect on its audience. Just as he did with *Platoon* and *Born on the Fourth of July,* Stone employed a highly dramatic script, compelling music, innovative cinematography, and capable editing to create a movie about a subject of enormous complexity and turn it into an unforgettable experience for the audience. The large cast of characters, featuring numerous Hollywood stars in both leading and cameo roles, the combining of both documentary and fictional footage, and the dramatic juxtaposition of color and black-and-white scenes are used with great skill to convey Stone's message. After finishing viewing the film, numerous people felt a profound sense of betrayal, distrust, and anger directed at their government for having deceived them about what really happened in Dallas on November 22, 1963.[2]

"Our film's mythology is different," Stone wrote shortly after the movie's release, "and hopefully, it will replace the *Warren Commission Report,* as *Gone with the Wind* replaced *Uncle Tom's Cabin* and was in turn replaced by *Roots* and *The Civil War.*"[3] Such assertions, which Stone made frequently in late 1991 and early 1992, infuriated his numerous critics as much as the flaws in the film itself. Oliver Stone claimed to be not merely a Hollywood producer and director but also a historian, relating the truth about the assassination in a more credible manner than individual researchers or government agencies. That untold millions of moviegoers accepted Stone's version of the Dallas tragedy as the only accurate one clearly aroused the ire and indignation of the Warren Commission's defenders among the mainstream press and media. Thus, *Newsweek* felt compelled to warn its readers in large letters on the front cover of its December 23, 1991, edition, "The Twisted Truth of 'JFK': Why Oliver Stone's New Movie Can't Be Trusted."

Not long before he began filming *JFK*, Oliver Stone told the *Dallas Morning News* that he was a "cinematic historian" and that the movie would be a "history lesson." Stone went on to express the desire that he "would be remembered as a good historian as well as a good dramatist." Stone thus squarely separated himself from most of his colleagues in the business of producing and directing movies, for he envisioned himself as a member of the historical profession, using film, rather than scholarly literature, as the medium through which he conveyed the results of his research. This approach to his art could be seen in several of his earlier films, which focused on Vietnam, as well as his later work, *Nixon*, but none so clearly transmitted Stone's intention of depicting a historical event on film as sharply as *JFK*. In many respects, this movie rendition of the Kennedy assassination provides a solid test of Oliver Stone's credentials as "a good historian as well as a good dramatist."[4]

JFK opens with a lengthy montage of black-and-white newsreel film, commencing with President Dwight D. Eisenhower's famous warning about the military-industrial complex dictating American foreign policy. It then covers the assassination, using a highly partisan version that advocates a conspiracy and cover-up reaching to the very highest levels of government. But its true focus remains fixed on the character of Jim Garrison, played by Kevin Costner and depicted in the screenplay in a highly sympathetic vein. Garrison in fact comes off as the white knight in shining armor, the hero who tries valiantly to rescue the truth about the assassination from those government officials who concealed it. Throughout the movie, Garrison encounters obstacles in his quest for the truth, obstacles placed in his path by the same officials who conspired to cover up the truth behind the assassination. For example, one of the central characters in the movie, David Ferrie, dies mysteriously just as Garrison is about to have him arrested for being a conspirator in Kennedy's death. The film leaves little doubt that the conspirators murdered Ferrie to prevent him from revealing what he knew about the assassination.

The movie focuses on Garrison's prosecution of New Orleans businessman Clay L. Shaw for conspiracy to murder John F. Kennedy. Stone portrays Shaw as an arrogant homosexual whose tastes run to young men. In one scene, Shaw, dressed in drag, engages in horseplay with Ferrie, a notorious homosexual. Both are unmistakably portrayed as coconspirators. Aside from the movie's homophobic theme, it clearly depicts Shaw as the villain and as one of the masterminds in the plot to kill JFK. The depiction of Shaw's trial juxtaposes Garrison's noble quest for truth with Shaw's evil and ultimately successful attempt to conceal it. In the movie version of the trial, Shaw is branded as a CIA collaborator. Portrayed by Tommy Lee Jones, the Shaw character comes across as cold, aloof, and menacing, frequently radiating that impression of sinister detachment in which Jones excels. After his acquittal, the triumphant Shaw proclaims to the press that he will return to his French Quarter domicile and fix himself a fancy meal.

Although *JFK* uses the Garrison investigation and the Shaw trial as its prime focus, the central theme of the movie concerns Stone's interpretation of the conspiracy to assassinate President Kennedy. From the beginning, the film gives the audience no suggestion of the subtleties and complexities of the ongoing controversy over the assassination. Instead, Stone drives home the point that it was a conspiracy over and over. The famous Zapruder film of the motorcade on Elm Street, graphically showing the impact of the fatal shot on Kennedy's head, is shown numerous times throughout the movie. During the climactic scene of the Shaw trial — Garrison's summation to the jury — both actual documentary footage and concocted scenes reveal such sinister events as a deliberate distortion of the medical evidence from the autopsy to make it appear that Kennedy had been shot only from behind when in fact he had been shot from different directions. In dramatic tones, Garrison tells the jury, "Do not forget your dying king. Show the world that this is still a government of the people, for the people, and by the people." Garrison then swings to face the movie audience directly and admonishes them, "It's up to you."

One of the movie's highlights is a sixteen-minute dialogue between Jim Garrison and X. Portrayed by Donald Sutherland, X is a retired military officer who has access to many of the secrets the Pentagon possesses, secrets concerned not so much with national defense as with enhancing the military-industrial complex's stranglehold on America. X tells Garrison that he has uncovered the real truth behind the assassination, that it indeed resulted from a conspiracy. He then relates the reason for the killing of the president: Kennedy's decision to begin withdrawing American troops from Vietnam. X explains to Garrison that with more than $100 billion in defense contracts at stake, the "people in the loop" simply could not stand by and allow him to de-escalate U.S. involvement in Vietnam. With Kennedy out of the way, they would have a compliant Lyndon Johnson in the White House, a man who would surely be much more amenable to turning Vietnam into a full-scale conflict. The film intimates that Johnson himself was in on the plot to kill the president.

Legions of critics assailed Stone for *JFK*'s gross historical errors. Indeed, the movie comes replete with inaccuracies and distortions. As a native of New Orleans, I cringe whenever I see a movie using that city as the setting, with the characters conversing in a phony drawl more appropriate to residents of Plains, Georgia, or Hope, Arkansas, than to the Crescent City. Stone falls into that trap, and he even has Garrison, a native of Iowa, speak in the drawl. With the notable exception of John Candy playing Dean Andrews, the casting proved entirely incongruous. Costner playing Garrison, Tommy Lee Jones playing Clay Shaw, Joe Pesci playing David Ferrie, and the real Jim Garrison playing Earl Warren all failed to match the physical appearance, the demeanor, the speaking voice, or even the mannerisms of the characters they were portraying.

Of greater concern to the historian are the innumerable factual errors with which *JFK* abounds. A small list of events in the movie that never occurred will illustrate the pervasiveness of Stone's inattention to accuracy: David Ferrie is arrested at a CIA training camp for anti-Castro Cubans involved in covert activities; Clay Shaw visits Guy Banister's office; Jim Garrison lives in the French Quarter; David Ferrie virtually confesses to participating in a plot to assassinate President Kennedy; Lee Harvey Oswald speaks Russian fluently; X and Garrison meet in Washington at the Lincoln Memorial; Garrison goes to the sixth floor of the Texas School Book Depository building; Garrison cross-examines Dr. Pierre Finck, one of the autopsy pathologists, at the Shaw trial; Oswald prints his own "Hands Off Cuba!" leaflets. In addition, Stone deliberately employs entirely fictional characters in the film: Willie O'Keefe, portrayed by Kevin Bacon, is used to reinforce the homophobic subtheme of the film, and X is loosely based on retired air force colonel L. Fletcher Prouty, a well-known advocate of an assassination conspiracy.

JFK unleashed a firestorm of criticism, much of it coming from academics and journalists who had absolutely no expertise in the assassination. One exception was George Lardner, Jr., of the *Washington Post*, who allegedly received a purloined copy of the original draft of the screenplay from Harold Weisberg, a longtime Warren Commission critic. Having witnessed firsthand many phases of the actual Garrison investigation and prosecution of Shaw, Lardner quite properly denounced Stone for using Garrison as his central character and for casting him in such a sympathetic light. Entitling his article "Dallas in Wonderland," Lardner launched a scathing attack on Stone, pointing out the factual errors as well as the "absurdities" in the screenplay. Terming the Garrison investigation a "fraud," Lardner excoriated Stone for his wild speculations and character assassinations of people such as Clay Shaw and Earl Warren.[5]

Coming six months before the public release of *JFK*, Lardner's article proved a precursor for a series of vicious attacks on Stone by members of the mainstream press and media, as well as by other prominent persons. Hodding Carter found that the movie contained "countless buckets of manure, large measures of legitimate doubt, drippings of innuendo and pages of actual history." Anthony Lewis assailed Stone's implication of Chief Justice Earl Warren in the assassination cover-up as "contemptible." George Will labeled Stone "an intellectual sociopath, indifferent to truth," and stated that by combining "moral arrogance with historical ignorance," the director had produced a film of "execrable history and contemptible citizenship." In the *New York Times Magazine*, David Belin, a junior counsel for the Warren Commission and the author of two books defending the commission's lone assassin thesis, denounced what he termed "The Big Lies of 'JFK.'"[6]

Typical of the scholarly response to *JFK* was a paper written by political scientist Robert S. Robins and psychiatrist Jerrold M. Post and presented at the 1997 meeting of the American Political Science Association. Robins and Post contend that Stone's movie embodies "political paranoia as cinematic motif," using the "paranoid theme" to add "narrative power and commercial value to the film." Labeling *JFK* a docudrama because it dramatizes historical personalities and events for the screen, Robins and Post report that it made a powerful impact on its audiences by reinforcing false beliefs they already held before viewing the film. Stone, in other words, deliberately aroused in his audiences a feeling of anger and betrayal, making them more likely to believe the conspiracy theories he promotes. *JFK* embodies the paranoid motif because it offers a distorted sense of reality, a simple "us against them" moral stance, and engages in powerful emotional persuasion bordering on political propaganda. The paranoid message, therefore, completes Stone's artistic statement. By persuading the public that the assassination and, by implication, many other momentous events are the products of "malign" conspiracies, Stone has engaged in "intellectual pollution" of the most reprehensible kind.[7]

The reviews of *JFK* from journalists and political commentators proved harshly critical, but those from film critics generally praised the film's artistic creativity, its inventiveness, and its magnetic impact on the audience. Roger Ebert, for example, called *JFK* "hypnotically watchable," calling it a "masterpiece of film assembly."[8] As many film critics pointed out, the movie employs a variety of cinematic techniques to convey to the audience an enormous amount of information in a little over three hours, and it does so with conviction and style. A vast array of characters, plots and counterplots, and conspiracy theories is skillfully woven together into a unified theme — that John Kennedy was murdered as the result of a conspiracy — and in a manner that the audience can readily grasp.[9]

One of Stone's most effective devices is to introduce the movie with a montage of newsreel film showing Eisenhower's warning about the military-industrial complex, Castro at a political rally, Kennedy himself telling Walter Cronkite of his doubts about whether the United States can win the war in Vietnam, and excerpts from Kennedy's famous American University address in 1963, in which he rejected the old cold war belligerency and proffered the olive branch to Nikita Khrushchev. As Art Simon observed, this introductory material sets the stage for the film even before the Garrison story is introduced. The viewers, therefore, have already been exposed to one of the fundamental underlying themes of the film: that Kennedy's death resulted from his administration's strong movement away from confrontation and toward accommodation with its erstwhile enemies.[10]

The film seems to overpower its audience with numerous layers of imagery: the main cast acting out the scenario of the Garrison investigation; the black-and-white images of Oswald, Jack Ruby, and others; the color images from the Zapruder film; the deliberate showing of the image of Lyndon Johnson on the screen while "X" tells Garrison of the "perpetrators" carrying out their "coup d'état." So powerful is this imagery, so profound its impact on the audience, that the Garrison-Shaw story seems almost a petty tale inserted merely to give the film continuity. Everyone knows from the beginning that the truth lies outside New Orleans and inside the corridors of power in Washington. Garrison's role in the film can thus be viewed as more symbolic than real, for the reality of the assassination conspiracy lies not in the murky anti-Castro or gay scene in New Orleans but in the determined opposition to the policies of peaceful coexistence that Oliver Stone claims President Kennedy tried to pursue.

One of the main criticisms leveled at Stone came from his use of the controversial Jim Garrison as the movie's principal character. Numerous writers, such as Edward Jay Epstein, James Kirkwood, and, most recently, Patricia Lambert, have detailed the innumerable flaws in Garrison's investigation, in particular, the utterly fraudulent case against Clay Shaw. Garrison's arrogance and pomposity, his cryptic remarks to the press that the truth about the assassination was lurking "behind the looking glass," and his railroading of uncooperative witnesses such as Dean Andrews have been thoroughly examined and need not concern us here.[11] Relying heavily on Garrison's own highly biased account, *On the Trail of the Assassins,* as the basis for much of the movie, Stone fails to maintain the spirit of objectivity that historians must respect.[12]

Stone also drew fire for his insistence that the assassination resulted from a conspiracy. Using Jim Marrs's *Crossfire* as his main source, Stone clearly loaded the film with evidence that pointed to a conspiracy and deliberately omitted that which pointed to a lone assassin.[13] The result, of course, is a highly prejudiced view of the Kennedy assassination. Viewers are shown virtually none of the evidence pointing to Oswald's complicity. None of the witnesses who saw or heard shots coming from the Book Depository is portrayed. The strong evidence that Oswald murdered Dallas police officer J. D. Tippit forty-five minutes after the assassination is omitted.[14]

Another criticism of Stone is his hagiographic depiction of John F. Kennedy as a champion of truth, justice, and peace. Stone's Camelot-like version of Kennedy's administration hardly accords with the facts. During Kennedy's nearly three years as president, the United States financed and masterminded the abortive Bay of Pigs invasion of Cuba, attempted on at least six separate occasions to have Fidel Castro assassinated, nearly doubled the national defense budget, and increased the number of American troops in Vietnam from around 1,000 to more than 18,000.[15] These acts of hostility and belligerency belie Kennedy's oratorical commitment to peaceful coexistence in which Stone places so much credibility. In short, Stone's depiction of Kennedy is highly biased and one-dimensional.

In an article entitled "*JFK*: Historical Fact/Historical Film," Robert A. Rosenstone raises several questions pertinent to any discussion of Oliver Stone's status as a historian: How does a film differ from the written word in the manner in which it depicts a past event? Are the responsibilities of the film director and producer toward historical facts the same as those of the traditional academic historian? Can a film, which by its very nature compresses a highly complex event into a neat cinematic story with a beginning, middle, and end, be evaluated by the same criteria by which one assesses scholarly works? The answers to these questions, Rosenstone argues, are not as simplistic as they appear. As he points out, "the Hollywood historical film will always include images that are at once invented and yet may still be considered true; true in that they symbolize, condense, or summarize larger amounts of data."[16] Rosenstone maintains that because Stone made people think about the past, made them question some of their traditional values, "whatever its flaws, *JFK* has to be among the most important works of American history ever to appear on the screen."[17]

Although Rosenstone's insightful comments need to be taken into consideration in evaluating any film that claims to narrate an actual historical event, Stone's insistence that he is a historian compels an assessment of that claim. Using Garrison as the protagonist in *JFK* clearly constitutes Stone's most vulnerable area. The movie's implication that Shaw indeed participated in a conspiracy to assassinate President Kennedy simply has no substantial evidence to support it. In the actual trial, the jury took less than one hour to arrive at a unanimous verdict of not guilty because Garrison had provided no solid basis for his case. The dubious testimony of Perry Raymond Russo, the use of a convicted drug dealer as a witness, and giving credence to the utterly incredible story of Charles Spiesel, who had sued New York City for placing him under "hypnosis" and "mental torture" and who had fingerprinted his own daughter upon her return home from college to ensure that she had not been replaced by an alien double, are among the innumerable transgressions that made Garrison's prosecution of Shaw a travesty of justice.[18]

Nevertheless, Garrison did assist in bringing the shortcomings of the Warren Commission to the public's attention. For the first time, the famous Zapruder film was shown at the Shaw trial, a film that provides a graphic vision of a shot from the front. Garrison also denounced and attacked the federal government, especially the CIA, for covering up the truth about the assassination. Although some of Garrison's wilder accusations have been proved absolutely false, his claims of a massive cover-up have been proved true. Garrison also deserves credit for first bringing to public attention the mysterious activities of Lee Harvey Oswald in New Orleans in the spring and summer of 1963, when Oswald publicly posed as a Marxist but covertly associated with individuals on the opposite side of the political spectrum.

The question of whether the Kennedy assassination resulted from a conspiracy has been debated since before the public release of the Warren Commission's report in September 1964, and that controversy remains unresolved. The mainstream press and news media, as well as most academics, strongly support the lone assassin conclusion of the Warren Commission. However, few journalists and virtually no scholars have conducted any serious research into the assassination, and their criticisms of the advocates of a conspiracy have generally assumed the guise of name-calling and innuendo rather than legitimate scholarly dissent. On the other side, those who espouse the conspiracy view have frequently distorted evidence and have often devised bizarre theories ranging from the barely plausible to the absurd.[19]

One might argue with Oliver Stone's version of the assassination conspiracy, but his critics have engaged in unfair smear tactics by attacking him for arriving at that conclusion. Works by such authors as David Belin and Gerald Posner have concluded that Lee Harvey Oswald bore sole responsibility for the assassination, and a recent exhaustive study by Dale Myers found that Oswald murdered Officer Tippit and that no credible evidence of a conspiracy exists.[20] Other studies, by Sylvia Meagher, Josiah Thompson, and this author, have concluded that Oswald could not possibly have acted alone and that substantial evidence of a conspiracy does indeed exist.[21] In short, Stone's film version of the assassination conspiracy certainly deserves criticism, especially his implication that Lyndon Johnson was involved in it, but those who have attacked him for advocating the conspiracy theory display their ignorance of the growing literature on the crime.

One of the areas in which Oliver Stone remains most vulnerable to criticism is his opinion that an unidentified cabal of military-industrial-intelligence movers and shakers ordered Kennedy's assassination because he intended to withdraw all American troops from Vietnam. As Marcus Raskin observes, the Kennedy administration encouraged, fostered, and intensified the "culture of violence" that the cold war had engendered. Kennedy's policy of "flexible response," developed by Robert McNamara, not only necessitated a $13 billion increase in national defense spending in less than three years but also compelled the United States to promote a defensive-offensive "war fighting capability on all levels of violence from nuclear war to counterinsurgency."[22] The culture of violence that permeated Kennedy's administration, Raskin argues, was abetted in no small measure by the president's frequent bellicose public statements, including the one he intended to deliver in Dallas that fateful Friday in November. The possibility that certain lower-level government figures connected with the "conflating of crime and political intrigue in the covert and military world of that time" plotted the president's murder, Raskin contends, cannot be dismissed.[23]

With the exception of *Uncle Tom's Cabin,* Harriet Beecher Stowe's explosive novel dramatizing the horrors of the institution of slavery, *JFK* probably had a greater direct impact on public opinion than any other work of art in American history. The revelations in the movie of a massive cover-up of several million pages of documentary evidence on the Kennedy assassination by various agencies of the federal government generated a groundswell of public demand that those agencies release for public perusal all the evidence they had suppressed for three decades. Spurred to action by irate constituents, members of Congress held public hearings during the spring and summer of 1992 and discovered, to their astonishment, that there was indeed a voluminous amount of documentary and other evidence relating to the assassination that various agencies had deliberately withheld from the public record.

The result was the President John F. Kennedy Assassination Records Collection Act of 1992. Passed by Congress and signed into law by President George Bush, the act mandated the appointment by the president of an Assassination Records Review Board (ARRB), whose responsibility was to locate, identify, review, and release all assassination records as expeditiously as possible. The act stipulated that the National Archives and Records Administration serve as the repository for the collection, with the "presumption of immediate release" of all records. Appointed by President Bill Clinton in 1993, the ARRB consisted of historians Anna Nelson, Henry Graff, and Kermit Hall; archivist William Joyce; and U.S. District Judge John Tunheim, who chaired the board. With adequate funding and staff, the board held public hearings, located and identified records, and transmitted to the new branch of the National Archives in College Park, Maryland, several million pages of evidence from the files of numerous government agencies. Shortly before the ARRB's legal mandate expired in September 1998, it issued a final report that specifically credited *JFK* with stirring up public opinion to pressure Congress into passing the legislation.[24]

The materials released thus far provide no "smoking gun" that conclusively proves either the lone assassin or the conspiracy theory of the assassination. But in many respects, the review board uncovered and made available to the public materials that sustain the arguments of Oliver Stone and other Warren Commission critics that there was a conspiracy among various government officials and agencies to suppress information relevant to the assassination controversy. For example, the Lyndon Baines Johnson Presidential Library in Austin, Texas, released transcripts of Johnson's telephone conversations in the immediate aftermath of the assassination through the publication of the Warren Commission's report in September 1964. In one such conversation, Johnson and his close friend and mentor Senator Richard Russell of Georgia, a member of the Warren Commission, discussed the cornerstone of the commission's lone assassin thesis: the notorious single-bullet theory that maintained that a bullet fired from Oswald's rifle entered President Kennedy's neck, exited from his throat, and penetrated Governor Connally's chest, wrist, and thigh, shattering two thick bones and emerging virtually intact. Both Johnson and Russell emphatically expressed their utter disbelief in that controversial theory.[25]

Other examples include an original copy of a draft of the Warren Commission's report, which placed the entrance wound in Kennedy's back. This draft, which the review board obtained from the private files of Warren Commission chief counsel J. Lee Rankin, contains the handwritten alteration by commission member Gerald Ford that changed the location of the bullet wound from the back to the neck, a distortion of the evidence to make it conform to the single-bullet theory.[26] Another example of the newly released material involves correspondence between Rankin and commission member John J. McCloy. In his review of the final draft of the report, McCloy informed Rankin that he was not persuaded that all the shots came from the sixth floor of the Texas School Book Depository building, nor, in McCloy's estimation, had the commission proved that Lee Harvey Oswald had fired all the shots.[27]

In the summer of 1998, the AARB made public the transcripts of depositions it had taken with several of the key personnel involved in the autopsy. These depositions lend credence to Stone's assertion in *JFK* that the medical evidence had been tampered with to make it appear that Kennedy had been shot only from behind. In one deposition, Dr. James J. Humes, the head of the team of pathologists that performed the autopsy, admitted that he had burned both his original autopsy notes and the original draft of the autopsy and substituted later versions.[28] In other depositions, former FBI agents Francis O'Neill and James Sibert, both present at the autopsy, and James Stringer, the photographer who took the autopsy photographs, insisted that the extant photographs of Kennedy's brain do not replicate the actual condition of the organ on the night of November 22, 1963.[29] Douglas Horne, the ARRB staff member who supervised the digitizing of the autopsy photographs at Kodak's headquarters in Rochester, New York, wrote a lengthy report in which he claimed that a deliberate falsification of the evidence pertaining to the president's head wounds took place in the week following the assassination.[30] Saundra Spencer, a navy photographic technician, testified under oath that the autopsy photographs she processed at the Naval Photographic Center in Anacostia, Maryland, were not the same as the photographs currently stored in the National Archives.[31] It should be mentioned that previous reviews of the medical records by medical experts have both supported and attacked the lone assassin thesis. However, the recently released information does provide a sound documentary foundation for Stone's version of strange events occurring at the autopsy.[32]

Arguably the most controversial contention of the movie is the assertion that if Kennedy had lived, the whole course of American history would have changed for the better. Stone maintains that Kennedy had decided to drastically ease the tensions of the cold war. After the Cuban missile crisis of 1962 brought the United States and the Soviet Union to the brink of nuclear war, Kennedy, according to Stone, realized how dangerous American-Soviet hostilities had grown. Therefore, in 1963, he initiated a series of dramatic steps to reach an accommodation with Khrushchev. In June he gave his famous American University speech, calling for lasting peace and an end to the nuclear arms race. In July he and Khrushchev installed the so-called hot line between the White House and the Kremlin, and in August they signed the nuclear test-ban treaty.

JFK implies that these measures alarmed the military-industrial-intelligence establishment, whose very existence depended on a continuation of cold war animosity, but nothing terrified it more than Kennedy's reversal of U.S. policy in Vietnam. After publicly stating in September 1963 that Vietnam was not America's war, the president signed National Security Action Memo (NASM)

263 the following month, authorizing the withdrawal of 1,000 American troops from Vietnam. That same month, the White House forecast that all remaining American troops would leave Vietnam by the end of 1965. This action would free the administration to make sharp reductions in defense spending and shift limited resources to domestic issues. That is why, Stone alleges in *JFK*, Kennedy was assassinated. An unnamed cabal of influential individuals in the military-industrial-intelligence complex, eager to escalate American involvement in Vietnam, decided that Kennedy had to be eliminated. This scenario forms the shakiest part of the movie's foundation. Stone offers no evidence of such a plot, and he fails to mention that when Lyndon Johnson did in fact escalate American involvement in Vietnam into a full-scale conflict, it was at the urging of such advisers as Robert McNamara, McGeorge Bundy, and Maxwell Taylor, all of whom had been appointed by Kennedy.[33]

Shortly after *JFK* was released, Oliver Stone was asked what he wanted people to learn from his movie. Stone responded that he wanted "a shift in consciousness . . . a realization that our history from 1961 to 1963 is a superficial one." He then stated that "history needs to be rewritten."[34] *JFK*'s numerous factual inaccuracies, its glorification of the Garrison investigation, its unfounded theory of an assassination conspiracy involving people at the highest levels of government and industry, and its efforts to rewrite the history of the Kennedy administration from a decidedly biased and controversial perspective hardly qualify the film as the definitive account of this monumental event. Nevertheless, Oliver Stone performed a great service. He aroused so much interest in the assassination that a whole generation of scholars is currently conducting research into the newly released documents. He gave the establishment a much-deserved blow to the solar plexus. His allegations of a systematic suppression of millions of pages of documentary materials by various government agencies have been proved true by the release of those materials under the act that he played a critical role in having enacted. He certainly generated a new era of controversy about the assassination. For all of *JFK*'s faults and shortcomings, few producers and directors can claim such an impact from their movies, and few historians can claim such an impact from their works.

Heaven and Earth

Better than any other feature film from Hollywood, Oliver Stone's *Heaven and Earth* shows a Vietnamese perspective of the Vietnam War. It gives audiences glimpses of the tropical paradise that turned into hell as French, American, South and North Vietnamese, and Vietcong soldiers fought for control over the land's future. Through the story of one woman's experiences in those tragic years, the movie communicates an important message. It shows that the people of that paradise did not wish to fight the Americans or the French or anyone. They wanted peace and freedom, but the outsiders wouldn't let them have it without a tremendous struggle. As the movie demonstrates, war uprooted the Vietnamese people from their stable villages and ancestral homes. It turned the friendly Vietnamese people against each other and tore tranquil communities apart in orgies of hate, violence, and retribution. No wonder Hollywood was reluctant to touch this story. A Vietnamese picture of the war is painful to view.

Heaven and Earth's contribution to the public's thinking about Vietnam means a great deal to me, because I am the woman portrayed in the film. The movie traces many of the major events of my life from the time the war came to my village in 1962 to when I moved to the United States and settled in southern California. As the author of two books about these experiences and as someone who served as an adviser to Oliver Stone in the making of *Heaven and Earth*, I feel particularly close to this film. Perhaps I am too close to qualify as a judge of the film's treatment of history. I do not pretend to stand as an impartial observer. Nevertheless, I do hope that my personal connection to the movie enables me to deliver some useful insights on Oliver Stone's interpretation of the Vietnam War.

Ever since I first arrived in the United States in 1970, I felt that Americans needed to get a better understanding of the Vietnamese people's perspective of the war. I especially sensed that need when I moved in with my American husband's family in San Diego. Some of the friends who visited the home, people associated with the U.S. Navy, were not very comfortable with my presence. I was a constant reminder of a war that was killing their relatives and friends. These friends acted as if the fighting in Vietnam were my responsibility, especially when they watched the news and heard reports about casualties. Often they used derogatory names to describe the Vietnamese enemy. For instance, when viewing pictures of body bags, one said, "We should go over there and kill all the gooks." Another insisted that America must bring the war to a close by killing every communist in Vietnam.

I felt sad and lonely and very much an alien during those moments. The "gooks" they were talking about were my people. I could not tell my husband or the visitors about the secrets of my earlier life. I had been a supporter of the Vietcong and an enthusiastic follower of the heroic leader Ho Chi Minh. I wanted to say to everyone sitting around the television set: "Let me tell you what a 'gook' is, what those people represent to me. They are freedom fighters. You know nothing about who we are and what we fight for." But, of course, I could not speak in such a way. I was timid and scared — terrified, in fact — when I heard the references to "gooks."

To relieve my tension and feel some catharsis, I began to write down lots of my experiences in Vietnam. At first, I had no idea of writing a book. How could I? Lacking a formal education, especially any training in the craft of writing, I could not imagine that I would do anything more than record these memories for my personal use. At least the activity gave me solace. Silently I was answering those angry Americans who disparaged my people.

As my notes piled up over the years, the idea of combining the material into a book grew more appealing. I felt increasingly confident that I had something important to say. I wanted Americans to know about my beloved land and to understand how my people lived and struggled in the war. In the mid-1980s, I signed up for a two-day seminar on writing in San Diego. It cost $375, a significant financial burden at the time, but I happily paid the fee. I was determined to explore opportunities to get my story out to the public, and the seminar seemed to be a good way to get started. We broke into small discussion groups and told the stories that had motivated our interest in writing. Nervously and sometimes in tears, I recounted a few of the extraordinary scenes of human suffering I had witnessed during my years in Vietnam. Several people at the seminar gave me enthusiastic support and urged me to keep writing. One of the individuals at that seminar later helped me make valuable connections.

Over the next year, I sent my manuscript to several publishers and movie producers, and each time I received a rejection. Some readers in the publishing business guessed that the public would not demonstrate much interest in a book that was sympathetic to the Vietcong, America's enemy. Others thought that Vietnam had been in the public eye for too long and that Americans did not want to hear about the war anymore. Too many people associated

Vietnam with body bags and funerals, with antiwar demonstrations and political clashes, they said. Americans wanted to forget Vietnam and move on.

I was beginning to despair about the chances of getting my story published when *Platoon* appeared in the movie theaters. I considered not going to see the movie, because I thought Americans hated my country. I worried that Hollywood was going to portray my homeland in an ugly manner. And what did a filmmaker know about my country, anyway? How could he understand the paradise of lush green rice paddies that had been turned into the hell of war? I tried to resist going to the theater, but eventually curiosity got the best of me. Frequent commentary about the movie in the media and scenes of people standing in long lines at the box office excited my interest. I wanted to know what all the commotion was about. Eventually I paid $5 for a ticket (very costly at the time), sat down in a crowded theater, and waited anxiously to see if the story that was about to unfold on the screen would, at least, reveal a few truths about the Asian society I had left behind sixteen years before.

To my great surprise, *Platoon* was different from anything I had ever seen in the cinema. This wasn't another John Wayne picture showing American GIs as victims and heroes. It presented an honest and truthful view of tragic times. The villagers in *Platoon* were familiar to me, because I was one of them. The GIs were believable, too. They were very much like the Americans I had known. *Platoon* reminded me of the many young Americans I had met during the war years, people for whom I felt a great deal of love and sympathy.

I had entered the theater eager to see if *Platoon* could teach Americans some valuable lessons about the war. Instead, I discovered that the film had taught me a lesson. By the end of the picture, when the helicopter takes off from a hill and flies over the rice paddies and Charlie Sheen delivers his monologue, I realized that American GIs had been involved in a war they did not understand. U.S. soldiers had been dropped into a strange and foreign land. The politicians and generals had asked them to deal with a country and a people they knew nothing about. Like the soldiers in *Platoon,* they showed fear and confusion in their eyes as they moved through the jungle, the kind of fear and confusion that could make some of them kill their own people.

Popular and critical reception of the movie challenged my assumptions about public disinterest in the Vietnam War. The enthusiasm for *Platoon* suggested that, at last, Americans might be ready to face harsh truths about their involvement in Vietnam. Oliver Stone had succeeded in getting Americans to look honestly at the GI's story. Now I was determined to show Americans the Vietnamese people's story.

Within a short time, my efforts paid off. An editor who had been present at the seminar in San Diego took an interest in my case. He was a Vietnam War veteran, and he thought that my recollections would fascinate Americans who knew little about the Asian experience in the war. The editor informed Sandra Dijkstra, head of a literary agency, about my work. She put me in touch with Jay Wurth, a talented writer who helped shape my notes into a story. Dijkstra also negotiated a contract for me with Doubleday.

In February 1989, I had good reason to celebrate the Vietnamese New Year Tet, for I was in New York City to promote the forthcoming publication of *When Heaven and Earth Changed Places.* The release date for the book was still three months away, but already I was on the cover of the *Los Angeles Times Magazine.* Articles about me were turning up in *People* and in other prominent magazines and newspapers. Once Doubleday released the book, I received invitations to participate in nationally televised talk shows on NBC and CBS. Many more opportunities followed, and before long, I found myself on a whirlwind tour across the country.

While I was on a flight to New York for television appearances, I heard some passengers talking about a review of my book that had appeared in the *New York Times Book Review* (a picture of me and my son Jimmy appeared on the front cover of the issue). Then the passengers began to stare at me. They sensed that I might be the subject of the review. I was very shy at the time and did not want to draw attention to myself, so I pretended that I had no connection with the story. Nevertheless, I continued listening, eager to hear their comments on the book.

That article in the *Book Review* by David Shipler helped draw Hollywood's attention to my story. Shipler wrote, "If Hollywood had the courage to turn this book into a movie, then we Americans might finally have a chance to come to terms with the tragedy in Vietnam." Almost immediately after Shipler's article appeared, a number of people who wanted to make my story into a movie flooded my agent's office with calls. I was very pleased with this display of interest, but I was also concerned that the filmmaker who purchased the right to dramatize my life might take great liberties and shape the story in a way that was not truthful. I worried that I might not even recognize myself on the screen. Fortunately, Oliver Stone was among the many who were taking an interest. He had read Shipler's review, and he had also seen the feature story about me in the *Los Angeles Times Magazine.* When Robert Kline, a film producer and also a Vietnam vet, asked Stone if he had any more Vietnam stories to tell, Stone pointed to the cover story and said, "I want that girl." Kline just happened to have a copy of my book with him, and he turned it over to Stone.

When I told my literary agent about my fear that Hollywood filmmakers might distort my book, she understood my concern. Dijkstra informed me that one team of inquiring callers seemed especially right for the job of moviemaking: Oliver Stone and Robert Kline. She believed that Stone could do a fine job interpreting my experiences in view of his work on *Platoon* and *Born on the Fourth of July*. When she mentioned *Platoon*, I remembered how much that movie had impressed me and how its success had inspired the effort to get my own story told. Eagerly, I agreed to meet with Stone and Kline.

As soon as I met Oliver Stone at Bob Kline's Newport Beach home, I had a good feeling about him. Oliver was warm, funny, and confident. His face was kind and gentle, and his body language very noble. In Vietnamese we call this *di tuong*. I had met my "soul" partner on earth. A day after that meeting, my agent communicated the good news that Oliver Stone had agreed to direct the movie and Robert Kline would produce it. Then I knew that my agreement with God was working. I had asked the Lord to help me get my story out so that I could try to make the world a better place. I thought it was my karmic destiny to communicate understanding of a Vietnamese perspective. Now that dream seemed to be coming true. I had been blessed with a great agent in Sandra Dijkstra and an excellent collaborator in Jay Wurth. With Robert Kline and Oliver Stone designing the screen version of my story, it looked like I could bring my message to millions of people.

Not long after our first meeting, Oliver graciously invited me to visit with him and his family at his homes in Santa Monica and Santa Barbara. When I made my first appearance, I was nervous and shy. As we began to talk about my book, however, I felt more comfortable. When Oliver asked me what I wanted to see in the movie, I described some of my worries. I told him that I had always heard that Hollywood directors tried to make a true story more "commercial," stressing sex and violence. I was very concerned that the same thing would happen in the film about me. "Not like *The Doors*," I pleaded. Oliver laughed and explained that my book involved an entirely different kind of story. When I added that I didn't want to see myself portrayed as a female Rambo, he really had a good laugh. I laughed, too. That weekend we smiled a lot and got to know each other and built a mutual trust.

A few years after our first meeting, I received the screenplay from Oliver. I was greatly surprised when the script arrived in the mail, because I never thought that he would let me be part of his production team. I was even more shocked when I discovered how true to my life he had remained throughout most of the screenplay. Word by word, line by line, he presented a realistic picture of what my people had gone through during the war. The script was authentic not only because Oliver based it on my book but also because he informed it with his own recollections. Oliver had lived with the villagers. He knew the scenes of wartime Vietnam firsthand.

Later, when Oliver and I were returning to the United States after scouting locations in Vietnam, I accidentally helped him finish his screenplay. At the time, Oliver was very frustrated because he didn't have a good ending for the story and he couldn't decide on the kind of strong male role he needed. During our flight from Vietnam, I was working on the manuscript of my second book, *The Child of War, Woman of Peace*. Oliver asked me what I was doing. When I told him, he took the manuscript and began to read. After going through only about twenty pages, he looked over at me and smiled. At last, Oliver had what he needed to complete the story and define the character of the leading man. Right then and there, Oliver optioned my second book. He combined details of the two books to create the story for *Heaven and Earth*.

As production work began, Oliver treated me like a partner, and I was grateful for the opportunity to remain closely involved in the movie project. He brought me in as technical adviser, a job that was supposed to involve two weeks of activity. But after I helped the team of production designers replicate a Vietnamese village, Oliver was so impressed that he would not let me leave the set. He consulted with me frequently on the story as well. When he had to make changes or combine or omit scenes, he always made sure that I understood why adjustments needed to be made. Oliver also kept me by his side in front of a monitor on the set, making sure that I approved of the look of the various scenes before shooting began.

I was pleased with the casting of Hiep Thi Le for my role in the movie, and I had an opportunity to work directly with her. Oliver sent Hiep to my home to spend two days with me before shooting began. Hiep knew about life in Vietnam personally. She had spent her first nine years there. Hiep was from Danang province, and amazingly, her mother had lived in the same village where I had lived. Hiep was not a Hollywood superstar. She was a lovely Vietnamese immigrant with no acting experience. We bonded quickly and established a sort of mother-daughter relationship. When on the set, however, I could not approach her directly to provide guidance for her portrayal. Oliver insisted that I communicate all such recommendations to him once the shooting was under way. He did not want the young actress to become confused listening to advice from two individuals.

I also liked the way Tommy Lee Jones portrayed my husband. For the movie, Oliver combined a couple of my American husbands into one character. He jokingly told me that he had to compress the characters, because if he tried to portray all my romantic relationships with men, the movie would have to be six hours long. I thought that was very funny.

Compression was certainly necessary in portraying my experiences after arriving in America, because so much had happened since 1970. In 1971, I accompanied my husband, Ed Munro, back to Vietnam. While we were there, the Vietcong overran the town where we lived (the movie shows this event, but it leaves the impression that the assault occurred before I left Vietnam for the first time). The company Ed was working for sent him home after that attack, while I remained in Vietnam. At the time, I was in love with another man, who rescued me by helicopter during some of the fighting (in the movie, my fictional husband Steve performs the rescue). Ed died in 1972. My relationship with the helicopter rescue hero ended, and later I married another American, Dennis Hayslip. Dennis went to Vietnam in 1975 and succeeded in getting my sister and her two Amerasian children out of the country just two days before the fall of Saigon. Dennis died in 1983, and as the movie indicates, I did not remarry. I returned to Vietnam in 1986 after realizing considerable economic success in California as a landlord and a restauranteur. During that visit, I was saddened to see how poor — indeed, desperate — the Vietnamese people were in the aftermath of war.

As the movie indicates in its final captions, I later devoted a good deal of time to humanitarian causes in Vietnam. Eventually, I stepped away from business activities and devoted much of my time to creating the East Meets West Foundation, which established health clinics, schools, and orphanages and built water systems in Vietnam. More recently, I created the Global Village Foundation, which focuses on maintaining the unique heritage and infrastructure development in rural villages in the Vietnamese countryside. Its first project is to develop a model community in my ancestral village of Ky La, which is located near Danang. As *Heaven and Earth* suggests, ancestral ties are very important to the people of Vietnam. My family has strong roots in Ky La; it has lived in the community through many generations. My mother, played by Joan Chen in *Heaven and Earth,* still lives in the house of my father's ancestors, the home where I grew up. She is ninety-three years old.

If asked to point out what *Heaven and Earth* leaves out, I would draw attention to two matters. Obviously, Oliver could not give adequate attention to all the themes I wanted to see addressed, and I recognize that a motion picture could not cover everything, but I feel that it is important to identify these two shortcomings.

The first concerns the movie's rather limited treatment of the way people lived in Vietnam. *Heaven and Earth* shows some aspects of the daily life of the Vietnamese people, especially in the opening scenes, but I would have preferred to see a more extensive portrayal. I spent a lot of time instructing Oliver and members of the production team about how the Vietnamese cooked, communicated with each other, worshipped, and slept. I even explained how the Vietnamese planted rice and nursed their crops until harvest time. Oliver enjoyed hearing my detailed descriptions, and suggested that I teach a course at UCLA about the Vietnamese economy, society, and culture. His movie had to focus on different, more exciting subjects, though. Very little of this portrait of daily life ended up on the screen.

The second absence in the movie concerned depictions of violence and cruelty. Oliver had already received much criticism for his portrayal of American savagery in the Vietnam War, especially for scenes in *Platoon*. Some critics said that his portraits were too dark and sinister. They complained that the pictures of rape, murder, and destruction gave American GIs a bad image. Critics said that Oliver's movies were too negative, often presenting U.S. soldiers as cruel and inhuman. While I admit that this critical picture is not the only truth about the war, I must say that it is surely *one* truth. Many soldiers *did* treat my people brutally, not because they were evil but because they had been victimized by the propaganda of hate. The war made all of us into monsters, Vietnamese as well as Americans.

I never understood the critics' way of thinking. Didn't they know that war is violent and ugly? Didn't they recognize that there were many My Lai–style massacres in Vietnam that were not covered in American newspapers and television news reports? These critics should face the unpleasant facts. The fighting killed thousands of innocent women and children. Military action brought a holocaust to Vietnam. Americans have to face that disaster honestly so that it cannot happen again.

Heaven and Earth showed some of this horror through its view of a torture camp and in a few other brief enactments. But those scenes had to stand for many more terrible actions that I witnessed, actions that soiled the American military's record in my country. Oliver Stone staged other examples of American violence and cruelty, but eventually he cut them out of the movie. I was disappointed, but I recognized that pressures to limit unpleasant scenes can affect a movie as well as a book. I had originally written many pages describing ugly incidents in the first draft of my book, but I had been encouraged to slice out much of it. My extensive reporting on atrocities seemed likely to turn off readers.

People should realize that it is important to confront the unpleasant side of history. In Vietnam we say *su that hay mac long* — the truth always hurts. All of us must face the truth. We have to deal with the consequences of our actions. Why write a book or make a movie? To deliver a message. That message may disturb us, but we must hear it. Argument and debate help us to wake up, to see life more clearly. Often a husband and wife fight in order to communicate better. If their dispute improves understanding, they can make love after they make up. Americans must experience that kind of argument as they look at their record in Vietnam. They will be more capable of love and understanding after they confront the angry disputes about what they did in Vietnam.

Although I have these objections concerning the movie, overall, I am pleased with *Heaven and Earth*. Oliver Stone is a strong man and has a strong point of view and tried hard to present a woman's story, which was not easy. Oliver told me from the beginning that he intended to tell my story the way my book told it, and he pretty much kept that promise. It was the studio people and critics who wanted to diminish the presentation of violence and cruelty in the film, not Oliver.

Heaven and Earth finished Oliver Stone's important trilogy on the Vietnam War. In *Platoon*, he gave us the story of a young man going off to war for the first time and believing with all his heart and soul that he was doing the right thing for his country. *Born on the Fourth of July* continued that theme and told of a soldier's abandonment after he returned home and Americans treated him as less than a hero. *Heaven and Earth* provided thoughts for Americans who could not forgive and move on. Those people still had much karma to work out. I hope that *Heaven and Earth* helped them in their struggle.

Before the release of *Heaven and Earth* in December 1993, many people in the United States regarded Vietnam as a hellhole and saw the communists in the country as monsters who needed to be exterminated. Perhaps those who viewed the movie found their attitudes changing. *Heaven and Earth* revealed that the enthusiasts of Ho Chi Minh's revolution were not simply "gooks," "VC" (Vietcong), "NVA" (North Vietnamese Army), or any of the other epithets American soldiers used to identify them. Those people were human beings. Stone portrayed the Vietnamese people crying and bleeding just like other people of the world. I still remember that years ago Americans followed with great humanitarian sympathy the story of one little American girl who had fallen down a deep hole, while another, bigger humanitarian story failed to excite their attention. I, too, felt concern for the welfare of that little girl, but I wanted Americans to realize that another, broader kind of tragedy needed their attention as well. Two million of my people died in the Vietnam War. Thousands were left handicapped. Poisoning injured or killed thousands. More tons of bombs fell on my little country than in all the American theaters of action in World War II. The American military also released 71,253,000 liters of toxic chemicals and 18,000,000 gallons of Agent Orange. If *Heaven and Earth* helped some Americans recognize that good people were victims of that kind of warfare, the movie provided a valuable service to humankind.

After the release of *Heaven and Earth*, Oliver called me to explain that the press had not been very kind to the film, and there were not many people in the theaters. I told him that was okay. Too many Americans were still in a deep sleep about Vietnam. They were not ready for the truth. But our message would surely get out to thousands, and that was important.

I am proud of what Oliver Stone accomplished. He stirred the souls of the American people, challenging their sense of morality and fairness. In *Heaven and Earth* and in his other movies about Vietnam, he attempted to show what war in Southeast Asia meant to the people whose lives were profoundly affected by it — the U.S. soldiers and the Vietnamese civilians and soldiers. Oliver Stone did not deliver a pretty picture. But why should he? The war brought much death, destruction, and human suffering. By facing the negative directly and honestly, Oliver left us something that is surely positive.

Way Cooler Than Manson

Natural Born Killers

*What characterizes the film is a complete lack of consistency
to the point of being deliberately, totally illogical — which is fun.*

— Oliver Stone[1]

Natural Born Killers (1994), Oliver Stone's most radical and controversial movie, dissects late-twentieth-century American violence, satirizes its
exploitation by the media, meditates on it as an aspect of the human condition, and, depending on whose lawyers you choose to believe, has contributed to it through copycat killings. A "now movie" in the vein of *Easy Rider*
(1969), *Natural Born Killers (NBK)* is anything but historical, yet all these
topics are of interest to historians of violence — at least they are to me. After
watching the film five times in as many years, I have come to the conclusion
that Stone was right. *NBK* is illogical, whether judged by historical, sociological, aesthetic, or theological standards. It is, in fact, a virtuosic mess. But
by patiently sorting through the mess, we can learn something about recent
trends in American violence and what, if anything, movies have contributed
to it.

THE ROAD TO BATONGAVILLE

"I wanted to have fun," Oliver Stone told an interviewer the summer *NBK*
was released. "I really wanted to do a combination of a road movie, like *Bonnie
and Clyde,* and a prison film, like *The Great Escape* and *Papillon.*"[2] His Bonnie
and Clyde turned out to be Mickey and Mallory Knox, a pair of psychopathic
lowlifes lifted from a Quentin Tarantino script and launched into cinematic
hyperspace.[3] Stone shrewdly cast Woody Harrelson, the hulking son of a real-
life killer, as Mickey and, less shrewdly, Juliette Lewis, a white-trash specialist,
as Mallory. Mal, as she is known, has a little problem — a lecherous father and
an idiot mother. Enter Mickey, exit problem. Dad drowns in the fish tank, Mom
burns in her bed.

Mickey and Mallory wed in a pagan ceremony, exchanging rings of intertwined snakes. They get their kicks on Route 666, a stretch of desert highway they terrorize for three weeks. They wipe out bunches of ordinary people in ordinary places — a store, a slumber party, a roadside café — always leaving one survivor to tell the tale to the slavering media. They eventually rack up fifty-two victims — a number connoting randomness, as in a deck of cards. Yet supernatural determinism is the apparent metaphysical basis of the film. The victims are fated to die. Mickey and Mallory are fated to kill. Demons possess them.

The plot turns, as in many stories of love and violence, on an act of adultery. Mickey intimates that he wouldn't mind a brief ménage à trois with Mallory and a terrified hostage, bound and gagged in their motel room. Mallory storms out and takes her rage for a drive. Mickey rapes the hostage — a shot deleted from the theatrical release but restored in the director's cut on video. Mallory pulls in for gas, seduces a garage jockey on the hood of a Corvette, and then shoots him dead.

Already lost in a moral desert, Mickey and Mallory soon find themselves stranded in a real one. "Right now," Mickey says, "I'd go down on a lawman for a gallon of gas." They stumble upon the hogan of an Indian shaman, played by Russell Means. Forewarned by a dream, he knows that these demons have come to claim his life — not that they mean to. The shaman dies when Mickey awakes from a nightmare about his abusive parents, gun blazing. "Bad, bad, bad, bad, bad, bad, bad, bad," Mallory shouts at Mickey. "You killed life!"

They pay for it. Literally snakebit, they stumble into the Drug Zone, a surreal pharmacy lit gangrenous green, in search of an antidote. A phalanx of police led by self-appointed supercop Jack Scagnetti (Tom Sizemore) closes in. Scagnetti grabs Mallory. He yells to Mickey, holed up in the pharmacy, that he'll cut off her breasts if Mickey doesn't surrender. He does. Behind him we catch a glimpse of a sign, "Take Your Medicine." It's administered à la Rodney King. Mickey is stomped into submission as a breathless Japanese correspondent delivers a blow-by-blow account.

Mickey and Mallory are convicted in a circus trial. (In one particularly gruesome scene, which Stone decided to delete, Mickey stabs a witness to death with a pencil.) Hero and heroine are shipped off to Batongaville Prison, where the bodies keep piling up: "three inmates, five guards, one shrink, all in one year's time." Warden Dwight McClusky, Tommy Lee Jones doing a redneck shtick, conspires with Scagnetti to kill Mickey and Mallory during a transfer to a looney bin. Wayne Gale, a Geraldo Rivera–style journalist played with unctuous genius by Robert Downey, Jr., has other plans. He wants to interview Mickey live after the Super Bowl on his "American Maniacs" show. Millions tune in. The inmates are watching. A riot erupts, ignited by Mickey's line, "I'm a natural born killer." Mickey seizes Gale, his crew, and two guards as hostages. He frees Mallory, who stabs the loathsome Scagnetti in the throat and shoots him in the head. Fade to red.

Gale, meanwhile, decides that he fancies real violence more than the video version. He crosses over and starts banging away at the guards, crying out that he's alive for the first time in his life. It's a short life. After Mickey and Mallory bluff their way out of Batongaville, shotguns taped to their hostages' heads, they quickly dispose of Mr. Media. "Killing you and what you represent is a statement," Mickey explains to the pleading Gale. "I'm not 100 percent sure exactly what it's saying. You know, Dr. Frankenstein killed Frankenstein." Gale flings out his arms in the manner of Goya's "The Third of May, 1808" — a nice ironic touch. Mickey and Mallory blast away as Gale's camera records the execution. Flash forward to Mickey and Mallory in a ticky-tacky van, two kids romping around, another in the oven: natural born parents. They got clean away with it.

THE CRITICAL REACTION

In a sense, Oliver Stone got away with it, too. A feature-length experimental film with upwards of 3,000 shots, weird camera angles, multiple formats, morphing, cartoons, avant-eclectic sound track, and headache-inducing montage is not the most obvious route to box-office success. In less talented hands, the film could have been a commercial and critical disaster. It was neither. Stone and his editors worked on the film for eleven months following just fifty-three days of frenetic shooting. "We wanted an impressionist feeling, but there was no randomness," coeditor Harry Corwin recalled. "Every two-frame flash was thought out."[4]

Warner released the film in August 1994, after Stone cut 150 shots to avoid an NC-17 rating. (He restored these deletions in a video release that I am treating as the authoritative version.[5]) The timing was nearly perfect. Violent crime rates, though down from their peaks in the early 1990s, were still scandalously high, and O. J. Simpson had unwittingly provided the world's first live slow-motion trailer. *NBK* enjoyed the biggest opening of any Oliver Stone movie and went to number one immediately. After three weeks it began to sink, though it ended up grossing more than $50 million in the United States and nearly £4 million in the United Kingdom. Measured against a cost of $34 million, the film was a modest hit.[6]

Critical opinion was divided. Several heavyweights praised the film. Roger Ebert, in a four-star review, called it a "wonderland of murderous satire" that served as "a slap in the face, waking us up to what's happening."[7] *Time* and *Newsweek* published favorable reviews, as did *Variety*. But other critics, including some long-standing Stone supporters, hooted."Like bad sex and a bad drug trip combined," complained David Denby.[8] "If America is a party, with its mindless sitcoms, pseudo-newscasts and tabloid sensationalism," wrote Hal Hinson in the *Washington Post*, "Stone crashes it and pukes in the punch bowl. It's a purgative work, but one that does Stone more good than it does us."[9] (Stone agreed with this last judgment, or at least evoked a similar metaphor. "It felt at one point like I was throwing up on canvas," he said. "It was about capturing that mean season, from '92 to '94, when there was one bloody tabloid scandal after another."[10])

Internet commentary, which *NBK* sparked a great deal of, was also polarized. "The problem with using the jabber of trash culture against itself: It's still jabber," Tom Keogh wrote in an electronic review.[11] Scott Renshaw's complaint that Stone looked like "a colossal hypocrite attempting to cash in on exactly what he spends two hours clucking his tongue at" found many echoes.[12] Yet the film also quickly developed an international cult following, with Nietzscheans, Jungians, and garden-variety Web surfers singing its praises. It generated its own electronic fan magazine, the *Batongaville Times*.[13] Plugged-in kids blew kisses. "I thought it was a terrifly great movie," one wrote, "and what really gets people is that im only 12 and I first saw the movie when I was 8 or something like that but if thre was such thing as mickey and maylory than I would be there greatest fan."[14]

COPYCATS

Kids older than twelve have allegedly offered the sincerest form of praise, that of imitation. Accounts of *NBK*-inspired slayings have come from places as diverse as France, Georgia, Massachusetts, New York, Tennessee, Texas, and Utah. The Columbine High killers, Eric Harris and Dylan Klebold, were reportedly big fans. One southern Georgia couple, Ronnie Beasley and Angela Crosby, supposedly watched the movie nineteen times without stopping. They embarked on a crime spree that included carjacking, theft, kidnapping, and murder. Beasley shaved his head like Mickey's; he and Crosby used Mickey's and Mallory's names in correspondence to each other after they were apprehended.[15]

The best-known case, however, is that of Ben Darras and Sarah Edmonson. They were so taken with the movie that they watched it six times in one night. Setting off in Sarah's Nissan Maxima, they robbed and killed Bill Savage, a cotton gin manager in Hernando, Mississippi; detoured for a day's sight-seeing in New Orleans; and then shot and paralyzed Patsy Byers, a convenience store clerk in Ponchatoula, Louisiana. Byers's lawyer, Joe Simpson, sued Stone and Warner, citing a principle of Louisiana law that any act of man that causes damage to another through negligence can be compensated in court. "If [Stone's] found negligent," Simpson said, "you're looking at $20 to $30 million." Attorney and best-selling novelist John Grisham, who happened to be a friend of Bill Savage, also jumped into the fray. Likening *NBK* to a defective product, he argued that the director and production company were both liable. "The film was not made with the intent of stimulating morally depraved young people to commit similar crimes," he observed, "but such a result can hardly be a surprise." Unsafe at any speed.[16]

A Louisiana district court judge initially dismissed Byers's suit, but his decision was reversed and remanded by the Louisiana Court of Appeal. In October 1998, the Louisiana Supreme Court, and then in March 1999 the U.S. Supreme Court, declined to reverse the appellate court decision. This did not mean that Stone and Time Warner had lost, only that the suit against them could go forward. Patsy Byers was no longer in the picture — she had died of cancer in 1997 — but her husband, Lonnie, decided to press on. As I write, in late April 1999, the case is still in its pretrial phase.

The Supreme Court's action spooked Hollywood and brought forth dire warnings in liberal, libertarian, and journalistic circles. The suit, editorialized the *Montreal Gazette,* "could produce an artistic chill of the kind not seen since Ayatollah Khomeini's fatwa against Salman Rushdie." Ed Quillen, writing in the *Denver Post,* called it a contender for the "dumbest American lawsuit currently in litigation. . . . After all, millions of people saw 'Natural Born Killers' without launching murder sprees along our Highway 666."[17] The thick edge of the wedge proved the most popular editorial gambit. We'll end up with lawsuits against Shakespeare festivals because *Hamlet* (all those dead bodies!) rubbed somebody the wrong way.

Attorney Simpson denies this. The appeals court decision says only that the plaintiffs deserve a chance to prove that Stone *intended* to urge viewers to emulate the criminal conduct of Mickey and Mallory. To get past the protected-speech defense, Simpson has to prove that Stone deliberately designed the film to provoke lawless activity, as evidenced by certain incautious remarks he reportedly made. The most important of these is his description of audience reaction quoted in a newspaper interview: "The most pacifistic people in the world said they came out of this movie and wanted to kill somebody." Should Stone lose — and Simpson concedes that the odds are ten to one against that happening — it would not necessarily serve as a precedent for litigation against films based on content alone.[18]

Stone's attorneys think that the protected-speech defense is ironclad. Given that *NBK* is a work of fiction, that the crime in question did not occur immediately after the viewings, and that millions of moviegoers did not behave in similarly violent fashion, they believe that they are entitled to summary judgment. Cases like this one have a chilling effect by forcing artists and studios to fend off lawsuits. Litigious interrogation of an artist's intentions (as opposed to, say, those of the author of a nonfiction book urging readers to murder their enemies and showing them how to do it) is always a bad idea in a free society.[19]

But the question remains, Do ultraviolent movies like *NBK* really inspire homicidal mimesis? Law is one thing, real life quite another. And one of the startling features of late-twentieth-century American life is the extent to which the electronic environment has encroached upon, and partially supplanted, face-to-face social interactions. We all walk around with electronic personae in our heads. Some of them are so pervasive that no one can escape them — Elvis, JFK, Madonna. Others reflect our own interests and needs — this soap opera star, that sports hero. Researchers have discovered that, for many of us, these media figures are socially real. Though we may never meet them in the flesh, we act like them, dress like them, talk like them, talk about them, talk *to* them, fantasize about them, and mourn their passing. When Anthony Lane wrote that Princess Diana's true family numbered in the millions, he expressed a truth as deep as the banks of flowers laid outside Kensington Palace. Wallace Stegner said it simply: "We are not so far from our models, real and fictional, as we think."[20]

Watching *NBK* again and again on acid, as Darras and Edmonson supposedly did, would have burned Mickey and Mallory into their electronic repertoires, and not necessarily as figures of satire. The film is so intense that LSD is almost beside the point. Stone says that when the Motion Picture Association of America ratings board demanded cuts to avoid an NC-17 rating, it often couldn't specify which scenes. The board's real problem was the film's terrifying, chaotic energy. He's absolutely right about this, but he shrugs off the implications of millions of young viewers watching a movie that is, emotionally if not technically, out of control.[21]

The production company itself fell under the movie's spell. Producer Jane Hamsher's memoir, *Killer Instinct,* is full of fights among the actors, the prisoners, and the producers themselves. At one point, Woody Harrelson threw ninety-pound Juliette Lewis against the hood of a car and twisted her arm behind her in a half nelson. Screaming obscenities, she yelled at him to "'Knock it off, . . . I'm just an actress, playing a part!'" But at that moment, was she? Hamsher's comment on the shooting atmosphere — "We were no longer just making a film, the film was making us" — is arresting. So is her description of how she felt when a riot scene, with scores of prisoners as extras, briefly turned into the real thing. "I was the only woman in the place," she recalled. "I should have been terrified, and even now I don't know why I wasn't. There was something in the air that was so electric, so kinetic, so visceral and cinematic and real that I felt utterly and completely alive. Whatever the reason, no concern for my safety — or lack thereof — ever entered my mind."[22] Notice the conjunction of "visceral" and "cinematic" and "real." Whether her choice of words was intentional or a slip of the pen, it reminds us that fiction-life boundaries can blur, that the cinematic can be experienced as the real. So, yes, there is a social psychological basis for suspecting *NBK* of potentially malign influence. It is not unique in this regard. A number of other films, including *The Basketball Diaries, The Burning Bed, Child's Play 3, A Clockwork Orange, Colors, The Deer Hunter, Fatal Attraction, Interview with the Vampire, Magnum Force, Menace II Society, New Jack City, Nightmare on Elm Street, The Silence of the Lambs,* and *Taxi Driver,* have been cited in connection with copycat behavior.

Copycat killings are nevertheless extremely rare. Compared with the fundamental causes of lethal violence in America — ghetto isolation, multigenerational poverty, family decline, illegitimacy, gangs, guns, drugs, and alcohol — *NBK* is a drop in the proverbial bucket. A harder question is whether a steady diet of violent fare makes a difference. What about the kid who habitually chases *NBK* with a little *Pulp Fiction* and *Terminator* action? Here the evidence is mixed. Media mayhem appears to be more of a triggering or exacerbating influence than a primary cause of violent behavior. Mostly, it affects less academically talented boys who are already aggressive but who become more so after viewing violent episodes. Unfortunately, these same boys are among the most avid moviegoers and consume a disproportionate amount of Hollywood's macho fare. That is, the most violent movies are watched by the most violence-prone group. The movies have also gotten progressively bloodier. It seems quaint to recall that *Death Wish,* with a body count of eight, was a highly controversial film when it was released in 1974. By the late 1980s, action films like *Robocop* (1987), *Die Hard* (1988), and *Rambo III* (1988) were averaging just under sixty bodies per movie.[23] With *NBK,* who knows? Fifty-two plus nine in prison plus dozens more slaughtered in the Batongaville riot and Wayne Gale as an afterthought — triple digits, at least.

Nor is the influence of violent movies confined to the local cineplex. When popped into VCRs or broadcast on television, their effect is magnified. By age eighteen, the average American, in the course of twenty-five viewing hours a week, has reportedly seen 200,000 acts of televised violence and 40,000 murders. (For blacks, the figures are closer to 300,000 and 60,000, given that they

spend as much as 47 percent more time watching television than whites.[24])
Carnage on this scale is bound to desensitize. Stone agrees. He flashes "too
much t.v." across Mickey's and Mallory's torsos while they are standing in the
hogan. The point of view is the shaman's. It is what he glimpses in their —
and, by extension, our — troubled souls.

As a piece of cinema, this is very effective. As an explanation for violence in
the real world, it is doubtful, or at least in need of qualification. Although
overexposure to media violence has inspired some crime, particularly in
undersocialized males like Mickey, it is not, in statistical terms, anything other
than a minor factor. To grasp the point, think about violent crime rates in the
United States over the last four decades. They rose during the 1960s and 1970s,
came down in the early 1980s, rose again in the late 1980s and early 1990s, and
have since steadily declined. In explaining these ups and downs, criminolo-
gists evoke social forces far more tangible than media violence. The decline since
1992, for example, is likely due to a combination of an aging population, a more
prosperous economy, the abatement of the crack epidemic, more efficient and
aggressive police tactics, and the mass incarceration of young minority men.
Yet most studies of television violence have found an increase in the number
of violent scenes during the 1990s, notably in cable movies and cartoons. Web
sites and computer games have also become increasingly graphic. If, as psy-
chologist Jonathan Freedman points out, media violence is the master vari-
able, why haven't crime rates been going up rather than down in recent years?[25]

This doesn't excuse media violence, but it reduces the charges against it. The
most plausible charges are, in descending importance, the inspiration of copycat
crimes, tragic in outcome though small in number; the further coarsening of
an already cynical and voyeuristic culture; the false conviction of millions of
viewers that the world is a meaner and more dangerous place than it actually
is; the ruination of potentially good movies (e.g., *The Matrix*) in the interest
of audience appeal; and the exacerbation of contemporary cinema's besetting
vice — sensory overload at earsplitting volume.

AMERICAN MANIACS

The issue of causation aside, does *NBK* accurately reflect the pattern of violence in the larger society? Stone has touched at least one very deep nerve.
Americans are more afraid of being killed by strangers or maniacs than they
were in the past, and with good reason. The settled middle class, as historian
Roger Lane puts it, "has only at rare times worried about murder, mostly a
matter for other folks. But this is one of those times: even as homicides by
ordinary adults are falling in number, the most troubling kinds have been ris-

ing, from ideological bombings and serial killings to the more common murders by strangers, criminals, and deeply alienated teenagers."[26] Stone himself has emphasized the randomness of American violence.[27] Mickey and Mallory are the bogeymen just around everyone's corner.

But sheer randomness is a better description of what happens in warfare than in most American homicides. Listen to Stone on Vietnam:

> We burned the villages, we did a lot of damage. Not on the My Lai scale, but we did it on a steady basis. It was random. We'd be pissed off on certain days. We'd walk up to a village and an old gook lady would be going down the trail. One of the guys would be pissed off and he'd say, "Hey, gook, come here." She wouldn't hear or else wouldn't turn around because she was scared and just kept walking for a few more steps. The guy wouldn't even ask her a second time. He'd just raise the fucking '16 — *boom, boom, boom* — dead. No questions asked. . . .
>
> I saw people die. I killed. I almost was killed. Almost immediately I realized that combat is totally random. Life is a matter of luck or destiny, take your pick. Two soldiers are standing two feet apart: one gets killed, the other lives. I was never a religious person, but I became spiritual in Vietnam. Organized religion is for people who fear Hell, but true spirituality is for people who've been to Hell. Possibly, I was saved for a reason. To do something. To write about the experience, maybe. To make a movie about it.[28]

You can make a case that, experientially and psychologically, *NBK* really belongs to Stone's Vietnam oeuvre. Change a few words in the passage above, and you have something Mickey might have said to Wayne Gale during his interview. Mickey's skill and familiarity with weapons — honed by Dale Dye, the ex-marine who also trained the actors in *Platoon* — are transparently martial.[29] He bayonets a bystander during an armed robbery, deftly stealing his hat as he runs him through. It's a gesture that, however implausible, reminds us of the last time American soldiers casually lifted souvenirs from dying civilians. It's easy to flash Mickey, man of the 1990s, back to the 1960s and imagine him as a kind of Super Bunny, pumping his shotgun and lighting up the villes.

People get shot randomly in this country, too. It happened to my own father, critically wounded by two stray bullets fired during a botched motel robbery. But, as a statistical matter, random violence most often occurs in inner cities near drug markets or gang war zones. The modal victim is an African American kid minding her own business when she catches a stray round from a drive-by. (In gang parlance, such people are "mushrooms." They pop up in the wrong places and get mowed down.) Criminologically speaking, the mise-en-scène of *NBK* is wrong. Random death on a desert highway might come in the form of a drunk in the passing lane, but not a couple of white psychos on their honeymoon.

Another problem with Mickey and Mallory is that they are serial *and* mass murderers. The labels provoke an exchange between Wayne, who calls him a serial killer, and Mickey, who says that technically he's a mass murderer. In fact, he's both, which is vanishingly rare. The serial-mass distinction is either-or, not both-and. Mass murderers take out many victims at once and attract instant and massive police response. Patrick Henry Sherrill, the most infamous of the postal killers, shot fourteen people to death. Charles Whitman picked off sixteen (including, we learn in a cinematic aside, Scagnetti's mother). James Huberty got twenty-one, George Hennard twenty-two — a twenty-third victim died later in the hospital. Mass murderers are disturbed persons who are as much suicidal as homicidal, and they do not escape. They kill themselves, die in a barrage of SWAT bullets, or passively surrender.

Serial killers are those who kill three or more people over at least thirty days, sometimes much longer. They are typically white and middle class, prey on individuals, often act out sexual fantasies, and can evade the police for a long time. Ted Bundy had a run from 1974 until his arrest in 1979 during which he killed eighteen women.[30] A man and woman driving around in a 1970 Dodge Challenger convertible, their faces all over the papers and television, staging mass killing after mass killing, and then disappearing without a trace after escaping prison is, to put it mildly, at odds with reality.

To permit Mickey and Mallory to get away with all this mayhem, Stone depicts police and prison officials as utterly feckless, when they aren't busy strangling people or plotting crimes of their own. Although the chief object of Stone's wrath is the media's exploitation of violence, he has another and, to my mind, less justified target: the ineptitude and sadism of police and prison officials. Bad cops and wardens surely exist, but the average run is far more professional and efficient than the clownish gestapo of this fable. A real Mickey and Mallory wouldn't have lasted three days on the lam, let alone three weeks. Nor would they have added nine more victims to their string while in prison. Ultradangerous inmates like Willie Bosket, known to his keepers as "Dr. Hannibal Lecter," may attempt once to kill a guard, but they do not get a second chance, let alone a ninth. Bosket spends his days isolated from other prisoners, surrounded by four video cameras, ensconced in a special cell from which even the electrical outlets have been removed.[31] Mickey, by contrast, sits in a normally furnished cell, shaves his head before a mirror with electric clippers, and writes letters to Mallory with a pen. No wonder the bodies keep piling up.

Goofs large and small abound in *NBK*. A daylight breakout *after* the Super Bowl? But cataloging implausibilities (an ingrained habit of historians) takes us only so far. The film is, after all, over-the-top satire. It's a long way from the conventional realism of *Platoon* and *Wall Street* or even the crackpot realism of *JFK*. *NBK* is intended less as a convincing portrayal of contemporary American violence than as an indictment of the media's appropriation of it.

Here Stone is on more solid ground, and the numbers back him up. From 1989 to 1991, national evening news broadcasts for all three networks averaged 67 minutes per month on crime stories. In late 1993, the amount had more than doubled to 157 minutes. The crime time kept increasing, thanks in no small part to the O. J. Simpson frenzy, which had spawned no fewer than 1,449 national news stories by 1996. Local news programs, strobe-lit with blue lights, were worse still. One study of late-night news in Denver found that over half of all news coverage was devoted to crime, including more than two-thirds of all lead stories. Related issues such as poverty got no coverage at all. Nor was the crime mania restricted to conventional news broadcasts. Police-blotter and tabloid fare, narrowly focused on the violent, sordid, and sensational, proliferated in the 1990s. To research the Wayne Gale role, Robert Downey, Jr., simply hung out with *Current Affair* reporter Steve Dunleavy, hence the Australian accent.[32]

In fact, the obsession of the American mass media with violent crime had become so obnoxious by the time Stone was making *NBK* that he came up against a self-satirization problem. Some subjects — North Korean politics comes immediately to mind — are so crazy in their normal operations that they do not lend themselves well to satire, even over-the-top satire, because it's essentially redundant. It's like holding up a distorting mirror inside a funhouse. Things are already pretty twisted.

Put another way, *NBK* doesn't have much to tell intelligent viewers, at least not at the level of surface theme. Notice that Stone doesn't have this problem in other films. What was it really like in Vietnam? How does Wall Street operate? Who murdered JFK? What made Nixon tick? Those are great, juicy themes. But TV as exploitative drivel? Sorry. We knew that one already.

Tommy Lee Jones, a man whose IQ is a good seventy points above that of the character he portrays, observed, "We were really thinking about Molière all the way through this. . . . You don't have to be a very sophisticated person to know this is not an exploitation film. This is an *art* film."[33] Of course it is — if you comprehend art films. But what if you think like the kids interviewed for "American Maniacs"?

Teenager 1: Mickey and Mallory are the best thing to happen to mass murder since Manson.

Teenager 2: Yeah! But, uh, they're way cooler!

NBK ran into a classic high-low problem. Serious viewers were inclined to dismiss it as shooting a mile-wide target with a mile-long cannon. Not-so-serious viewers dug the cannon. "If Stone were the sort of embattled artist he likes to imagine himself," Michael Shnayerson wrote, "his art would be seen, or heard, or read by only a small, sophisticated audience." But, as a mass-market filmmaker, "he communicates with a far larger, less educated audience — one that may, for example, take his screen violence literally, and not see a 'moral order turned upside down.'" Stone, Shnayerson continues, seems oblivious to any sense of responsibility his role confers. "Worse, shown the ways in which confused youths interpret his sophisticated message, he does not seem inclined to reflection concerning his artistic methods."[34]

FYODOR STONE

NBK need not be understood solely in terms of violence — whether violence in America, violence in the media, or violence purportedly caused by the film itself. As Hamsher relates in her memoir, Stone decided early in the game that he wasn't interested in simply making a timely satire about a couple of gun-happy lowlifes in a celebrity-mad society. He regarded Tarantino's script (much to Tarantino's displeasure) as a blueprint for something bigger. "He has a sort of '60s glamorization of Indian/desert spirituality that he wanted to integrate into the film," she wrote, "whether it belonged there or not."[35]

Garry Wills, a champion of Stone's work, believes that it does. He argues that Stone's films are really about the cosmic showdown behind the news, the perpetual heavenly war of clashing spiritual principles. Though he may have become the whipping boy of the Religious Right, Wills writes, "Stone is one of the few filmmakers who regularly treat religion in a serious way. Some refuse to consider his religious thrashings important, because . . . they take exotic forms — the religion found in and beyond excess." Wills goes so far as to call Stone a cinematic Dostoyevsky, "making great American novels on film."[36]

Stone has made some great movies, perhaps some great religious movies, but *NBK* is not among them. I say this because, to qualify as religiously great, a work of art needs at least a modicum of theological consistency. Stone may have had fun making *NBK* a tangle of inconsistencies, but they frustrate deeper interpretation. Why, for example, do Mickey and Mallory kill innocent people? Mal (evil) answers with a song, "I guess I was born, naturally born, born bad."

Mickey tells Gale that killing's in his blood. His father was violent and his father before him. His gene pool is a "flaming pit of scum" into which God threw him. He kills unselfconsciously. "The wolf don't know why he's a wolf," he tells Gale. The born-killer riff is reinforced by the predatory images — hawks, scorpions, snakes, praying mantises — that appear throughout the film. It's pure cinematic Darwinism.

Yet Stone undercuts the biological determinism with flashbacks showing Mickey and Mallory as abused children. Mallory's father has beaten and raped her for years. She has a younger brother only because, we are told, her father wandered into the wrong room — her mother's — one night when he was too drunk to know the difference. The shaman's diagnosis: Mallory has the sad sickness. Mickey's got it too. Flash back to his faithless, foul-mouthed mother. "I hate you, you little asshole!" she screams. Flash again to his father blowing his brains out. Young Mickey is blond, innocent — a frightened angel, not a wolf. He's not born bad, he's made bad by his vile parents, his white-trash culture, his media-trash culture. God didn't throw him into the pit. We did it by our collective failure to purge our violent, voyeuristic society. That, after all, is the moral point implicit in the satire. Stone made it explicit in an interview: "These two kids are desensitized, at the beginning of the movie, totally to their environment — by their parents, by their upbringing, and above all by television."[37] There's nothing genetic about the tube.

To confuse matters further, warden McClusky offers a third perspective on evil. His is the traditional one of personal responsibility that discounts both genetic and environmental determinism. Shrink-talk is bunk. "It's all pride. It's arrogance. It's bullshit," he tells Scagnetti. Mickey and Mallory are just a couple of evil scumbags who deserve to die, the sooner the better. Scagnetti, their would-be executioner, has himself strangled Pinky, a beautiful young prostitute, to get inside Mickey's head. "Mickey, I'm comin' to get ya!" he shouts over her lifeless body. It's hard to view Pinky's death as anything other than an instance of willed, hypocritical maliciousness with a nasty misogynist spin. It's even harder to work out where NBK stands on the problem of evil, a stumbling block if we're to take it seriously as a religious work.

The death of the Indian shaman is another puzzle. Why is his shooting so bad, why is it the act on which the film turns, why is it the one mortal sin that sends Mickey and Mallory to Batongaville hell? It makes no sense, after all, to chastise a cat for killing a songbird. The bird, however beautiful, is just another meal. The cat — Mickey — is supposed to be a natural born killer. But the Indian was somehow different. "You killed life!" Mallory screams at Mickey after he shoots the Indian. So what were all the other victims? Life unworthy of life?

Apparently so. In the climactic interview with Gale, Mickey admits that he's sorry about the Indian. The shaman, as Wills points out, lived outside the media-polluted world. He was a cosmic fellow traveler, a natural man with his roof open to the heavens. (We glimpse an upside-down flag hanging on his wall, presumably the one that covered the casket of his son, who was killed in Vietnam. It's another symbol of his alienation from American society and its self-imposed troubles.) His death was a mistake, a bad shot, a puck flipped into the wrong net. But Mickey feels nothing about the others. He's just fate's messenger. Those people weren't innocent. They had some sin, some awful secret. Or they were already dead inside, so much brush waiting to be cleared. Nothing's wrong with killing the inauthentic and the doomed — an attitude closer to existential fascism than to true religion. Gale's coming "alive" by killing the guards is more of the same. *NBK* isn't a religious movie. It's a religious movie manqué.

Stone didn't even pick the right ending. The alternative version,[38] in which another escaping psycho named Owen shoots Mickey and Mallory, is morally, aesthetically, and sociologically superior. "Kurtz, he dead," works a lot better for this bloodbath than a clean getaway. But the happily-ever-after ending, Stone says, "had more juice."[39] Whatever its shock value, it's thematic poison. *Bonnie and Clyde,* for all its historical inaccuracies, at least got the message right. The price of homicidal rebellion in America is death, not tooling down the endless highway in the latest model from Van-O-Rama.

HARD FOUL

NBK, then, is a misfired attempt at outrageous satire with contradictory religious overtones: essentially, a failed experiment. This does not mean that Stone is a failed director. At a time when tripe aimed at fourteen-year-olds dominates the industry, Stone stands out. A seeker who made a remarkable odyssey from Goldwaterite to grunt to radical auteur, he is near the top of a short list of working American directors who make serious political films for an adult audience. All artists have their creative flops. John Updike wrote *Marry Me.* Woody Allen directed *Stardust Memories.* Stone did *NBK.* It happens.

Think of Stone as a baseball slugger who has a strong tendency to pull the ball. Sometimes his long shots stay fair, as in *Platoon:* home run. Sometimes they loop left, as in *JFK:* foul ball. Sometimes they *hit* the pole, as in *Nixon,* a mighty shot that caromed foul for most historical umpires but fair for *Citizen Kane* fans. *NBK* is an easier call: hard line drive, low, foul, beaned some kids in the cheap seats.

Nixon

IS IT HISTORY? *Stephen E. Ambrose*

Oliver Stone wants not only fame and fortune but also respect. To achieve it, he went to unprecedented lengths in promoting his movie *Nixon*. Since *The Birth of a Nation*, Hollywood has found treasure in the American past, from war, historical romances, and the lives of presidents. To one degree or another, the producers have pretended that their movies were based on fact. But never before has a producer issued an advance copy of his script, much less one including hundreds of footnotes, done in approved graduate-student fashion, citing some eighty books, numerous oral histories, tapes of Nixon's meetings, and other sources; opening essays by John Dean, Daniel Schorr, Alexander Butterfield, Stanley Kutler, Paul Nitze, and others, as well as an interview with Stone; and concluding with photo-offsets of numerous Watergate documents.

This scholarly blitz impressed reporters and reviewers, but it is fraudulent. Stone's peacocklike display of his scholarship is too thin to cover his basic contempt for real scholarship. His devotion is to drama, and were he to change Nixon's name to Dixon, Henry Kissinger's to Missinger, and label the movie fiction, no one could quarrel with him over his scholarship or inventions. But he insists that he is more than a dramatist and producer, that he is a historian. In this essay, I judge him on that basis.

Stone claims that he has discovered what the journalists and professional historians missed, the truth about Nixon. The film opens with a prologue on a black screen:

> This film is an attempt to understand the truth of Richard Nixon. . . . It is based on numerous public sources and on an incomplete historical record.
>
> In consideration of length, events and characters have been condensed, and some scenes among protagonists have been conjectured.

The last sentence hides a multitude of lies.

Oliver Stone wants to participate in the historical debate on the character of Richard Nixon without conforming to the canons of history. He feels free not merely to conjecture but also to invent scenes that never happened, to give one man's words to another, and to assign Nixon posts that he never held. He imagines a Nixon who took a dark secret to his grave with him, a man whose character, while complex, was contemptible.

A man's drinking habits and his language are important expressions of his character. Stone makes them central to Nixon's. He has Nixon drinking steadily and heavily throughout the film and using foul language regularly. He cites Tom Wicker and me as his sources on Nixon's drinking habits. In his 1991 biography of Nixon, Wicker wrote that he had found only one authentic case of Nixon's being drunk — when he was in Moscow as vice president. In my biography, I wrote that H. R. Haldeman told me that he had never seen Nixon drunk, and following a couple of paragraphs on the subject of Nixon's drinking, I concluded, "Whatever Nixon's problems in life, and Lord knows there were many, alcohol was not one of them."[1]

Maybe Stone is right about Nixon and booze, and Wicker and I are wrong. But he cannot cite us as his sources for a portrayal of Nixon popping pills and knocking them back with straight scotch whiskey. If I felt as free as Stone to conjecture, I might conjecture that he put forward those padded footnotes confident that few would ever read them or check them.

Nor will most viewers realize that they are getting a cruel distortion of the language Nixon ordinarily used. In Stone's movie, he has Nixon saying "fuck" throughout — in one scene, eight times. In fact, Nixon was a shy Quaker boy who seldom used locker-room language. The bulk of the "expletive deleted" words that Nixon blocked out on his transcript version of the tapes were "hell" and "damn." I have listened many times to the available tapes, some sixty hours' worth, recording conversations between Nixon and his closest advisers when they were in deep trouble, and I never heard him say "fuck." William Safire told me that Nixon sometimes said "asshole." He used "son of a bitch" regularly. In general, Nixon's language was mild, especially in comparison with that of Harry S. Truman, Dwight D. Eisenhower, Lyndon B. Johnson, and John F. Kennedy. Stone creates the opposite impression.

Stone insists that precisely because he ignores the canons of history, he gives a sharper, more sensitive portrait of Nixon than do the professional historians, chained as they are to the documents. The novel *All the King's Men* and the movie *Patton* are examples of what he means. And certainly there are those (not I) who think that Robert Penn Warren got closer to Huey Long's character than T. Harry Williams did in his biography and that George C. Scott's performance gave a clearer view of George Patton than Martin Blumenson's biography.[2]

By changing Long's name, Warren gave himself the fiction writer's freedom to make things up. Nevertheless, he stuck closer to the truth than Stone did. Examples of Stone's inventions include Nixon's saying about John Kennedy, "We were like brothers, for Christ's sake"; Pat Nixon's demanding a divorce; Mao's telling Nixon, "You're as evil as I am. . . . Others pay to feed the hunger in us. In my case, millions of reactionaries. In your case, millions of Vietnamese." Can anyone imagine Mao's talking to Nixon like that? In fact, yes. Here, as elsewhere, Stone counts on his audience's believing that it is possible that Dick and Jack were friends, that the Nixon marriage was always on the verge of breaking apart, and that Mao would say such things to Nixon.

The first canon of history is that you cannot put words into people's mouths. Stone not only does that, but he regularly takes lines he likes from the actual speakers and puts them into the mouths of others. Kissinger gets Nixon's line to Mao: "But your writings have changed the world, Mr. Chairman." Alexander Haig gets Barry Goldwater's line to Nixon: "No one I know feels close to you." Nixon gets John Ehrlichman's "twisting in the wind" line. Sometimes Stone gets the right man with the right line but gets the timing wrong. In 1973, Haig is leading Nixon through a hospital corridor. "Clear the path!" Haig shouts. "Clear a path. I'm in charge here."

Perhaps these are peccadilloes. The central piece of fiction in the movie is not. It is the creation of a Nixon–Fidel Castro–Kennedy connection. Stone has Nixon involved in a CIA assassination plot against Castro, which somehow played a part in the Kennedy assassination and left Nixon with a terrible secret and guilt about Kennedy's death. All this leads to a flash of insight on Nixon's part that is the climactic vision of the movie.

Details are wrong. In the movie, Nixon tells Haldeman, "You open up that scab [referring to the CIA and Castro] and you uncover a lot of pus." What Nixon said was, "You open that scab [Howard Hunt] there's a hell of a lot of things . . . this involves the Cubans, Hunt, and a lot of hanky-panky."

In the movie, Nixon tells Haldeman that there was a CIA project to kill Castro and insists, "It was our idea. We felt the invasion [Bay of Pigs] wouldn't work unless we got rid of Castro. So we asked ourselves — who else wants Castro dead? The Mafia, the money people." So they hired the Mafia. Nixon says that Eisenhower approved the plan and ordered it put into effect before the 1960 election.

Haldeman, astonished, blurts out, "Eisenhower approved that?"

Nixon replies, "He didn't veto it. I ran the White House side."

Haldeman later tells Ehrlichman that Nixon's involvement in the Castro affair "in some crazy way got turned on Kennedy."

According to Stone, it was during the June 10, 1972, conversation with Haldeman (the first meeting of the two men after the Watergate burglars were arrested, now infamous because of the 18½–minute gap in the tape) that the truth came out. "It seems that in all of those Nixon references to the Bay of Pigs, he was actually referring to the Kennedy assassination," Stone quotes Haldeman. In threatening the CIA with exposure, Nixon was "reminding [Director Richard] Helms, not so gently, of the cover-up of the CIA assassination attempts — a CIA operation that may have triggered the Kennedy tragedy and which Helms wanted desperately to hide." Those words come from Haldeman's memoir *The Ends of Power*, cowritten with Joseph DiMona. Haldeman later repudiated the book and those words specifically.[3]

Christopher Wilkinson, one of Stone's cowriters, insists in his introduction to the book that the words are nevertheless accurate and that Haldeman reached his conclusion on June 10, which was why Nixon manually erased the 18½ minutes. Wilkinson argues that "it is reasonable to assume that whatever was on the 18½ minute gap was substantively different from any of the other *blatantly incriminating* material Nixon exposed."[4]

No, it is not reasonable to assume. We do not have to assume anything. Haldeman's handwritten notes on that meeting exist. Although hardly verbatim, they are clear on the subjects discussed. Nixon's first order was to sweep the Oval Office for bugs (not his, of course). Next he told Haldeman to get to work on public relations by accusing the Democrats of crimes of their own — "hit the opposition with their activities," as Haldeman took it down.

Stone's Bay of Pigs–assassination business is all fantasy. Richard Bissel of the CIA did raise the question of assassination with Eisenhower, but he was rebuffed. Eisenhower said that political assassination was beyond the pale (in 1963, he expressed deep shock at Ngo Dinh Diem's murder) and that if the CIA got rid of Fidel Castro, Raul Castro would take power, "and that's worse."

Vice President Nixon never headed any CIA project. Stone calls him the "action officer" for the Bay of Pigs and assassination attempts. His source is Howard Hunt's memoirs. But no assassination attempt was made in the Eisenhower administration. And what Nixon wanted in fall 1960 was not Castro's death but a successful invasion and overthrow of the regime before the November election — a so-called October surprise.

This gets us to Nixon's dark references to the Bay of Pigs and the CIA. They were about the training of Cuban exiles by the CIA and the Bay of Pigs planning going on in the Eisenhower administration in 1960. After Kennedy became president and the Bay of Pigs landing was tried and failed, the Kennedy people put it out that it was all Eisenhower's fault because it had been his plan.

Eisenhower furiously resented this charge. He felt that the CIA and Kennedy had bungled the operation and rightly insisted that he had never signed off on a plan.

Nixon was on the extreme outside of all this. When he said in the movie, "We protected the CIA from the Bay of Pigs," Stone jumped to an unjustified conclusion, but he made his interpretation persuasive to the audience by leaving out the last nine words of Nixon's sentence: "and a hell of a lot of other things." Nixon was speaking generically, not specifically. Stone does not use Nixon's line that the CIA plots "have nothing to do with ourselves." The Nixon-Castro-Kennedy connection is akin to Stone's fantasy that JFK was about to take us out of Vietnam when a conspiracy formed by the military-industrial complex assassinated him.

Beyond giving us his version of Richard Nixon's character, Oliver Stone offers an interpretation of who rules America and how the system works. This is bold but not wise, more imaginative than informative.

The philosophical insights came to the Stone team of writers in a coup d'oeil when they suddenly realized that "for Nixon to have become President in 1968, Jack Kennedy had to die, Lyndon Johnson had to be forced into retirement, Dr. King had to die, Bobby Kennedy had to die, Hubert Humphrey had to be eviscerated in Chicago." Some might feel that there was an element of chance in all this, but Wilkinson writes:

> It almost seemed that Nixon was being helped, helped by something dark, something sinister, something frightening. Some *thing.*
> And we call it The Beast.
> The Beast became a metaphor for the darkest organic forces in American Cold War politics: the anti-Communist crusade, secret intelligence, the defense industry, organized crime, big business.

Plus the CIA.

The Beast was within Nixon and controlled him. "You're just a mouthpiece for an agenda that is hidden for us," a voter says to the movie Nixon during a TV debate — nicely summing up Stone's view of the United States and the world.

Kennedy, Stone asserts (he has Nixon say it), never knew about the assassination plot against Castro, but the CIA kept it going: "It had a life of its own. Like a kind of 'beast' that doesn't even know it exists. It just eats people when it doesn't need 'em anymore." CIA director Helms, according to Stone, agreed. In the movie, Helms says that the plot was "not an operation as much as an organic phenomenon. It grew, it changed shape, it developed insatiable, devouring appetites."

In the climactic scene, Nixon himself realizes that the Beast is in charge. He is at the Lincoln Memorial, talking with a nineteen-year-old college student. She says, "You don't want the war. We don't want the war. The Vietnamese don't want the war. So why does it go on?" Nixon is rendered speechless by this statement. She goes on, "You can't stop it, can you? Even if you wanted to. Because it's not you. It's the system. And the system won't let you stop it."

Nixon mumbles that more is at stake here than what she wants, or "even what I want."

"Then what's the point?" she asks. "What's the point of being president? You're powerless."

Nixon reels under the power of her insight. Later he tells Haldeman: "She understands something it's taken me twenty-five fucking years in politics to understand. The CIA, the Mafia, the Wall Street bastards."

"Sir?" Haldeman interjects.

"The Beast," Nixon explains. "A nineteen-year-old kid. She understands the nature of 'the Beast.'"

Toward the end of the movie, Nixon vows to do something about it. "Whoever killed Kennedy came from this . . . this *thing* we created. This Beast. That's why we can't let this thing go any farther."

Enough. This is sophomoric Marxism circa 1950. The gross simplification of how and by whom the United States is run misses the complexities of the system and assigns to the unseen and scarcely defined Beast an evil intent that accounts for all the evil done by the United States and in its name since 1945 (if not before) without a single piece of evidence of serious thought or study by Stone.

Does it matter? William Shakespeare took liberties with the histories he dramatized, and I do not suppose that we are worse off because his vision of Henry IV does not correspond with the facts of English history. But the Bard was not depicting contemporaries, and he did not have an agenda for social, economic, and political change in his country. Stone thinks that the United States is rotten because of the sinister forces that rule. He used both Kennedy and Nixon to prove it. He wants to change the country and points to the Kennedy assassination and the Nixon presidency as proof of the need for radical political action. In that sense, it matters greatly that he has distorted the past.

Aside from Stone's puerile conspiracy theses, does he advance the debate about Nixon's character, accomplishments, and crimes? In a movie in which key events are ignored, central scenes are made up, and Nixon uses words he never used, how could he? *Nixon* may be great entertainment, perhaps even great drama — that is for the movie and drama critics and the public to decide. It is not history.

ON *NIXON*   *George S. McGovern*

Oliver Stone's *Nixon* was not a film that I was eager to see. Stone is a brilliant and creative artist, and Nixon had long fascinated, sometimes appalled, and sometimes impressed me as a politician. But devoting more than three hours of the Christmas season to watching my old nemesis of 1972 depicted on the screen was not a prospect that thrilled me. My family and I went to an early Washington showing of the film primarily so that I could write a review. So what did I think about the film?

I though it was superb — the best film I had seen in a long time. It riveted me to the screen from start to finish. I walked out of the theater prepared to nominate the movie and the director as the best of the year. Anthony Hopkins, who played Nixon, is surely one of the great actors of our time, and he captured Nixon in a remarkably convincing way. Joan Allen, who played Pat Nixon, deserved to be named the best supporting actress of the year.

Anyone with even a casual interest in American politics would like this film. I write these words despite the fact that I am described by the screen Nixon as "that pansy, poet, socialist." This description has seemingly not diminished me in the eyes of my wife, daughters, and son — whom I observed laughing appreciatively. There may be a reason for this: Nixon never once mentioned my name in public in the 1972 presidential campaign. He would neither debate me nor appear on the same stage or even in the same city. So I think my family was cheered to hear my name at long last on Nixon's lips — courtesy of Oliver Stone and Anthony Hopkins.

Some others mentioned in the film come off much worse. Gordon Liddy, one of the Watergate insiders, is referred to by both Nixon and Bob Haldeman as "a fruitcake." They clearly regard him as a contemptible nut. Henry Kissinger will not like his portrayal at all. But this is not a film about Kissinger or Liddy or me or anyone other than Richard Nixon.

I think the central character is treated fairly, with balanced consideration of his complicated and contradictory nature. It has been reported that the Nixon family is very unhappy with this treatment — particularly Julie and Tricia, the Nixon daughters. But I wonder if they have seen the film or are judging it on reports from others. I know and like these two young women well enough to believe that if they look at the film without prejudice, they may come to appreciate it. They might even see a rather sympathetic portrayal of their dad's better qualities and their mother's special strengths.

This is not a documentary film to be judged primarily for its attention to historical accuracy. It is a drama in which the director has sought to present his insights relative to Nixon as a person and as a political leader. I think most of those insights are well conceived and grounded in reality. For example, Nixon boasts of his political skill as a longtime anticommunist in promoting détente with the Soviet Union, opening up relations with China, and disengaging American forces from Vietnam without a right-wing rebellion. "I'm the only politician who could have gotten away with this, and I was able to do it because I've fought the Communists for so many years that my credentials to deal with them are accepted," Nixon says in effect on the screen as he did during his life. He is doubtless right about all this.

The screen Nixon may also be right in contending that disengaging American forces from Vietnam without a domestic political upheaval from the right wing was his most difficult political achievement. Early in the Nixon administration, I went to the White House to see the new national security adviser, Henry Kissinger. My purpose was to argue that the new administration should quickly end American involvement in the disastrous Vietnam War. I assumed that Kissinger must have realized by 1969 that the deepening American military involvement had been a tragic mistake. Acting on this assumption, I said that President Nixon could simply say that his predecessors, Presidents Kennedy and Johnson, had in good faith committed forces to Vietnam and that Nixon had supported these efforts. But it had become clear that this course could no longer be consistent with out national interest and the realities facing us in Vietnam. Kissinger readily conceded that the war was a terrible mistake. But, he said, if the president were to pull out now, the American right wing would go out of control across the country. The president would lose his most committed constituency. We couldn't govern the country, he said.

He may have been right in this political judgment. But it disturbed me deeply, as it does now, to realize that we were continuing to slaughter the Vietnamese people and our own soldiers not because it was a military necessity but purely for domestic political reasons. Nothing in the movie lends comfort to any other conclusion.

As the screen Nixon says to his wife when she complains about his lifetime obsession with politics, "Everything is politics. You're politics. I'm politics." Oliver Stone is right in seeing Nixon's four-year prolongation of the Vietnam War as "politics." It certainly bore no relationship to the realities facing us in Southeast Asia.

Stone drives this point home when he has a college student confront Nixon during his nighttime visit to the war protesters' vigil at the Lincoln Memorial following the May 1970 killing of four students at Kent State. "You don't stop this war," she said, "because you can't. The system won't let you." Back at the White House, Nixon confesses to an aide, "That nineteen-year-old kid told the truth."

Nixon on the screen accepts a number of political realities. "It's the cover-up, not the deed that's the real problem here," he says at the height of the Watergate investigations. "They can't impeach me for Cambodia. The president can bomb any country he wants," he asserts.

At an earlier time, he understood that the deaths of John and Robert Kennedy had opened the way to the White House for him, just as he had known that a second presidential campaign against John Kennedy in 1964 would have been hopeless. "Nobody is going to beat Kennedy in 1964," he told those who suggested that he should run again after his razor-thin defeat by Kennedy in 1960.

He also knew, as the film underscores, that the shooting of George Wallace in 1972 virtually assured his reelection to the White House that year. I have always believed that if Wallace had not been shot, the Alabama governor, running as an independent, would have taken the South and a number of northern states from Nixon in 1972. This might not have ensured my election, but at least it would have made for a close battle between Nixon and me — more on the order of the Nixon-Humphrey campaign when Wallace did run as an independent. Curiously, neither Humphrey nor his 1968 campaign is referred to in the film.

The absence of Wallace in the presidential campaign of 1972 is just one factor that contributed to Nixon's considerable margin of victory. There are other elements, too, that made a difference in what otherwise could have been a much closer and less predictable contest for the White House.

Second, the confusion over my selection of Thomas Eagleton as my running mate and the subsequent decision to drop him cost millions of votes that had nothing to do with ideology. Third, when the national convention had me give my acceptance speech at 2:30 A.M., after nearly all Americans except my wife and children had gone to bed, I missed my best chance to talk meaningfully to a hundred million Americans. I was on in prime time only in Guam. Fourth, Nixon's vast television budget for negative advertising created an image of me as an unstable radical surrounded by long-haired hippies, pot-smoking draft dodgers, antiwar rebels, abrasive women, and militant blacks. These were factors that fed the landslide of 1972.

The Stone film gives considerable attention to Nixon's difficult boyhood years in explaining his later political conduct: his economically pressed family; his demanding, hardworking father; his deadly serious Quaker mother, who told him, "You achieve strength in this life, happiness in the next"; the death of his two brothers; his small-town, unglamorous childhood years; his painful shortcomings as a stubborn but untalented football player who was used as a tackling dummy by larger players. This background stood in sharp and painful contrast to the wealth, travel, sophistication, grace, elegance, and diversity of presidential opponent John Kennedy. Nixon was a product of Whittier College, Kennedy of the Ivy League. Nixon was scorned by the working press, Kennedy was adored.

The film demonstrates repeatedly Nixon's feelings of inadequacy and resentment toward what he regarded as Kennedy's undeserved advantages. He comes to believe that the press as much as the public despised him not because of his policies but because he was an unappealing person. "It's not Vietnam they hate; it's me. I'm the enemy," he cried. The screen Pat Nixon agrees. "They'll never love you no matter how many elections you win," she tells her husband. Another commentator in the film describes him as "the darkness reaching out for the darkness."

Nixon believed that his problems with the national press corps began with his prosecution of Alger Hiss as a member of the House Committee on Un-American Activities. If Nixon is right about this, it would be a tribute to the national press corps. Actually, the contempt for Nixon began somewhat earlier, with his slanderous campaign for the House of Representatives in 1946. In that first bid for federal office, Nixon maligned one of the ablest patriots ever to serve in the Congress — Jerry Voorhis of California — a favorite of the Washington press corps. Nixon followed that campaign four years later with an equally odious and slanderous campaign for the U.S. Senate against Helen Gahagan Douglas.

With the recent death of Alger Hiss, we have understandably been treated to yet another round of arguments about his guilt or innocence. He was charged with betraying his country by passing secret documents to his accuser — Whittaker Chambers, then a communist and later an anticommunist. I have nothing to offer that would hold up in a court of law relative to the charges against Hiss. But I would like to say what I believe about Hiss and the way his case was handled. I think that Alger Hiss was a public-spirited patriot to the United States and to the basic values of American democracy. Those who knew him best testified that he was a capable, constructive, and conscientious public servant, including Dean Acheson. He was brought down during the most hysterial period of the cold war on trumped-up charges by two men whose reliability we have reason to doubt — Whittaker Chambers and Richard Nixon.

Chambers, a shabby ex-communist, was in all probability trying to redeem his own bad record and to make a few fast dollars selling a book about his sensational charges. But it was Congressman Nixon who, in 1948, held up on national TV the microfilm he and Chambers contended would prove Hiss's guilt. Nixon said that the microfilm documented "the most serious series of treasonable activities which has been launched against the government in the history of America." In truth, as Victor Navasky reported in *The Nation,* it "turned out to consist of material about life rafts and other ephemera available on the open shelves of the Bureau of Standards."[5]

The perjury charge that was used to send Hiss to prison turned on his denial in court of knowing Whittaker Chambers during the latter's communist days. At the time Chambers supposedly knew Hiss, Chambers was going under another name. In any event, the material that Chambers claimed he got from Hiss and Nixon asserted was so damaging was actually harmless stuff readily available in the public record to anyone.

Although I have no way of proving the innocence of Hiss, his attackers never convinced me of his guilt. I can only say that if and when I go to meet that universal judge of us all, I would rather stand in the shoes of Alger Hiss than in those of his two principal accusers: Whittaker Chambers and Richard Nixon.

Ten years after Nixon was forced to resign the presidency, I went to see him in New York. I found him a more mellow and considerate man than he had been during his more active political career. In the conversation, I gave him credit, as does Stone, for his policy of peaceful coexistence with the Soviet Union and for opening the door to Communist China. But we need to remember that in Nixon's earlier political career he was an unscrupulous, Red-baiting demagogue going after liberals as though they were traitors.

I think that Oliver Stone truthfully interpreted Richard Nixon as an ambitious, insecure, self-loathing, sometimes paranoid figure. Nixon also possessed, as Stone shows, considerable political astuteness and imagination that carried him to the world's most powerful office — only to destroy himself by his own paranoia at the moment of his greatest electoral triumph. Stone's portrait of Nixon is both brilliantly and accurately drawn, and I salute him for enriching and dramatizing our knowledge of an important but tragic chapter in our recent history.

ON *JFK* AND *NIXON* *Arthur M. Schlesinger, Jr.*

Few contemporary filmmakers are so intensely involved with history as Oliver Stone. Few reshape — or, as he would say, deconstruct — history with such technical virtuosity. He is endlessly resourceful in his effort to coerce assent by quasi-realistic simulations of the past. A magician of montage, he drives his movies ahead at a slam-bang pace. A Stone film bombards with images, sounds, cuts, and flashes, like a music video. It artfully mimics documentaries with jerky, gritty, black-and-white, cinema verité sequences as if filmed by a handheld camera. No one can tell where fact ends and fiction begins.

But how do *JFK* and *Nixon* relate to the realities of history? (I will bypass postmodernist claims that history is all fiction anyway.) *JFK* purports to tell the story of the murder of a president of the United States. The premise of the movie is not unreasonable. It is that in 1963 President Kennedy was planning to end American involvement in the Vietnam War as part of a broader project to wind down the cold war.

No one can say for sure what Kennedy would have done had he lived; it is hard enough to know what living presidents are going to do about anything. But there is strong evidence that Kennedy had no intention of sending combat units to Vietnam and was intending to withdraw American "advisers" attached to units of the South Vietnamese army by 1965.[6] Robert McNamara, his secretary of defense, and McGeorge Bundy, his national security adviser, have both recently declared their belief that Kennedy would not have Americanized the war as his successor did in 1965.

Oliver Stone's premise is thus defensible. But the conclusion he draws from it is indefensible. It is that, outraged by Kennedy's policy of winding down the cold war, a cabal of evil men in high government positions organized a great conspiracy based on the Joint Chiefs of Staff, the CIA, the FBI, the military-industrial complex, anti-Castro Cubans, homosexuals, and the Mafia for the purpose of murdering the president and, with the aid of Lyndon B. Johnson, covering up the dirty deed.

Serious conspiracy arguments can be made about Kennedy's murder. But *JFK*'s conspiracy theory derives largely from charges recklessly hurled about by the New Orleans con man Jim Garrison and from the fantasies of Fletcher Prouty (the Donald Sutherland character). Stone subsequently defended himself by identifying his film with Akira Kurosawa's *Rashomon,* in which each witness offers a different version of an episode of feudal violence in a Japanese forest. *JFK,* he suggests, is in the same way a theoretical exploration of "possible scenarios of who killed Kennedy and why." But Stone's explosive style overwhelms any idea of the film as a dispassionate analysis of alternative theories. As he made clear in an interview with Mark Carnes, he really does believe that "somewhere from one of these possibilities came the directive, the order, the need to kill Kennedy, and it was probably held to a very small group, ten or twenty people, a Julius Caesar–style murder."[7]

Oliver Stone is an earnest, appealing man. He is a patriot. He fought bravely for his country in the horror of Vietnam. He has surely earned the right to brood and agonize over the reasons he and so many others were sent to kill and die in a pointless war. His Vietnam films *Platoon* and *Born on the Fourth of July* have a documentary power and moral realism that make them serious contributions to the history of our times.

But artists have fantasies, too, to which they are often hopelessly loyal — and their fantasies often hopelessly abuse the truth. Virtual history is not enough. The impact of *JFK* on the unwary young, born long after the events and remote from the atmosphere of the time, should not be underrated. Too many seem to think that Stone is telling it as it was.

Of course there is dramatic license, and the plea is not per se unreasonable. Artists are right to utilize their comparative advantage over scholars and to exploit their freedom to go beyond facts and documents into the realm of imagination and invention. Still, except for supreme artists like Shakespeare, Tolstoy, Verdi, and Delacroix, dramatic license should not be corrupted by ideology, as it certainly has been in *JFK*.

Nixon seems to me an incomparably better film. It is more faithful than *JFK* to the facts and to the spirit of the times. I noticed only one major error. The movie appears to accept Nixon's claim that Kennedy had been briefed about the CIA's Cuba operation during the 1960 campaign. This claim, denied at the time by Allen Dulles, the CIA director, has been authoritatively refuted.[8]

The portrait of Nixon himself is, if anything, excessively forbearing. The disgraced president is presented as the product of a cold and stern father and a distant mother preoccupied with his ailing brothers. He chauffeurs his girlfriend on her dates with other men, and he lacks the charm, money, wit, polish, and class of the hated Kennedys. "In the end," Stone has said, "it's tough not to feel some compassion for a guy who just never thought he was good enough to join the establishment." Nixon emerges less as an agent than as a victim.

Stone pulls punches, for example, in portraying Nixon's Vietnam policy as one of peace with honor. In fact, the United States could have gotten out of the war in 1969 if it had abandoned the demand for concurrent withdrawal of North Vietnamese troops from South Vietnam — a demand that was finally dropped in 1972. The subdued critique of Nixon's policy in the movie hardly explains the violence of the antiwar protests. At the end, we feel less outraged by Nixon than sorry for him.

Nixon's great defect is Stone's continuing compulsion to see history in terms of conspiracy. Periodic cuts to swaggering Texans and sinister Cubans remind us of the "ten or twenty people" who pull the strings behind the scenes. The climax comes on the steps of the Lincoln Memorial, where a New Leftist makes Nixon recognize what the movie designates as "the Beast." Nixon muses, "She understood something it's taken me twenty-five fucking years in politcs to understand. The CIA, the Mafia, the Wall Street bastards."

Christopher Wilkinson, Stone's collaborator on the *Nixon* script, calls the Beast the "metaphor for the darkest organic forces in American Cold War politics: the anti-Communist crusade, secret intelligence, the defense industry, organized crime, big business . . . a headless monster lurching through postwar American history, instinctively seeking figureheads to wear its public face, creating them when need be, destroying them when they no longer serve its purpose."[9]

This conspiratorial obsession is something that Stone shares with Nixon, which no doubt is why his portrait of Nixon is so sympathetic (aided, of course, by Anthony Hopkins's superb performance). In the function of conspiracy within the movie, however, there is a major difference between *JFK* and *Nixon*. In *JFK*, the obsession with the Beast is organic to the plot. In *Nixon*, it is an additive that impairs the whole and could have been deleted without harm to the rest.

But Stone is too much a true believer for such a deletion. John Kennedy, Martin Luther King, Robert Kennedy, Richard Nixon — "these four men," he told Mark Carnes, "all ran up against 'the Beast' and were removed or killed as a consequence." He rejects scholars who observe that the Beast is a constant in American history, taking a succession of forms: the Illuminati and the Masons, the Papists and the Elders of Zion and the Communist Party, the Council on Foreign Relations and the Trilateral Commission. Stone wants to hear no more of Richard Hofstadter and *The Paranoid Style in American Politics*: "I find that so condescending. Hofstadter is trotted out every time. . . . Caesar, Lincoln, popes left and right, kings — they have all been removed as the result of conspiracies. Why should American history be any different? Even Franklin Roosevelt was almost removed by a coup d'état."[10] (When was that?)

"Anyone who reads history," Stone tells us, "has to acknowledge the power of conspiracy." History, in his view, is made at night. Appearances are an illusion; reality subsists in the shadows, where Stone's ten or twenty people secretly plot the basic decisions. This is a tidy, schematic view of history. But is this the way people really behave in a messy and unpredictable world?

"The crowning attainment of historical study," wrote the British historian Sir Lewis Namier, "is a historical sense — an intuitive understanding of how things do not happen." One doubts that things happen in the ordered way proposed by conspiracy theorists. Against the view that history is shaped by conspiracy is the view that it is more likely to be shaped by what our British brethren call "cock-up."

My own impression both as a historian and as a sometime participant in public affairs is that cock-up is generally a better explanation than conspiracy. Misconception, misperception, accident, chance, ignorance, fatigue, stupid-ity — these surely are greater factors in human history than premeditation and plot, even if they do not make such gripping movies.

Of course, dramatic license is inevitable in the translation of history into fiction, drama, opera, painting, cinema. But even license must have its limits. This is perhaps especially true for film, the most lifelike of arts, playing upon — preying upon? — vulnerable audiences herded in darkened halls. One might conclude that the film's ease of verisimilitude confers a special responsibility not to mislead, especially about the recent past.

PART III
STONE RESPONDS

On Seven Films

WALTER LAFEBER ON *SALVADOR*

I was trying to say, look, this is what's really happening in El Salvador right now in the 1980s and nobody here in the United States is paying attention outside of the official news, and that news is not giving you a sense of the damage being done there and to the rest of Central America. I wanted the movie to strike home, "in your face," in the moment, like the agitprop films of the Soviets during the revolution. I now realize how against the grain I was. No wonder the film died at the box office. America as a revolutionary state? Impossible with our media.

I think LaFeber points out clearly that I am not setting out to distort history, but rather that I am seeking the meaning of it. It's interesting to read now the original *New York Times* review by Walter Goodman. He says, "Taking his cinematic as well as political lead from the work of Constantin Costa-Gavras, he [Stone] offers an interpretation of history . . . laying blame on conservative forces in the United States for abetting the horrors in El Salvador."[1] As far back as 1986, a critic like Goodman, who seriously damaged the film's prospects in New York with his review, at least understood that I was offering an "interpretation of history." I am still amazed at the uproar many of my films have caused since then — but only a moron would consider them documentaries.

A lot of Hollywood movies utilize the copy "based on a true story" in their advertising, which is a way, I suppose, of defending a movie from those who don't understand the distinction between the literal and the dramatic. *Tora, Tora, Tora,* a cited favorite of conservatives, actually has front titles that say: "All of the events and characters depicted are true to historical fact." I think that's far more pretentious than anything my films have stated. Perhaps Toplin is right in calling me a "docudramatist," if the idea behind it is that I integrate the documentary "effect" with the drama. But if so, this artistic form was originated, at the very least, by the novelist E. L. Doctorow in *Ragtime* (1981), though I have a sneaking suspicion it was done way before him.

Just to set the record straighter, if at all possible, Richard Boyle was *not* one of the first to inform the world of the martyrdom of Oscar Romero. He tended to exaggerate his own importance, to be sure, but to the best of my knowledge, he *was* one of the first to show up at the crime scene of the murdered American nuns. And he did have special feelings for Jeannie Donovan, one of the victims.

I disagree with LaFeber saying that, "nearly all the U.S. training of that military was done by uniformed officers either in the United States or at the U.S.-operated School of the Americas in Panama." From my own research, as well as from talking to several of these people, I believe that several Salvadoran death-squad commanders studied the techniques the United States employed against the Vietcong and the North Vietnamese Army in *Vietnam* during the 1960s. I also remember once staying in the same out-of-the-way hotel on the outskirts of San Salvador as several mysterious members of the Chilean military, who were there training their anticommunist allies in the techniques they learned in the 1970s, from their own U.S.-fomented civil war followed by the Terror (unleashed, not so ironically, by Nixon — the other Nixon, not the one created by Ambrose).

I am confused by LaFeber's assertion that the James Woods character "is a sounding board for Boyle's and Stone's hatred of the 1980s, especially its 'yuppie' phenomenon," as I did not share Richard's contempt for yuppies. I felt negative emotions in the late 1960s when I had just returned from Vietnam, but by the early 1980s, these feelings had changed, and as a dramatist, I was far more detached and thought that there were many positive aspects that resulted from the "yuppie culture."

LaFeber also wrote, "Stone admitted this [understating and avoiding some realities] when he noted, 'I've edited some of the violence.'" I did so because this film was made cheaply by a small British company. I had no profile as a director and was not in any position to argue the cuts made for reasons of violence or sex with the Motion Picture Association of America (a voluntary censor board). Orion Pictures chose *not* to pick up the film for distribution because of the violence, and it was finally distributed by Hemdale, the company that had made it, with little promotion money, a few mixed reviews, and miserable results at the box office. This deeply depressed me, as I was on the outskirts of Manila preparing *Platoon* for the same company, and it took a great act of will to go on and make that film in the face of *Salvador*'s failure. It was not until *Platoon* picked up "word of mouth" and became an international success later in 1986 that *Salvador* was recognized in video, which led to the Academy Award nomination of Woods as best actor and Boyle and me as screenwriters. It also led to my being nominated twice in the same category for original screenplay —

Salvador (with Boyle) and *Platoon* (by myself). I don't know if this had ever happened before, but in any case, I won for neither film.

LaFeber cites me for accuracy in not creating a false middle, which is often the fate of American political dreamers and historians, who tend to point to the great middle ground of compromise to solve any country's problems. That middle did not exist in Salvador, primarily because President Duarte did not have the confidence of the people, and because the United States was perceived by those same people to be pulling the strings behind the scenes.

The differences between Archbishop Romero's actual speech and the speech in the film are small, and I don't feel the need to discuss them. Perhaps I did understate what the Salvadorans endured in 1980, but this goes to the heart of a larger issue. I once said, about *Platoon,* that it is impossible to approximate on film the horror of war. Film, at best, is an illusion, which can never substitute for the savagery of real violence; a further point is that the violence we see on television and in many fantasy-action movies is far too sanitized, too melodramatic, or without consequence or true meaning. And if we're to be honest about life through our representation of it in our art, we must at least *try* to show violence and nonviolence at their best and worst — as well as love and sex in all its extremes and mystery. Unfortunately, our societal code will not permit that in our country at this time, and as a result, we have false violence, false modesty, hypocrisy in most things, and, for the most part, a puritan, titillating, ignorant sense of sex — resulting, I believe, in a distortion of the true strength of our social fabric.

In the matter of revolutionaries on horseback, LaFeber is wholly correct. It was a genuine mistake, as was the one I made placing Ron Kovic at Syracuse University in *Born on the Fourth of July* (discussed later in this chapter). Sometimes these details are poorly researched or communicated. But similarly, we must recognize that historians also make mistakes. We all do, but I am now convinced that any mistake I make is brought into the spotlight to discredit the entity known as "Oliver Stone." For instance, when I went to Syracuse, New York, in 1998 for a college lecture, I was queried by an aspiring politician on the network news about a mistake I'd made and publicly acknowledged in 1990. It was my depiction of a violent, riot-breaking Syracuse police department in *Born on the Fourth of July.* Little did I realize what I was in for when my *second* apology for the *same thing* made the national wires and dozens of newspapers — the theme being "Stone Wrong Again." This is interesting, because I am clearly on the record in the media as acknowledging my mistake the first time during the film's release. So why suddenly highlight a nine-year-old mistake again, if not to actively discredit me? I don't cry easily, but it is frustrating to continually read negative interpretations of my actions rather than positive ones. Most people are mixed bags — let's say fifty-fifty. Why, then, do some "media darlings" get a 99 percent approval rating from our modern morality czars — even if they get married many times, pay for transvestite sex, have babies with sperm-bank fathers or egg-donor mothers, demand astronomical sums to act in a movie, and sometimes behave with extraordinary egotism at the expense of fellow workers in the film crew, all of which help destroy the social fabric far more than any debatable idea in any film could?

I know by now that I have few friends in the "editor class" of our society, especially when I see stories drafted by young, "impressionable" journalists who have actually met me and found themselves rewritten by their editors to reflect the negative or, as they would say, to restore "more balance." This is a problem in general with our media — very little personal responsibility is taken; some people who do take responsibility are often pictured as egotistical "final cut" directors in the film business. Now everything seems to be rewritten or "marketed" or "spun" by an "editor class" that, for want of a better word, functions as propagandists and censors. Recently, a young woman interviewing me from a list of questions felt that she had "to include one because I was told to," although she had no idea why she was asking it. The question was: "Mr. Stone, how true is this movie this time?"

You can perhaps understand why I sometimes get angry inside. There's so little you can do, except change your name. But you can't even do that anymore in a society where there are few secrets — except in conspiracies. We all seem to live in glass houses. In essence, we have stripped all spirituality of its meaning, all awe, almost all of the "private conscience" Jefferson and the founders defended so eloquently — in the cause of secularism and commerce in human souls.

In any event, if I had known, which I don't think I did (this is going back fifteen years now), that the rebels were on foot only and not on horseback, would I have left that out? I don't know, frankly. I was a young man, and that was my first important film. I was struggling desperately to make that final battle scene memorable. Horseback epitomized the old ways the rebels had of fighting a highly modernized military machine created by the Pentagon. Even today in Mexico, it is impossible for the Chiapas Indian insurgents to fight on a level playing field against superb American satellite technology provided to the Mexican army. But as a passionate filmgoer for a great many years, it still thrills my soul to see the rebels attacking tanks on horseback, set to the powerful and romantic music of the late Georges Delerue. You could say that Boyle and I were born romantics.

I was proud of Boyle's speech to the colonel and the CIA station chief. It was blunt, to the point, and said everything I had to say about American foreign policy in third-world countries since World War II. I thought at the time I wrote it, This may be preachy, but look at it this way, Oliver, you probably won't get another chance to make a film like this again. So — say what you got to say with the resources you have. Make every film as if it's going to be your last breath on earth.

The fact that I'd written *Scarface* got us into the Arena Party headquarters in San Salvador and almost permitted us to get three-quarters of the film made there, using the best American technology that belonged now to the rebel-hunting Salvadoran army. This proposition fell through when our "adviser" was killed playing tennis.

The intelligentsia of our time, who I wish had supported the film, did not. I don't know if they recognized how difficult it was simply to get that film made at a budget of something like $2.5 to $3 million. It was nearly impossible, and next to my most recent film, *Any Given Sunday,* it was the most difficult and chaotic film I've ever shot, worth a book in itself.

PLATOON

The Vietnam War and Personal Experiences

I went to Vietnam in 1965 as a teacher of English, history, even mathematics, in the Chinese Cholon district of Saigon. The Chinese were, in general, a prosperous merchant class whose children were educated at this Catholic private school, the Free Pacific Institute, which I believe was connected to a fiercely anticommunist Taiwanese organization. I later heard that this organization was CIA connected and/or funded. The property-owning Chinese community felt threatened by the Communists and despised and feared them; remember that 1965 was also the year of the Chinese genocide in Indonesia, not far to the southeast of Saigon. These Chinese people ended up suffering greatly during the war and, envied for their financial success, were mistrusted by both the North and the South — my first serious run-in with jealousy as a controlling emotion of human affairs.

I ducked out to be a wiper in the American merchant marine. The wiper is the lowest skilled man on the ship. He cleans toilets and blows out the main boiler in the engine room twice a day; it was dangerous, and I was scalded several times. It's a job one used to be able to pick up in a foreign port without union papers, as the previous wiper would often desert.

I came back to the States and then went to Mexico, where I wrote a novel, *A Child's Night Dream,* which was published by St. Martin's Press in 1997. I also went back to Yale briefly, but then dropped out a second and final time. That's when I returned to Vietnam, "volunteering" for the draft, which meant two years of duty instead of three; I furthermore insisted on being sent to a front-line rifle company quickly, before the war would be over.

I didn't go because I was gung ho about the war itself. I think you have to see *Platoon* to understand this distinction. Gung ho implies Ron Kovic's marine attitude. I went because I wanted to go to the bottom of the barrel; these tendencies, I think, grew from the nature of my novel, which describes a nineteen-year-old man wrestling with death — as well as his own personal problems at home in New York City.

The day I arrived at the 25th Infantry in Cu Chi, I experienced a sharp reality check when I "cut point" (leading the platoon into the jungle, using a machete to chop through the dense foliage) for about six hours. I was about as tired as a living person can get; we were fighting the North Vietnamese Army (NVA) regulars, at first thinking that they were the Vietcong (VC). They were so light compared with us. I was carrying sixty pounds of equipment. I was overweight for the degree of Vietnam's humidity. In short, I wasn't really ready. But I got ready over the next few weeks. To survive, I had to. I was wounded quickly twice within three months of combat, stretching from September 1967 through the Tet Offensive in January 1968. I received the Bronze Star for valor in August 1968 during my stint with the First Air Cavalry Division. But my most surprising experience was probably seeing almost the equivalent of a civil war going on in every one of the four units I was in (three of them front-line combat units).

That tour of duty taught me, in some perverse way, that the enemy was truly in us. There was a vast difference of values in our culture, not only at home but also in Vietnam. For instance, there were the "heads" and there were the "straights" or "lifers." The heads were the guys who would do marijuana, which I came to believe was far healthier and meditative than alcohol on our bodies. It acted as a form of release for stress, which was something I tried to show in the movie — that "grass" was a means by which we survived and kept a portion of our humanity intact. Others were drinking, some heavily — all this "in the rear" base camps, of course. These men — we called them "straights" — were often, I found, the most dangerous people to be around, especially if you were a civilian. They were more likely to rape, kill, shoot, and burn down villages — if there was any evidence of civilian support for the NVA; sometimes these villages had no choice in the matter, as the VC and NVA put pressure on them, too. These men were the dangerous ones. If you were Vietnamese, you would've been worried if an American patrol came around. It was pretty tough to be a Vietnamese civilian at that time.

One important point I was trying to illustrate in *Platoon* was that the "heads," the guys doing dope, were maintaining some sense of their humanity. In war, we need that balance, let's say, between the masculine and feminine. We would decorate our arms with bracelets and bandannas and listen to "soul music"; we grew into the embodiment of an entire subculture, mostly black, whereas the straight, mostly white southern "lifers" were a drinking culture. I'm generalizing, but there was definitely more reward to be had acting as a "redneck" in one's appreciation of poker, beer, whiskey, or country music. Such pleasure in these activities would often lead to promotion.

As a result of that experience, I've come to believe in the power of the herb, cannabis, to heal and relieve the mind, and I wholeheartedly support its legalization in this country. It's a rotten deal for 50 percent of the space in our prisons to be filled with so-called "criminals," many of them marijuana people, most of them nonviolent, their "crimes" victimless other than themselves. Instead, we have become a culture of punishment. But punishment, unfortunately, has *nothing* to do with enlightenment.

In an essay I said that "I killed." To clarify that, I killed only enemy soldiers as far as I know. I say that because there was so much confusion in that war. But I didn't witness any My Lai–type killings.

In *Platoon,* they burned an entire village. But that was infrequent. Sometimes we would burn a hooch, or a section of a village, because we might have found some kind of NVA or VC supplies or markings. These villages were quite spread out, so you didn't have lieutenants and captains supervising everywhere. I think this might be misunderstood. We were not running around like the crazy rapists and looters pictured in the My Lai massacre. Murders occurred more in the context of walking through these villages, sundazed, irritated, and very angry over alleged paranoias, when sometimes one of our soldiers might randomly "pop a gook," an ugly characterization for killing something like a bug. Sometimes individuals, out of frustration over language barriers, would yell at the villagers to do something "*didi mau!*" ("now! fast!"), but the villagers would not understand, and then a frustrated soldier might beat or shoot that villager. In sheer anger, I once shot several rounds at the feet of a very old man to make him dance, squirm, and beg, as shown in the movie. I saw some near-rapes. Once I stopped two girls from being raped and, perhaps, killed. Another time I saved a soldier from drowning. I say this because in the continuing war for balance between life and death, positive, life-preserving actions were crucial to the survival of our individual souls.

But there was a great deal of killing, regardless. And, ultimately, killing Vietnamese did have an emotional impact on me, but not in the short term. In the short term, I felt all right. In the long term, it became a consequence you deal with for the rest of your life, because you *don't* forget.

I still remember the details vividly. I remember the moment — the man's face. Very rarely in modern combat, as the firepower is so huge, do you see the enemy's face or the men you might have killed. In this case, I actually saw the man I killed, with a grenade, trapped in his spider hole. In several other instances, I came face-to-face with the enemy at a frighteningly close distance of several yards. Those are the things you never forget — and you shouldn't. And yet, with everything else, with all the stuff I saw going down over there, the guys getting demoralized, the uselessness of it all, that's exactly what I tried to do — forget.

After I came back, I didn't protest and become militant as Ron Kovic did. Ron had been radicalized, particularly by his Bronx VA hospital sojourn. I went back to a weird world in the East Village in New York with no friends or contact with any veterans. I found myself in a highly civilized world ignoring the Vietnam War. It was a moneymaking world. President Johnson had refused to raise taxes for the war, and as a result, there was an artificial boom going on. Money was a new lifestyle in itself, as opposed to a means to an end. It was, in effect, a precursor to the 1980s. Nobody I knew even *talked* about Vietnam, making it a very difficult situation to return to. I lived in a small apartment with walls I painted red. I smoked Vietnamese grass and ingested plenty of unsupervised acid in what a psychiatrist might describe as highly negative situations — such as riding the subway for hours in New York City. I was, I suppose, by the standards of society, a "bad boy," but I eventually married and cleaned up my act by going to New York University film school on the GI Bill. I didn't want to think about Vietnam anymore.

But I couldn't help but see more and more protests on TV, everywhere. And then Nixon came in January 1969 and, contrary to his electoral promises, kept the war going for *four more years*. I thought at first that he was going to solve the problems as a right-wing guy who had the power to withdraw our forces with honor; it often happens that way in history, but he lied and kept the war going for various political reasons (see my discussion in the next chapter on *Nixon*).

At NYU, I was exposed to some of the radical thinking of the time and joined a cooperative in making a documentary called *Street Scenes*. Breaking all the rules of film hierarchy, we all declared ourselves equal — director, cameraman, sound man, and so on — a form of socialist filmmaking that didn't work at all. We filmed crowds in Wall Street protesting the Cambodian invasion and fighting with the reactionary construction workers ("America! Love it or leave it!"). They smashed several of our cameras. If anything, this symbolized, as did the film *Joe*, about a working-class stiff who didn't understand the deep change of values in this country, the cultural divide starting to happen in America.

But I don't think I was truly educated in liberal, progressive politics until 1975, when I wrote *Cover-Up*. By then, I'd done a lot more reading and talking to people experienced in the analysis of politics. I was mostly centered on building a career in film, driving a cab, working as a temp, as a messenger boy, and at a sports film company. Retreating into the romantic theaters of the French New Wave was a way of avoiding this madness. At first I defended our troops and, in vaguer fashion, the war, as Kovic did in *Born on the Fourth of July*. But by 1973–1974, I could no longer support this position. I wrote the first draft for *Platoon* in a burst in the summer of 1976, with the idea of putting down on paper some of my strongest inner feelings that I had never expressed before, not wanting to see them vanish down the accelerating memory hole. That was pretty much the film that audiences would see ten years later on the screen, and it was about as different from *The Green Berets* as a film could be (see Halberstam's essay, pages 112–16).

When we saw *The Green Berets* in an outdoor military theater in Cu Chi (or was it Cam Ranh Bay?), we laughed hard. Although it might have made a ton of money, the film was a disgrace and bore no connection to real war, as it showed the Vietcong dropping like flies beneath John Wayne's guns. Believe me, they were much tougher. It was like some awful World War II movie and wasn't taken seriously. But it does still show you the mentality of our country then. I felt the same reaction, actually, when I saw *Courage Under Fire* some twenty-five years later. Critics may have loved it, but I despised the film — the Arabs dropping, in close order, once again, like flies beneath our weapons. What rubbish!

The Army and the Marines

The marines were extremely different from the army in their approach to war. One thing I did not want to do was make "a marine movie," which is what I attempted later with *Born on the Fourth of July* (1989). There was a difference. Many regular army were draftees. The marines had a proud tradition, and at the beginning of the war, they were all volunteers. I don't remember in what year, but they later resorted to the draft as well. They seemed crazy to us, an organization willing to lose a few extra men in order to accomplish what could probably be done by being a bit more patient, using our overwhelming air and artillery support to weaken the enemy; not always, but more often than not, this latter strategy worked.

The marine tactic required that when you were hit by enemy fire, you didn't stop and call up "chickenshit" choppers in support (in any case, there weren't that many helicopters in support; that was also true for several army units, such as the 25th Infantry, whereas we benefited from many helicopters in the First

Cavalry Division). Instead, they went and took the enemy head-on. Many of us believed that the marines took far heavier casualties for that reason. In the army, we wondered why they abided by the age-old military tradition of a charge. They seemed clearly rock-headed to us in achieving their objectives, but they were respected and often feared.

Making Platoon *and Other Inductive Movies*

I didn't design *Platoon* as an antiwar movie. I simply didn't think in those abstract terms, because they categorize and kill off the ambiguities of this life experience. I was only thinking about making it true and gritty, from the inside out. As such, I worked as a dramatist, not as a historian. *JFK* wasn't about Jim Garrison. Garrison was the way in, and then the movie took on the larger themes of the Kennedy assassination and its consequences. *Natural Born Killers* began, in a way, by saying, "Why don't I try to make that genre one time? A road movie combined with the prison-movie genre." The result: a new hybrid. In any case, *Natural Born Killers* became something else, too. It grew. In the same manner, my recent football film *(Any Given Sunday)* has grown into something far more complex than when I started. But, whatever its design, *Platoon* came along at a time when Hollywood was still wary of making any films whatsoever about the enigmatic Vietnam War.

That was the nature of Hollywood then, and probably now. Francis Ford Coppola *(Apocalypse Now)* tackled it, but he tackled it in a Wagnerian, mythic way, as did Michael Cimino *(The Deer Hunter)*. Both were great films, but they were not exactly realistic, and that was okay with me, because *Platoon* addressed that niche. The success of both those epic movies certainly killed off the chances in the late 1970s and early 1980s of making *Platoon.* Jane Fonda attacked the war in *Coming Home,* but not many people went to see that movie, unfortunately, because it was very grim. But she did tackle it.

First Blood in 1982 and *Rambo* in 1985 were very successful. We can't forget them or their impact. It was especially difficult for an idea like *Platoon* to go up against the message these films were propagating. It was a tough time for me and my way of thinking. I was turned down on *Platoon* so many times I couldn't begin to add them all up. By the standards of that time, the movie was considered grim, and Hollywood didn't like "downers"; it wanted to make money. A "downer" might be the truth, but who cared? Hollywood wanted — and wants — to make money. Truth has never been an issue for most Hollywood people. But I eventually got lucky by hanging in there, and *Platoon* was finally made, not by an American company, ironically, but by a small British one, Hemdale, with some participation from Orion, an American distributor, both of which have, unfortunately, gone out of business.

Obviously, the movie reflected the impact of my Vietnam experience, but my childhood prior to Vietnam has had an impact, as has my life *after* Vietnam. I didn't traumatize my thinking over there, if that's what my critics mean. It was not an issue of arrested development. My life has moved through many different phases and types of films since then.

Tom Hanks, in *Saving Private Ryan,* had a strong Custer-like quality that he underplayed brilliantly. Hanks decided that he had to save, it seems, the whole Allied front by making that final stand at the bridge. The point was: *sacrifice.* I understood why when I saw Stephen Ambrose's name attached as a consultant to the film and knew right away that the movie was going to be about heroism. As such, I think that though the film is well made, it's ultimately a false movie in that regard. As a young man, I talked to quite a few World War II veterans from both the European and the Pacific theaters. I think the movie is false to the concept of what a platoon leader can achieve. I was in a fair amount of combat in three different units, and I think most men in combat are pretty much the same — except for specialized commandos. They would have thought that their leader was nuts and probably would have blown his head off long before the platoon had lost its fourth man. People simply don't want to die. And soldiers, whatever they say, are still human beings, no matter in which century they serve. They are *scared.* Patriotism can sometimes be, we finally find out, a highly dangerous emotion. And men who sense that they might die because of poor leadership turn on their leaders. In many ways, *Platoon* resembled the madness of Stanley Kubrick's *Paths of Glory* in its depiction of platoon warfare.

But Ambrose seems to be on some sort of sacred mission and, though he never served one day in combat, is certainly close to the cultural zeitgeist at this point in time. These cycles turn, however, and I only hope that some good historian comes along and deconstructs Ambrose's sentimentality and heroism as the distortions they are — quite like General Custer, in his way, which is probably Ambrose's best history. I still advise you not to go to war, Mr. Ambrose. Your deductive thinking may be in for a shock.

But to return to *Platoon,* I placed the actors in the charge of ex-marine captain Dale Dye for two weeks, night and day, for various arduous military exercises. I told Dale what I wanted done, then he carried out those orders, adding, with my permission, some very good ideas of his own. I wanted my actors to experience loss of sleep over a period of two full weeks. I wanted alternating three- and four-man foxholes. That way, on certain nights, the actors, rotating on guard a third or fourth of the night, could not possibly sleep well. I wanted night provocations — noise, attacks. I wanted pseudo-mortar rounds. I wanted my actors to have a 360-degree experience of war, as much as possible. There was to be no letup. This was not a base camp situation. The idea was: now you are in the field, you are at risk twenty-four hours a day. Two weeks is a very short time, but actors are by nature highly imaginative. I wanted them to come out of that boot camp in the Philippine jungle with the "thousand-yard stare" on their faces. That is *very hard* to achieve, but we did. I also hired Stanley White to help as Dye's master sergeant, a homicide detective for twenty-plus years who had been in Vietnam and was the basis of the Mickey Rourke character in *Year of the Dragon.*

I had seen too many World War II movies where people didn't look worried enough or tired enough or even young enough, for that matter. Screen soldiers, in general, were too old, and comfort had compromised that "thousand-yard stare." In the infantry, I remember that the dirt was embedded in my skin and became part of my body during the fifteen months I slept like a feather, on my nerves.

Barnes and Elias

Sergeant Barnes has become something of a legend. This is a fictional name. I couldn't use the real one. But I carried his radio for a short while, and I knew him a little. He was intimidating by any standard, as he'd been shot seven or eight times, and part of his face was demolished. He'd been hospitalized almost a year in Japan, married a woman there, *and then volunteered to return to Vietnam.* That's pretty heavy. He came back with thick, coarse plastic surgery added to his face, but he was certainly a good if cruel soldier, able to creep up on the enemy, and he certainly knew how to kill. He was, as in the movie, silent and almost Ahab-like in his desire for revenge.

Elias existed as well, but I used his real name, as he was dead and I regarded the role as a form of tribute to him. I was somewhat surprised, still, to see his full name on the wailing wall in Washington — Juan Angel Elias (we knew him only as Elias). His daughter wrote me a beautiful letter years ago, thanking me on behalf of her unknown father. He was a cross of Mexican, Indian, and American from New Mexico, I believe, a real rock and roller — sort of a Jim Morrison, fun-loving, handsome as a devil, with Tyrone Power looks, shiny black Indian hair, a great fighter. Like Barnes, he had put in two or three tours of duty. I met him in the Long Range Reconnaissance Patrol (nicknamed "LURPS") in the First Cavalry. They'd be dropped deep in the jungle, three to eight men, sometimes more. Functioning as reconnaissance parties, they would scout the trails with binoculars and call in artillery and retreat. They were not supposed to engage in combat, but there were times when they would be overrun and disappear into the jungle for days and days. After I left the LURPS to go to another unit in the First Cavalry Division, I heard that Elias had been killed in a freak "friendly fire" accident in May 1968. I was *stunned* that he would allow himself to die. Many mourned him. But it was the basis of his death that formed the fictional turning point of my film. I'd estimate that 15 to 20 percent of our casualties, probably more, were from our own "friendly" fire.

WALL STREET

I relied on a number of Wall Street successes and failures to help me authenticate the film's look. Also, my father worked on Wall Street most of his life and introduced me to many people of all value systems, creeds, and greeds. I still vividly remember the musty offices without light down on the Wall Street of the 1950s. We talked to crooks who'd been busted, to SEC prosecutors, pretty much to anyone with a story willing to talk to us. Kenneth Lipper certainly came in handy once we were ready to shoot and helped us approximate the many changing, modern details.

Several critics of *Wall Street* complained about its black-white moralizing. Some identified it as "Wall Street bashing." But if anything, in view of the responses I've received through the years, it seems to me the opposite is true. Gordon Gekko (Michael Douglas) turns out to be, perversely, the most seductive character in the piece. In the same way that years later Mickey and Mallory emerged from the cauldron of *Natural Born Killers* or, years earlier, Al Pacino in *Scarface,* Gordon Gekko became a devil, a Mephistopheles for the 1980s. And yet he was a hero to so many young people of that and this hyped-up time. People still come up to me all over the world, exclaiming, "Great movie! I loved Gordon Gekko!"

If he was so blackly painted, how was it that people liked him so much and Michael Douglas won an Academy Award as best actor in 1987? Is this black and white? His oft-quoted "Greed is good" speech is interesting, as he, at many points, represents a commonsense point of view. Sometimes the things that are the most dangerous to us are also the most seductive, as in the case of Charlie Sheen. The movie is about excess — the excesses of capitalism. My dad used to say that on paper, communism made sense, but capitalism, unfair as it might be, was the only thing that actually worked in the world's checkered history. He also warned that when taken to excess, capitalism would go out of whack. That's how cycles of boom and bust resulted.

What corporations have done to American life now is very dangerous. They're buying most everything in vertical and lateral diversifications, branching into specialized areas of work they are not, on the surface, qualified to work in; in an urge to heighten their specialized attractiveness to Wall Street capital, they're making subdivisions of subdivisions of divisions. Pretty soon we'll be betting on options of options. Needless to say, the morale of the employees and the inventors and the creative people has been diluted by this "fear of fear." It seems almost everyone in society that I know — judges, attorneys, actors, studio executives, writers, the upper, middle, and lower classes — are living in some form of fear, part of an interconnected system with a capital "S" that is highly subject to flux. When people feel that they work but are offered no security and thus can give none, and the prisons are as full as they are, and every political leader has to be a multimillionaire to win, when corruption and anger prevail, then that system has gone amok.

Martin Fridson on Wall Street

Fridson sets the film up as a target for things I never said; much more modest claims were made. To be held to this highest standard for a film with business as its background is a form of flattery, but in no way did the film proclaim itself an avatar of the 1980s. In the quotes that I've seen in preparing this essay, I referred repeatedly to tradition, especially to my father's viewpoint, which offered me a perspective on Wall Street going back to the 1930s.

I referenced the film *Executive Suite* (1954) several times; directed by Robert Wise and starring William Holden, Fredric March, and Barbara Stanwyck, it was a good film and probably the last serious business film that I'd seen. I wanted to renew that tradition, and on the heels of *Platoon* and the Oscar in May 1987, I plunged right in. I mention this because Fridson accuses me of opportunism in taking advantage of the October crash of 1987. I cannot help but laugh at how errant a notion this is, given the one to one-and-a-half years generally required to make a film. I would have to have been a great prophet, and if I were, wouldn't I have made a fortune first, at least enough so I wouldn't have to struggle to make my next film with some amount of freedom?

I always had a business film in the back of my mind. As a child, my father and I would walk out of a movie together and he'd usually say, "Huckleberry, we could've done it better!" And I'd ask how, and we'd argue about the plot and so forth, which turned into a fabulous learning experience for me at fourteen and fifteen. Whenever business was mentioned, Dad would say that the film was silly in this or that way and that the portrayal of the way business really works was not believable.

Also factored into my decision was my feeling that there was a sort of curse to the Oscar. If you look at the record, many directors don't work for a long time after they win one. It's hard to go back in, the likelihood being you'll never win again, at least "for a long, long time," as Richard Brooks once told me backstage at the Oscars. The fear of failure becomes a disease, like making the cover of *Time* magazine. That was all the more reason I wanted to get to work. I decided a long time ago, maybe after Vietnam, that I didn't want to live my life in fear and make my decisions in such a way.

I also wanted to make an honest business film that my father, who was gone by then, would have been proud of. I wanted to expand my film vocabulary as quickly as I could, as I had been struggling for almost fourteen years to make my own films. I had experienced much frustration and betrayal, and I wanted to make up for that bad time and move on quickly, in case it all ended, and put a lasting vision down on film. Thus I made ten films, several of them large of scope, over ten years in an effort that eventually exhausted me.

If you look back at the zeitgeist, the media at the time, seeking a simplistic tale of crime and punishment to reflect the October 1987 crash, actually tied *Wall Street* both to the crash and to the 1980s. But how and why would I make a claim that this was a definitive film? It hardly seemed such to me. On the contrary, the film reflected a spirit of expansion. I remember saying something to the effect that the Reagan years had brought a quantum leap of energy to America. I associated *Wall Street* in many ways with my script of *Scarface* (1983), wherein I saw the life in Miami — with its big, new, vulgar culture of money, the nouveau riche — as paralleling a Wall Street where the new players were kids aged twenty-five, thirty, making *millions* of dollars. It was unheard of. I guess it's no longer amazing with Internet capitalism. But it was certainly a new phenomenon then. In my father's day, men who made millions of dollars were few and usually much older.

My dad made me very aware of the white-collar scandals of the 1950s and 1960s, of people like Jimmy Ling, of the many stock scandals of the era, of the ultimate zero-sum game wherein capitalism dictated that there be more losers than winners. My father himself came out somewhere in between. As Fridson admits, there was a jump in the number of white-collar convictions for insider trading in the 1980s. Money became paramount, and in the pursuit of it, people were willing to break the law in great numbers, especially young people coming straight from college, with ethics like baby sharks.

Fridson's essay seems totally hooked on the negative. He doesn't address the continuing popularity of the film, which is on television almost every week. People seem to enjoy the film. I think of *Wall Street* as a *Scarface* of business, Gekko replacing Tony Montana in showing crooks in a new dimension. As the greasy mechanic in *U-Turn* (Billy Bob Thornton) said, "You think bad, and bad is what you get." I think the same is true for the Martin Fridsons of the world. He insists that I claimed *Wall Street* to be the definitive 1980s film. The media, as a result of the 1987 crash, interpreted it that way, but I am being dishonestly credited, as it was certainly not intended that way; nor do I think that the film was the definitive view of the 1980s. There were too many other things happening in that decade — Iran-contra and Reagan, for starters.

Fridson writes about "unspectacular ticket sales." That's another way, I suppose, of putting down a film that made $45 million at the domestic box office. That was a lot of money then, especially for a highly verbal film. It wasn't a huge hit, but it certainly was profitable for Fox and continues to be, judging from the steady volume of residuals through thirteen years.

There was, incidentally, an interesting background to this. Fox had two big films ready for Christmas release in 1987, but a studio generally doesn't want two of its biggest films competing against each other in the same season for the audience's brief attention span. For that reason, I think, Barry Diller (head of Fox) made a decision to dump our film out there (in some 1,500 to 2,000 theaters) near Christmas, while rolling out the well-made, more cultivated, and excellent Jim Brooks film *Broadcast News*. Given its large amount of insider dialogue and action, *Wall Street* was not a film to be distributed in Gainesville, Florida, in a supermarket mall on its first weekend. It just wouldn't fly. Not in Arizona or the Midwest, either. You're playing business roulette. But it was clear that Diller felt he owed Brooks's film the class treatment, releasing it to spectacular reviews and in slower motion — what was once called a "rollout," allowing the film to "build" until it had sufficient critical mass to allow it to be played in the Fort Walton, Floridas, and Indianapolises of our country, always in the hope that Oscars might bring further attention and money to the film.

It was thus sweetly ironic that, as it turned out, *Wall Street* was nominated for an Oscar, much to Fox's surprise, which at the time thought of Michael Douglas as more of a softer B star from television; and then Michael went on to win the Oscar. He has never looked back since. At the end of the day, the box-office equivalent for both films was almost similar. Yet I believe that we would have made more money if *Wall Street* had been released with more care.

So why not see the glass as half full? See the amount of dialogue throughout the film that addresses the audience intelligently. *Wall Street* was about a young man growing up, going through his own version of discovery of the corruption of life. Personally, it marked an ability to make other kinds of films, a broadening of my language and vocabulary. I don't believe that there has been a film since that has achieved what *Wall Street* has in this complicated realm of money and desire.

Fridson faults me for earning a grade of seventy in economics. Didn't Einstein flunk physics or math? At least I got a seventy; I could have received a fifty, as I did in Greek classics at Yale. Like geometry, it was difficult for me. I didn't have the aptitude. That doesn't mean I didn't understand the results of it.

Fridson claims greed to be the novel element in the film, but the Michael Douglas character never says that greed is a *new* phenomenon. In the stockholder speech midway through the film, he says loudly that "greed is as old as the evolutionary spirit itself." The speech, I believe, was a solid defense for a way of thought that characterized the hard practicality of my father's generation, the same World War II approach, based in common sense, that he learned from Eisenhower. Gekko was saying, look, we need hostile takeovers because the system is infected. Sick! These companies we're supporting are living on indulgence and fat, the arrogance and prosperity of the 1950s, and as a result, we've been overtaken by the Japanese and Arabs. We must *now* reshape this situation and make money for all stockholders, not just the rich few.

I perceived a piece of Kirk Douglas in Michael — the mental brilliance and opportunism of the immigrant. I had known Michael socially as an astute businessman but felt that he had softened his image in pictures and TV too much. I was looking for the Michael that would come across tougher, even nastier, on-screen. He turned out to be a fortuitous choice.

Charlie Sheen did research off and on for months prior to shooting. Yes, he was stiff, but he was also stiff in *Platoon,* and *that* is his acting essence, a quality that I liked. He was young, somewhat awkward, and in the presence of older men, and thus he behaved ultra-cautiously. Ultimately, he anchored the movie. I doubt seriously that Michael would've won the Oscar if Charlie hadn't been believable enough as that anchor.

Fridson includes a criticism of my depiction of pandemonium on the trading floor of the stock exchange. I worked one partial summer (1964) on the cocoa and sugar markets of old Paris, and I think anyone would tell you that the human mind is given over to fits of panic and chaos, especially when money is flowing rapidly between contracts due in Jakarta, ships stuck in Dominica, and financing staggered in London. With Ken Lipper's and coproducer Ed Pressman's stepfather's help, we were able to access the floor of the exchange, talk to the traders, and ask them to act out a hectic experience. I never implied that it was *always* hectic. If you remember the scene in the film, it's about the movement of a volatile stock. And when a small to medium stock like this *moves,* aggravated by insider rumor and outsider hope, it moves *fast.* In fact, the futures of entire countries such as Mexico can now be radically moved on any single day by forces way out of their control. So we find, as in war, boredom intermixed with swift, surprising action. The scripted scene from the movie was played by real brokers on the floor *during trading hours.* We were on the actual floor for about an hour and a half. This may well have been a first.

When Bud's dad, Carl Fox (Martin Sheen), speaks about "creating something," that was my father's favorite mantra. He believed in a Wall Street that
provided funds to business for research and development, which permitted him
to feel good about what he was doing. Fridson sees the film in simpler terms,
as a populist view of financiers as parasites. He misunderstands. I agree with
Carl Fox, but I also think that Wall Street is integral to our society, as it *can* do
much societal good, raising funds for important research and large cash-
needing enterprises. But, history being ambivalent, Wall Street also became a
haven for all the excesses of the 1980s and 1990s, an excuse to raid other people's
pockets for the enhancement of small clusters of individuals with no interest
in developing companies they had purchased on a short-term basis. This speed
of investment, sometimes in and out of "a position" within minutes or hours,
truly reflects a world that is, in all regards, impatient, highly secular, and judged
only by result — the means justifying any end as long as it is dollar profitable.
That, in effect, was the 1980s, symbolizing the great clash in history between
practical and idealist forms of behavior.

BORN ON THE FOURTH OF JULY

I think the militaristic John Wayne stereotype influenced many young men
to enlist in the military and support the war. Ron Kovic certainly was one such
person. I was more influenced by Tarzan, Errol Flynn, and Clark Gable, and
definitely Hemingway. And I tremendously enjoyed the James Bond stories by
Ian Fleming. I loved the rectitude of male heroes that, in that era, was a domi-
nating impulse. It certainly colored my decision to join up and go to Vietnam.
But that kind of idealism and romance quickly burned away when I actually
went into combat and saw how ugly war really was. I tried to show that side of
it — idealism meeting reality — but without losing sight of the Eliases, who I
thought of as the good guys, the heroes of my youth. Anyone who knows
better and makes of war a stirring, moving experience has made a fraudulent
movie. Such a picture becomes a cliché, for example, the commonplace World
War II movie. I particularly liked the Korean War films because they were so
cold and scary. For example, Anthony Mann's picture *Men at War*, with Robert Ryan and Aldo Ray, shook me deeply.

In the film, I tried to be as accurate and truthful as I could to Ron's memory
and mine. Several incidents and facts were changed, and some mistakes were
made. For example, there was no police breakup of a riot at Syracuse University, although there were numerous protests across the country against the
American invasion into Cambodia in May 1970, resulting in four killed by the
National Guard at Kent State and two at Jackson State; 440 colleges were closed

down or disrupted in early May. Though it was a stupid mistake on our part, and I apologized to the Syracuse police at the time in the media, it hardly reinvented reality to say that there was a vast upheaval in this country.

Nor was Ron Kovic gassed in Miami, though he was removed violently from the Republican convention hall while Richard Nixon was speaking, which was described in his book. That *was* the point — that Ron had come to Miami as one of the leaders of the veterans' movement and was front and center, ever the marine, trying to shout Nixon down.

He *was* gassed and beaten in a demonstration we did not dramatize — in Los Angeles, where he was betrayed by an undercover policeman, who appears in the movie at the convention. I did not dramatize the Los Angeles scene because of length. What is at stake here? The truth essentially was that Kovic was not given credibility by our establishment as a veteran of that war. And as a dissident, he was not encouraged to speak publicly. In fact, he was beaten and gassed in Los Angeles and silenced in Miami, where running confrontations with the police continued for days.

Nor did Kovic visit the parents of the soldier from Georgia he believed he killed in combat. This we freely admitted at the time of the movie's release. It certainly stands as a dramatic interpretation, but I believe it also has a broader meaning. In writing in detail to a large public about killing this man and how the Marine Corps covered it up, Kovic was releasing his innermost feelings on paper — which we *externalized* by having him tell this directly to the parents and wife of the man in Georgia, where they actually lived. Ron told me that he had thought of going there but did not. As the boy's name in the book had been fictionalized, one reason I believe he chose not to go was the renewed pain this revelation would cause them in knowing how their son actually died.

One could certainly argue that Kovic was scared of actually meeting them, for whatever reason, but to go to the lengths of misinterpretation that presidential candidate and TV opinion-maker Pat Buchanan did in criticizing the film was despicable. By suggesting that Kovic had never killed the man, that he had made it all up because the marine records didn't reveal so, is to overlook the obvious fact that in a war where we sustained well over 15 percent "friendly fire" casualties, the military records of that corrupt time continually attributed deaths, both American and Vietnamese, to fictional causes.

The point we tried to make was that Kovic found himself in Mexico in a hell of hedonism — a private world of girls, cardplaying, and drinking — and that by returning to his homeland, he decided to reenter the public arena. Confessing to the parents of the dead soldier was his first step toward reintegration. Raised as a Catholic, and convinced that he'd murdered his own man

("Thou shalt not kill, Mom, thou shalt not kill women and children") in a typically confused combat situation straight out of the pages of Stephen Crane, Ron experienced emotions of self-horrification aimed at everything he had ever believed about war — almost a perverse joke played on him by ancient gods. It was, next to his paralysis, perhaps the biggest single event of his life; he *had* to come to terms with himself. And that, I believe, was the reason he allowed himself to be hit in the spine by the second bullet that paralyzed him for life.

After that, driven by his Catholic guilt, he felt that he could acquit himself only by leaving Mexico and returning to his native land to join the public debate, enter the flow of history, and confess to the world in a book defining his actions; certainly the parents of the dead soldier would have been a part of that audience. Thus I believe that this is a valid and powerful form of artistic license. Perhaps to others it is the wrong sort of liberty, but to my thinking, it is *not*, as it follows in the spirit of Ron's tell-all book. This fundamental and risky usage of dramatic license is as strong an example I can think of to illustrate what a dramatist does.

THE DOORS

Jim Morrison is more than a talented musician to me. He's a Dionysian cultural figure, an icon, and a poet — a powerful poet. I think he is misunderstood. The trial in Miami destroyed him. I don't think he was guilty. What's really interesting about the movie — if you pay attention — is that it provides a chronology. The songs are in chronological order and change across his short but intense career. The songs represent the mood of his life in each chapter. The later music, which many people don't understand, I find to contain some of his most creative poetry. There are no easy simplifications. Is the film about a fallen star and self-indulgence? Not really, because I think that some of Jim Morrison's best work was at the end, when he was at his fattest, unhappiest (?), and sloppiest. Out of his death, Orpheus-like, arises this fertility. The *American Prayer* album, which frames the entire movie, is the key, I believe, to his character.

The movie also helps us recall extraordinary times, invoking young people to awake, to think for themselves. There was such a time when young people did so. It was okay. I wasn't saying that we should all die with him. Obviously, he was a creature of excess.

Excess, yes. But, strangely so, by living a larger life, you inflate your life, you learn and see more of life, and you die a wiser man. As long as you don't hurt other people. That's when it becomes an issue. Excess is a fragile line. At times

Jim did hurt other people. I think we each have to find the line for our own excess. I, too, have been a creature of excess.

Morrison, in a sense, had to be destroyed — like Dionysus, mutilated in order to be reborn. But I believe he did what he had to do in his allotted twenty-seven years. He lived out his karma.

Was the film a look at a sex and drug rebellion? Yes, in part, but that is not why I made the movie. I made it because I deeply admired Jim Morrison's honesty and artistry.

James Farr sets me up as another straw man when he claims that I pronounced the movie as *the statement* on the 1960s and that the Doors were the definitive band of the decade. I never claimed that the movie represented that era. It was a *part* of that era, that's all. In numerous interviews, I repeatedly stated that the Beatles were the mainstream group, and I described the Doors as dark, a special taste, like the American Rolling Stones.

Farr also implies that I believe in Morrison's incantations: "Break on through. Kill the Pigs. Destroy. Loot. Fuck your mother. All that shit. Anything goes. Anything." Again, a misunderstanding. It is past tense. I expressed these radical feelings in 1968–1969, coming out of Vietnam and the East Village in New York, when I was as close to becoming a political anarchist/revolutionary as I would probably ever be. I do not share those feelings now. Among other factors, my mother is far too old.

At further risk of repeating myself — as one wag said, "the reason I'm repeating myself is *you're not hearing it!*" — Farr should realize I do not consider myself a "cinematic historian," and never have. It still astonishes me, call me naïve, that a serious historian or, for that matter, any person would be so eager to destroy the integrity of another person's reputation by not researching and reproducing his quotes in the proper tense and with *full* context.

To learn about the 1960s, you need to look at, for example, Andy Warhol and Norman Mailer and the works of many others. I never intended to present the essence of the 1960s in one voice, as I am not capable of doing so. By example, I did pay homage to the music of the Temptations and Smokey Robinson and the Miracles in another of my films, *Platoon*.

As for "Unknown Soldier," I didn't use it because I thought it was one of their worst songs, and Paul Rothschild, the band's music producer and later the movie's music producer, agreed. It's literal, in my mind, and unnecessary in a film that makes amply clear Jim's rebellion against not only Vietnam but also the collapse of traditional values in the 1960s.

Farr says that Morrison is too serious. But throughout the film, we see Val Kilmer playing at various roles, putting on just about everybody, including the continuing mockery of himself as self-professed "clown." Ed Sullivan is certainly one of his targets, as are members of his band. He mocks and yet believes in the power of poetry in seducing Meg Ryan's character on a Venice rooftop. Later on a Hollywood ledge, he plays a game of death with her, demanding that she jump with him in order to prove her love. I think Jim is constantly putting people on in this vein of black Irish humor he had.

I read more than seventy-five transcripts gathered from people who had known Jim, provided per our contract with Jerry Hopkins, coauthor of *No One Here Gets Out Alive*.[2] These contained all the basic raw elements that were supposed to go into the book, but, in commercializing it, Hopkins ended up using little of the material — a boon to us, really, as it opened up a whole new reservoir of thinking. I don't think many fans of the film realize, partly because of the intense negative propaganda assiduously manufactured by band leader Ray Manzarek, that many of the scenes they think are pure fiction were actually based on these transcripts, which were as wild as stories go about any man — drinking blood with one woman, playing with knives and drugs, daredevil suicide stuff; there must have been thirty to forty women of different types, each with a differing view of Jim, in these manuscripts. The biggest mistake I made in my dealings was to composite too many of these women under the sobriquet of Patricia Kenneally, who later demonstrated that she didn't really understand the dramatic process of absorbing other women's actions and on one national television show stated her intention to strangle me and was rumored to be putting various curses on me. Another evil witch to watch out for in my life. With time, *The Wizard of Oz* grows clearer to me.

All kinds of people were represented, including people many others have never heard of who knew him from various sexual situations. It was eye-opening, as *Citizen Kane* was in its way, as each of these people had a varying awe, dislike, love, or jealousy of Jim. These extracts were priceless, as were my meetings with the respective families; the late Bill Graham, who smoothed the way; and the angry Ray Manzarek, who did everything in his power — to this day still does — to trash the film, which reignited a dead career and made him millions of dollars that he continues to accept. Still, *The Doors* script was always problematic, even when we shot it, but the music helped fuse it together. I rewrote it in the summer of 1989 in Santa Barbara, more as a tone poem than a normal screenplay. The concept was that the thread to his life was there all along in his lyrics. I picked the songs that fit and wrote each piece of the movie as a mood to fit that song. It was like a musical; in fact, I undertook it instead of a long-planned *Evita*. The motivations of the characters were murky to some, clearer to others. I trusted his lyrics to tell his tale. I tried not to put my rationalizations about motivations between us and those songs.

Morrison, hardly a mainstream personality, never Elvis-popular, was a self-professed shaman who listened to an inner state that he brought to the tribe in poetic form. A shaman must be connected to the earth, to the sky, to the holier forces. Yet Jim, taking the edge off his intensity, also saw himself as a clown; most witnesses attested to his sweetness, brilliance, and, of course, that sense of promise. Yet few realize how much he truly achieved in his short lifetime. I prefer to think of him as a holy fool, a contrarian in our tribe. Long may they live.

There's a great character I've seen in Chinese films, that of the crazy old warrior drunk on rice wine, weaving and diving and laughing, yet possessed of a total physical and mental consciousness with which to fight the demons. In Jim Morrison we had a man who was on a serious, death-framed quest. The success of simply being a rock singer would never have been enough for Jim Morrison. He was a changeling, his own god, in pursuit of his dreams and fleeing his furies. He did what he came here to do.

HEAVEN AND EARTH

I did not make this film in response to critics' complaints that my films neglected or denigrated the role of women. I wanted to make it because it was the completion of a cycle of stories that would at least give credit to the other side, which nobody had yet done in Hollywood. Our Vietnam movies had always been about Americans and, as such, were ethnocentric if not racist. Here was a chance to do something different. I found a story I grew to love when I read Le Ly Hayslip's book.

What intrigued me and ultimately compelled me to make the film was that strange combination of suffering and forgiveness in Le Ly, which became associated in my mind with Buddhism. That this spiritual practice allowed her to forgive the enemies who had hurt her so deeply amazed me. It was such a great and generous gesture of the heart and mind. I joined Nyingpa Buddhism as a result of it, which, I gather, is the wildest form of mountain Buddhism and at many junctures in its history has been fiercely attacked by other sects in an attempt, never without strong resistance, to outlaw it. It's a spiritual practice, born in Tibet from a rugged race of wild ways and wilder visions. My teacher, Kusum Lingpa, comes from there. Rinpoche Chogyam Trungpa wrote the best English documents I know of explaining Nyingpa; one such title, "Crazy Wisdom," illustrates the many and ironic contradictions that exist in this life. One of the qualities of spirituality is, as F. Scott Fitzgerald suggested, a fine mind's ability to hold two contradictory thoughts at the same time, its capacity to contain multitudes of feeling; the nature of contradiction itself is engulfed in the amorphous nature of "id" or "crazy wisdom."

The production itself was a major challenge for me. In the book, there were six or seven men involved in her life. I cut that down to one man — played by Tommy Lee Jones — only because of time, as the film was already two hours and twenty minutes long. Ultimately, in my opinion, there were not sufficient differences among these men to warrant different characters. Focusing on the one character also opened up the role for Tommy Lee Jones and thus helped finance it. He gave a very powerful performance in my opinion.

Le Ly herself was very supportive. I worked closely with her. She was on the set and was particularly helpful in the rural details — how to grow rice, how to live on the edge of a rice paddy, and so forth. We trucked Vietnamese refugees from northern Thailand to the south and trained them in the rice fields that we built with American "super rice."

The film was, unfortunately, a heartbreaker for me on its release on Christmas Day 1993. The reviews were dreadful, dismissive. But to this day, it is still one of my favorites, because it is tender and beautiful and still makes me cry in certain scenes, like the one in which the screen Le Ly comforts the despairing, suicidal Tommy Lee Jones character ("different skin, same suffering"). I still wonder, if I had been an Asian woman instead of a white American male, would the notices have been a little more generous?

NATURAL BORN KILLERS

Mickey and Mallory are in an impossible situation. They are born of a decadent culture. As for the argument of nature versus nurture, which appears in Courtwright's essay — I always saw it as a combination. I wasn't pushing one over the other. Mickey may say, "I'm a natural born killer," but I don't really believe him. I think that he has grown into one. They were raised horribly, so horribly that the only way to do Mallory's backstory was as a television sitcom. We had a canned laugh track over Rodney Dangerfield because you couldn't — you *wouldn't* — want a realistic depiction of Mallory's home life. I made the point numerous times to interviewers at the time that I had made realistically violent films in *Platoon, Born on the Fourth of July,* and *Salvador.* I said, this is not real. Why do you continue to say in your reviews: it's violent, it's violent, it's violent? That's obvious, now try looking again: you might see that it's also *looking at* violence in our contemporary society and *showing* at the same time, through its weird graphics and montage, just how nutty it's gotten. *NBK* is a frame for that looking. The fact that it's never been done like this is exactly what makes you look again and maybe *think* about where we were as a social collective in that mean decade we called the 1990s, with its emphasis on negativity, anger, and trivia.

Having just returned from making *Heaven and Earth* in rural Thailand, where Buddhism is practiced and nonviolence revered, I found myself back in America, as if a painter throwing up on a canvas that which I saw and powerfully felt — more tabloid news, more commercialism, more aggression, more media, more of everything that's rotten. I felt sick. It was also a personal time of searching for more honesty in my life, a time of divorce and pain.

Courtwright quotes me as saying that I wanted to have fun. Yes, I wanted to have fun — in the way a painter might play with and interpret chaos into surrealism. Fun not at the expense of a human being, but fun in the act of escaping a landscape of madness and culture wars, and of creating inside the mind. I never sought to hurt anybody. In all the much-ballyhooed news of copycat crimes emanating from *NBK*, not one shred of evidence has yet presented itself in court. Many kids *did* like the film, because it was different. It was also cut extremely fast; it was the most intricately cut film I've ever worked on. It was in the *JFK* tradition but went beyond it. It took ten months to edit. It was edited and concocted as a poem would be, with its own rules of thought and song. For me, and for several directors whose opinion I respect, it was a groundbreaking technical film. It had its own rules.

There were times when I was confused. I found it overly chaotic, and I was concerned at one point. I took the film up to Seattle with Warner Brothers' permission, and I previewed it for two audiences on two separate nights, to see whether they understood the movie, to see if I was, so to speak, "in the ballpark." We had good enough ratings on both nights to know that we were close. Then we made more changes to clarify some of the more chaotic moments. Essentially, we released it in the graveyard of the summer, late August 1994, probably because the studio was unsure of its prospects and everyone was running away from the widely praised *Pulp Fiction* by the same author of our original piece, who had publicly disowned *NBK* before having seen it. Yet we broke all records for that week of the summer. It was an $11 million weekend, which was pretty big in those days.

Courtwright says that some young viewers are emotionally if not technically out of control. But I wonder, why does *NBK* have to be understood by everybody in the same way? In a PG film, theoretically, everyone is supposed to understand it. But in adult films, more is allowable. Courtwright, in a sense, makes the same argument that many liberals make. It's an argument that's very dangerous to our American concept of a private conscience that cries out "leave me alone — it's my mind," as long as one can control it from hurting others. The argument, this time started by John Grisham, that *NBK* is a "defective product" starts with the assumption that one should take responsibility and *feel bad.* They'll defend your right to make it, yes, but only if you feel guilty — which is really another form of censorship. I refuse to give in on that. I say, look, I feel very good about the film; I'm proud of this damned film. It's one of the best films I've ever done. I can't be blamed for the literal interpretation of it by certain morons and unstable people, any more than the Bible can be blamed for its culture of violence. It just is the way it is. And moviemakers go as far as they can in reflecting what they feel and see and are sensitive about.

I see a culture essentially damned by television; a prison system that is highly punitive, with half its inmates there on drug charges and victimless crimes against the self; and a police force bordering on that of a police state. The Fourth and Eighth Amendments are nearly gone. "Due process" is a joke to any poor person. And now the First Amendment is about to go on trial, all to the amusement of media that want to sell products and just love a fight — *any* fight. It doesn't matter if it's your basic freedom to express yourself at stake. In fact, if you say that you are protected by the First Amendment, you are often jeered at by the media for using it as an excuse — as if you *needed* an excuse; you *don't.* The First Amendment is written in stone by the hands of our founding fathers.

In this ugly mix, Mickey and Mallory Knox are antiheroes who come out heroes to those who empathize with them. This is often the case in films, but few give the film credit for allowing the possibility that these two kids *change.* And that includes Courtwright.

There are two parts in the film. The road movie ends with the bust in the supermarket. The second part consists of the prison sequences and the breakout. In the first part of the second half, Mickey (Woody Harrelson) joins Mallory (Juliette Lewis) in expressing his feelings of change. He's writing a letter to her. Through the wall, we see her dancing. And you hear the words he is saying. Mickey is not the brightest guy in the world, but he's saying that *he is feeling things he's never felt before.* Prior to that, when the Indian shaman (Russell Means) was killed, Mallory had undergone an abrupt shift of consciousness, yelling, "Bad! bad! bad! bad!" at Mickey, meaning that she, too, had felt, *for the first time in her life,* the sacredness of this life. From that point on, Mickey and Mallory have only one desire in the world: to reunite their love. They are essentially no longer interested in killing. They kill from then on only as a means to escape their modern prison, wherein the system is so corrupt and dehumanized that the warden (Tommy Lee Jones) puts out a contract on their lives. The final murder is perhaps their most climactic, in that it involves Wayne Gale (played by Robert Downey, Jr.), representing the media, which has so debased

American culture. Mickey tells Wayne he's going to shoot him. Mickey doesn't know why, but he's going "to make some sort of statement."

So Mickey and Mallory kill him, leaving the camera running on empty, as they make good their escape into the underground, where they never have to kill again. And then they are seen in a van on some American highway, with newborns, living happily ever after in a Rousseau-like state of innocence.

If Mickey and Mallory had been the same couple in the second half that they were in the first, that would have been a movie without hope for me, without redemption. I doubt I would have made that, sucker that I am for a higher meaning to our lives than its short brutishness. I'm American and French. It's a weird mix. My mother was Catholic and my father Jewish. I don't share a lot of the same guilt patterns that our Anglo culture seeks from its citizens. I'm beginning to see America as this weird split between North and South, between the English side of us and the Italian-Spanish-French side of us. Alongside the African Americans, the Asians, and the Native Americans, this country is constantly shifting shape, growing, absorbing, and reinventing itself. Yet the crux of the establishment in thought and power comes from Britain, the British-American connection. This baffles me, because it was the French who helped us the most during the Revolution. Yet the French are often disliked by Americans and naturally ridiculed by the media.

We have become a culture of fear and punishment. We have more people in jail than ever before. We have this exaggerated fear of drugs and sex while we exalt our love of firearms, hunting, patriotism, property, and money. It's a love of barbaric behavior. And there is great pride in that. I witnessed it on the football field in my new movie, *Any Given Sunday*. It's a tough culture to grow up in as a kid. You are either on the football team or you are not. There was a reason for those kids at Columbine High School to do what they did. I think they felt discriminated against, pushed around. They decided that they were going to do some pushing of their own. Being pissed on, they got pissed off. But in the end, much of this supposed "copycat behavior" is media inspired. The television news is addicted to showing violence for ratings. The news often references *NBK* because it's an easy film to reference, but they're missing the aesthetic. It *did* have a following, but more because it was a light show, like *Fantasia*, like *2001*, than because it was a model of behavior. The movie had a striking acceleration of imagery. I called it "splinters to the brain" at the time.

John Grisham took up this line about product liability. If an idea, an illusion like a movie, can be deemed a defective product and can be sued as such in our society, then we must realize that this could destroy the basis of our culture — all works of art, pseudo-art, wanna-be art, whatever art, it doesn't matter. Take Beethoven's angry symphonies and say they drove you to madness, that you killed because of it, and that you are therefore not responsible for your own behavior. Twinkies made Dan White kill Harvey Milk. What will America come to when everyone sues everyone else? It will be paradise for lawyers, but also a sickness. Perhaps we can start taking responsibility for our own lives by mandating that if you sue and lose, you have to pay the defendant's costs of defending himself — with some limits set to prevent large corporations from using money to win inside the justice system.

The interview between Mickey and Wayne in the prison is based on an unedited version of a Geraldo Rivera interview of Charles Manson done many years ago. Rivera puts himself in a morally arrogant position; he clearly thinks himself a better person than Manson, as he ignores something very intelligent about Manson. I'm not saying that Manson isn't warped; he is. He grew up as tough and as cruelly as any child could, but he did not actually *kill* anybody. He talked about it, that's all, but that was enough, apparently, to set off the actual murderers. In the power of his eyes, Manson's like the fictional Hannibal Lecter. In being so much brighter and cunning than the superior Geraldo, Manson gave me the idea of Mickey playing mental chess with Wayne and coming up with some pretty interesting ideas about the recognition of violence in each one of us. It is one of my favorite scenes.

In saying that "goofs abound," Courtwright is not aware that I did not set out to be realistic, as in *Platoon, Born on the Fourth,* or *Heaven and Earth.* They were purposeful goofs, satiric in intent. Satire, by definition, is a work holding up human vices and follies to ridicule or scorn. I'm glad Courtwright at least notices when we flash "too much TV" across Mickey's and Mallory's torsos. The rest, I think, eludes him totally.

He says that there are sophisticated people who will get the film, but he worries about the kids who say, like the teenager on "American Maniacs," "Mickey and Mallory are the best thing to happen to mass murder since Manson." This puts us all at the feet of the lowest common intelligence in the audience. Most "products," then, would have to be on the order of a Jerry Lewis/Adam Sandler comedy, because once you enter this arena, *everything* is PG-13. We worship at the feet of our children. We regulate for their purpose. This is wholly wrong, and it makes children out of adults, not the reverse.

If you are raised with a sense of values by your parents and teachers with a sense of the spiritual, however it's achieved, you would have no interest in hurting or taking the life of somebody else. You would know that murder is bad. Your moral values system would have been set on its foundation. You would never cross that line. You also would know that movies are sometimes wildly exaggerated — Jerry Lewis or *Natural Born Killers.* Sometimes, of course, these movies are a little sneakier in thought than comedies — and they become *satires.* And sometimes these movies play with subversive ideas. The kids talking about Mickey and Mallory in the movie are not necessarily killers. Very few people actually commit violent crimes, and when they do, we generally find a long trail of evidence going back a long time.

How can Courtwright disagree that there was plenty of murder on the old frontier? In nineteenth-century America, people were randomly and barbarically killed. There was much homicide in American history way before television.

Courtright says: "It's even harder to work out where *NBK* stands on the problem of evil, a stumbling block if we're to take it seriously as a religious work." I would refer him to the interview between Wayne and Mickey, in which Mickey defends his point of view. But I think Mickey is incorrect in describing himself as a natural born killer, because he is not. We have in us the killer brain, but we also have a culture that has moved away from that violence. Yet we still seem to possess the remnants of the old brain in all aspects of our culture, up to and including war made by respectable men in establishment positions.

In that same voiceover, Mickey wants "out." He wants to go away somewhere and have a family and never kill again. So if that's an answer, it's not an easy answer. That's why I cut the other ending, the killers receive their just deserts ending. It wasn't due to the reasons Courtwright ascribes. It's because I really felt they should get away. There had to be some hope for the future. They were the new Adam and Eve in the way that our contemporary society is remaking us into pre-cyborgs. Although Mickey and Mallory had killed in the old culture, now that the media were dead, they would be the new model parents for a new culture.

The other ending was shot essentially as a "prevent defense," partly because Warner Brothers was nervous, and partly because I was not sure. A film is a journey, and where you end is not necessarily where you think you're going when you begin. If it is undertaken in good conscience, no finer experience can happen to a filmmaker. It has always been "the Hollywood ending" to have the killers killed in the end.

When I asked my fourteen-year-old son the other day, "What do you think? Should you be watching these violent video games?" He said, "I think it's just the opposite. If you don't have them, you're more dangerous. I go to those video games a lot, and they're violent, but after I finish them I feel released."

I did take the unedited long form of the film and I mixed it, as I sensed it was going to be cut somewhere along the line. Warner Brothers still has that print in a vault somewhere. Few have even seen it, as Warner refused to release it theatrically. They don't realize its value. I tried to take that version to

England but eventually showed it on tape to the British censor, who said of the original cut, "This film is far more clearly a satire." In exaggerating and holding for a longer time on certain sometimes gruesome imagery, the film made its point, that of a satire. By cutting it, the censors made it harder to understand its intent.

In an essay I wrote for the press kit at the time of release, I described my intentions in part at that time:

When we set out to make *Natural Born Killers* in late 1992, it was surreal. By the time it was finished in 1994, it had become real. In that warped season, we saw Bobbitt, Menendez, Harding, King, Buttafuoco and several other pseudo-celebrities grasp our national attention span with stories of violence, revenge and self-possession. Each week America was deluged by the media with a new soap opera, insuring ratings, money, above all, continuity of the hysteria.

Tomorrow — tonight — Mickey and Mallory Knox can happen, without doubt. And they, too, would have their hour in the sun — and, by the next two issues of *TV Guide,* would give way to the next predator in the ratings war, which, like the polls that monitor the President's daily popularity or whether or not we should send troops to Ruritania this month, become some sort of the equivalent of the "popularity contests" we all had to suffer through as kids. The desserts, as I remember, never went to the deserving but to the gossiped about, which is more important to the American psyche than to be perceived as an A student. The scientist, as we learn in our culture, is unknown; Billy the Kid is not. Only the Greeks created great victims in their dramaturgy — Elektra, Medea, Antigone, and Oedipus we are not. But we are a species that inflicts, we are a people who do unto others — Vietnam, sports, lawsuits come immediately to mind.

Violence is salvational in the American epic tradition (at least it was in James Fenimore Cooper and Jack London and Ernest Hemingway), the law of survival, the natural law, now perverted by the politically correct PG access of "family entertainment" safely preaching to us that violence is incorrect. Is it? Or is it the way of the world where, under every peaceful blade of grass, tiny yet feral bugs devour other bugs in cycles of destruction and creation?

On *Nixon* and *JFK*

NIXON

Stone on Ambrose

Stephen Ambrose complains that I have Nixon drinking too much and using foul language. Co-screenwriter Steve Rivele counted the number of drinks in the film, and they were of an insignificant amount. Perhaps Ambrose was confused by the framing device used in the film — that of cutting in and out of Nixon alone in the Lincoln Room of the White House, reliving his life through this *one* night. It's not that we thought that Nixon was a heavy drinker at all; he was hardly in Winston Churchill's league (but who was?). What we were trying to show was a man who reflected the notorious tensions of his last year in office. Most likely his slurring had to do with the medication he was taking for the phlebitis (blood clotting) in his leg; Ambrose, I think, misses the humor in the opening sequence of Nixon awkwardly trying to open his pill bottle, then dropping them all over the floor and crawling around after them.

Ambrose says that H. R. Haldeman told him that he had never seen Nixon drunk. I had to laugh. Haldeman, the vigilant Doberman pinscher of Nixon's regime, would say anything that a good number-two man in any corrupted organization would say. Support the boss at all costs, even if it means jail time, which in Haldeman's nightmare of a case came true. And, by the way, only in jail did Haldeman go public with damning comments about Nixon's involvement in the enigmatic Bay of Pigs incident — which Ambrose discounts because it does not fit the theme he has deduced from Nixon's life.

The film was also much criticized for its foul language not only by Ambrose but also by loyalists and others. It took Stanley Kutler of the University of Wisconsin five years of litigation to gain access to the presidential tapes, and it is through his valuable historical contribution that 200 additional hours were released.[1] (Forty hours had been released in April 1974, providing us a broad outline of Nixon's "abuse of power and obstruction of justice.") At last we discover the angry labyrinth of Richard Nixon's world, his brilliant mind often interrupted by a rough and brutal language, in keeping with his paranoid and lonely character. Ambrose argues that Nixon mostly used "damn." Not really — it's "Goddamn!" or "Jesus Christ!" or "shit!" and "cocksuckers," the latter sometimes in reference to "the Jews," whom Nixon set apart in a category of almost personal enemy; in general, he seemed to characterize groups of people in a racist way, often referring to "wetbacks," "kikes," and "wops." No wonder Nixon fought so hard to keep these transcripts from public view. Even the president's congressional allies, his friends, and friendly columnists were appalled. Senate minority leader Hugh Scott called this vocabulary "shabby, disgusting, and immoral"; Vice President Gerald Ford found it "a little disappointing"("two-inch" Ford is always reliable for euphemism and damage control [see my comments on *JFK*]); William Safire, a longtime Nixon speechwriter before he became a conservative *New York Times* columnist, thought the conversations revealed a man "guilty of conduct unbecoming a President." The Reverend Billy Graham, a strong supporter, could not "but deplore the moral tone implied" and was dismayed that "situational ethics" had infected the White House. (What is "situational ethics"? If he means the context of the job, then is it not the president's higher purpose to rise above such Mafia-like talk?) I believe intuitively that Nixon's physical inferiority (his football experience at Whittier College, for instance) left him enamored of tough-guy language and made him act tougher than he really was. (Or is such conjecture allowable by Ambrose's standards? Aren't all historians frequently compelled to engage in such conjecture?) This is why Nixon delighted so much in the hard-nosed football analogies of a coach like George Allen of the Washington Redskins. He was one of Nixon's heroes, as was the character of General Patton, played by the indomitable George C. Scott in the movie that Nixon watched several times on the eve of his decision to invade Cambodia. So, on this matter, when Ambrose says that Nixon's language was mild in comparison with that of Truman, Eisenhower, Kennedy, and Johnson, I think he borders on the ridiculous.

Ambrose speaks of padding our footnotes in the Nixon book. If anything, people in my position know that anything we put out may come back to haunt us one day. Footnotes are no different, especially as we knew that we were going to be judged in a community of scholars. In fact, I sometimes now feel in writing screenplays that I err too much on the side of reason at the expense of the Dionysian, dramatic side being held in check.

Since my qualifications to interpret the past are often dismissed on the basis that I am not a historian, we should raise the issue of Ambrose's qualifications and remember that he is a problematic, conservatively oriented biographer of Eisenhower and Nixon (the former he reveres greatly, the latter he finds near-great). Yet both biographies omit substantial shadow areas in each administration, which is a disservice to present and future students of this time; more importantly, these biographies are taken by the gullible mainstream media as authoritative. This is far more dangerous to the minds of students than any single movie I could concoct out of toads, livers, and whatever witchcraft Ambrose thinks I practice. I say this not only for public reasons but also for private ones. I find many of Ambrose's statements about me ("fraudulent," "peacocklike display of his scholarship," "his basic contempt for real scholarship") offensive as well as highly subjective and ideological — not at all a proper historian's language. Lastly, it should be noted that Ambrose, who often celebrates martial figures, has never served one day in combat.

Ambrose also complains about the film's fictionalizing of Pat Nixon seeking a divorce. Haldeman, Woodward and Bernstein, and Fawn Brodie all mention it. Several staff members have been quoted about the Nixons' icy relationship, going back as far as the 1962 gubernatorial loss in California. Their relationship was perhaps the worst-kept secret in D.C., that lovely town on the Potomac of arranged marriages and discreet heartbreak. The columnist Bob Scheer, one of our consultants on the film, also helped us in describing their relationship from his interviews with both Dick and Pat independently. Their marriage was, in any age, by any standard — Arabic, Chinese, or American — one of "face," respect paid, children well raised, the rewards of a life lived on the surface where nothing is wrong, except that everything is wrong in the picture. In other words, as with much of Nixon's life, don't look too closely.

One aspect of this life is the fierce defensive perimeters put around it. The estate of the late president has been adamantine in its legal battle with the government over the tapes. I even recall Nixon, then an old man, going out of his way in an interview with David Frost to attack *JFK* without, of course, having bothered to see it, claiming that I was making up things about Kennedy's Vietnam policy that I hadn't even said. Again, the straw-man approach. Similarly, his daughters, Julie and Tricia, attacked *Nixon* a few days before its release in nationally prominent news stories, although they hadn't seen a frame of it.

Ambrose is certainly correct when he says that we invented the dialogue of Mao telling Nixon, "You are as evil as I am." Their dialogue was probably perfunctory and broken down by diplomatic protocol into small, specified, and more prosaic categories — or perhaps not. We certainly can be faulted for being wrong, but *not* for taking the dramatic liberty. Our reasoning for this was that Mao, known for his peasant bluntness and bemused by Nixon's passive position, may have acted with caustic "face" in dangling the carrot of official recognition. Nixon had risked much in coming, and he needed to return with something major in his pocket. The late Harrison Salisbury portrayed Mao, perhaps unfairly (much disinformation exists on Mao), as an escalating opium addict during the 1950s.[2] Under the influence of morphine and aware of his forthcoming demise, Mao might conceivably talk bluntly (see my response to the issues of literalness in historical drama in chapter 3).

Regarding the assassination plots against Castro, this is very difficult to penetrate and understand. But I have no doubt whatsoever that Nixon knew of the invasion plan in 1960 before he left office as vice president. Richard Nixon said it himself in 1964: "I had been the strongest and most persistent advocate for setting up such a program."[3] And he told Kennedy after the Bay of Pigs that the best move would be "to find a proper legal cover and go in."[4]

Newsweek's Evan Thomas challenged our reading of *Nixon* in this matter:

> Legitimate historians have wondered about Nixon's role in the assassination plots against Castro, but no one has offered evidence directly linking Nixon. Stone cites two sources. One is H. R. Haldeman, who wrote in his 1978 memoir, "The Ends of Power," that during Watergate he suspected that Nixon was obsessed with a CIA plot that somehow led to the assassination of JFK. But Haldeman later disavowed this version. . . . Stone's other source is E. Howard Hunt, who wrote in his memoirs that Nixon played some kind of supervisory role in CIA operations aimed at overthrowing Castro. . . .
>
> It is impossible, of course, to absolutely dispose of Stone's elaborate theory linking Nixon, the CIA, the mob and the Kennedy assassination. Nixon did eventually learn of the assassination plots, possibly after he became president, and it's true that the White House tapes recorded him saying that an investigation of the CIA's role in the Bay of Pigs could produce a larger scandal. "You open up that scab and you uncover a lot of pus," said Nixon. But in the movie, Stone conveniently cuts out what else Nixon said: that the CIA plots "have nothing to do with ourselves."[5]

In reference to this latter statement, when you listen to Nixon on tape, you should be aware of how he hesitates, fumbles, and then repeats himself as if in retreat from his first statement. He often seems to be catching or watching himself, remembering he's on tape for the public record. Yet he conceded after his resignation that he never thought these tapes would be made public and that they were intended for his archival use only. His behavior thus straddles contradictory emotions throughout the tapes — pure work-oriented dialogue, fear, confession, shame, anger, and finally denial. If Thomas finds it "convenient," that's a dramatist's judgment call; we are faced with dozens of those decisions in any given scene. But even so, Thomas's argument is disingenuous at best. As discussed in my comments on *JFK*, Kennedy inherited the plot and all its antecedents of intervention from the Eisenhower administration. Furthermore, in any reasonable military plan to invade a country, it must be considered of paramount importance to assassinate the leader of the enemy and, in so doing, perhaps avert the need for an invasion and the subsequent loss of life. If Eisenhower condoned going after Hitler in World War II, then why not Castro? It would make sense to the military mind — as would the dropping of the A-bomb on Japan, canceling out the need to invade. But I don't personally believe that JFK would have condoned the assassination of Castro, particularly as he nixed the October 1962 Pentagon-planned invasion of Cuba in favor of a protracted back-channel negotiation with Cuba through individuals such as United Nations Ambassador Adlai Stevenson, New York lawyer James Donovan, ABC news reporter Lisa Howard, and French journalist Jean Daniel.

Toplin refers to two sources I use to back my interpretation of the scene. However, it is actually four, possibly five sources that we noted in the book of the movie, including General Robert Cushman (who became deputy director of the CIA under Nixon), a man widely noted for his loyalty to his commander in chief through the years. Cushman also performed the key role of Nixon's military aide in the 1950s, and then served as Vice President Lyndon Johnson's military aide, strangely enough, *during* the Bay of Pigs. It was Cushman who told Hunt in 1960 that Nixon was the "project's action officer in the White House." Nixon himself becomes a source later, as previously noted. The fifth source would be Eisenhower, who had instructed when the operation was authorized in March 1960 that "everyone must be prepared to swear that he has not heard of it."[6] In fact, when Eisenhower and Kennedy met the day before the inauguration, a meeting that I gather did not go well, judging from Eisenhower's facial expressions the next day on television during the inauguration, "'President Eisenhower said with reference to the guerrilla forces which are opposed to Castro, that it was the policy of this government, to help such forces *to the utmost*' . . . it was his recommendation that this effort be *continued and accelerated*."[7]

Beyond the fact of E. Howard Hunt writing in his memoirs that Nixon had played some kind of supervisory role in CIA operations aimed at overthrowing Castro, we have the surprising revelations of the post-Watergate Haldeman coming "to understand that 'the Bay of Pigs' was really a code word for the assassination track. In all of these Nixon references to the Bay of Pigs, he was actually referring to the Kennedy assassination . . . to the cover-up of the CIA assassination attempts on the hero of the Bay of Pigs — Fidel Castro; a CIA operation that may have triggered the Kennedy tragedy and which Helms [and Nixon] tried desperately to hide."[8] Think about that for a moment: Haldeman himself breaking down to reveal this. Why?

Ambrose simply dismisses Haldeman's claims by telling us that Haldeman later retracted this statement from the book. How easy — but Ambrose neglects the charismatic effect Nixon had on Haldeman and that this retraction came only *after* Haldeman had been released from prison and had an awkward rapprochement of sorts with his former, now penitent boss. It is a trait of subjective historians — and dramatists, mind you, whether for good or ill — to use those quotes they like and dismiss those they do not, and then justify it. Why doesn't Ambrose work backward for a change and allow for the fact that Haldeman said what he said and follow inductively the implications of that?

Amidst the thousands of hours of tape, why is it that, to the best of our knowledge, just this one 18½-minute gap is missing when the talk is getting interesting? What is being acknowledged by this? Or by Nixon's recoiling at the mention of Howard Hunt working for the White House? What was the "hell of a lot of things" he referred to in the underlying "scab" he didn't want opened? Why did Nixon constantly refer to the Bay of Pigs as something he didn't want exposed, even though it took place under a different president, one from the opposing party who had defeated him? Why did he ultimately resign his presidency instead of revealing what he knew? Again, we're in "magic bullet" or "neuromuscular reaction" territory. To quote Nixon accurately, "this is sort of a comedy of errors, bizarre . . . Hunt . . . knows too damn much and he was involved, we have to know that. And if it gets out . . . this is all involved in the Cuban thing, that it's a fiasco, and it's going to make the FB — ah CIA — look bad, it's going to make Hunt look bad, and it's likely to blow the whole, uh, Bay of Pigs thing, which we think would be very unfortunate for the CIA and for the country at this time, and for American foreign policy, and he's just gotta tell 'em 'lay off' . . . I don't want them to get any ideas we're doing it because our concern is political."[9] As if dogshit were stuck to his shoes, Nixon continually circles this same subject: "This involves these Cubans, Hunt, and a lot of hanky-panky . . . you open up that scab and you uncover a lot of pus." This is what we said in the movie, but what Nixon actually said was, "you open that scab there's a hell of a lot of other things in it that we just feel that this would be very detrimental to have this thing go any further. . . . This involves these Cubans, Hunt, and a lot of hanky-panky."[10]

Ambrose says of the 18½-minute gap, "We do not have to assume anything. Haldeman's handwritten notes on that meeting exist." Is Ambrose saying that he buys the Haldeman theory of history? Does that mean he also believes in toto the memoirs of Henry Kissinger? As there is no questioning going on, this is just not serious history to me. It seems that Ambrose is so conservative and respects authority so much that anything a general or a secretary of state says is final. This is a serious flaw in a historian. It's almost as serious — if it were not so blackly funny — as when Haldeman asks Nixon in our movie, "How is this national security?" To which Nixon replies, "Because the president says it is. My job is to protect this country from its enemies, and its enemies are within the walls." It reads quite hilariously on paper, but when you actually dramatize it, with a star player like Anthony Hopkins giving it the wonderful human edge he does, it becomes even funnier, and in fact clearer. That is one of the deep joys left to me — writing and watching drama employing living beings.

Although Nixon was a statesman for peace, trained in the footsteps of Winston Churchill and Charles de Gaulle, both of whom he much admired, by the end of his life he had failed to reach his objective because of the flaws in his character. This is ultimately what the movie is about. I've grown to think that if Kennedy was prologue, then Nixon was epilogue, and that the framing device — of using these two powerful young men to understand our country in those turbulent years — has probably given me as much satisfaction in my work as anything in my lifetime, comparable to completing the three Vietnam films as a cycle. As with Kennedy, I finally believe that there was a fundamental mystery about Nixon, the dark man of the sonnets and secrets, part paranoid Macbeth, part wholesome, fear-struck Quaker, and much more, all of which he took with him to the grave. It is this quality that is important, not actually who said what to whom about what, what the Bay of Pigs meant or didn't mean, who Hunt was, or the Cubans. *Nixon* was not about conspiracy and layers of reality, as was *JFK*. It was about a conspiratorial mind-set that destroyed the greatness in a man.

Ambrose says that I think the United States is "rotten" and that I want to "change the country." Change the country? I must wonder why that prospect worries Ambrose; there is also a vast assumption on his part, as he has no evidence whatsoever — except for my radical remarks in 1969 following my duty in Vietnam. At the risk of repeating myself, I have great love for this country, and I believe that my movies have had a positive impact on it, raising points and asking questions that merit an answer or an investigation. I did — and do — want to see many things in this country *change,* and there is certainly nothing wrong with that, unless you have a society of silent consent and planned conformity. Ambrose truly reveals himself with the line, "He wants to change the country." Presumably Ambrose does *not* want to change the country, and in so stating reveals the true inner meaning of the conservative movement in this country, abetted by men such as him with falsely nostalgic journeys to the American past of Lewis and Clark and the Second World War. Why cannot these men, locked to a past, fearful of the future, confront the harshness of the present?

Nixon and Covert Operations

Roberts and Welky say that Nixon may have been involved in the Bay of Pigs "in some way," but it's a point they don't pursue. In fact, the only point of evidence that says he was not involved comes from Richard Bissell, a veteran of the cold war CIA, denying that Eisenhower or Nixon knew anything. Naturally, that's who Ambrose believes, when in truth we should trust Bissell about as much as we do Allen Dulles, who was fired by Kennedy, to serve on the Warren Commission; Dulles told the commission nothing of the secret war against Cuba. Talk about a fox in the chicken coop. Is Bissell going to betray his president? Of course not. He was a loyal man, at least to Eisenhower and Nixon, but I'm not so sure about Kennedy. There's just too much counter-evidence to Bissell's prevarications; he cannot stand up to the known results of our foreign interventions during the Eisenhower administration. Bissell died recently and never had to account for his apparent gangsterism on the international scene. Nor will Richard Helms — at age eighty-six, one of the nation's last keepers of the flame — unless he is questioned and investigated, which, given his aura of respectability, I highly doubt will happen in this day and age.

But we should not forget that Nixon had often been to Cuba in the 1940s and 1950s and maintained a strong relationship with conservative Florida Senator George Smathers (to the extent that Nixon could enjoy intimacy with anyone — even with Bebe Rebozo, hardly a word was spoken). Nixon was also an intimate of the Dulles brothers (John Foster and Allen), even something of a protégé as a vice president, and had periodic, almost weekly meetings with them. He was probably the most operative vice president we had up to that point, insofar as Eisenhower was perceived to be the Reagan of his day — a grandfather president who played golf and napped, although I believe he was far more active than people gave him credit for. Nixon was the worker bee, going around the world, getting to know everybody who counted, promoting American interests and covert activities in the name of anticommunism, espousing the domino theory in Asia, Africa, and our own backyard in South America, all in serious preparation for his presidency in 1960. By that modus operandi alone, Nixon *had* to know of the covert missions in these various countries, unless, of course, he was the equivalent of Vice President Dan Quayle in 1988–1992. But by all accounts, Nixon was brilliant and involved. Ex-president George Bush evolved in the same manner, professionally upbeat, generally smiling, revealing only the tip of the iceberg. Like Nixon, Bush — vice president, then president, ex-CIA chief, ambassador to China and to the UN, Yale man, oil man — stood at the heart of our empire. As vice president, he performed some of the dirtiest work for President Reagan, particularly in the oil-rich countries of the Middle East. Similarly, there should be little question in the detached observer's mind that Vice President Nixon was in the loop on Dulles's numerous covert missions, particularly as he wanted so badly to be president. The assassination attempt on President Sukarno of Indonesia, for instance (some say the target was really Chinese Premier Chou En-lai, which I find quite believable), could have been another possible by-product of his trips to Asia. And when he finally became president, Nixon — in getting rid of Salvador Allende in Chile in 1973 and fomenting a huge civil war and reign of terror in that country — was really going about business as usual. He'd had quite a lot of practice, under Ike's wing, in the 1950s.

Ambrose implies that I am saying that Nixon was in some way "in" on the assassination of JFK. Nothing could be further from the truth. What I was trying to express was that two Kennedys had died by the time Nixon came to office in 1969, paralleling in a strange way the deaths of his own two brothers in his youth. I think there is great significance to this. This is not to say that he was responsible for the death of Kennedy, but that, as with his brothers, it was through their sudden deaths that he was given the mantle of leadership, which can lead to a vastly accelerated pressure on oneself to succeed, resulting in a syndrome of suffering known as "survivor guilt" — the notion being that one's success is due to the death of another. In an important scene with Haldeman set in the Executive Office Building, I tried to show that Nixon must have had *some* feelings about Kennedy's death and *may have felt somewhat responsible* because of his deep involvement in the Cuban campaign prior to Kennedy's arrival, which may have resulted in blowback and the president's murder. Furthermore, the death of John may well have necessitated Robert's demise in 1968, which, given the strange circumstances of his murder in Los Angeles in 1968, is still open to speculation. As there was a strong likelihood that antiwar candidate Kennedy would have beaten Nixon at the polls, this opened the door for Nixon's presidency, a very interesting theme that I believe was first raised by Fawn Brodie in her book *Richard Nixon: The Shaping of His Character.*[11] I think the importance of a state of near–civil war existing between Kennedy, Nixon, and the country, as well as the opening and closing effects of their presidencies from 1960 to 1974, is something historians have not paid enough attention to, without ideology restive in the background.

In all those newsreels we saw in movie theaters as kids, it seemed that Richard and Pat Nixon were always traveling the world, waving and smiling in prearranged photo opportunities, but then one sweet day in 1958, we were mystified and a little shocked to see rocks thrown at them in Venezuela and their car almost upturned. The innocence in us wondered why the crowd was so anti-American? Perhaps because "you can smile and smile and be a villain," as Hamlet, a fiction, once put it.

Ron Rosenbaum summed it up poetically in his review in the *New York Times Book Review* of *Inside the Oval Office: White House Tapes from FDR to Clinton,* by William Doyle:

> He fails to do justice to the deepening and darkening picture of the Nixon Presidency that has emerged with the release of hundreds of hours of new tapes since Nixon's resignation, most recently those transcribed and published by Stanley Kutler last year.
>
> But it may be true that no single book can ever do justice to the encyclopedic dimensions discovered, the fathomless depths of the Nixon character. He contains multitudes and complexities, and the more we read of his tortured conversations and his tormented soliloquies, the more he becomes not just another beleaguered President, but a dark mirror of the American character. It is worth noting that any citizen can — and really should — pay a visit to the National Archives Repository in suburban Maryland just outside Washington, and listen in to Nixon's Oval Office tapes. On a recent trip, I felt myself mesmerized listening to the President's tearful, shaken, half-slurred (you can hear the ice rattling in his whiskey glass) appeal to Billy Graham for absolution of his guilt for firing those closest to him (Haldeman and Erlichman) to protect himself from the consequences of crimes he ordered them to commit. This experience confirmed for me a feeling about Nixon and his tapes: the window they offer into the poisonous alchemy of self-aggrandizement and self-loathing that led to his destruction makes Nixon, more than anyone, the author of the great American novel of this century.[12]

These words encompass eloquently the reasons I wanted to make this movie. At the center of our century — along with Wilson, the two Roosevelts, the Kennedys and Reagan — is this lonely man of high idealism, paradox, corruption, and mystery, the bete noir of American politics.

Stone on McGovern

George McGovern, interestingly, points to the screen Nixon in contending that disengaging American forces from Vietnam, without domestic political upheaval from the Right, was his most difficult political achievement. We gave Nixon the benefit of the doubt in a scene on his favorite yacht, the *Sequoia,* one night out on the Potomac discussing the imminent Cambodian invasion with his inner circle. Herein he lays out his concept of appeasing the Right by "triangulating" the Soviets, Chinese, and Vietnamese through means of the Vietnam War — its most important aspect being to *divide* China from Russia over their competing support of North Vietnam. Crediting this cold war motivation as well as their natural disinclination to lose "face," many feel that Nixon and Kissinger dragged the war on for four more years.

This behavior makes me wonder again and again why a political hard-core minority has such power over our country. And why do men like Nixon or Kennedy or Johnson or, more recently, Bill Clinton continually cave in to the fear of the Right as if it were necessary to prove their toughness? It truly illustrates that proverbial Roosevelt quote: "We have nothing to fear but fear itself." Why, when they finally reach the heights of the presidency of the United States, instead of the great soaring freedom of the eagle, must they chain themselves down like Nixon's Prometheus, forever churning in the morass of their compromised humanity, searching for forgiveness? There was forgiveness all along. It was in Nixon — if only he could have seen it and forgiven himself. Why take four more years, 35,000 American boys, and a million more Vietnamese with him?

George McGovern saw this because he lived it — the perplexing strength of the Right, which effectively destroyed his political career. What is this political grouping, really? It is a minority of idiosyncratic interests, disguised by their moral superiority, coming together to block change. They are malevolently sour about a world changing way too fast for their taste. People like Richard Mellon Scaife, contributing to Tom DeLay and Newt Gingrich, claiming to know God better than the rest of our nation's misguided pagans; widows with inherited millions; religious zealots; lobbyist machines; and corporate coffers have contributed to the vastly inflated importance of special interests on our political landscape. When and how shall we ever break this cycle of dependency? With an electoral sweep of a third party? With laws against distorting financial influences in elections? Or with another revolution, some 250 years after the first?

McGovern has written a generous essay. There are many cynics in the journalistic profession who have no idea how *one kind word* can motivate a dog in the corner, cringing from the stick, to try again to be a great and trusting dog. Similarly, generosity of spirit knows no bounds when it comes to healing the soul of a nation.

George McGovern endured the humiliation of defeat with great grace. I think he would have become as fine a president as we ever had, if only. . . . But nonetheless, I am deeply honored by his insight.

JFK

Stone on Kurtz

Michael Kurtz says the newly released documentary evidence from the Assassination Records Review Board provides "a kind of defense for Oliver Stone." I think more important than my defense is the information in those documents, which probably would have never seen the light of day, at least in our lifetime, had the film not caused the uproar it did.

This is an important legacy for the film. Kurtz is correct that although no smoking gun has come out on either side of the debate — who, after all, would put such a "black op" on paper? — there's a clear historical record of a cover-up taking place. If not for the release of these documents, we'd never have known about ex-president and Warren Commission member Gerald Ford altering the placement of where one bullet entered Kennedy, *raising it two to three inches* from the upper back to the lower neck, to provide a stronger case for the Warren Commission's Oswald premise. That's clearly tampering with evidence. We'd never have heard the conversation between President Lyndon Johnson and Senator Richard Russell in which they both admitted to not buying the Oswald lone gunman theory for a single second. We'd never have known that Warren Commission member John J. McCloy (former U.S. high commissioner to Berlin and chief disarmament adviser to Kennedy) was never satisfied with the lone gunman resolution. This was one point I was trying to make in the movie: why were these files kept from the public's eye, unless they flew in the face of what the commission was trying to promote?

Kurtz says that I fail to mention that all the advisers who pushed Johnson in the escalation of 1965 were originally men that Kennedy had put into positions of power, such as McNamara, Taylor, and Bundy. Also, Michael Beschloss's *Taking Charge* claims that Johnson was deeply troubled by the pressures placed on him by the Kennedy men, who wanted to turn Vietnam into a full-fledged war.[13] Really? Johnson had such a hard time that on Sunday afternoon, after burying Kennedy, he went to the first meeting of his new administration, as shown in the film, and what was it about? Vietnam! He was not postponing business, was he? Why not? On the day of the president's burial, could he not *wait* a day? In that meeting, Johnson reassured his generals and staff that he was committed to Vietnam — from which meeting NSAM 273 resulted.

What about these advisers? X, who was played by Donald Sutherland, was mostly based on Colonel Fletcher Prouty, a twenty-three-year career military officer and flyer who spent nine of those years in the Pentagon as the first-ever "focal point" officer between the CIA and the air force for clandestine operations, per National Security Directive 5412. He often briefed the Joint Chiefs on CIA plans and would have been at the "nerve center" of the most secret enterprises of our military-industrial complex; at various times, he met with Secretary of State John Foster Dulles at his home for private briefings, and later briefed Allen Dulles of the CIA. Prouty resigned his commission in 1964, in disgust over what he considered a cover-up in the murder of John Kennedy.

X implied in the film that Kennedy was ahead of his chief advisers because he was doubting what he was hearing. Why, for instance, was he continually sending civilian observers to Vietnam as his eyes and ears? Prouty personally expressed to me his strong doubts about both McGeorge Bundy (national security adviser) and General Maxwell Taylor (chairman of the Joint Chiefs of Staff), particularly Bundy's canceling of American air strikes in support of the jeopardized Cuban invasion force at the Bay of Pigs, *without* discussing it with Kennedy. Taylor was an ambivalent figure, back and forth on Vietnam. He was against it; then he was for it. Major John Newman, who had more than twenty years' experience as a military intelligence officer when he became a consultant to our film, also highlighted Kennedy's doubts about the Pentagon in detail in *JFK and Vietnam*.[14]

NSAM Argument

Roberts and Welky argue that NSAM 273 reaffirmed the policies of NSAM 263. *Not at all.* There is a very important distinction between the two in terms of semantics, which altered the nation's path toward war in Vietnam, and a seismic change in tone from 263 to the follow-up memorandum to 273, issued in January 1964. From late November to January 1964 — in just two months — we find a significant reversal of policy in regard to the U.S. commitment to Vietnam. How so?

On October 5, 1963, a meeting was held in which the Pentagon and the White House discussed the possibility of removing troops. Robert McNamara (secretary of defense) and General Maxwell Taylor had just returned from Vietnam and had authored a memo (dated October 2) that offered their recommendations for a new policy. This meeting, in turn, led to the writing of NSAM 263 (dated October 11), which distilled the McNamara-Taylor memo with JFK's own viewpoint.[15]

The first paragraph of 263 asserted that the ensuing policy statements were to remain classified *at the highest levels,* which contradicts the Roberts-Welky argument that this was all a public relations ploy. The second paragraph was the operative one. There were two points that were to serve as new U.S. policy: the first was that 1,000 troops would be withdrawn by Christmas of 1963. Roberts and Welky acknowledge this but ignore the second point: *that all U.S. personnel would be out by the end of 1965.* The second portion of this paragraph again stipulated that no formal announcement should be made in regard to this policy. Why?

Either Nixon or Goldwater was the likely candidate for the Republican nomination in 1964 over the liberal, divorced Nelson Rockefeller, and Kennedy didn't want to be attacked for "losing" Vietnam in the same way that the Republican Right had, in the 1952 election of Eisenhower, successfully accused the Democrats under Truman of "losing" China in 1950. This was a familiar refrain of the cold war, although we never "had" either China or Vietnam in the first place.

The third paragraph of NSAM 263 referred to telegram 534, which had been sent by the State Department to Ambassador Lodge in Vietnam. This cable gave final U.S. acknowledgment that the coup against President Diem was going to take place. When this coup backfired and Diem was killed, Kennedy was by all accounts shocked.

NSAM 273, written by Bundy, was very specifically worded and subtle. Formalized on the day Kennedy was buried, 273 stated that we would retain the objectives of U.S. policy with respect to the withdrawal of U.S. military personnel *as stated in the White House statement of October 2, 1963.* This was referring to the McNamara-Taylor draft, which didn't use the specific language of withdrawal that reflected the direction JFK wanted and added on October 11.

The referral to October 2, as opposed to October 11, yielded major ramifications. In fact, by the end of 1963, although there were several pseudo-withdrawals, troops being rotated back and forth as they were later — in the secret Central American War of the 1980s — there was to be no 1,000 troop withdrawal. In other words, in those nine days, Kennedy had taken a weakly worded recommendation from Taylor and McNamara and turned it into a far stronger policy without stipulation, and after his death, his wishes were being sidestepped.

The wording of the January 22, 1964, Memorandum For the Secretary of Defense (Follow-Up Memo to NSAM 273) written by Taylor, presumably with the full support of the new president, displayed an assertiveness absent in either 263 or 273. Its purpose was "to make clear the resolve of the President to ensure victory over the externally directed and supported communist insurgency in South Vietnam. In order to achieve that victory, the Joint Chiefs of Staff are of the opinion that the US must be prepared to put aside many of the self-imposed restrictions which now limit our efforts, and to undertake bolder actions *which may embody greater risks.*" It continued: "To do this, we must prepare for whatever level of activity may be required, and being prepared, must then proceed to take whatever actions as necessary to achieve our purposes surely and promptly."[16] This, in effect, allowed for U.S. covert troops — SEALs, Green Berets, and so forth — to infiltrate North Vietnam alongside South Vietnamese commandos. All this *less than two months* after JFK's assassination? And there's no difference? I can't imagine a greater swing in intention than that expressed in these two documents, 263 and the Follow-Up to 273. And what did this Follow-Up lead to? Of course, to our increased covert warfare in the

North, leading to the inevitable friction that prompted the alleged North Vietnamese strike at the U.S. vessel the *Maddox* in the Gulf of Tonkin on August 2, 1964 — which, through time, has been revealed as a bogus instigation that, as President Johnson desired, resulted in an unofficial but legitimized (by Congress) "CIA war" in Vietnam.

Perhaps the most disturbing aspect of this skullduggery, aside from the war itself, was that so many people in power, who knew better, would say that there was no difference between 263 and 273. Remember — it is important — that NSAM 273 *never directly referred* to NSAM 263. It referred to the meeting — the White House statement of October 2, 1963 — *nine days before.* It was a crucial distinction that subtly set us on a course of war the very Sunday afternoon that Kennedy was being buried, as the nation watched through the smoke of the funeral pyre, too distracted to notice that not all the faces were crying.

It is clearly my belief that Kennedy would never have allowed us to escalate our commitment so disastrously in Vietnam. Roberts and Welky claim that the conciliatory speeches I quote were anomalous. If speaking on network television with Walter Cronkite and giving Senate majority leader Mike Mansfield his word were "anomalous," then what would have constituted normality to these two? We have McNamara's observations on this in his book *In Retrospect: The Tragedy and Lessons of Vietnam.*[17] We have Arthur Schlesinger, Jr.'s. We have Kennedy's groundbreaking American University speech, where he called on the Soviets, as well as Americans, to reexamine their cold war ideologies, reminding one and all that "in the final analysis our most basic common link is the fact that we inhabit this planet. We all breathe the same air. We all cherish our children's future. And we are all mortal." We have Ted Sorensen noting in his 1965 book, *Kennedy,* that in November 1963, Kennedy was eager to make clear our aim to get out of Vietnam. Sorensen said that Kennedy had always been doubtful about the optimistic reports filed by his military.[18] Finally, there was Robert Kennedy in 1968 speaking frankly to his press secretary, Frank Mankiewicz, later a publicist for our film. He confided to me that Robert Kennedy, a critic of the Vietnam War, had come to question the official account of his brother's death and indicated that if he won the presidency, he would initiate a new investigation.

JFK, the CIA, and the Bay of Pigs

Kennedy had learned a searing lesson from the optimistic prognostications he had received from the CIA on the Bay of Pigs; as a result, I believe, he was applying a "two-track" approach to Vietnam. He was going along with the CIA and the Pentagon (which, it should be noted, were also divided on this enterprise), but with the probable intention of turning on them if the 1964 election became a strong personal mandate. This is the way politics is played, "two tracks" at the same time, as we often do in our own personal lives, even using several parallel tracks when necessary. Schlesinger admits that "Oliver Stone's premise in *JFK* is far from unreasonable. There is strong documentary evidence as to his [JFK's] long-run purpose. From the beginning to the end of his administration, he steadily opposed repeated military recommendations that he introduce an American expeditionary force."

Former Speaker of the House Tip O'Neill (who took Kennedy's congressional seat) was told by Kenny O'Donnell, a close adviser to the president, that Kennedy always planned to withdraw the troops after the 1964 election. O'Neill saw this as obvious, commenting that Lyndon Johnson was under the influence of Pentagon officials to a much greater extent than Kennedy had been. O'Neill, in his book *Man of the House*, interestingly pointed out that Kennedy, an Ivy Leaguer who had served in World War II, was more inclined to question authority than Johnson, who was enamored of tough talk and cowboy ethics.[19]

I once met Kennedy's defense secretary, Robert McNamara, and remember his evocative parting comment to me on his president, "I shall never look on his like again." He has since written a book in which he said bluntly that Kennedy would not have gone ahead with the war. Whether he knew that in 1963–1964 is another question. McNamara was pictured at the time as a "whiz kid" technician, a doer rather than a thinker, but whatever he was (and I am sure it was complex), I found him, at age seventy-nine, to be deeply meditative on his historical role. I felt sorrow for him in his effort, born of the highest idealism, to come to terms with his dark past, one of "the best and the brightest" of a generation that had crashed, so ironically, on the primitive, rocky shoals of Asia.

Kurtz writes that Robert Kennedy made frantic efforts to conceal the seamy side of his brother's administration, going so far as to ask for the complete removal of all files from the Oval Office and other locations before the new president arrived back from Dallas. In my opinion, the reason Robert Kennedy went for the official line from 1963 to 1968 was that he simply could not let the CIA-mob assassination attempts on Castro be discovered by the American public of the 1960s. Not only would it have blackened the memory of his dead brother, who at that point was a martyr, but it also would have kicked back to the Eisenhower-Nixon administration, which had begun the invasion plot against Cuba in March 1960. At that time, in 1963, it was *unheard of* for an American president, much less the American government, to be involved in subverting foreign governments.

Yet all along, as a materially rich but spiritually poor nation, we were living inside the framework of a corrupt and clandestine culture, the birthright of the Nazi "big lie." From 1948 on, the CIA had been seriously violating its "national security" charter. President Dwight Eisenhower, the ex-general and, ironically, of German descent, was perhaps the primary agent in allowing this state of affairs to be. There is some question about this, and many would argue on Eisenhower's behalf. But many others have no doubt that in some way Eisenhower allowed this culture to be set up and said okay to it. (My father, a devoted Republican his entire life and a wartime lieutenant colonel on Eisenhower's financial staff, always used to mutter as he threw down the newspaper that Secretary of State John Foster Dulles was really "running the country." And after General Walter Bedell Smith, whom my father knew and respected, along with "Ike," left the CIA, John Foster's brother, Allen, fittingly became director of the agency — that is, until Kennedy fired him.) Schlesinger writes:

> Who authorized the CIA to try to murder foreign leaders? The answer remains obscure. In the [Patrice] Lumumba case [the elected prime minister of the Congo], Eisenhower said something in the meeting of the National Security Council that at least one person present understood as an assassination order. . . . The Castro authorization is even less documented. Richard Bissell (at the time CIA Chief of Operations) assumed that Allen Dulles had cleared the idea with Eisenhower, using a "circumlocutions approach" in order to maintain "plausible deniability." . . . Dulles must have glimpsed a green light somewhere in 1960. Could it have been flashed by the Vice President of the United States? "I had been," Richard Nixon said in 1964 of the invasion project [Cuba], "the strongest and most persistent advocate for setting up and supporting such a program. . . ." Brigadier General Robert Cushman, Nixon's military aide and later his deputy director of the CIA, described Nixon to Howard Hunt in 1960 as "the [Cuba] project's action officer in the White House." "Apparently," H. R. Haldeman later wrote, "Nixon knew more about the genesis of . . . the Bay of Pigs than almost anyone."[20]

Of course, it was Nixon's own continual allusions to the Bay of Pigs on tape that remained singular to the heart of the Watergate affair. The CIA, pure and simple, had *no* business on American soil, and when the *New York Times* got wind of training and personnel camps not only in Guatemala but also in Florida and Louisiana, it assented to a Pentagon request to probe no further. It would have been so *unlike* Nixon's customary behavior regarding anything having to do with containing communism for him not to *know*, in some detail, of all these illegal maneuverings on American soil — especially as it was he who had brought the Castro "communist" problem to Eisenhower's attention. Kennedy, meanwhile, seemed to have only limited and incomplete access to these plans. Richard Reeves, a critic of *Nixon* in a front-page *New York Times* cultural piece, and certainly no ally of Kennedy's contribution to our history, wrote in *President Kennedy: Profile of Power*: "Kennedy had been briefed twice about the CIA plans, but he knew few of the details except that there were more than 1,000 Cubans being trained by the CIA in Guatemala. The operation had been authorized in March, 1960 by Eisenhower who had instructed, 'Everyone must be prepared to swear that he has not heard of it.' The idea was to duplicate the U.S. role in the covert overthrow of two leaders who might have been hostile to their interests, Premier Mohammed Mossadegh of Iran, in 1953, and President Jacobo Arbenz Guzman in Guatemala, in 1954."[21]

Reeves goes on to say, "A month later when he had been President for three weeks Kennedy read another piece on the exiles in the *Times* and dictated a morning memo to McGeorge Bundy. 'Has the policy for Cuba been coordinated between Defense, CIA, and State? Have we determined what we are going to do about Cuba? If there is a difference of opinion between you and the other agencies I think they should be brought to my attention.'"[22] This indicates that Kennedy was clearly out of the loop here, which raises two questions: (1) Was Kennedy really briefed in any detail by the CIA about Cuba before the famous third debate between Nixon and Kennedy? Nixon claimed that this betrayal of information on Kennedy's part lost him the 1960 election. (This claim, conversely, makes it clear that Nixon must have known about our Cuban plans in some depth in 1960 when the debates occurred, which is something Ambrose and others continue to deny.) And (2) Did the CIA continue "off the shelf" to try to kill Castro, using the mob and various other methods right up to the meeting with its newly recruited assassin, AMLASH, in Paris on the day Kennedy was murdered, *without* seeking even the tacit permission of the president of the United States?

This issue raises hackles on both sides of the ideological barrier. I have tried to approach this, as a member of a younger generation, inductively and with detachment. Bear in mind that I was once an eighteen-year-old boy at Yale endorsing Barry Goldwater, heckling Hubert Humphrey, and disliking Democrats because my father did. Schlesinger says confidently that Kennedy knew nothing; Ambrose and other Kennedy haters say that he was steeped in blood, conveniently forgetting the Eisenhower-Nixon role in this mess. But I can't help feeling that Ambrose and his fellow conservatives, who seem to be flourishing these days in their mainstream media attempts to destroy Kennedy's real meaning to the American people, despise Kennedy for his military failings at the Bay of Pigs particularly because, they claim, he blamed it on Eisenhower. Yet as a young man, I distinctly remember Kennedy going out of his way to apologize directly to the Cuban exiles at the Orange Bowl in Miami in December 1962 (some say that this speech sealed his death warrant). Eisenhower was spared any public questioning on this matter, as he had always possessed the respected traits of aloofness and, most importantly, gravitas; in sharp contrast was the sweaty workmanship of Nixon, who was fortuitously dismissed from the national political stage after his 1962 gubernatorial defeat in California.

To the detached mind there can be no question that we sought to destabilize more than a dozen foreign governments in the Eisenhower-Nixon years. William Blum's excellent book *The CIA, A Forgotten History* details operations (primarily CIA related) during the Eisenhower years in British Guiana, Cambodia, Chile, China, Burma, Costa Rica, Guatemala, Indonesia, Iran, Tibet, the Philippines, Ecuador, and Vietnam.[23] Nor should we forget the impact and intent of the "Eisenhower doctrine" in the Middle East, conferring upon our government the right to intervene militarily in the countries of that region.

One day in June 1953, John Foster Dulles, waving a secret memorandum, announced to a group of top D.C. policy makers, "So this is how we get rid of that madman Mossadegh," the left-leaning prime minister of Iran who was one of the first leaders in the region to question Western hegemony over its oil interests. Did this make Mossadegh a "madman?" In Dulles's book, yes — as well as a communist; he had to go. Apparently no one in the room objected to his departure, according to Kermit Roosevelt of the CIA in his book *Countercoup*.[24] There were no probing questions as to the consequences; no legal or ethical issues were raised. The subsequent overthrow (and later execution) of Mossadegh in August 1953 was an American-only initiative, whereas only a few years earlier President Truman had insisted that Mossadegh be kept in power to prevent a Soviet takeover of Iran. Our actions ultimately led to the shah of Iran being overthrown in 1979 and the revival of Islamic fundamentalism throughout the Middle and Near East, a disastrous result.

In Asia, particularly in China, Burma, and the Philippines, we became much more involved than before. While we supported the Nationalist Chinese who had found a home in Burma, the Red Chinese invaded in 1961 as a combined force with the Burmese to successfully throw out the U.S.-supported Chiang Kai-shek forces. Burma subsequently denounced the United States and moved closer to China. But Burma was not the only jumping-off spot for CIA-organized raids into China, which had good reason to be paranoid of us, as would the North Vietnamese later that decade. There have been continual, never-dismissed stories of our practicing bacteriological warfare in China during the Korean War. The Chinese claimed that they killed 106 American and Taiwanese agents who parachuted into China between 1951 and 1954 and captured 124 others. We maintained this futile program of covert espionage until at least 1960, with the same frustrating results as our venture into Chinese Tibet, which helped ignite the Tibetans and led to the exile of the Dalai Lama. To this day, some continue to blame the Chinese for this, while ignoring our own efforts to destabilize the Chinese regime from Tibet, Taiwan, and other places. I think we must ask ourselves why so many of our interventions have backfired. The wheels of justice, they say, grind exceedingly slowly — but they grind exceedingly fine. Blowback has a conscience.

In Vietnam, we should remember that Eisenhower's administration heavily supported the French war and for some time seriously considered committing combat troops. And we prevented elections from being held in 1955, under UN supervision, in order to stop the clear favorite, Ho Chi Minh, from uniting the country under his form of agrarian communism. It's astounding that Ambrose continues to defend Eisenhower by implying that he could be so innocent, so dignified, and so above it all as to golf and nap *through eight years of major foreign interventions.* The same was said years later by our media about Ronald Reagan when he was president — how old he was, how out of touch. But we now know that Reagan was a far smarter fox than people gave him credit for, and he most certainly knew what he wanted internationally. In the minds of all three of these Christian cold warriors — Reagan the actor, Dulles the missionary, and Eisenhower the general — we as a nation were fighting a duel to the death on behalf of Christian, property-owning capitalism against atheistic, property-sharing communism — the "evil empire" — and we would destroy the enemy *by any means necessary,* including ends that would justify those means.[25]

Although much is made of John Kennedy's involvement in the assassination of Castro and very little of Dwight Eisenhower's, one must still wonder what, if anything, Kennedy knew of the assassination. Did he authorize the CIA to continue its attempts to murder Castro in 1961–1963? There is still "no evidence that any Agency official ever mentioned it to any President — Eisenhower in 1960, Kennedy after 1960, Johnson after 1963. . . . The practice of 'plausible denial' had, as Colonel William R. Corson, a veteran intelligence officer, put it, 'degenerated to the point where the cover stories of presidential ignorance really are fact, not fiction.'"[26] If that's the case, consider a scenario in which Eisenhower kicked off the first approval in the matter of Premier Patrice Lumumba in the Congo (or, more likely, earlier in Iran against Mossadegh or in the Philippines against President Elpedio Quirino or in Guatemala against President Jacobo Arbenz). Thereafter, it is conceivable that the CIA continued to operate "off the shelf," almost as a sovereign nation within a nation, carrying out our official policies in covert ways, including assassination, and protecting its leader by *not* telling him. Pretty heavy. It's improbable, but given the arrogance of the Dulles clan, it's possible — very insanely possible.

But it is still not clear to me that Kennedy knew what was really going on. He was, for one, using go-betweens to Castro, such as anchorwoman Lisa Howard and lawyer James Donovan. He even sent a message to Castro days before his death via Jean Daniel, the editor of the Parisian *L'Observateur*, signaling that he was looking, with French president de Gaulle's encouragement, for a path of reconciliation with Cuba. Two days later, the day Kennedy was murdered, the CIA's Task Force W (another unit established to overthrow Castro by any means necessary) was meeting in Paris with AMLASH, the code name for a new rip-off artist calling himself the next assassin of Castro (by now living out his twenty-sixth life?). Is Kennedy running "two tracks" here? For various reasons, I doubt it.

But if "the argument that the Kennedys knew and approved of the assassination plan comes down, in the end, to the argument that they *must* have known — [then certainly] an argument [can be made] that, of course, applies with equal force to Eisenhower and Johnson." Schlesinger asserts that regardless of whether "the CIA people believed they had an original authorization [to assassinate] of some yet undiscovered sort from Eisenhower, they never inquired of Kennedy whether he wished these risky and . . . [sinister] adventures to continue." He also says, "It appears that the CIA regarded whatever authorization it thought it had acquired [under Eisenhower] in 1960 [against Castro in Cuba] as permanent, not requiring review and reconfirmation by new Presidents or, even more astonishingly, by new CIA directors. For neither Bissell nor Helms even told John McCone what his own Agency was up to."[27] Confirming this, Fletcher Prouty told me that after Allen Dulles was fired, the first job given to his clandestine group in the air force was flying Kennedy's new CIA appointee, John McCone (not to be confused with John McCloy of the Warren Commission), around the world for several months of on-the-job training under the tutelage of the various station chiefs of the CIA. This action, in Prouty's opinion, was intended to keep McCone out of the loop in Washington, D.C., during the crucial planning stages of the assassination of John F. Kennedy.

Additionally, evidence has surfaced that "Eisenhower never even properly discussed what was happening in Vietnam with Kennedy. After reading a position paper on Vietnam he [Kennedy] responded 'This is the worst yet. You know, Ike never briefed me about Vietnam.'"[28]

I am sure there's tainted evidence to be brought to both sides of Kennedy's intentions. But let us remember several of Kennedy's conversations with people he respected or trusted, such as Tad Szulc, the Latin American correspondent for the *New York Times*, telling him that the "U.S. morally must not be part[y] to assassination," and then telling Richard Goodwin, special assistant to the

President, "If we get into that kind of thing [assassination], we'll all be targets." That same month, Kennedy said in a public speech, "We cannot, as a free nation, compete with our adversaries in tactics of terror and assassination."[29] Recall that Kennedy had not been in office when the major portion of our covert destabilizations of foreign governments was going on — Lumumba's murder among them. His only such experience would have been the deaths of Ngo Dinh Diem and his brother in Vietnam in early November 1963, to which Kennedy reacted with great shock. Perhaps, in his Harvard-trained mind, he could accept the abstract concept of removing a foreign leader from power, but the actual murder of a political opponent had far dirtier implications. This was not, to people such as Kennedy and others like him, the American way.

Even his young adversary, Castro, said during Kennedy's last days, "Personally, I consider him responsible for everything, but I will say this: he has come to understand many things over the past few months; and then too, in the last analysis, I'm convinced that anyone else would be worse."[30]

Thus I continue to be amazed at the hatred directed at Kennedy by many progressive people who fail to accept the realities of the way our system works. Intellectuals may expect idealistic leaders to come from the common man and behave impeccably in the public arena, in which case Kennedy would certainly not be their man — his "Camelot" as much an optical illusion as Eisenhower's golf game — but in the end, we all define our characters by our choices. And whatever his critics say, I am convinced that John Kennedy was neither Dwight Eisenhower nor Lyndon Johnson, and he would never have condoned the assassination of foreign leaders, with or without "plausible deniability," nor ordered half a million U.S. troops to Vietnam to fight in a civil war with no exit strategy or much upside.

Another important aspect has been overlooked in this controversy. As early as June 1961, Kennedy rocked the Pentagon and the CIA with NSAMs 55 and 56; this issue was raised in the film, as Colonel Prouty went to great lengths to describe to me the shock these NSAMs caused in the corridors of power. Essentially, Kennedy was making good on his promise "to splinter the CIA into a thousand pieces" after the disastrous Bay of Pigs — by turning over to the Pentagon the execution of *all* cold war operations, thereby renouncing the CIA's perceived and illegally acquired role of destabilizing foreign governments during the Eisenhower-Nixon era. NSAM 55 stated: "They [the Joint Chiefs of Staff] should know the military and paramilitary forces [a reference to the CIA's cooperation with Cuban right-wing elements, as well as the "secret war" being waged in Laos and Vietnam] and resources available to the Department of Defense, verify their readiness, report on their adequacy and make appropriate recommendations for their expansion and improvement."[31] What Kennedy was trying to do here was basically *regain control* of the CIA, so that misadventures like the Bay of Pigs would not happen again.

In NSAM 56, Kennedy went further:

> It is important that we anticipate now our possible future requirements in the field of unconventional warfare and paramilitary operations. A first step would be to inventory the paramilitary assets we have in the United States Armed Forces, consider various areas in the world where the implementation of our policy may require indigenous paramilitary forces, and thus arrive at a determination of the goals which we should set in this field.
>
> The President requests that the Secretary of Defense, in coordination with the Department of State, and *the CIA,* make such an estimate of requirements and recommend ways and means to meet these requirements [signed by McGeorge Bundy; cc: Secretary of State, Director of the CIA, General Maxwell Taylor].[32]

To inventory the CIA's notorious "black budget," much less all the other overlapping intelligence budgets we were paying for, would be a vast and daunting effort for any president, even for the conservative Nixon, who, in his Bay of Pigs conversation with Haldeman, revealed his frustration over his inability to get the full file on the Bay of Pigs from Richard Helms at the CIA. Prouty told me that neither of these two NSAMs was effectively carried out, as in all bureaucracies there is a vast gap between intention and execution, especially when the employees are reluctant to change. The CIA therefore continued to operate for its own ends with a growing budget for war in Vietnam, as well as a separate "black budget," whose whereabouts and contents remain highly secret to this day.

Jim Garrison

I believed Jim Garrison, but I never intended this movie to be a biography, as *Nixon* was. Ellen Ray, who published an excellent magazine called *Covert Action Information Bulletin* (now called *Covert Action Quarterly*), introduced us. I wasn't as naive as some would paint me. I probed him and, in fact, had a rough first meeting with him when some of my questions delved into his possible involvement with the Mafia. I think Garrison truly despised the concept of the Mafia, and a flawed pride made him thin-skinned about being questioned about something that had no trace of evidence or merit in his mind. After spending time together during the course of the filming, Jim Garrison became as much a hero to me as Ron Kovic and Le Ly Hayslip. They were all heroes in the true sense of the word — people who had achieved much but paid a stiff price for it. Incidentally, neither Zack Sklar, my cowriter who knew Garrison well, Kevin Costner, who played him, nor I ever detected anything other than an elegant southern drawl coming from his lips. I wonder how he could have gotten himself elected in a town as chauvinistic as New Orleans if he'd used his Iowa-born accent, as claimed by Kurtz? Garrison's death, shortly after our film's release, was a great blow to the many who knew and loved him. But this I know with my eyes and heart: not only was he very happy that *JFK* had been made, but, more importantly, he died a man proud of his strenuous life and difficult accomplishments.

When Garrison started the case, he had enough evidence for a grand jury indictment, which is hardly the frivolous case depicted by his many critics. Twenty-two jurors heard the evidence. Additionally, in a preliminary hearing, a *three-judge panel ruled that there was enough evidence to go to trial.* Nonetheless, by the time the trial started nearly two years later, several of the witnesses had been killed or were suspiciously dead, men such as the eccentric, macho David Ferrie; Eladio del Valle, who was mutilated with a machete in Florida; Lee Bowers, the railroad man; and the prostitute Rose Cheramie. Crucially, all Garrison's out-of-state subpoenas were denied by state governors, such as Reagan in California. The U.S. attorney in Washington refused to subpoena federal government witnesses, such as former CIA director Allen Dulles and his assistant, Charles Cabell. NBC, then a kingdom owned by Brigadier General David Sarnoff, a very close friend of the Pentagon, ran an outrageous one-hour documentary destroying Garrison's reputation. It was so patently unfair and one-sided that Garrison complained to the Federal Communications Commission and was granted a free half hour to respond on the same network. His reply is still available — a historic first attack on the military and CIA branches of our government, delivered with no evidence of nerves, eyes cool and straight into the camera, all six feet seven inches of him standing alone against a desk, with no notes whatever, just a great lawyer's intellect speaking with common sense and from the heart.

Much has also been made by his critics about the charges against Clay Shaw being dismissed quickly, thus proving that Garrison had no case and that this was therefore a vindication of the Warren Commission. These critics never mention that the trial was delayed a year and a half, during which a great deal of chicanery went on. Files disappeared, and once they were turned over to Shaw's defense team by Tom Bethel, a "volunteer" in Jim's office. As noted, witnesses also disappeared, and every request by Garrison for extradition of out-of-state witnesses was refused — something that had never happened to him before the Shaw case. His office phones were tapped. The FBI followed him. In all likelihood, discredited witness Charles Spiesel, an accountant from New York who approached the Garrison prosecution team shortly before trial and claimed, almost too perfectly, that on a trip to New Orleans he'd met David Ferrie and spent a night out with him and Clay Shaw during which they discussed murdering Kennedy, was either a nut or a "plant," spy talk at that time for a successful penetration of the enemy camp.

A desperate Garrison made the mistake of putting him on the stand and went through the details as they had discussed. Then the defense came in and asked *extremely specific questions,* which led to Spiesel testifying that the New York police had hypnotized and tortured him in the past and that he fingerprinted his daughter each time she returned from college to make sure that she was still who she claimed to be. Garrison and his staff were naturally stunned. All previous credibility linking Shaw to Ferrie had been lost.

The CIA itself orchestrated a campaign to discredit Garrison in the public eye; a memo dated April 1, 1967, outlined a strategy for using "media assets" to say that Warren Commission critics are politically motivated, financially motivated, do sloppy research, and so forth (things we still hear today). Shaw's defense was closely watched by the CIA, and Richard Helms, director of operations in 1963, was asked at a staff meeting if the agency was doing enough to help Shaw.[33] In 1979, Helms testified under oath that Shaw was a "domestic asset," which made Shaw a perjurer to begin with. The House Select Committee concluded in its investigation in 1979 that there was "reason to believe Shaw was heavily involved in the anti-Castro efforts in New Orleans." Thus the question was not whether Clay Shaw got a fair trial, but whether Jim Garrison got one.

I tried to make it clear in the film that Garrison *knew* his case was weak but continued for various reasons: "I didn't know exactly how Shaw was involved, but with Shaw I grabbed a toehold on the conspiracy. I wasn't about to let go because of technicalities." For one, he knew that Shaw was hardly the innocent he proclaimed himself, that he had strong OSS/CIA connections dating back to the war. Later, after the trial, Garrison found out from Bertrand Russell's secretary, Ralph Schoenmann, that Shaw had been a board member of a company thrown out of Italy for espionage. Shaw had played an extensive international role as an employee of the CIA trying to bring fascism back to a leftist Italy through the front organizations Permindex and Centro Mondiale Commerciale, which were subsidiaries of his International Trade Mart in New Orleans. The Italian left-leaning press investigated these allegations and eventually exposed the company's activities, which included financing a French opposition organization that had attempted to kill President de Gaulle on numerous occasions. Once this became public knowledge, Italy threw Permindex out of the country. There were many clandestine elements to Shaw's life; he was, in a sense, a true "Mask of Dimitrios." Crucially, Shaw had consistently used the alias "Clay Bertrand" in the homosexual underworld of New Orleans and was lying about it. Kevin Bacon's character, Willie O'Keefe, was a composite of several homosexual witnesses — among them Perry Russo, David Logan, Raymond Broshears, and William Morris — who knew or cavorted with Shaw and had seen him with David Ferrie, Perry Russo, and, perhaps, the enigmatic Lee Harvey Oswald. Yet Garrison made a conscious decision not to call any homosexual witnesses or imply that Shaw was homosexual (Russo was not "out" then) and thus lost potential witnesses to the Shaw-Bertrand connection. Several other witnesses of a nonsexual nature did testify.

Shaw claimed under oath that he had never known either Oswald or Ferrie. But four people in Clinton, Louisiana, had noticed Oswald in a voter registration line, accompanied by two men, in the autumn of 1963. The descriptions of the two men matched those of Clay Shaw and David Ferrie. The town marshall, a bit suspicious, checked out the license plate of the car they were in and discovered that it was registered to Clay Shaw's Trade Mart organization.

Vernon Bundy, a heroin user, was another Garrison trial witness who said that he saw Oswald and Shaw together. He was sitting on a wall at Lake Pontchartrain ready to shoot up, looking around to make sure the coast was clear, when he saw Shaw giving Oswald a wad of money. The defense predictably attacked Bundy as a heroin user who couldn't be trusted. Yet he was the first to correctly point out that Shaw had a slight, though discernible, limp in his walk. How could he have known that unless he'd seen him before?

The film was much maligned for its portrayal of Shaw as a depraved homosexual. I couldn't care less what his sexual orientation was, and Garrison clearly tried to keep away from the homosexuality issue, which was an issue only because it was a crucial link to establishing a physical connection between Ferrie and Shaw. Shaw claimed under oath never to have known Ferrie — which was his second lie on the stand. There was a photograph, however, found of them in drag together (which we used in the movie). There was no way, in my opinion, that Shaw could not have known Ferrie. That's why that scene was in the movie.

If it had been a photograph of them carousing with women, I would have had a scene showing that. It's frustrating, because there's one faction that attacks me for making up facts as I go along, and another that attacks me because I adhere to what the evidence was, which just happens to stand in the way of a particular agenda. Once you fall into a politically correct way of thinking, you're in danger of destroying the concept of truth. No one with a brain is going to walk away from *JFK* thinking that all gays are president killers or that their homosexuality was the reason these particular men may have been involved. The chief villains in this scenario were men in Washington, D.C., and

I presume they were heterosexuals for the most part. But who really cares? This was a trumped-up claim that veered toward frivolousness but for the fact that it agitated an already excitable, overly defensive group.

Even if Shaw/Bertrand was not directly involved in conspiracy, bringing the case was a means of advancing the Oswald-Ferrie connection. In that regard, Garrison could be faulted on narrow legal grounds, but I truly believe that his motives were pure and patriotic. At a time of great conformity and at great personal discomfort and risk to himself and his family, Garrison was the first and only public official to object to this public burial of Kennedy and raise the questions that many wanted raised. In the film, the character X confronts Garrison with his choices at the later stages of his investigation: "Be honest. The best chance you got is to come up with a case, something, anything, make arrests, stir the shit storm! You gotta hope to reach a point of critical mass where other people will come forward and the government will crack. Remember, fundamentally people are suckers for the truth and the truth is on your side, bubba. I hope you get a break." (Although Prouty had never met Garrison until the film was made, their thinking on the murder was remarkably alike.)

That never quite happened. Garrison was hoping that people in other states, especially in Texas, the scene of the crime, would have the guts to step forward. But fear and conformity triumphed in the end, as they often do in real life.

Garrison's case was further damaged when Judge Haggerty dismissed the testimony of police officer Habighorst, who had booked Shaw when he was first arrested and asked Shaw if he had any aliases. Shaw, without thinking, perhaps under the shock of arrest, wrote down "Bertrand." Haggerty now argued that because Shaw didn't have his lawyer present at the time, the evidence was inadmissible. Never mind the fact that this was standard booking procedure that had never been questioned before in court. Although further evidence would continue to emerge in later years, without that testimony — the link that tied Clay Shaw to "Clay Bertrand" to David Ferrie and possibly to Lee Harvey Oswald — Garrison was sunk. If Habighorst's testimony had been allowed, what would have happened?

When Garrison came out with the original charges, there was so much negative publicity and pressure on him that he *did* make errors of judgment, as we all might under such pressure, particularly by trusting "volunteers" who subverted his investigation. He was accused of bullying witnesses and using hypnosis and sodium pentathol (truth serum) to lead impressionable witnesses to invalid conclusions. There was such a jumble of smears thrown at Garrison that, as usual, the smears were too easily confused with the truth. Read Garrison's last book for a specific, point-by-point analysis of the bogus charges against him — not one of them proved, yet to this day repeated over and over by the echoing, think-alike media.

The "smear campaign" against Garrison was as crude as, but unfortunately more effective than, the two trials brought in 1972–1973 by the federal government against Garrison, which are described in full, colorful detail in his last book. Basically, the accusations stemmed from a roughly spliced together sound tape, similar in its crudeness to what J. Edgar Hoover was to do to Martin Luther King, Jr., a few years later, trying to prove that Garrison was accepting a bribe in a pinball machine scam from his former chief investigator, Pershing Gervais (whom Garrison dropped from his staff after hearing from an attorney that Gervais would get a particular case dismissed for $750 in cash), now a local New Orleans lowlife under government pressure to "rat" Jim out. The trial, rarely mentioned by Garrison's critics, was so obviously a frame and so poorly presented that it collapsed with a quick not-guilty verdict. But it's interesting to note how little attention *that trial* ever received, unlike the Shaw trial.

Jim Garrison came in as district attorney on a sweeping program of reform. He had a reputation for closing a host of sleazy joints. He didn't know Carlos Marcello, the reputed boss of the region who operated largely out of Jefferson Parish, next door to New Orleans but as different in its politics as New Jersey is from New York. Garrison told me, with utter conviction, that he saw Marcello *once* — in a restaurant. In New Orleans, that land of great myths, whopping stories were told of Garrison by his many enemies, political opponents, ex-cons, and the like. But I don't really believe Jim ever took a bribe. There was something very straight, Lincoln-like about him. He was well spoken and well read, a southern gentleman given to courteous behavior, especially around the beautiful women he had an eye for. He often made humorous allusions from history to contemporary affairs, and he conveyed a sense of great integrity in all matters. He'd been an artillery pilot for the U.S. Army for five years (through World War II) and then a field artillery officer for another eighteen years in the National Guard. In his last book he candidly discussed the so-called psychological problems he experienced in his second war in Korea. Much was made, of course, by the media of Garrison's "nervous breakdown," when in fact he was diagnosed as only needing some psychotherapy to deal with what he had seen during his military tenure. To have his name dragged through the mud — accusations that he was gay, wore a dress, and went after Shaw because he'd been spurned — must have pierced his proud heart. He was a man of such conviction that he would write a second book, *On the Trail of the Assassins,* about this case almost twenty years after his first book, *A Heritage of Stone.* Very few people return to such a subject unless they *truly* believe in it.[34]

Did he have a mistress? Yes, and she eventually became his second wife. The fact that he married her after divorcing his first wife indicates, if anything, that Garrison was a highly committed man. But the important point to remember is that his first wife didn't believe in his case and wanted him to stay away from the one thing he was most passionate about — "let justice be done, though the heavens fall!" They separated *after* the events depicted in the movie.

Though Garrison was very popular (he was elected three times as district attorney, and later to the State Court of Appeals), he was despised by the main newspaper of New Orleans, the *Times-Picayune,* for political reasons. Its reporting of the case was highly biased, as it certainly didn't want stories about crazy Cubans and Lee Harvey Oswald circulating around New Orleans; it was bad for advertising and bad for the garden-club image of the city that a small, aristocratic group, including Clay Shaw over at the "respectable" International Trade Mart, wanted to project.

Another fact often omitted by the critics is that the jury at the trial, when polled, *all said that they believed there had been a conspiracy to kill JFK, but that the evidence was not sufficient to convict Clay Shaw.* The case can be likened to Hemingway's story *The Old Man and the Sea:* after catching the biggest fish in his sea, the fisherman ties it to the side of the boat and heads back to shore, but by the time he gets there, all that is left of the fish is a skeleton picked apart by sharks. Garrison certainly had a bayou full of his own sharks to deal with, and his Ahab-like obsession to gain a foothold in the quicksand is one of the great American stories of the underdog against the system.

The "Jim Garrison" in my film is perhaps an idealistic archetype to many. The director Frank Capra took this approach. Alfred Hitchcock also used this approach throughout his career in nonpolitical movies. Cary Grant and Jimmy Stewart often played these roles for the two directors. That is the dramatist's license, to create an attractive hero to guide and anchor the audience and, in this case, take it through a long jigsaw of a movie. But what is consistent between the real-life Garrison and the on-screen Garrison played by Kevin Costner is the sincerity of his quest for justice. Jim was as passionate about a sense of fairness and justice as any man I've ever known. But life teaches us in the end that "no man is an island." Jim came close to being great. If he had won the case and had somehow opened up the whole thing, he might have been the greatest single American hero since Charles Lindbergh, who certainly had the darker sides that Jim was reputed to possess. The media could have had their own "field day" with Lindbergh, if they had so chosen. But that would have involved telling the truth. The lie is generally much more colorful and sells far better.

In the end, Jim Garrison may have lost in the eyes of our media, which too readily echo one another rather than do the original hard work of investigation, and so he goes down in history as one of the footnotes rather than as one of the heroes. But in my book, he stands out as a giant.

On Toplin's Remarks about JFK

Kennedy, Toplin says critically, was depicted at the beginning of the film as an impressive president. I think that's not quite the case. I think that by 1963, he had begun to fully grasp his role as our national leader in a turbulent time and realized that the burden of promoting change rested squarely on his shoulders. Note the American University speech in the film; his speech to the nation on civil rights with regard to the Birmingham situation; his visit to the Berlin Wall; his call for U.S.-Soviet cooperation, including a unified space program; and, most importantly, his initiatives with Khrushchev to sign the Nuclear Peace Treaty of July 1963. Put yourself inside his new thinking on Vietnam and Cuba, and you will begin to understand this man as the progressive he had always considered himself. I believe that these changes would have yielded their fruit after the 1964 election. But our portrait of him was the official one that we knew *at that time*. If you study the film closely, it starts out in an objective sense with a "television story." It is the Kennedy of that period, painted as a charming, idealistic, good-looking president, which is what the American people remember him as. But in that same "pseudo-documentary" segment, I thought we made clear that the civil rights issue had made him hated in much of the South. Our contemporary accounts now emphasize that Lyndon Johnson enacted the actual legislation of civil rights change, as if in denigration of Kennedy's timidity, but they ignore the singular fact that it was Kennedy who first signaled these changes by adopting a wholly different policy from Eisenhower's benign neglect.

At that point, *JFK* introduces Jim Garrison (Kevin Costner), hooked to his TV during those three catatonic days, along with the rest of the country. It seems that we all saw it one way — the way it was so confidently told to us by "the Media," which leapt into major prominence in our public consciousness as an *entity* that fateful day. (How close in sound, ironically, to that Greek tragedy *Medea*, the "mother" of a sensational crime.) After that, the movie moves from black and white and muted colors to more saturated colors several years later as Garrison meets Senator Russell Long (Walter Matthau) on an airplane; this is where we enter the investigation, unpeeling the onion, visiting and revisiting Dealey Plaza in layers of time. The opening functions as prologue. It shows the way Kennedy was painted *then* — as an impressive president: young, strong, and popular.

I disagree with Toplin when he suggests that *JFK* somehow seduced many viewers into betraying their common sense. Polls in the 1960s and 1970s showed that the majority of the public had overwhelmingly strong doubts about the Warren Commission's conclusion that Oswald had acted alone. Then there was a drop-off of interest for many years, not revived even after the House Select Committee contended in 1979 that there was a "probable conspiracy." The Justice Department deigned not to pursue it, so the assassination topic remained a small, cottage industry as the country grew sick of the self-analyses and critiques it had put itself through. Even the name "Kennedy," it seems to me, was being quietly set aside by our official historians, as a short-term footnote of a president. Then our film arrived on the scene in 1991, with the force of a tsunami wave, and those initials, "JFK," have now become commonplace as a designator, I believe, of something both heroic and tragic that happened in our history.

Questions about the Assassination of JFK

Some critics, who go after a movie because they want to destroy its impact, attack the messenger or go after the few details that may be wrong here and there in order to suggest that *all* is wrong. Media celebrity Sam Donaldson got his two cents in over the issue of the phone system in the film, making it his major point of rebuttal on his TV show *Prime Time,* saying that he had been in Washington that day and the phones *were* working; he still mentions it proudly to this day. But I wonder: why doesn't he address the dozens of other things we may have gotten *right?* Furthermore, it amazes me that he won't acknowledge that many phone lines *were* down, many of them *key* phone lines. Many people experienced it. William Manchester described Senator Ted Kennedy desperately running around to find a working phone.[35] The lines at the Justice Department and the White House were intermittently working or dead. There seems to have been selective brownouts, perhaps from overload, but we don't really know. What we do know is that there were a lot of *coincidences* that day, and not just in the Washington phone system — things like one-third of the 49th Armored Division being airborne back to the United States from Germany.[36] When you string dozens of these coincidences together, it becomes an amazing body of circumstances crying out for serious thought and investigation, not the type undertaken by the Sam Donaldsons of the television news world.

Why, for example, wasn't Kennedy protected properly by military security in Texas, especially with the civil rights hatred directed at him and the near-beating of Adlai Stevenson, a two-time presidential candidate, a few weeks before? *There was just no military presence in Dallas that day,* which is amazing and still goes unanswered, partly because the army's military intelligence shredded all the files. And what of the open windows all along the parade route? That was a Secret Service rule — to secure all windows overlooking an open-car parade like this one. And why was the car, against all standing rules for the president's safety, allowed to drive so slowly before, during, and after its fatal turn from Houston onto Elm? Why was the parade route changed — with the permission of Mayor Earle Cabell (who, ironically, was also the brother of General Charles Cabell, the number-two man at the CIA who was fired by Kennedy) — and shown in the newspapers several days in advance, taking the president's caravan right under the book depository building, where the car would be forced to make an ultra-slow turn instead of going straight through Dealey Plaza to the freeway? People could have seen him just as easily in the middle of that plaza from the grass on both sides of the car, instead of from Elm Street. And then the president would have had sufficient distance from all windows — unless, that is, someone wanted him inside an L-shaped ambush (a military tactic allowing for enfilade fire, which we learned in the army was the ideal trap against our Vietnamese enemy). That spot was Dealey Plaza.

Another reasonable question: why didn't Oswald, if he was in the sixth-floor window, shoot Kennedy as the car was coming up Houston Street toward him? He would have had the same time element but gotten off clearer shots. Instead, Oswald supposedly let Kennedy pass him and fade away, forcing him to shoot through foliage that was relatively thick at the time on a tree high enough to impede a clear shot. (Afterward, the tree was, for no apparent reason, immediately pruned and cut back by Hoover's FBI. Hoover claimed that the tree had shed its leaves by November; however, the tree was a Texas live oak, which sheds its leaves the first week of March.) That's just not a sniper's way. And as we know, the time element more or less established by the Zapruder film — 5.6 seconds — is a nearly impossible time frame to fire three shots with precision from the window, especially with a rifle as badly made as the Italian World War II rifle allegedly bought by Oswald (through the mail using the easily traceable alias "A. Hidell"). Both the FBI and CBS television conducted tests to prove that Oswald could have made those shots in the time frame allowed. In both instances, they had to "improve" the deficiencies of the rifle before even coming close. Still, it took several rifle experts several passes to even approximate that shooting skill. And Oswald, per his marine records, was a less-than-average shot. When I tried it during our filming, I found it impossible, as an ex–infantry soldier, to allow myself *any time to aim* — assuming that I was able to load and reload the rifle *twice* in the time required. And when one takes into account the *noise* from Dealey Plaza, the cheering — the pressure must have been as intense as war itself.

I believe, as Garrison did, that figures from the CIA and/or military intelligence, be it army, navy, or air force, would be the most logical masterminds of something as complex as a coup d'état featuring a public execution in broad daylight and a cover-up to follow. The cover-up is the hard part. But neither Garrison nor I *ever* made a statement about *who* killed Kennedy, because we didn't know; we could only speculate. Colonel Prouty has been the most outspoken in suspecting Ed Lansdale, the ex–advertising man who became the legendary spook of "ugly American" fame. He masterminded our Filipino intervention in 1953 but then failed in Vietnam when Dulles sent him over to lead our first efforts in 1954 (we had supported the French war from 1947 to 1954). Enamored, as General MacArthur was, of the Far East as his field of play, Lansdale was hoping to return as ambassador to Vietnam to make good on his legend as our chief problem solver (Joseph Conrad could not have invented a greater character than Lansdale). Prouty, who knew him well, told me that Lansdale had been verbally promised the ambassadorship by Kennedy, but through the efforts of George Ball and others, was denied the position. Lansdale instead was appointed to two crucial "in-house" positions in D.C. — managing Operation MONGOOSE, the "official" invasion force targeting Cuba in 1962, and a lesser known assignment with the "Camelot" think tank at American University.

In a March 6, 1990, letter to Jim Garrison, Fletcher Prouty wrote:

Then with the failure of the Bay of Pigs, caused by the phone call to cancel the air strikes by McGeorge Bundy, the military was given the job of reconstituting some sort of Anti-Castro operation. It was headed by an Army Colonel; but somehow Landsdale (most likely CIA influence) got put into the plans for Operation Mongoose . . . to get Castro . . . ostensibly. The U.S. Army has a think-tank at American University. It was called "Operation Camelot." This is where the Camelot concept came from. It was anti-JFK's Vietnam strategy. The men running it were Lansdale types, Special Forces background. Through 1962 and 1963 Mongoose and Camelot became strong and silent organizations dedicated to countering JFK. Mongoose has access to the CIA's best "hit men" in the business and a lot of "strike" capability. Lansdale had many old friends in the media business such as Joe Alsop, Henry Luce among others. With this background and with his poisoned motivation I am positive that he got collateral orders to manage the Dallas event under the guise of "getting" Castro. It is so simple at that level. A nod from the right place, source immaterial, and the job's done. The "hit" is the easy part. The "escape" must be quick and professional. The cover-up and the scenario are the big jobs. They more than anything else prove that

Lansdale mastery. Lansdale was a master writer and planner. He was a great "scenario" guy. I still have a lot of his personally-typed material in my files. I am certain that he was behind the elaborate plan and mostly the intricate and enduring cover-up. Given a little help from friends at PEPSICO, he could easily have gotten Nixon into Dallas, for "orientation," and LBJ into the cavalcade at the same time, contrary to Secret Service policy. He knew the "Protection" units and the "Secret Service," who was needed and who wasn't. Those were routine calls for him, and they would have believed him. Cabell (Mayor of Dallas, brother of second man to Dulles, Charles Cabell) could handle the police. The "hit men" were from CIA overseas sources, for instance, from the camp near Athena, Greece. They are trained, stateless, and ready to go at any time. They ask no questions, speak to no one. They are simply told what to do, when and where. They are told how they will be removed and protected. After all, they work for the U.S. Government. The "tramps" were actors doing the job of cover-up. The whole story of the power of the cover-up comes down to a few points. There has never been a Grand Jury and trial in Texas. Without a trial there can be nothing. Without a trial, it does no good for researchers to dig up data. It has no place to go and what the researchers reveal just helps make the cover-up tighter, or they eliminate that evidence and the researcher.

This was, no doubt, extremely covert work, but it was also *routine* for professionals. And as Prouty made particularly clear in his book *The Secret Team*, it can be controlled, contrary to what cynics usually say.[37] These critics often assume that everyone gossips as much as they do, but in reality, a few dedicated men (I would estimate anywhere from eight to twenty) could pull it off. I doubt that there were more than that. It doesn't take a "vast conspiracy," which are the words my critics like to put in my mouth. If you get a few good military men or ex–Green Berets or commandos of some kind, these men are sealed by oaths of honor; they are trained not to betray one another, not even under torture. This is wholly conceivable in the world of men like Prouty; it's even ordinary, in a sense, just another " black op." You may not even know who your target is until minutes before — it could have been anybody in or around the motorcade, but then you realize that it's the president in your sights. There is, among most professional assassins, no moral doubt whatever. In any case, you're "protected," because there's just no security around. Perhaps you have a moment of shock, but a trained professional does not think. He pulls the trigger. The lightning of history is made, but on the radar screen of the killers, it is no more than a blip. Furthermore, members of the team don't really know *who* they're working for. The person who gives them direct orders is the only one they know; he, in turn, may be in touch with another "cell" in the operation. One team doesn't know what another team is doing, or if it's even there. It's all done on a "need-to-know" basis. True guerrilla, or terrorist, warfare is based on the culture of stealth, hardly this huge complex described by critics, who don't seem to understand the cell-like structure of covert operations (which, by the way, we encountered in depth in our North Vietnamese foe).

Consider also the late John Connally, the Texas governor who Toplin numbers among *JFK*'s critics. I had dinner with Connally, and he told me, as he had publicly stated on several occasions, that the "magic bullet," the one that supposedly hit him and Kennedy in seven different places, was not possible. He had felt a slight delay between hearing one bullet hit Kennedy and then another hitting him; he was absolutely sure that the bullet that hit him was *not* the same one that hit Kennedy — which makes the three-bullet scenario impossible.

But it was natural for Connally to back the Warren Commission. He was governor of Texas, a close friend to Johnson, and a potential presidential candidate as late as 1980. What was he going to do — say what he was really thinking? If Lyndon Johnson privately asked his old Washington neighbor J. Edgar Hoover during their first conversation after the assassination, "How many shots were fired?" followed by, "Any of them fired at me?" and then, "Were *they* aiming at the President?"[38] you must think that perhaps Johnson thought that "they" had been shooting at him also — as they had shot at his friend John Connally. That statement exonerates Johnson of any participation in the crime, in my opinion (the cover-up is another matter), which is another lie continually perpetrated by the film's critics. But it *also* raises the larger point: given more than one shooter, just who were "they"?

If you walk it, what first strikes you about Dealey Plaza is how close and theatrical everything looks, and you might also notice how many good shooting angles there are. The key sight line is from the fence on the grassy knoll toward the president's oncoming car. We've now heard several scientific theories justifying the gunman being behind Kennedy, but the Zapruder film, shot from close to this fence, clearly shows the president's head flying *backward* when hit — in many opinions, from a bullet to the head fired from behind the fence. Inside that L shape from Houston to Elm, Kennedy was a dead duck. He was never going to be allowed to leave Dealey Plaza alive. And the man, or men, at the fence were the insurance in case the first or second team in the buildings above missed. And, as Prouty pointed out to me, there might even have been a team at the overpass, waiting in case all the teams missed. When you go for a kill like that, you do *not* leave your target wounded. Like a lion, Kennedy would have been far more dangerous wounded. That day, Dealey Plaza was, in military terminology, a "kill zone." And with that shot at noon to the front of his head, they not only blew out Kennedy's skull, they also struck a lightning bolt of fear in our collective heart. They reminded us of something we may have forgotten. No longer would we follow the path of the young and different drummer.

I didn't play with the Zapruder film, whatever critics said. It is shown exactly as it is, and it is also slowed down. Some scientists say that there could have been "a neuromuscular reaction" that would account for Kennedy's head shooting backward on first impact (had the shot come from the rear in the book depository), but you don't have to be a combat veteran to know that generally the target goes with the impact and velocity of the bullet.

On top of that, we were told that the other fatal bullet, the first or second, the so-called magic bullet, went into the rear of Kennedy's lower neck. But now, thanks to the documents released by the Assassination Records Review Board, we find out for sure what many have said for so long — that the bullet went into Kennedy's upper back. That was Gerald Ford's "clarification." This is very important, because Ford's change allowed the minute physical possibility that the magic bullet could have hit Connally — who was in the seat in front of Kennedy — in the inner thigh, accounting for *seven wounds* to two men. Those odds are long on any day. Let's say it's possible. But if you lower the bullet entry wound another two to three inches and it enters Kennedy's upper back, where it actually did, according to several eyewitnesses at the first hospital in Dallas (before the botched autopsy in D.C. under the strict control of the military), then the magic bullet becomes as ridiculous as it sounds.

We're talking *Alice in Wonderland* history here. You see something with your own eyes, and they tell you, "That's not what you saw." This is what they told Jean Hill, the woman in the red coat in Dealey Plaza, who was standing very close to the president at the moment of fatal impact and who was one of our best, most articulate witnesses. She was a woman of much conviction, not easily scared off her testimony by the intimidating FBI officials who questioned her, as shown in the film. There were, all in all, so many coincidences — the three-bullet scenario (one missed and nicked a bystander at the overpass), the Zapruder film, the "magic bullet," Kennedy's head going backward. The existence of a "magic bullet" and another bullet exploding the president's head backward and to the left represents *two enormous coincidences that happen in six seconds*. Some might say, well, these are the quirks of nature. The sensible mind might allow for one such incredible coincidence, but two bullets that behave so irregularly back to back?! To quote the folksy Senator Russell Long, "That dog don't hunt!"

There *had* to be a fourth bullet. There may have been a fifth or perhaps a sixth, as Garrison speculates in the film. But all it needs is a fourth bullet, and it *has* to be a conspiracy — in that it was *nearly* impossible for Oswald to fire three accurate shots in the time frame allowed; therefore, four shots is *utterly* impossible. Nor does the three-bullet theory hold water. It's not based, for me, on 5.6 seconds. It's really the issue of three bullets versus four. Tied to this is the important issue of hand-to-eye coordination and speed. Did you ever try to load the Mannlicher-Carcano, the kind of rifle allegedly used by Oswald? Italian infantrymen in World War II used to call it the worst rifle ever made by man, and infantrymen tend to value their weapons. To reload that rifle takes more than a moment. High-caliber riflemen could barely execute the Oswald scenario — with three, four, five, or even six shots, and they weren't even aiming. You have to *know* and *possess* your target. It can't be a moving target. It can't be through foliage. Then factor in the pressure of the crowd, the noise. Even to try to do it all in *ten seconds* is very difficult for anyone, much less a supposedly untrained ex-marine with psychological problems. Plus, Oswald is said to have run down several flights of stairs right after, where a policeman crossed him at the second-floor Coke machine, calm as a clam, just ninety seconds after the murder.

I don't believe Oswald was even in that window. I believe he was the "designated patsy" of the unit and knew a limited amount, enough to have him liquidated quickly and without trial. In the absence of a conviction, Oswald should always be correctly identified as "the alleged assassin" but is rarely described that way in any of our media.

Also bear in mind that assassins through history have generally proclaimed their acts. When they've killed for a political reason, as Oswald is supposed to have done, they've been proud of it. But Oswald clearly said to all the cameras, "I didn't shoot anybody, no sir. I'm just a patsy." His crucial twelve-hour testimony to the Dallas police, we are told, was never recorded, nor were any notes ever kept, contrary to any known departmental procedure.

Tom Wicker's and Anthony Lewis's critiques were very disturbing to me, as well as George Lardner's and Dan Rather's. Tom Wicker wrote a long article in the *New York Times* basically recycling the charges made against Garrison in the NBC documentary that Jim protested to the FCC about. He neglected to mention that not one of the witnesses NBC quoted would repeat their charges under oath, and that several witnesses had been offered bribes by NBC producers to smear Garrison. Perry Russo was offered a job in California to recant his testimony against Shaw and denounce Garrison. Russo, a gay, macho New Orleans cabdriver with strong right-wing opinions who I came to know and respect for his honesty and conviction, refused. But none of that made its way into Wicker's article. Wicker seemed outraged that our film might cause audiences to distrust their government. It's sad when a journalist of Wicker's stature has to be reminded that in a democracy the government has to earn the people's trust. It's not a given. Dan Rather was the first newsman to see the Zapruder film. He thought Kennedy's head had gone backward and at first said so, but then recanted and reported that the head had gone forward (thus justifying the Oswald scenario). Rather's report of the head reaction remained the official mythology for many years — until the release of the Zapruder film, largely through the efforts of Garrison at the Shaw trial, where it was first shown to a public jury.

On CBS's *48 Hours,* Dan Rather asked me some twenty questions about *JFK.* There were minefields in every single question. As I had been "edited" before by CBS, I insisted that between each question I be allowed to talk to my researcher. I wanted to have my words precisely stated, as I knew how they cut film on the news. It took close to two hours to deal with these twenty questions, and though my answers were, I thought, thought-provoking, when the interview aired, CBS presented only one question, and even that response was abbreviated into trivia. I cannot help but believe that had my answers been full of holes, they would have been aired.

Similarly, on the esteemed *Nightline,* the producers stunned me at the very beginning of the show with an astounding five-minute propaganda piece on Garrison. They never told me about it or presented any evidence of their hearsay charges against Garrison. They gave me approximately a minute or two to respond, which was ridiculous, given the complexity of the charges, and then they cut to a commercial. When I questioned my researcher on several of the outlandish statements made against Garrison, someone in the production booth taped that private conversation, which later appeared on radio, trying, I suppose, to make me look like a fool who didn't know his facts. It was a strangely resonant event for me, having read in Jim's book of his awful treatment by Johnny Carson on the *Tonight Show* and of the attempt in a bathroom to frame him as a homosexual.

Fundamentally, I believe that this murder was about "blowback." In Afghanistan, the CIA trained and equipped the Muslim mujahideen to fight the communist Soviets. Years later, these same clients blew up our World Trade Center, whereas the Soviets became our potential allies. This reminds me once again of the almost Graham Greene black-but-humorous bitterness in all these "ugly American" dealings. Truman wants Mossadegh, Dulles does not. He wants the shah back. He gets him, and his son. Years go by. Nixon and Kissinger (imagine fifteen years before, Eisenhower and Dulles) now want to get rid of the shah; he's becoming too dominant a player in that part of the world. And within a few years, by 1979, he's gone, and his American support with him, to be followed by a repressive, fundamentalist regime that vows, at several points, to exterminate us and our values in genocide-like terms. The moral of the story is becoming clear to me: as I said in another way earlier, the wheel of our karma turns slowly, but it turns exceedingly fine. When you actually finance and train people to kill, they go out and kill, generally your enemy, but in the end, they kill anybody who tries to take back their power or get in their way. "Be careful what you wish for," a wise philosopher (I believe Goethe) once said. All over this known world, we have trained and abetted police, military, semiterrorist, and paramilitary troops to achieve whatever objectives we wanted at the time. But, as we have come to learn, the objectives change but the men do not. And then they become the very monsters that suddenly want to kill us in the most brutal way. (Think of our empire, for a moment, besieged by Attila the Hun at the gates of Rome.) Ask the mythic Dr. Frankenstein. Or go to Central America, Chile, or Argentina and ask the members of the not-so-mythic death squads about the "good-old-boy" network in training camps at Fort Benning, Georgia, the Panama Jungle School, the mountains of Colorado for our Tibetans, Athens, Greece, for some fine shooting, and so forth. The camps just keep moving around.

I believe that the Bay of Pigs blew back on Kennedy. There are generally two theories espoused. The first is that the right-wing Cubans committed the assassination because they wanted revenge for the Bay of Pigs fiasco. But I don't understand how they could have pulled it off by themselves, as they had to not only stage a well-organized military operation on American soil but also create an entire profile for a guy called Lee Harvey Oswald and sell that to the media and the American public. And then they had to have Jack Ruby commit his crime, never reveal anything until he changed his mind in jail, and then abruptly die of cancer. "Sheepdipping" was, and may still be, a term used in espionage, meaning to create a suspect by "contaminating" him. Our military intelligence had several such disaffected Oswald types available, generally young, rootless men who might think that they were better off in the USSR or China, or they might simply go AWOL and "vanish."

There were reports on several Oswald types who defected to Russia around the same time — disaffected loners, alienated from our system. Imagine the possibility that military intelligence of the CIA puts several agents in the Soviet Union who are military defectors. They might not even know yet how to gainfully employ these agents; they are solely "patsies," each in their isolated cells, allowed to think that they're somebodies because they have connections to higher-ups. It always seemed that Oswald had "handlers" along the way (even in Russia), one probability being George de Mohrenschildt in Dallas, possibly

Ruth Paine in Dallas, another possibly Clay Shaw in New Orleans. Nor can we overlook the phone call Oswald is supposed to have placed, while in custody, to a man in North Carolina he had called before. For such a small-timer, it still amazes many detached observers how worldwide Lee Harvey Oswald's contacts were — the first human Web site.

In any event, given the money and time required for such long-term thinking, one day one of those agents "sheepdipped" with a profile (e.g., Oswald "as communist") might pay off handsomely. The Nazis had many such people working for them during World War II in the Soviet Union. We were quite eager to inherit that network in our larger, more important war against communism, in which cause we were willing to import a great many Nazi scientists, medical experts, and war criminals after the war. Of course, that's not the normal, Ambrose version of reality.

The other blowback theory is that someone high up in the U.S. military or the CIA was furious about the Bay of Pigs fiasco, which had deeply embarrassed the United States. Additionally, and most importantly — and wholly overlooked by our contemporary historians — there was Kennedy's subsequent failure to carry out the Pentagon's planned October 1962 invasion during the Cuban missile crisis. Many powerful people were increasingly wary of Kennedy's moves. I believe the idea grew naturally to get rid of Kennedy before he could win another election in 1964, from which a dynasty might conceivably start rolling with Robert Kennedy's victory in 1968. Most dangerous of all was the mind of John Kennedy — which, for whatever reasons, was changing our country's main strategic thinking on Vietnam, Cuba, and, most importantly, the Soviet Union. Even an end to the cold war was feasible by 1968.

The following excerpt from the script details a variety of other Kennedy initiatives that could have excited resistance:

"X" (to Garrison): Don't underestimate the budget cuts Kennedy called for in March of '63 either — close to fifty-two military installations in twenty-five states, twenty-one overseas bases, you're talking big money. You know how many helicopters have been lost in Vietnam? About three thousand so far. Who makes them? Bell Helicopter [more than 5,000 were ultimately lost, with a replacement figure in the billions]. Who owns Bell? Bell was near bankruptcy when the First National Bank of Boston approached the CIA about developing the helicopter for Indochina usage. How 'bout the F-11 fighters? General Dynamics in Fort Worth. Who owns that? Find out the defense budget since the war began. $75 going on $100 billion . . . $200 billion'll be spent there before it ends. In 1950 it was $13 billion. No war, no money. *Sometimes I think the organizing principle of any society is for war.*

The authority of the state over its people resides in its war powers [emphasis mine]. Even Eisenhower, military hero of WWII, warned us about it: "Beware of the military-industrial complex," he said. Kennedy wanted to end the Cold War in his second term. He wanted to call off the moon race in favor of cooperation with the Soviets. He signed a treaty with the Soviets to ban nuclear testing, he refused to invade Cuba in '62, and he set out to withdraw from Vietnam. But all that ended on November 22, 1963.

Thus, given the numerous toes being stepped on and the billions of dollars lost, you certainly have a motivation to blow that president's mind "into a thousand pieces" (exactly what Kennedy warned he wanted to do to the CIA, and tried to implement by firing its three top leaders and issuing NSAMs 55 and 56). When striking at a snake, make sure you kill it before it kills you.

In any event, I think that any viable theory one chooses ultimately suggests a coup d'état. What's not well known is that this would not have been the first such attempt in American history. In fact, I am amazed that Schlesinger ignores all the evidence of a coup d'état in the works against President Franklin Roosevelt in 1933–1934. It was a moment, to be sure, out of one of Frank Capra's best movies, *Meet John Doe,* which captured so well with its speeches and mobs the feeling that our country was falling into the grip of fascism, which was then popular in Germany and Italy, our bulwarks against Russia.

Roosevelt's New Deal policies were scaring the hell out of the nation's wealthiest, and a small-core group made up of J. P. Morgan, Jr. (J. P. Morgan & Co.), Colonel Grayson Murphy (Wall Street chief of Grayson-Murphy), Hugh Johnson (head of the National Recovery Administration), Iréné du Pont (chairman of du Pont), and Bernard Baruch (noted philanthropist and a Roosevelt confidante), among others, planned to have General Douglas MacArthur, of later World War II fame, lead troops into Washington, D.C., on a protest march and then privately announce to President Roosevelt that he was taking over as secretary of general welfare, which would make him the de facto leader of the nation, reducing Roosevelt to a mere puppet figure. Once this had taken place, they would reinstitute the gold standard, along with many other reforms.

However, General MacArthur had lost much prestige after he ran roughshod, with horses and tanks, over the bonus marchers in 1932 — a protest in which impoverished, depression-racked World War I veterans camped out near the Capitol to recoup promised bonuses reneged on by their government. There was no way, in fact, that MacArthur could lead the country — although he would cannily wait to assume a leadership position *after* the coup had taken place. Ironically, the same thing almost happened again during the Korean War, with MacArthur acting like his own warlord before Truman fired him.

The cabal instructed Gerald MacGuire, a trader for Grayson-Murphy, to approach two-time Medal of Honor winner, ex-marine major general Smedley Darlington Butler in 1933 to lead their revolt. They were correct in their assessment that he wasn't a big fan of Roosevelt's New Deal policies but wholly misunderstood his deep-seated commitment to our democracy.

General Butler strung the conspirators along in a 1930s John Buchan 39 *Steps* or 1960s James Bond fashion, leading them to believe that he was with them, but finally helping to expose the plan. Others, such as the founder of our modern military intelligence, General Ralph Van Deman, and young J. Edgar Hoover at the nascent FBI, were also involved — mercifully, on the side of Roosevelt. They were heroes, pointing out once again, especially in Hoover's case, the paradoxes of our history — all of it paradox.

This ugly affair prompted congressional hearings (the McCormack-Dickstein hearings of 1934, available on record, and led by the same John McCormack of Massachusetts who later became Speaker of the House) that concluded that everything General Butler had charged had been substantiated. Yet we got only part of the story from the hearings. The other part never came out. There is little reason to wonder why, when you understand the concentrated power and names of the plotters. Lieutenant Colonel William Corson, now in his eighties, retired from the Marine Corps, and a member of military intelligence during World War II, Korea, and Vietnam, whose father, Ray Corson, had been an integral intelligence figure working for General Van Deman, corroborated the story and told me of some startling, behind-the-scenes events showing how the coup was thwarted.

The media did their best to ridicule this story. Henry Luce at *Time* played a leading role. He even attacked General Butler's credibility in the mainstream, calling the affair a "plot without plotters." It was all very sad, not only because Butler was one of our great unknown American heroes, but also because Luce (born in China to missionary parents and married to the conservative doyenne of American politics, Clare Booth Luce) played a similar role later in Vietnam and, in effect, was a significant influence on America's tilt toward Asian interventionism. The commercially conscious and respectable *New York Times* gave the story scant attention. It took the stronger, more liberal presses of the day — *The Nation, New Masses* — to get it out to the public. Yet no one, with the depression in full swing, really paid attention. There were other, more important problems pressing — as always in real life.

Roosevelt also clearly wanted it swept under the rug. The committee's report excluded many of the most embarrassing names — former New York governor and 1928 Democratic presidential candidate Al Smith, General Hugh Johnson of the National Recovery Administration, and a number of admirals and generals who were privy to the plot. Roosevelt was responsible for that. He still had to work with these people and felt that it was in the best interest of the country to move on. However, he did tell General MacArthur, according to Corson, that the general would never set foot in this country again while he, Roosevelt, was alive. And the "American Caesar" never did, to the end of his life compromised by his traitorous addiction to power over the masses.[39]

Another insight of historical importance is the fact that Eisenhower was a close aide to MacArthur. Although he participated in the bloody rout of the World War I veterans, who had gathered in a tent city in D.C. to ask for bonuses reneged on by their government, with MacArthur (and Patton), it is unclear whether he was privy to MacArthur's traitorous thoughts. I hardly claim to know, but I wonder. Given the nature of Eisenhower's secret enterprises with the Dulles brothers in the 1950s, I believe one should take a far deeper and darker look at our most benign president. Often in history, there are precedents for a person's behavior, shown as much as twenty years earlier, but with a different outcome.

Schlesinger on JFK and Nixon

Schlesinger says that I describe a "great conspiracy" in the JFK murder. As I've explained previously, it's not that way at all. He also dismisses the "fantasies" of Colonel Fletcher Prouty. I must wonder, why are they fantasies? Please give us specifics. It is not enough to ridicule a man's entire career, as the media would. I respect Schlesinger too much, but somehow, I think the intellectuals, the professors of the world, when working in the beehive cells of government, have no idea of the complexity of covert operations going on parallel to their own activities.

Schlesinger says that dramatic license should not be corrupted by ideology. Doesn't Tolstoy dislike Napoleon a priori in *War and Peace?* Isn't ideology in the background of Schlesinger's calling Prouty's career of distinction and hard-earned insights "fantasies" or dismissing Jim Garrison as a "con man"? I'm not at all comfortable with a historian thinking that. I think a historian, by profession, should stay inductive; otherwise, it speaks of an agenda and is a perfect example of the deductive thinking that some critics accuse me of. Having experienced so many political changes in my life, I'm aware of the seductions of ideology and have tried to steer clear of any one way of thinking. I avoid in my work, I think, easy categorization; many people on the Left attacked me for being too empathetic to Nixon. In fact, I'm neither Left nor Right, finding some positions on either side attractive or abhorrent. If anything, I consider myself, for want of a better definition, an independent thinker, hovering somewhere near the "radical center." A beautiful quotation, coming from no less a figure than the enigmatic Albert Einstein, sums up a life of tribulation and success, equally mixed and soured, as was Garrison's: "So many things have been written about me, masses of insolent lies and inventions that I would have perished long ago, had I paid any attention. One must take comfort in the fact that time has a sieve, through which most trivia run off into the sea of oblivion. Without being overly arrogant, I suspect the same could be said for any man or woman who dares enter the arena."

Schlesinger goes on to say about conspiracy, "One doubts that things happen in the ordered way proposed by conspiracy theorists." He harps on conspiracy, ignoring the fact that history, to my mind, is rather a blend of natural accident, the conscious decisions of individuals, and sometimes conspiracy. Nor is conspiracy neat and clean, as Schlesinger describes. As in the case of the Kennedy assassination, there are many differing points of view. It's something of a disordered mess, and there are many dangling clues. *JFK* was a thriller to me, a mystery story, a "why-dunit" even more than a "whodunit." In the course of my research, I became more and more convinced of a state of being that was inconsistent with the principles of the founders. Money and power have corrupted our Republic. This conclusion is not a belief-based dramatic license corrupted by ideology, but rather one of inductive thinking. Ideology didn't make the film. Character made the film.

Says Schlesinger: "History, in his view, is made at night." Yes. Much is, but not all. "Appearances are an illusion." Yes. And I don't think there are too many sensible people who would disagree with me. Schlesinger also says that I believe reality happens "in the shadows, where . . . ten or twenty people secretly make the basic decisions." Not always, but I think most people recognize that there are often people in the shadows. Similarly, one person can make history with a single decision, as did Schlesinger's hero, John Kennedy. Inside a cell-like structure, leadership can be as large or as small as necessary. Most people, I believe, would reasonably accept that. If they don't, then I think they'd better think again. After all, it was Schlesinger's leader who, by the converse of the historic coin, was struck down in Dallas on one fateful afternoon of our history, in a decision made by one or more individuals.

James Petras seems to understand some of my thinking:

The fact that the film was attacked in the mass media for its politics months in advance of its screening by critics who had neither viewed nor even read the final screenplay speaks to the knee-jerk political reflexes that have become so much part of the mass media's subservient defense of the American political elite. These intellectuals in uniform are prepared to do battle in the name of State Truth, even before they know their adversary's message, facts or logic. . . . Fear that the public will make a connection between private discontents and the public sphere at its highest levels has provoked the semi-official media mongers to launch an unprecedented attack on the making of the film, followed by a series of vicious ad hominem and political attacks on Stone himself.

Petras then goes on to cite in particular Bernard Weinraub of the *New York Times,* "whose call to 'blunt the highly charged message' was an example of the kind of media arm-twisting that the film exposes. Stone will soon have ample material with which to make a sequel of *JFK*." He then concludes by saying, "Stone has turned the negative reviews of *JFK* into a powerful indictment of the mass media."[40]

But when I agreed to address the National Press Club in January 1992, it was not so much to indict as simply to defend my film. I said in part:

This is not history, this is myth. It is a myth that a scant number of Americans has ever believed. It is a myth that has sustained a generation of journalists and historians who have refused to question it, and above all who close ranks to criticize and vilify those who do. So long as the attackers of that comforting lone gunman theory could be dismissed as kooks and cranks and the writers of obscure books that would not be published by "reputable" publishing houses, not much defense was needed. But now, that myth is under attack by a well-financed — and I hope — well-made motion picture with all the vivid imagery and new energy the screen can convey. Now, either enormous amounts of evidence have to be marshaled in support of that myth, or else those who question it must be attacked. There is no evidence; therefore the attack is on.

There is as yet no marketplace of history for the years of the Kennedy assassination and immediately afterward. Let us begin to create one. What I have tried to do with this movie is to open a Jeffersonian stall in that "marketplace of ideas" he described and offer a version of what might have happened, as against the competing versions of what we know did not happen that fateful day.

Posner's Case Closed

Colonel Prouty once told me something to the effect that "the scenery is for the suckers, and there's plenty of them here. Oswald, Shaw, Ruby, Ferrie, all that group — they're just scenery. They distract you, make you take your eye off the ball. Stick to Kennedy, stick to the motivation, the why-dunit, that's where the answer lies."

In the vein of allowing myself to be distracted once again by the scenery, I should mention Gerald Posner, who is media famous in this country as the author of the "widely credited" assassination epic *Case Closed*.[41] I used the quotation "widely credited" because it appeared in a recent *New York Times* book review of another book. In fact, you could pretty much find those words anywhere you looked in the establishment press, as one publication supports the other in supporting Gerald Posner. I doubt that many of these people have actually read the book or, for that matter, know much about the case, but somehow, in some way, known or unbeknown to the gods, Posner's book has been elevated to a stature comparable to the Bible in its authenticity. The very title, *Case Closed*, suggests a smugness of thought that should be repellent to most fair-minded Americans. When it first came out, it was already being touted on the cover of *U.S. News and World Report* as the factual answer to my movie. It was everywhere I looked and read in the mainstream press. Rarely have I seen a book receive such unanimous, intense, and surprisingly sound-alike praise. It's almost as if the copy for the review had been issued as a press release by Random House, or *Pravda* in the old Soviet Union.

There is not the time or space here to go into the many "straw-man" arguments that Posner put in my mouth, as well as the mouth of anyone else who disagreed with him. When the book first came out, I went to the twelve references to my name in the index, flipped to each one, and found in every instance that Posner was conveniently fitting his interpretation of events on the screen to his purpose and was using me, and other assassination dissidents, as straw men, that is, setting us up with weak, often out-of-context arguments that he could easily tear apart, along with those witnesses whose reliability he judged quite subjectively.

These types of books had been published before, especially in the 1960s and 1970s, and, as with Posner's book, few read them. But in this case of 1990s hyper-media onslaught, few could miss the wide dissemination of his conclusion, published by Random House in 1993 and featured in numerous establishment magazines and reviews. Posner was given every available prestige outlet on television, often without any opposing point of view presented.

Many fallacies abound in the Posner book, many subjective judgments, and much "straw-man" argumentation, but some of the fallacies that quickly come to mind and were never questioned by the media are: the Oswald-Banister Camp Street confusion, the validity of witnesses Jean Hill and Rose Cheramie, the palm print on the murderer's rifle, and the notorious computer analysis supposedly proving that Oswald did it alone.

There had never been a doubt in most reasonable minds, including in the conservative approach taken by *Frontline* on PBS, that Banister and Oswald were based in the same building at one time. Yet Posner thought it more credible to believe that Oswald made up a false address — one that just happened to house Guy Banister, who used him in his anti-Castro crusade as a "plant" and agent provocateur for the pro-Castro forces. But don't believe either of us — if one physically goes to New Orleans to the two addresses, one will understand clearly how both addresses enter the same building, which was also in the heart of the government section of New Orleans.

Posner attempts to discredit witnesses Jean Hill and Rose Cheramie with a holier-than-thou attitude, but if you want a sterling account of Hill's own story, read Bill Sloan's *The Last Dissenting Witness*.[42] She will tell you of seeing movement coming from the fence on the grassy knoll, as well as giving details on the threats and outright dismissal of her testimony by federal officials. The Cassandra of this tragic epic, Rose Cheramie, was in a hospital on November 20, 1963. Two days before Kennedy's assassination, she warned that the president was to be killed. Posner discounts this because she was a heroin user. Again, one should ask the morally smug Posner why it is that a heroin user would have a penchant for prophecy, worse eyesight, and a more unreliable memory than anyone else?

In regard to the palm print, Posner, not the film, ignored the chain of evidence. Initial tests for prints found only traces of a couple of fingers that couldn't be identified. There was no palm print when the rifle was sent to the FBI, yet in some sort of *X-Files* phenomenon, a full week later, the print was "discovered." Who would argue that Posner's rationality is more grounded in reality than what the movie presents?

In a nasty footnote, Posner offers up an ugly description of Larry Howard, the late director of the JFK Assassination Information Center, which looked into many of the omissions and flaws of the official exhibit on the sixth floor of the Book Depository, which is the one you will visit when you go to Dallas now, because Larry Howard has passed away and the museum, which always struggled, has closed. Howard provided our production with valuable insights and information and, in that capacity, was paid like any other consultant on a film. Why doubt his sincerity? Because he was paid by us? It makes me wonder, at deeper levels, why not one of us ever escapes the condemnation of others in this lifetime. The Bible had it right when it stuck to questions. Who shall throw the first stone? Who? Posner doesn't hesitate in numerous instances to seek to destroy the legitimate insights of dozens of people who have given much of their lives, often without reward, to questioning this case.

One of Posner's more deceptive maneuvers in the book is to present a "computer analysis" proving Oswald guilty — wholly ignoring the same computer's analysis proving Oswald *not guilty* of the same actions. The president of the computer company that created this model for analysis apparently was displeased over the use Posner made of his computers but was never clearly heard or else was ignored by the same crowd that adored Posner for reassuring them that the big bad wolf was not under the bed. What this man had to say was very important: there were *two* analyses; one was positive, the other was negative. Posner published *only* the one that found Oswald guilty. In any event, I won't even begin to get into what criteria were fed into the computer regarding Oswald that produced this result, but it seems to me that with the growing sophistication of our computers since the book's release, much more incisive and intelligent work can be done with a computer. For that matter, just allow any scratch of DNA to be taken from Kennedy, Connally, Oswald, or Ruby and you will further the case. But no one will do this because, as Prouty said, *there was no ongoing investigation* once the body was pulled out of Texas, and LBJ made sure that the Warren Commission was substituted for a real trial in Texas.

Posner eventually acknowledges the fact that Congress passed "historic" legislation to release all the files in conjunction with the Kennedy assassination because of the movie *JFK*. However, always ready to downplay the truth, he writes it as an aside in a footnote — once more in the name of building me up as a straw man to tear apart.

Thus goes the case, and one day we will all be dead, and what will it matter? Even the CIA, with all its untold billions, has now informed us that it can go no further in releasing any more documentation on its numerous interventions in the 1950s. Guatemala was tough enough; Iran would certainly be a disaster. The soup is thick. But what was the reason given in the media by the CIA? Lack of funds and time. That was pretty cynical, but by now, very little surprises me in this era, wherein we each have the potential of becoming either an "enemy of the state" or a "nonperson" part of a "nonevent." I pray that twentieth-century totalitarianism takes a long walk in the twenty-first century and never comes back again.

In the same vein, ask yourself, where were the rebuttals to Posner's book? In fact, go beyond that and ask yourself, have you ever seen any serious review in a major mainstream publication of an anti–Warren Commission book, letter, statement, or, for that matter, even a tiny quote? I don't remember one, not in the last ten years, not since the film was released. It appears, however, that there is no disagreement at all with Posner in our press, whereas nothing could be further from the truth. What is truly tragic in this Posner affair is that dissent itself is being stymied. The *New York Times* and *Washington Post* have been, perhaps, the most outrageous in their muzzling of dissent and their refusal to print *anything* that takes a reasonable view of a possible conspiracy in Dallas.

Such an unreasoning attitude toward dissent in the Kennedy murder — which, like Oedipus to the Greeks, has become our national taboo — should make us realize that as a nation we have become thoroughly corrupt and dishonest with ourselves. That's why I dedicated my movie "to the young, in whose spirit the search for truth marches on." I yearn for that day to come, when those stronger than I can return this country to the ideals, even a fraction of the ideals, in which it was birthed.

I pray for my country. I love it as much as any man. I served in its armed forces with some distinction, but that is not to say that I am a nationalist or a blind "patriot," all too often the last refuge of the scoundrel, the man who has not served and calls on his country to advance his ideology. My mother was French, an immigrant who came over here in 1946 — which makes me, I guess, half-immigrant. I am very proud of that for a reason: because I truly think that it is the immigrant population that has kept the best part of America alive — without money or class, with their lack of pretension and their contempt for elitism in any form, with their capacity to work hard, to confront, to fight, and to raise the tough questions and not to clamor weakly for conformity. These are the parts of the American character I love: the energy, the verve, the can-do spirit — the Jack London, Mark Twain, Tom Jefferson, George Washington, and Abe Lincoln in each of us. Unfortunately, the worst part of America came out in its reaction to John Kennedy's murder, in its desire to simplify, to deal with good guys and bad guys and a lone gunman — John Wayne theatrics. The European press was much more skeptical, because it saw in this assassination political forces at play. There was, when all is said and done, a status quo in the media at the time of the assassination that we can virtually call "silent consent," not a cover-up involving "thousands," as Schlesinger condescendingly described it, but simply silent consent involving the private conscience.

We have never really questioned the results of the Kennedy assassination. In the later 1960s, we experienced the hippie movement, race riots, many organized protests, and the drug culture, all this eruption of behavior a few short years after Kennedy's murder. I think there was, on a deeper, subconscious level, a significant erosion of trust in our government. On the conscious level, we moved on. We buried Oswald and we got rid of Ruby and the nightmare went away. But subconsciously, the tsunami wave silently occurred and continues to roll on. At the beginning of this new millennium, we must ask ourselves, with integrity, have we all become part of a commercial corporate state with ourselves as media-dominated consumer-slaves? Or are we still a true democracy, wherein private conscience and individual actions still matter?

I said at the time that the Warren Commission, from beginning to end, was a myth. I still believe so, and I believe that *JFK*, the movie, was made as counter-myth, which I believe truly represents the inner spiritual meaning of the assassination. Only in the twenty-first century, I think, will historians catch up to what we have tried to obscure, and they will point their fingers at us as a society of consent, fear, and mediocrity in this matter, but more tragically, they will point to John Kennedy's death as a key moment — and not a ridiculous footnote — in American history.

"In a dark time, the eye begins to see." — Theodore Roethke

Notes

PART I: STONE ON STONE'S IMAGE

1 Stephen Talbot, "Oliver Stone Keeps Telling Personal History," *Mother Jones* (March/April 1991): 46.
2 Oliver Stone and Zachary Sklar, JFK: *The Book of the Screenplay* (New York: Applause, 1992); Oliver Stone, Stephen Rivele, and Christopher Wilkinson, Nixon: *An Oliver Stone Film* (New York: Hyperion, 1995).
3 Robert Sam Anson, "The Shooting of *JFK,*" *Esquire* (November 1991): 93.
4 *New York Times,* December 21, 1995.
5 Bob Woodward and Carl Bernstein, *The Final Days* (New York: Simon and Schuster, 1976); Fawn Brodie, *Richard Nixon: The Shaping of His Character* (New York: W. W. Norton, 1981).
6 Personal letter from Howard Zinn to Stone; emphasis added.
7 Richard Reeves, *President Kennedy: Profile of Power* (New York: Simon and Schuster, 1993).
8 Mike Feinsilber, Associated Press, July 2, 1997.
9 Richard Hofstadter, "The Paranoid Style in American Politics," *Harper's Magazine* 229 (1963): 77.

PART I: A SACRED MISSION: OLIVER STONE AND VIETNAM

1 Stuart Fischoff, "Oliver Stone," *Psychology Today* 26 (September/October 1993): 69; Mark Rowland, "Stone Unturned," *American Film* 16 (March 1991): 42; *Oliver Stone: Inside Out,* produced and directed by Joel Sucher and Steven Fischler, Pacific Street Producers Group, 1992; Gavin Smith, "Oliver Stone: Why Do I Have to Provoke?" *Sight and Sound* 4 (December 1994): 12.
2 James Riordan, *Stone: The Controversies, Excesses, and Exploits of a Radical Filmmaker* (New York: Hyperion, 1995), 3–8.
3 Rowland, "Stone Unturned," 41–43; Riordan, *Stone,* 8–12, 20–22.
4 Riordan, *Stone,* 11–12, 17, 23.
5 Gary Crowdus, "History, Dramatic License, and Larger Historical Truths: An Interview with Oliver Stone," *Cineaste* 22 (fall 1996): 40; David Breskin, "Oliver Stone: The Rolling Stone Interview," *Rolling Stone,* April 4, 1991, 40.
6 Riordan, *Stone,* 24–25, 16, 27; Breskin, "Oliver Stone," 40.

7 Michael Singer, *The Making of Oliver Stone's* Heaven and Earth (Boston: Charles E. Tuttle, 1993), 4; Lisa Grunwald, "Why We Still Care," *Life*, December 14, 1991, 43, 39; Robert Sam Anson, "The Shooting of *JFK*," *Esquire*, November 1991, 96.

8 Riordan, *Stone*, 32–33; Susan Mackey-Kallis, *Oliver Stone's America: "Dreaming the Myth Outward"* (Boulder, Colo.: Westview Press, 1996), 11.

9 Riordan, *Stone*, 33–35.

10 Ibid., 35–40; Fred Schruers, "Soldier's Story," *Rolling Stone*, January 29, 1987, 26.

11 Chuck Pfeifer, "Oliver Stone," *Interview* (February 1987): 73; Pat McGilligan, "Point Man," *Film Comment* 23 (January/February 1987): 16; Fischoff, "Oliver Stone," 44; Smith, "Oliver Stone," 12; Breskin, "Oliver Stone," 40.

12 McGilligan, "Point Man," 16; Gary Crowdus, "Personal Struggles and Political Issues: An Interview with Oliver Stone," *Cineaste* 16 (1988): 20; Peter Blauner, "Coming Home," *New York*, December 8, 1986, 64; Riordan, *Stone*, 40, 42.

13 Singer, *The Making of Oliver Stone's* Heaven and Earth, 5; Riordan, *Stone*, 43, 11; Gerald Peary, "The Ballad of a Haunted Soldier," *Maclean's*, March 30, 1987, 61; *Oliver Stone: Inside Out*.

14 Riordan, *Stone*, 44; "Oliver Stone's Platoon Buddies Recall the War 20 Years Later," *People Weekly*, May 11, 1987, 83; Blauner, "Coming Home," 60, 64; *Oliver Stone: Inside Out*.

15 Riordan, *Stone*, 45–46; "Oliver Stone's Platoon Buddies Recall the War 20 Years Later," 84, 86; Gregory Cerio and Lynda Wright, "Oliver's Twist," *People Weekly*, January 22, 1996, 108.

16 Riordan, *Stone*, 48–50.

17 Ibid., 51–52.

18 Ibid., 52.

19 Ibid., 43, 53–54.

20 Ibid., 55–56; Schruers, "Soldier's Story," 53.

21 Riordan, *Stone*, 50, 57–59; Blauner, "Coming Home," 64; Lucia Hwong, "Political Commitment in Filmmaking: Oliver Stone," *Third Rail: A Review of International Arts and Literature* 9 (1988): 35; *Oliver Stone: Inside Out*.

22 Riordan, *Stone*, 60; Stephen Schiff, "The Last Wild Man," *New Yorker*, August 8, 1994, 50; Singer, *The Making of Oliver Stone's* Heaven and Earth, 6.

23 Riordan, *Stone*, 62–64; Schiff, "The Last Wild Man," 50; *Oliver Stone: Inside Out*.

24 Breskin, "Oliver Stone," 38, 41; Riordan, *Stone*, 65; Pfeifer, "Oliver Stone," 73; McGilligan, "Point Man," 16; Richard Grenier, "On the Trail of America's Paranoid Class: Oliver Stone's *JFK*," *National Interest* 27 (spring 1992): 77.

25 Riordan, *Stone*, 66–69, 72; Schiff, "The Last Wild Man," 50.

26 Riordan, *Stone*, 73, 76, 88–89; Mackey-Kallis, *Oliver Stone's America*, 11.

27 "Tough Guys Do Talk," *Newsweek*, December 11, 1995, 70; Garry Wills, "Son of Nixon," *Esquire*, January 1996, 72; McGilligan, "Point Man," 18; Riordan, *Stone*, 88–89.

28 Riordan, *Stone*, 92, 96, 97, 104, 108.

29 Mackey-Kallis, *Oliver Stone's America*, 13; Frank Eugene Beaver, *Oliver Stone: Wakeup Cinema* (New York: Twayne Publishers, 1994), 84.

30 Randy Roberts and James S. Olson, *John Wayne: American* (New York: Free Press, 1995), 535–60.

31 Singer, *The Making of Oliver Stone's* Heaven and Earth, 4.

32 McGilligan, "Point Man," 20; Mackey-Kallis, *Oliver Stone's America,* 64; Riordan, *Stone,* 196, 188.

33 Mahmaud Hussein and Regis Debray, "Oliver Stone," *Unesco Courier* 46 (July/August 1993): 5.

34 *Time,* January 26, 1987; *New York Times,* December 19, 1986; Riordan, *Stone,* 182, 213; Beaver, *Oliver Stone,* 97; Mackey-Kallis, *Oliver Stone's America,* 65; Pfeifer, "Oliver Stone," 73.

35 Peary, "The Ballad of a Haunted Soldier," 61; Richard Corliss, "Tom Terrific," *Time,* December 25, 1989, 75–76.

36 Kovic quoted in Roberts and Olson, *John Wayne,* 559.

37 Rowland, "Stone Unturned," 42.

38 Singer, *The Making of Oliver Stone's* Heaven and Earth, 6; Beaver, *Oliver Stone,* 142; Riordan, *Stone,* 276.

39 Singer, *The Making of Oliver Stone's* Heaven and Earth, 3.

40 Schiff, "The Last Wild Man," 48; Gavin Smith, "The Camera for Me Is an Actor," *Film Comment* 30 (January/February 1994): 26.

41 Anson, "The Shooting of *JFK,*" 96, 174; Riordan, *Stone,* 351; Smith, "The Camera for Me Is an Actor," 38; Richard Corliss, "Who Killed J.F.K.?" *Time,* December 23, 1991, 70.

42 Oliver Stone, "Who Defines History? Oliver Stone's Address to the National Press Club," *Cineaste* 19 (winter 1992): 24.

43 Kenneth Auchincloss with Ginny Carroll and Maggie Malone, "Twisted History," *Newsweek,* December 23, 1991, 46, 48; Corliss, "Who Killed J.F.K.?" 67; Evan Thomas, "Whose Obsession Is It, Anyway?" *Newsweek,* December 11, 1995, 68; Edward Jay Epstein, "The Second Coming of Jim Garrison," *Atlantic Monthly,* March 1993, 90; R. Emmett Tyrrell, Jr., "Stone Dead," *American Spectator* (February 1992): 11; Peter Collier, "Ollie Uber Alles," *American Spectator* (April 1992): 29.

44 Hussein and Debray, "Oliver Stone," 5; Smith, "The Camera for Me Is an Actor," 39; Beaver, *Oliver Stone,* 164; Oliver Stone, "Oliver Stone Talks Back," *Premiere* 5 (January 1992): 70; David Ansen, "What Does Oliver Stone Owe History?" *Newsweek,* December 23, 1991, 49; Fischoff, "Oliver Stone," 66.

45 Oliver Stone, "Where I Find My Heroes," *McCall's,* November 1992, 104; Hussein and Debray, "Oliver Stone," 7; Oliver Stone, "Was Vietnam JFK's War?" *Newsweek,* October 21, 1996, 14; Mackey-Kallis, *Oliver Stone's America,* 33.

46 Collier, "Ollie Uber Alles," 30; Auchincloss, "Twisted History," 48; Grenier, "On the Trail of America's Paranoid Class," 81; Stanley Karnow, "JFK," *Past Imperfect: History According to the Movies,* ed. Mark C. Carnes (New York: Henry Holt, 1995), 272–73; Neil Sheehan, Hedrick Smith, E. W. Kenworthy, and Fox Butterfield, eds., *The Pentagon Papers As Published by the New York Times* (Toronto: Bantam Books, 1971), 232–33, 210–13.

47 Singer, *The Making of Oliver Stone's* Heaven and Earth, 6.

48 Wills, "Son of Nixon," 72; Peter Biskind, "Stone," *Premiere* 9 (January 1996): 62; Mark C. Carnes, "Past Imperfect: History According to the Movies," *Cineaste* 22 (March 1997): 33; Stryker McGuire and David Ansen, "Hollywood's Most Controversial Director Oliver Stone Takes On Our Most Controversial President Richard Nixon," *Newsweek,* December 11, 1995, 70; Steven E. Ambrose, "*Nixon:* An Oliver Stone Film," *Journal of American History* 82 (March 1996): 1530.

49 Breskin, "Oliver Stone," 62.

50 Carnes, "Past Imperfect," 35.

51 Singer, *The Making of Oliver Stone's* Heaven and Earth, 4.

PART II: *SALVADOR*

1 Frank Eugene Beaver, *Oliver Stone: Wakeup Cinema* (New York: Twayne Publishers, 1994), 2, 5, 7.

2 Ibid., 69.

3 Norman Kagan, *The Cinema of Oliver Stone* (New York: Continuum, 1995), 82.

4 "Calendar," *Los Angeles Times,* December 1, 1985, 26, 28.

5 Christian Smith, *Resisting Reagan: The U.S. Central American Peace Movement* (Chicago: University of Chicago Press, 1996), tells this story.

6 "Calendar," 28.

7 Ibid.

8 Stone notes this in Beaver, *Oliver Stone,* 76.

9 Stone observed in an interview that the Boyle–Dr. Rock relationship is "really a Three Stooges situation" in which the two "sleazoids" dislike each other and "go nuts just being in the same room together." Gary Crowdus, "Personal Struggles and Political Issues: An Interview with Oliver Stone," *Cineaste* 16 (1988): 19.

10 "Calendar," 28.

11 Pauline Kael attacked this scene as a "posh, sinister version of 'The Last Supper,'" in the *New Yorker,* July 28, 1986, 79. But as noted later, a U.S. embassy account of the actual scene gives some support to Stone's version.

12 This and the following paragraph are drawn from Guy Gugliotta, "D'Aubuisson Kept U.S. on Its Guard," *Washington Post,* January 4, 1994, A1.

13 For example, Walter Goodman, "Screen: 'Salvador' by Stone," *New York Times,* March 5, 1986, C22.

14 Kagan, *The Cinema of Oliver Stone,* 91–97.

15 The policies of the 1960s and their unfortunate effects on Central America are traced in Walter LaFeber, *Inevitable Revolutions: The United States in Central America,* 2d ed. (New York: W. W. Norton, 1993), chap. 3, which has citations and a bibliography. A working definition of "oligarchy" was given by a Salvadoran oligarch: "It's an oligarchy because these families own and run almost everything that makes money in El Salvador. Coffee gave birth to the oligarchy in the late 19th century, and economic growth has evolved around them ever since" (Paul H. Hoeffel, "The Eclipse of the Oligarchs," *New York Times Magazine,* September 6, 1981, 23).

16 Dermot Keogh, *Romero: El Salvador's Martyr* (Dublin, Ireland: Dominican Publications, 1981), 96.

17 A superb analysis and firsthand description by an Irish scholar and journalist is Keogh, *Romero,* 99–115.

18 Crowdus, "Personal Struggles," 18.

19 Further discussion and references are in LaFeber, *Inevitable Revolutions,* 278–80.

20 The standard account is Mark Danner, *The Massacre of El Mozote: A Parable of the Cold War* (New York: Random House, 1994).

21 Quoted in Joan Didion, "'Something Horrible' in El Salvador," *New York Review of Books,* July 14, 1994, 8.

22 Raymond Bonner, *Weakness and Deceit: United States Policy and El Salvador* (New York: Times Books, 1984).

23 Didion, "'Something Horrible,'" 8.

24 A good analysis is Susan Mackey-Kallis, *Oliver Stone's America: "Dreaming the Myth Outward"* (Boulder, Colo.: Westview Press, 1996), 90, although the author confuses Frank Capra with Robert Capa in this quotation.

25 *New York Times,* March 5, 1986, C22.

26 Crowdus, "Personal Struggles," 19.

27 Ibid., 18.

28 *Washington Post,* May 27, 1996, A16.

29 Mackey-Kallis, *Oliver Stone's America,* 107.

30 The conversations in fuller form and in context are in ibid., 108–9.

31 George Herring, "Vietnam, Central America, and the Uses of History," in *Understanding the Central American Crisis,* ed. Kenneth L. Coleman and George Herring (Washington, D.C.: Scholarly Research, 1991), 181–91; Eldon Kenworthy, "The Selling of a Policy," in *Reagan versus the Sandinistas,* ed. Thomas W. Walker (Boulder, Colo.: Westview Press, 1987).

32 The major document on the U.S. military's evaluation of the long-term meaning of the Vietnam conflict is Secretary of Defense Caspar Weinberger's "The Use of Military Power," news release, November 28, 1984, Office of the Assistant Secretary of Defense (Public Affairs), Washington, D.C.

33 *Time,* January 26, 1987, 61.

34 William Deane Stanley, "Economic Migrants or Refugees from Violence?" *Latin American Research Review* 22, no. 1 (1987): 133–48.

35 Pat Gilligan, "Point Man," *Film Comment* 23 (January/February 1987): 19.

36 Kagan, *The Cinema of Oliver Stone,* 84; Beaver, *Oliver Stone,* 8.

37 *Washington Post,* April 4, 1986, D1.

38 *Los Angeles Times,* April 12, 1986, pt. V, 1, 8.

39 *Chicago Tribune,* April 25, 1986, sec. 7, 3.

40 *New Yorker,* July 28, 1986, 78–79.

41 *New York Times,* March 5, 1986, C22.

42 Kagan, *The Cinema of Oliver Stone,* 91, 96.

43 John F. Stone, "Manifestations of Foreign Culture: Salvador," *Journal of Popular Film and Television* 19 (winter 1992): 180–85.

44 Benjamin Schwarz, "Of Course We Knew," *Washington Post,* April 8, 1993, A21; Jefferson Morley, "Death from a Distance," *Washington Post,* March 28, 1993, C1; *Washington Post,* April 5, 1994, A24.

45 Robert Brent Toplin, *History by Hollywood: The Use and Abuse of the Past* (Urbana, Ill.: University of Illinois Press, 1996), viii.

46 *New Yorker,* January 19, 1998, 41.

John Dean Alfone, Linda Greenberg, William Kan, Dorothy Nelsen-Gille, Eric Rosenberg, and Steven Waite provided invaluable assistance in the creation of this essay. The author is solely responsible for any errors or omissions, however.

1 Kip Schlegel and David Weisburd, eds., *White-Collar Crime Reconsidered* (Boston: Northeastern University Press, 1992).

2 "The 100 Most Memorable Movie Lines," *Fort Worth Star-Telegram*, October 13, 1996, Arts sec. 1.

3 A hostile takeover is defined as a bid for a publicly traded corporation's stock, aimed at a number of shares sufficient to gain control and opposed by the company's board of directors.

4 The legal definition of insider trading is a complex subject. According to popular understanding, the crime consists of profiting illicitly in the stock market from information that has not been disseminated publicly.

5 Chris Welles, "The Platoon of Pros Who Helped Out on *Wall Street*," *Business Week*, December 21, 1987, 38.

6 James Lardner, *"Wall Street," The Nation*, January 23, 1988, 97.

7 Investment banker Kenneth Lipper's novelization of the movie, however, gives "Ann Darien Taylor" as the full appellation of the interior decorator portrayed by Daryl Hannah. The character's discarded first name adds an appropriate fashion note, as well as signifying an upscale female professional. See Kenneth Lipper, *Wall Street* (New York: Berkley Publishing Group, 1988).

8 John Simon, *"Wall Street," National Review*, January 22, 1988, 65.

9 Hal Lipper, *"Wall Street:* Paper-Thin," *St. Petersburg Times*, December 11, 1987, Weekend sec. 7.

10 Janet Maslin, "Morality Tales for Our Time," *New York Times*, December 20, 1987, sec. 2, 25.

11 Michael Kolbenschlag, "An Inside Opinion: Boesky Would Give the Film a 2," *Orange County Register*, December 13, 1987, F1.

12 Nigel Andrews, "Mammon-Obsessed Jungle Observed," *Financial Times*, April 29, 1988, 21.

13 John V. N. Philip, "The Gekko and the Fox; *Wall Street*, Directed by Oliver Stone," *Policy Review* (spring 1988): 78.

14 Derek Malcolm, "Wall Street Villainy," *Manchester Guardian Weekly*, May 6, 1988, 26.

15 John Gross, "The New Greed Takes Center Stage," *New York Times*, January 3, 1988, sec. 2, 1.

16 Dave Kehr, "Director Stone Plays Options Right in *Wall Street, Chicago Tribune*, December 11, 1987, A1.

17 David Edelstein, "Raiders of the Lost Market," *Village Voice*, December 15, 1987, 110.

18 David Sterritt, "Film," *Christian Science Monitor*, December 11, 1987, Arts and Leisure sec., 21.

19 David Denby, *"Wall Street," New York*, December 14, 1987, 87–88.

20 Peter C. Newman, "Wall Street's Gutter Ethics," *Maclean's*, December 28, 1987, 46.

21 Susan Festa, "Finance at the Peak of Excess," *American Banker*, December 31, 1987, 12.

22 Stanley Kauffmann, *"Wall Street,"* *New Republic,* January 4, 1988, 24.

23 Malcolm, "Wall Street Villainy."

24 Philip, "The Gekko and the Fox."

25 Richard Corliss, "A Season Full of Flash and Greed: Two Christmas Movies Tweak an '80s Devil," *Time,* December 14, 1987, 82.

26 Helen Dudar, "Michael Douglas, as Villain, Hits It Big on 'Wall Street,'" *New York Times,* December 12, 1987, 23.

27 Malcolm, "Wall Street Villainy."

28 "Michael Douglas Awarded First Acting Award, Second Oscar for 'Wall Street.'" Associated Press, April 12, 1988.

29 Lipper, *"Wall Street:* Paper-Thin."

30 Kauffmann, *"Wall Street."*

31 Newman, "Wall Street's Gutter Ethics."

32 Philip, "The Gekko and the Fox."

33 Vincent Canby, "Stone's 'Wall Street,'" *New York Times,* December 11, 1987, C3.

34 Lardner, *"Wall Street."*

35 Heather Evans, "Anatomy of a Movie," *Institutional Investor* (January 1988): 72–76. Note, however, that according to Richard Lormand, *(Reuters Business Report,* December 11, 1987), Sheen prepared for his role by spending time with David Brown, a one-time Goldman Sachs trader and confessed violator of the insider trading laws. Furthermore, reports Steven Rattner ("From Vietnam to Wall Street," *New York Times,* August 30, 1987, sec. 6, 2), Sheen took a six-week "course" designed by chief technical adviser Kenneth Lipper to expose the actor to a cross section of young Wall Streeters.

36 Michael Cieply and Connie Benesch, "'Wall Street' Makers Look for an Upturn; Financial Melodrama Doing Well in Big Cities, but Not Elsewhere" *Los Angeles Times,* December 19, 1987, pt. 6, 1.

37 Ibid.

38 Ibid.

39 Ibid.

40 Lipper, *"Wall Street:* Paper-Thin."

41 Alison Leigh Cowan, "Making 'Wall Street' Look Like Wall Street," *New York Times,* December 30, 1987, C1.

42 Festa, "Finance at the Peak of Excess."

43 Evans, "Anatomy of a Movie."

44 Cowan, "Making 'Wall Street' Look Like Wall Street."

45 Evans, "Anatomy of a Movie."

46 Connie Bruck, *The Predator's Ball: The Inside Story of Drexel Burnham and the Rise of Junk Bond Raiders* (New York: Simon and Schuster, 1988), 15, 135.

47 David Elliott, "Stone Bullish on Success of 'Street,'" *San Diego Union-Tribune,* December 18, 1987, D1.

48 Cowan, "Making 'Wall Street' Look Like Wall Street."

49 Ibid.

50 Ibid.

51 Geraldine Fabrikant, "Wall Street Reviews 'Wall Street,'" *New York Times,* December 10, 1987, D1.

52 Ibid.

53 Rattner, "From Vietnam to Wall Street."

54 Steven Rattner, "A View from the Trenches," *Newsweek,* December 14, 1987, 80.

55 Andrews, "Mammon-Obsessed Jungle Observed."

56 Philip, "The Gekko and the Fox."

57 Michael Cieply, "Hollywood Signs: Oliver Stone's New Film; Wall Street as a War Zone," *Los Angeles Times,* May 10, 1987, 24.

58 Lardner, *"Wall Street."*

59 Daniel Seligman, "Wall Street Mysteries," *Fortune,* January 18, 1988, 165.

60 "John Shad; Departing SEC Chairman Looks Back at His Six-Year Fight against Insider Trading," *Washington Post,* June 14, 1987, D2.

61 Martha M. Hamilton, "SEC Votes Insider-Trading Crackdown," *Washington Post,* September 2, 1982, C13.

62 David A. Vise, "Is Wall Street an Unprincipled Jungle?" *Washington Post,* August 22, 1986, C9.

63 Rattner, "From Vietnam to Wall Street."

64 Marc Cooper, "Oliver Stone: An Interview," *Playboy,* February 1988, 51–63.

65 See Nasser Arshadi, "Insider Trading Liability and Enforcement Strategy," *Financial Management* (summer 1998).

66 The film's internal evidence does not support the opinion of several reviewers that Gekko is modeled directly on risk arbitrageur Ivan Boesky. For example, both Maslin ("Morality Tales for Our Time") and Paul Farhi ("Corporate Bad Guys Not New to the Screen," *San Francisco Examiner,* December 28, 1987, C3) call Gekko "Boesky-like." Corporate raider Irwin "Irv the Liquidator" Jacobs goes so far as to characterize Gordon Gekko as a thinly disguised portrait of Boesky. In Jacobs's opinion, such attributes as Gekko's frenzied pursuit of the next deal, his lack of time for emotion, and his resort to profanity when thwarted were all reminiscent of Boesky. See Mike Langberg, "A Real Corporate Raider Examines 'Wall Street,'" *Chicago Tribune,* December 17, 1987, 17C. Ironically, Kolbenschlag ("An Inside Opinion") suggests that along with Boesky, Jacobs himself might be the model for Gekko. Reviewers' identification of Gekko with Boesky rests largely on the latter's unmasking as a criminal and his coining of the phrase "Greed is good" in a commencement speech. In fact, however, speeches by raiders Sir James Goldsmith and T. Boone Pickens, Jr., were additional sources of Gekko's tour de force at the Teldar Paper annual meeting, according to Welles ("The Platoon of Pros"). Unlike Boesky, but somewhat like takeover specialist Carl Icahn, Gekko appears to trade strictly for his own account, rather than investing on behalf of a limited partnership. Gekko's attempted takeover of an airline also smacks less of Boesky than of Icahn, who gained control of TransWorld Airlines in 1985. Edelstein ("Raiders of the Lost Market") is probably on the mark in describing Gordon Gekko as "a melding of Ivan Boesky, Mike Milken, Ronald Perelman, Donald Trump, [and] others."

67 Ann Reilly, "Antitrust Policy after the Steel Veto," *Time,* March 19, 1984, 85.

68 Seligman, "Wall Street Mysteries."

69 Robert Sobel, "Hubris Humbled: Merger Mania, Retribution, Reform — It's All Happened Before," *Barron's,* April 13, 1998, 24.

70 George F. Will, "The Angst of 'Wall Street,'" *Washington Post,* December 27, 1987, C7.

71 Cooper, "Oliver Stone: An Interview."

72 Andrei Shleifer and Robert W. Vishny, "The Takeover Wave of the 1980s," *Science* (August 1990): 745–49.

73 Rattner, "From Vietnam to Wall Street."

PART II: NEW LEFT, REVISIONIST, IN-YOUR-FACE HISTORY: OLIVER STONE'S *BORN ON THE FOURTH OF JULY* EXPERIENCE

1 The 1991 reprint of Trumbo's novel includes an introduction by Ron Kovic. See Dalton Trumbo, *Johnny Got His Gun* (New York: Citadel Press, 1991).

2 Ron Kovic, *Born on the Fourth of July* (New York: Pocket Books, 1976).

3 One might consult Oliver Stone's recent autobiographical novel, in which the central character, an adolescent Stone, projects himself into the future along a surreal journey into the jungles of Vietnam. Oliver Stone, *A Child's Night Dream: Oliver Stone* (New York: St. Martin's Press, 1997).

4 David Hackett Fischer, *Historians' Fallacies: Toward a Logic of Historical Thought* (New York: Harper Torchbooks, 1970), 135.

5 Actually, the first of Stone's Vietnam films was a nine-minute short entitled *Last Year in Vietnam,* which he made in 1967 while a student in Martin Scorsese's film class at New York University. Jean-Jacques Malo and Tony Williams, eds., *Vietnam War Films* (Jefferson, N.C.: McFarland, 1992), xiv.

6 One source says that William Friedkin was the planned director. See Robert Seidenberg, "To Hell and Back," *American Film* 15 (January 1990): 30.

7 Norman Kagan, *The Cinema of Oliver Stone* (New York: Continuum, 1995), 145.

8 Kagan, *The Cinema of Oliver Stone,* 145; Christian Appy, "Vietnam According to Oliver Stone," *Commonweal,* March 23, 1990, 187–89; Susan Mackey-Kallis, *Oliver Stone's America: "Dreaming the Myth Outward"* (Boulder, Colo.: Westview Press, 1996), 75.

9 The best example of such a film is John Wayne's *The Green Berets* (1968).

10 Michael Lee Lanning, *Vietnam at the Movies* (New York: Fawcett Columbine Books, 1994), 4, 127; Thomas Doherty, "Witness to War: Oliver Stone, Ron Kovic, and *Born on the Fourth of July,*" in *Inventing Vietnam: The War in Film and Television,* ed. Michael Anderegg (Philadelphia: Temple University Press, 1991), 253–54, 257, 259.

11 Kagan, *The Cinema of Oliver Stone,* 162–63; Oliver Stone, "A Filmmaker's Credo: Some Thoughts on Politics, History, and the Movies," *Humanist* 56 (September/October 1996): 3–6.

12 Stuart Klawans, review of *Born on the Fourth of July, The Nation,* January 1, 1990, 28–30.

13 Ibid.

14 Kagan, *The Cinema of Oliver Stone,* 163; Stone, "A Filmmaker's Credo," 3–6. For a negative evaluation of Stone's agenda, see Lanning, *Vietnam at the Movies,* and Peter C. Rollins, "Using Popular Culture to Study the Vietnam War: Perils and Possibilities," in *Popular Culture in the United States,* ed. Peter Freese and Michael Porsche (Essen, Germany: Die Blaue Eule, 1994), 322–23.

15 Richard Corliss, "Tom Terrific," *Time,* December 25, 1989, 74–79; see also Robert Scheer, "Born on the Third of July," *Premiere* (February 1990), 51–56.

16 Stephen J. Whitfield, *The Culture of the Cold War*, 2d ed. (Baltimore: Johns Hopkins University Press, 1996).

17 Stone cut a scene of Ron at the local movie theater engrossed in John Wayne in *The Sands of Iwo Jima*, which in his book Kovic says helped, along with similar movies like Audie Murphy's *To Hell and Back*, shape his image of war. Kagan, *The Cinema of Oliver Stone*, 148.

18 Devin McKinney, review of *Born on the Fourth of July*, *Film Quarterly* 11 (fall 1990): 46.

19 Stone had $18 million to spend on *Born*, actually a modest budget, and one he had to squeeze out of Universal Studios. James Riordan, *Stone: The Controversies, Excesses, and Exploits of a Radical Filmmaker* (New York: Hyperion, 1995), 274–76.

20 Ibid., 278, 294.

21 See Robert A. Rosenstone, "History in Images/History in Words: Reflections on the Possibility of Really Putting History into Film," *American Historical Review* 93 (December 1988): 1173–85.

22 See Gavin Smith, "For Me the Camera Is Another Actor," *Film Comment* 30 (January/February 1994): 26–43.

23 Winston S. Churchill, *The Second World War* (Boston: Houghton Mifflin, 1948).

24 Although Stone came from a comparatively privileged background, he was an enlisted man in the infantry and therefore a grunt, whose identity was determined not by previous civilian social status but by a military caste system.

25 For an excellent study of the distorted images of World War II, see Michael C. C. Adams, *The Best War Ever: America and World War II* (Baltimore: Johns Hopkins University Press, 1994).

26 Jean Seligmann, "Heroes with Handicaps," *Newsweek*, January 15, 1990: 59–60.

27 Paul Starr, *The Discarded Army* (New York: Charter House, 1973). For a positive portrayal of other facilities, see Max Cleland, *Strong at the Broken Places: A Personal Story* (Lincoln, Va.: Chosen Books, 1980); and Rick Eilert, *For Self and Country: For the Wounded in Vietnam the Journey Home Took More Than Courage: A True Story* (New York: William Morrow, 1983).

28 On the subject of veterans and protest, see Murray Polner, *No Victory Parades: The Return of the Vietnam Veteran* (New York: Holt, Rinehart and Winston, 1971); David Cortright, *Soldiers in Revolt: The American Military Today* (New York: Anchor Press, 1975); W. D. Ehrhart, *Passing Time: Memoir of a Vietnam Veteran against the War* (Amherst: University of Massachusetts Press, 1995); Richard Moser, *The New Winter Soldiers: GI and Veteran Dissent during the Vietnam War* (New Brunswick, N.J.: Rutgers University Press, 1996). For a statistical study showing that a majority of veterans polled were proud of their service, see Rollins, "Using Popular Culture to Study the Vietnam War," 324, 334.

29 Quoted in Seidenberg, "To Hell and Back," 56.

30 Riordan, *Stone*, 282.

31 Klawans, review, 29.

32 Quoted in Michael Norman, "Carnage and Glory," *New York Times*, July 7, 1996, sec. 2, 19.

33 For two excellent sources on this subject, see William H. McNeill, "The Care and Repair of Public Myth," in *Myth and the American Experience*, vol. 2, 3d ed., ed. Nicho-

las Cords and Patrick Gerster (New York: HarperCollins, 1991), 435–45; and John Hellmann, *American Myth and the Legacy of Vietnam* (New York: Columbia University Press, 1986).

34 Quoted in Eben J. Muse, *The Land of Nam: The Vietnam War in American Film* (Lanham, Md.: Scarecrow, 1995), 151; Stone, "A Filmmaker's Credo," 3–6.

35 Riordan, *Stone,* 304.

36 *New York Times,* January 15, 1990; Kovic, *Born on the Fourth of July;* Riordan, *Stone,* 303–5.

37 Appy, "Vietnam According to Oliver Stone," 188.

38 See Doherty, "Witness to War."

39 Michael Herr, *Dispatches* (New York: Vintage Books, 1991), 20, 46, 209; Doherty, "Witness to War," 257.

40 Quoted in Stephen J. Whitfield, "Limited Engagement: *The Quiet American* as History," *Journal of American Studies* 30 (April 1996): 84.

41 Christian G. Appy, *Working-Class War: American Combat Soldiers and Vietnam* (Chapel Hill: University of North Carolina Press, 1993); see also Rollins, "Using Popular Culture to Study the Vietnam War," 324, 334.

42 Quoted in Muse, *The Land of Nam,* 151.

43 Pauline Kael, "Potency," *New Yorker,* January 22, 1990, 122.

44 See Rollins, "Using Popular Culture to Study the Vietnam War," 324, 334.

45 Stone, "A Filmmaker's Credo," 4.

46 Peter C. Rollins identifies in the popular culture of the Vietnam War the American Adam motif: the scheme provides one way of condemning the nation while forgiving the soldier. See his "Using Popular Culture to Study the Vietnam War," 314–47.

47 *New York Times,* January 2, 1990.

48 Mackey-Kallis, *Oliver Stone's America,* 11.

49 Quoted in Kagan, *The Cinema of Oliver Stone,* 14–15; Mackey-Kallis, *Oliver Stone's America,* 11.

50 Doherty, "Witness to War," 255.

51 Natalie Davis, *The Return of Martin Guerre* (Cambridge, Mass.: Harvard University Press, 1983); John Demos, *The Unredeemed Captive: A Family Story from Early America* (New York: Alfred A. Knopf, 1994).

52 Melton A. McLaurin, *Celia, A Slave* (Athens: University of Georgia Press, 1991).

53 Simon Schama, *Landscape and Memory* (New York: Alfred A. Knopf, 1995). For an insightful commentary on the new narrative, see David Samuels, "The Call of Stories," *Lingua Franca* (May 1995): 35–43.

54 Winthrop D. Jordan, *Tumult and Silence at Second Creek: An Inquiry into a Civil War Conspiracy* (Baton Rouge: Louisiana State University Press, 1993).

55 Robert Brent Toplin, *History by Hollywood: The Use and Abuse of the American Past* (Urbana: University of Illinois Press, 1996), 3, 8; Rosenstone, "History in Images/History in Words," 1184.

56 Kagan, *The Cinema of Oliver Stone,* 5.

57 Riordan, *Stone,* 278.

PART II: THE LIZARD KING OR FAKE HERO?
OLIVER STONE, JIM MORRISON, AND HISTORY

1 Quoted in Susan Mackey-Kallis, *Oliver Stone's America: "Dreaming the Myth Outward"* (Boulder, Colo.: Westview Press, 1996), 101.
2 Roy M. Anker, "The Kingdom of Wish: Oliver Stone's Problem with History," *Fides et Historia* 25, no. 2 (1993): 90.
3 Ibid., 106.
4 Paul Baumann, "Sex, Drugs and Rock n' Roll," *Commonweal* 118 (May 3, 1991): 294–96.
5 Andrew Doe, *The Doors in Their Own Words* (New York: Perigee, 1991), 80.
6 Norman Kagan, *The Cinema of Oliver Stone* (New York: Continuum, 1995), 181.
7 Stephen Talbot, "60s Something," *Mother Jones* (March/April 1991): 48.
8 Robert Rosenstone, *Visions of the Past: The Challenge of Film to Our Idea of History* (Cambridge, Mass.: Harvard University Press, 1995), 71–79.
9 Mark Rowland, "Stone Unturned," *American Film* 16 (March 1991): 43.
10 Kagan, *The Cinema of Oliver Stone*, 166.
11 Ibid., 165.
12 David Breskin, "Oliver Stone: An Interview with the Director," in *The Films of Oliver Stone*, ed. Donald Kunz (Lanham, Md.: Scarecrow, 1997), 59.
13 Frank Eugene Beaver, *Oliver Stone: Wakeup Cinema* (New York: Twayne Publishers, 1994), 154.
14 Quoted in Kagan, *The Cinema of Oliver Stone*, 181.
15 Terence Rafferty, "Stoned Again," *New Yorker*, March 11, 1991, 81.
16 Quoted in Mackey-Kallis, *Oliver Stone's America*, 25.
17 Ibid.
18 "Splinters to the Brain," *New Perspectives Quarterly* 9, no. 2 (spring 1992): 53.
19 Ibid., 53, 48.
20 Quoted in Jerry Hopkins and Danny Sugerman, *No One Here Gets Out Alive* (New York: Warner Books, 1980), 19.
21 Doe, *Doors in Their Own Words*, 89.
22 Kagan, *The Cinema of Oliver Stone*, 181.
23 Ibid., 170.
24 Mackey-Kallis, *Oliver Stone's America*, 16.
25 Oliver Stone, "Where I Find My Heroes," *McCall's*, November 1992, 104.
26 Mackey-Kallis, *Oliver Stone's America*, 16–17.
27 Ibid., 8.
28 James Riordan, *Stone: The Controversies, Excesses, and Exploits of a Radical Filmmaker* (New York: Hyperion, 1995), 317.
29 Ibid., 311.
30 Beaver, *Oliver Stone: Wakeup Cinema*, 147.
31 Kagan, *The Cinema of Oliver Stone*, 166.
32 Breskin, "Oliver Stone: An Interview," 51.
33 Riordan, *Stone*, 335.
34 Ibid.
35 "Splinters to the Brain," 51.

36 Ibid., 53.

37 Riordan, *Stone*, 338.

38 Ibid., 343.

39 Talbot, "60s Something," 47, 48

40 Kagan, *The Cinema of Oliver Stone*, 164.

41 Rowland, "Stone Unturned," 42.

42 Kagan, *The Cinema of Oliver Stone*, 164.

43 Doe, *Doors in Their Own Words*, 85.

44 David Breskin, "Oliver Stone: The Rolling Stone Interview," *Rolling Stone*, April 4, 1991, 37–43.

PART II: OLIVER STONE, *JFK*, AND HISTORY

1 Oliver Stone interview with Associated Press, *Hammond Daily Star*, December 30, 1991.

2 Robert C. Maynard, "Truth Trapped by Secrecy Vacuum," *New Orleans Times-Picayune*, column of December 23, 1991.

3 Oliver Stone, "Oliver Stone Talks Back," *Premiere* (January 1992): 68.

4 "Director Oliver Stone Tells Why He Tackled the Big Story of His Time," *Dallas Morning News*, April 14, 1991.

5 George Lardner, "Dallas in Wonderland: Oliver Stone and JFK's Assassination," *Washington Post*, May 27–June 2, 1991, national weekly edition. See also Richard Zoglin, "More Shots in Dealey Plaza," *Time*, June 10, 1991, 64–66.

6 Hodding Carter, "'JFK' Stonewalls History," Newspaper Enterprise Association column, January 13, 1992; Anthony Lewis, "Stone's Fantasy," *New York Times* News Service column, January 13, 1992; George Will, "Oliver Stone Gives Paranoia a Bad Name," *New Orleans Times-Picayune*, column of December 23, 1991; David W. Belin, "The Big Lies of JFK," *New York Times Magazine*, February 17, 1992, 24. For other examples of scathing journalistic criticism of Stone, see David Ansen, "A Troublemaker for Our Times," *Newsweek*, December 23, 1991, 50; Kenneth Auchinloss with Ginny Carroll and Maggie Malone, "Twisted History," *Newsweek*, December 23, 1991, 46–49; Tom Bethel, "Conspiracy to End Conspiracies," *National Review*, December 16, 1991, 48–50; Richard Corliss, "Who Killed JFK?" *Time*, December 23, 1991, 68.

7 Robert S. Robins and Jerrold M. Post, "Political Paranoia As Cinematic Motif: Stone's 'JFK,'" abstract of paper presented at the 1997 meeting of the American Political Science Association.

8 Roger Ebert, *"JFK,"* *Chicago Sun-Times*, December 20, 1991.

9 Ibid.

10 Art Simon, *Dangerous Knowledge: The JFK Assassination in Art and Film* (Philadelphia: Temple University Press, 1996), 213–14.

11 See Edward Jay Epstein, *Counterplot* (New York: Viking, 1969); James Kirkwood, *American Grotesque: An Account of the Clay Shaw–Jim Garrison Affair in the City of New Orleans* (New York: Simon and Schuster, 1970); Patricia Lambert, *False Witness: The Real Story of Jim Garrison's Investigation and Oliver Stone's Film* JFK (New York: M. Evans, 1998).

12 Jim Garrison, *On the Trail of the Assassins: My Investigation and Prosecution of the Murder of President Kennedy* (New York: Sheridan Square Press, 1988). It should be noted that Garrison does have his defenders. See James DiEugenio, *Justice Betrayed: The Kennedy Assassination and the Garrison Trial* (New York: Sheridan Square Press, 1992), and William Davy, *Let Justice Be Done: New Light on the Jim Garrison Investigation* (Reston, Va.: Jordan Publishing, 1999).

13 Jim Marrs, *Crossfire: The Plot That Killed Kennedy* (New York: Carroll and Graf, 1989).

14 For a persuasive account of Oswald's complicity in the Tippit murder, see Dale K. Myers, *With Malice: Lee Harvey Oswald and the Murder of Officer J. D. Tippit* (Milford, Mich.: Oak Cliff Press, 1998).

15 See Marcus Raskin, "*JFK* and the Culture of Violence," *American Historical Review* 97 (1992): 493–95.

16 Robert A. Rosenstone, "*JFK:* Historical Fact/Historical Film," *American Historical Review* 97 (1992): 509.

17 Ibid., 511.

18 See Lambert, *False Witness,* 127–60. For comprehensive coverage of the trial, including pre- and post-trial developments, see *New Orleans Times-Picayune* and *New Orleans States-Item,* January 21–March 16, 1969.

19 For a small sampling of such works, see Charles Roberts, *The Truth about the Assassination* (New York: Grossett and Dunlap, 1967); David W. Belin, "The Second Gunman Syndrome," *National Review,* April 27, 1969, 534–35; Priscilla Johnson Macmillan, "Why Oswald Really Shot President Kennedy," *Ladies Home Journal,* November 1977, 122–43; James A. Bishop, *The Day Kennedy Was Shot* (New York: Funk and Wagnall's, 1968); Michael Canfield and Alan Weberman, *Coup d'Etat in America: The CIA and the Assassination of John F. Kennedy* (New York: Third Press, 1975); Jim Garrison, *A Heritage of Stone* (New York: Putnam, 1970). Michael L. Kurtz, "Conspiracy Theories in the Assassination of President Kennedy," paper presented at the 1997 meeting of the Southwest Social Sciences Association, provides a capsule review of most of the bizarre conspiracy theories.

20 David W. Belin, *November 22, 1963: You Are the Jury* (New York: Quadrangle Books, 1973); David W. Belin, *Final Disclosure: The Full Truth about the Assassination of President Kennedy* (New York: Scribner's, 1988); Myers, *With Malice.*

21 Sylvia Meagher, *Accessories after the Fact: The Warren Commission, the Authorities, and the Report* (Indianapolis: Bobbs-Merrill, 1967); Josiah Thompson, *Six Seconds in Dallas: A Micro-Study of the Kennedy Assassination* (New York: Bernard Geis, 1967); Michael L. Kurtz, *Crime of the Century: The Kennedy Assassination from a Historian's Perspective,* 2d ed. (Knoxville: University of Tennessee Press, 1993).

22 Quoted in Raskin, "*JFK* and the Culture of Violence," 494.

23 Ibid., 497.

24 Public Law 102–526, *U.S. Statutes at Large* 106 (1992): 3443–58; Assassination Records Review Board, "Executive Summary" and "Chapter Two," in *Final Report of the Assassination Records Review Board* (Washington, D.C.: U.S. Government Printing Office, 1998). See also Anna K. Nelson, "JFK Assassination Review Board, OAH, Foster Release of Top Secret Documents," *OAH Newsletter* 26 (February 1998): 5, 8, 10.

25 Michael R. Beschloss, *Taking Charge: The Johnson White House Tapes, 1963–1964* (New York: Simon and Schuster, 1997), 559–60.

26 "Ford Alters Location of JFK Wound," CNN Interactive *(www.cnn.com)*, July 3, 1997.

27 John J. McCloy to J. Lee Rankin, August 3, 1964, from the public release of 40,000 pages of J. Lee Rankin papers by the Assassination Records Review Board in September 1997.

28 Deposition of James J. Humes before the Assassination Records Review Board counsel, February 13, 1996; author's interview with Humes, March 18, 1997.

29 Depositions of James W. Sibert, September 12, 1997, Francis X. O'Neill, September 11, 1997, and John T. Stringer, July 16, 1996, before the Assassination Records Review Board counsel.

30 Report of Douglas Horne to the Assassination Records Review Board, September 1998.

31 Deposition of Saundra Spencer before the Assassination Records Review Board counsel, June 5, 1997.

32 For examples of medical reports defending the lone assassin thesis, see "1968 Panel Review of Photographs, X-Ray Films, Documents and Other Evidence Pertaining to the Fatal Wounding of President John F. Kennedy on November 22, 1963, in Dallas, Texas," President John F. Kennedy Assassination Records Collection, National Archives and Records Administration; Robert R. Artwohl, "JFK's Assassination: Conspiracy, Forensic Science, and Common Sense," *JAMA* 269 (March 24–31, 1993): 1540–43; John K. Lattimer, "Observations Based on a Review of the Autopsy Photographs, X-Rays, and Related Materials of the Late President John F. Kennedy," *Resident and Staff Physician Medical Times* 34 (May 1972): 34–63. For examples of medical reports supporting the conspiracy theory, see Charles G. Wilber, "The Assassination of the Late President John F. Kennedy: An Academician's Thoughts," *American Journal of Forensic Medicine and Pathology* 7 (1986): 52–58; Cyril H. Wecht and Robert P. Smith, "The Medical Evidence in the Assassination of President John F. Kennedy," *Forensic Science* 3 (1974): 105–28; David W. Mantik, "The JFK Assassination: Cause for Doubt," and "The President John F. Kennedy Skull X-Rays: Regarding the Magical Appearance of the Largest 'Metal' Fragment," in, *Assassination Science: Experts Speak Out on the Death of JFK*, ed. James H. Fetzer (Chicago: Catfeet Press, 1998), 93–139.

33 Beschloss, *Taking Charge,* 256–61, 494–510; Robert Dallek, *Flawed Giant: Lyndon Johnson and His Times, 1961–1973* (New York: Oxford University Press, 1998), 241–67, 371–79, 564–69.

34 Stone, "Oliver Stone Talks Back," 68. See also Oliver Stone, "'JFK' Strikes Blow for Open Debate," posted on the Internet newsgroup *alt.conspiracy.jfk* on October 31, 1996; Frank Morales and Paul DeRienzo, "Interview with Zachary Sklar, Co-Writer of the Movie 'JFK,'" *Shadow* (March 1992): 12–18. Other movies relating to the assassination include *Executive Action, The Parallax View, Winter Kills,* and *Flashpoint.*

PART II: WAY COOLER THAN MANSON: *NATURAL BORN KILLERS*

1 Quoted in Norman Kagan, *The Cinema of Oliver Stone* (New York: Continuum, 1995), 235.

2 Ibid., 227. Producer Jane Hamsher recalls Stone explaining his interest in making the film somewhat differently: "Everyone expects me to be the guy with the message. I just want to do something that's completely nihilistic" (*Killer Instinct: How Two Young*

Producers Took On Hollywood and Made the Most Controversial Film of the Decade [New York: Broadway Books, 1997], 77).

3 Tarantino's original script, "Natural Born Killers," is available at *http://www.mind.net/ nikkoll/scripts/qtnbk.html* (accessed September 4, 1997).

4 Kagan, *The Cinema of Oliver Stone,* 233.

5 *Natural Born Killers: Directors Cut,* Vidmark letterbox edition (1996). Tape 1 (hereafter *NBKDC*-1) opens with a brief statement by Stone and restores the shots he deleted to receive an R rating. Tape 2 contains "bonus footage," scenes that he cut for reasons other than ratings pressure. Several of these scenes, including the alternate ending, are of considerable interest. So are the interviews with Stone and the principal actors that appear on the second tape (hereafter *NBKDC*-2).

6 James Riordan, *Stone: The Controversies, Excesses, and Exploits of a Radical Filmmaker* (New York: Hyperion, 1995), 517. Gross figures are from "Business Information for *Natural Born Killers* (1994)" *http://uk.imdb.com/cache/title-more/business+70937* (accessed July 15, 1997); cost figures are from Kagan, *The Cinema of Oliver Stone,* 234.

7 Roger Ebert, "Natural Born Killers," *Chicago Sun-Times,* August 26, 1994, *http:// www.suntimes.com/ebert_reviews/1994/08/937174.html* (accessed July 15, 1997).

8 David Denby, "Dead Heads," *New York* 27 (September 5, 1994): 46–47.

9 Hal Hinson, "Natural Born Killers," *Washington Post,* August 26, 1994, D1, D7. See also Kagan, *The Cinema of Oliver Stone,* 246–52.

10 Jeffrey Wells, "Reborn to Raise Hell; 'Natural Born Killers': The Director's Cut," *Entertainment Weekly,* August 2, 1996, 66.

11 Tom Keogh, "Stone's Vision Is Stillborn," *http://www.film.com/filma/reviews/flat/ rev938.html* (accessed September 4, 1997).

12 Scott Renshaw, "Natural Born Killers," *http://www.inconnect.com/~renshaw/ naturalbornkillers.html* (accessed September 4, 1997).

13 *http://www.vermontel.com/~spyderx/batong.html* (accessed September 4, 1997).

14 "Re: Re: Re: Natural Born Killers," *http://bianca.com/shack/movies/reviews/0395/ t368.html* (accessed July 15, 1997).

15 Steve Levy, "Loitering on the Dark Side," *Newsweek,* May 3, 1999, 39; Trisha Renaud, "Killer-Flick Suit Clings to Life," *Fulton County Daily Report,* November 29, 1996 (electronic version).

16 "Dad Turns In Son over Thrill Killing," *Florida Times-Union,* August 15, 1997, A3, and "Stone Film Case Won't Be Blocked," ibid., March 9, 1999, A4; quotations from Michael Shnayerson, "Natural Born Opponents," *Vanity Fair,* July 1, 1996, 98–105, 141–44; further information from telephone interview with Joe Simpson, September 5, 1997. Grisham is not involved with Simpson's suit and has said little about the matter since his initial blast at Stone. *Natural Born Killers'* alleged role in these and other killings has been the subject of several TV documentaries, the best of which is New Zealand's TVNZ *Assignment,* episode 23, catalog no. ZASS1-96-23, tape no. 24106.

17 *Montreal Gazette,* March 23, 1999, B2; Ed Quillen, "What Could Happen If We Keep Blaming Hollywood," *Denver Post,* March 21, 1999, H-3.

18 Mary Swerczek, "Copycat Killing Suit Is Facing Test," *Times-Picayune,* March 22, 1999, A1; Adam Sandler, "'Killers' Raises Concerns," *Variety,* March 15–21, 1999, 12. The key appellate decision is *Patsy Ann Byers, et al. v. Sarah Edmonson, et al.,* 712

So. 2d 681; 1998 La. App. Lexis 1776. Inferring Stone's real intentions, whatever they may be, from his quoted remarks is an uncertain business. Hamsher's remark is apposite: "You never know what loony gibberish Oliver's going to come out with in the midst of an interview. Despite his omnipresence in the media, he has very little idea of how it actually works, or how to use it effectively, so he's always coming out with some incendiary half-baked comment that winds up getting him vilified" (*Killer Instinct*, 210).

19 These views were conveyed to me by Jack Weiss on April 16, 1999; I also spoke to Pete Kennedy on the same date and Joe Simpson for a second time on April 14, 1999. I am grateful to all three attorneys for their assistance.

20 John L. Caughey, *Imaginary Social Worlds: A Cultural Approach* (Lincoln: University of Nebraska Press, 1984); Anthony Lane, "Last Rites," *New Yorker*, September 15, 1997, 5; Wallace Stegner, "Who Are the Westerners?" *American Heritage* 38 (December 1987): 39.

21 *NBKDC*-1.

22 Hamsher, *Killer Instinct*, 162, 173, 175. I should add that Hamsher emphatically denies that either she or Stone bear any responsibility for the copycat crimes, notwithstanding her candid account of the atmosphere of violence surrounding the film's shooting or her critical portrait of its director, whom she likens to Caligula (164–65, 235, 257).

23 James Q. Wilson and Richard J. Herrnstein, *Crime and Human Nature* (New York: Simon and Schuster, 1985), chap. 13; David T. Courtwright, *Violent Land: Single Men and Social Disorder from the Frontier to the Inner City* (Cambridge, Mass.: Harvard University Press, 1996), 105–7, 249–51.

24 Courtwright, *Violent Land*, 249.

25 Freedman is cited in Robert Crew, "Lawsuit Based on Bizarre Idea," *Toronto Star*, March 13, 1999 (electronic version).

26 Roger Lane, *Murder in America: A History* (Columbus: Ohio State University Press, 1997), 352–53.

27 Kagan, *The Cinema of Oliver Stone*, 235.

28 Riordan, *Stone*, 58, 61.

29 Hamsher, *Killer Instinct*, 147–48.

30 Lane, *Murder in America*, 318–19; Tarantino, *Natural Born Killers*, 15.

31 Fox Butterfield, *All God's Children: The Bosket Family and the American Legacy of Violence* (New York: Alfred A. Knopf, 1995), xi.

32 Kagan, *The Cinema of Oliver Stone*, 230. News statistics are from Courtwright, *Violent Land*, 251–52; "TV News Focuses on Crime," *Florida Times-Union*, August 13, 1997, A6. Hamsher, *Killer Instinct*, 109, reports that Stone toyed with the idea of casting Geraldo Rivera in the Gale role but decided (wisely) against it.

33 *NBKDC*-2.

34 Shnayerson, "Natural Born Opponents," 144. Shnayerson contrasts Stone's behavior with that of Stanley Kubrick, director of *A Clockwork Orange* (1971), a film to which *Natural Born Killers* is often compared. "When British youths raped a woman to the tune of 'Singing in the Rain,' as Malcolm McDowell does in the film, director Stanley Kubrick was so appalled that he had his own masterpiece banned in Britain." Stone has denied all responsibility. He has, moreover, continued to produce or

otherwise sponsor extremely violent films, such as *Freeway* (1996) and *Gravesend* (1997). Looked at in its totality, Stone's work as a writer, director, and producer can only be described as that of a man more fascinated by lethal violence than repulsed by it.

35 Hamsher, *Killer Instinct,* 136, 119.
36 Garry Wills, "Dostoyevsky behind a Camera," *Atlantic Monthly,* July 1997, 96–101.
37 *NBKDC-2.*
38 *NBKDC-2.*
39 Kagan, *The Cinema of Oliver Stone,* 233.

PART II: *NIXON*

1 Tom Wicker, *One of Us: Richard Nixon and the American Dream* (New York: Random House, 1991); Stephen E. Ambrose, *Nixon,* 3 vols. (New York: Simon and Schuster, 1987–1991).
2 Robert Penn Warren, *All the King's Men* (New York: Harcourt and Brace, 1946); T. Harry Williams, *Huey Long* (New York: Alfred A. Knopf, 1969); Martin Blumenson, *Patton, the Man behind the Legend* (New York: Morrow, 1985).
3 H. R. Haldeman and Joseph DiMona, *The Ends of Power* (New York: Times Books, 1978).
4 Oliver Stone, Stephen Rivele, and Christopher Wilkinson, *Nixon: An Oliver Stone Film* (New York: Hyperion, 1995).
5 Victor Navasky, editorial, *The Nation,* December 9, 1996, 6.
6 See John Newman, *JFK and Vietnam* (New York: Warner Books, 1992), and Arthur M. Schlesinger, Jr., *Robert Kennedy and His Times* (Boston: Houghton Mifflin, 1978), chap. 31.
7 Mark Carnes, ed., *Past Imperfect: History According to the Movies,* enlarged ed. (New York: Henry Holt, 1995).
8 See John Helgerson, *Getting to Know the President: CIA Briefings of Presidential Candidates, 1952–1992* (Washington, D.C.: Center for the Study of Intelligence, 1996).
9 Stone, Rivele, and Wilkinson, *Nixon.*
10 Carnes, *Past Imperfect.*

PART III: ON SEVEN FILMS

1 Walter Goodman, "Screen: '*Salvador*' by Stone," *New York Times,* March 5, 1986, C22.
2 Jerry Hopkins and Danny Sugarman, *No One Here Gets Out Alive* (New York: Warner Books, 1980).

PART III: ON *NIXON* AND *JFK*

1 Stanley Kutler, *Abuse of Power* (New York: Free Press, 1997).
2 Harrison Salisbury, *The New Emperors* (Boston: Little Brown, 1993).

3 Arthur M. Schlesinger, Jr., *Robert Kennedy and His Times* (Boston: Houghton Mifflin, 1978).

4 Arthur M. Schlesinger, Jr., *A Thousand Days: John F. Kennedy in the White House* (Boston: Houghton Mifflin, 1965).

5 Evan Thomas, "Whose Obsession Is It, Anyway?" *Newsweek*, December 11, 1995, 68.

6 Richard Reeves, *President Kennedy: Profile of Power* (New York: Simon and Schuster, 1993).

7 Schlesinger, *Robert Kennedy*; emphasis added.

8 H. R. Haldeman and Joseph DiMona, *The Ends of Power* (New York: Times Books, 1978).

9 Kutler, *Abuse of Power*.

10 Ibid.

11 Fawn Brodie, *Richard Nixon: The Shaping of His Character* (New York: W. W. Norton, 1981).

12 Ron Rosenbaum, "Just Speak into the Lamp," *New York Times Book Review*, July 18, 1999, 13.

13 Michael R. Beschloss, *Taking Charge: The Johnson White House Tapes, 1963–1964* (New York: Simon and Schuster, 1997).

14 John Newman, *JFK and Vietnam: Deception, Intrigue, and the Struggle for Power* (New York: Warner Books, 1992).

15 NSAM 263 appears in *The Pentagon Papers*, ed. Gravel (Boston: Beacon Press, 1971–1972), 2:769–70. Colonel Prouty complained to me of irregularities in other editions, and he should know. He helped write much of the briefing material and memoranda that circulated through the highest levels of government.

16 Ibid.

17 Robert McNamara, *In Retrospect: The Tragedy and Lessons of Vietnam* (New York: Times Books, 1995).

18 Theodore Sorensen, *Kennedy* (New York: Harper and Row, 1965).

19 Tip O'Neill, *Man of the House* (New York: Random House, 1987).

20 Schlesinger, *Robert Kennedy*, 522–23.

21 Reeves, *President Kennedy*, 69–70.

22 Ibid.

23 William Blum, *The CIA, A Forgotten History* (Atlantic Highlands, N.J.: Common Courage Press, 1986).

24 Kermit Roosevelt, *Countercoup: The Struggle for the Control of Iran* (New York: McGraw-Hill, 1979).

25 For an interesting alternative viewpoint of this era, see John Loftus and Mark Aarons, *The Secret War against the Jews* (New York: St. Martin's Press, 1994).

26 Schlesinger, *Robert Kennedy*.

27 Ibid., 527.

28 Schlesinger, *A Thousand Days*.

29 Schlesinger, *Robert Kennedy*.

30 Ibid.

31 In *The Pentagon Papers*, ed. Gravel.

32 Ibid.

33 As reported by Victor Marchetti of the CIA in his book, with John Marks, *The CIA and the Cult of Intelligence* (New York: Alfred A. Knopf, 1974).

34 Jim Garrison, *On the Trail of the Assassins: My Investigation and Prosecution of the Murder of President Kennedy* (New York: Sheridan Square Press, 1988), and *A Heritage of Stone* (New York: Putnam, 1970).

35 William Manchester, *The Death of a President* (New York: Harper and Row, 1967).

36 See X's speech in Oliver Stone and Zachary Sklar, *JFK: The Book of the Film* (New York: Applause, 1992), 109.

37 Fletcher Prouty, *The Secret Team* (Englewood Cliffs, N.J.: Prentice-Hall, 1973).

38 Beschloss, *Taking Charge;* emphasis added.

39 For more on this failed coup, see Clayton Kramer, "American Coup d'Etat," *History Today* (November 1995): 42.

40 James Petras, "The Discrediting of the Fifth Estate: The Press Attacks on *JFK,*" *Cineaste* 19 (winter 1992): 15.

41 Gerald Posner, *Case Closed* (New York: Random House, 1993).

42 Bill Sloan, *JFK: The Last Dissenting Witness* (Gretna, La.: Pelican Publishing, 1992).

Selected Bibliography

PRINTED MATERIAL

"Abused Child Syndrome." *American Enterprise* (January/February, 1998).

Appy, Christian. "Vietnam According to Oliver Stone." *Commonweal* (March 23, 1990): 187–89.

Beaver, Frank Eugene. *Oliver Stone: Wakeup Cinema.* New York: Twayne Publishers, 1994.

Biskind, Peter. "On Movies, Money and Politics." *The Nation,* April 5–12, 1999.

———. "Stone." *Premiere* 9 (January 1996): 62.

Breskin, David. "Oliver Stone: An Interview with the Director." In *The Films of Oliver Stone,* edited by Donald Kunz. Lanham, Md.: Scarecrow, 1997.

———. "Oliver Stone: The Rolling Stone Interview." *Rolling Stone,* April 14, 1991.

Burgoyne, Robert. "Modernism and the Narrative of National in *JFK.*" In *Film Nation: Hollywood Looks at U.S. History,* by Robert Burgoyne. Minneapolis: University of Minnesota Press, 1997.

———. "National Identity, Gender Identity, and the Rescue Fantasy in *Born on the Fourth of July.*" In *Film Nation: Hollywood Looks at U.S. History,* by Robert Burgoyne. Minneapolis: University of Minnesota Press, 1997.

Cooper, Marc. "Oliver Stone: An Interview." *Playboy,* February 1988.

Crowdus, Gary. "History, Dramatic License, and Larger Historical Truths: An Interview with Oliver Stone." *Cineaste* 22 (Fall 1996): 38–42.

———. "Personal Struggles and Political Issues: An Interview with Oliver Stone." *Cineaste* 16, no. 3 (1988): 19–20.

Doherty, Thomas. "Witness to War: Oliver Stone, Ron Kovic, and *Born on the Fourth of July.*" In *Inventing Vietnam: The War in Film and Television,* edited by Michael Anderegg. Philadelphia: Temple University Press, 1991.

Fischoff, Stuart. "Oliver Stone." *Psychology Today* 26 (September/October 1993): 44–50.

Hamsher, Jane. *Killer Instinct: How Two Young Producers Took on Hollywood and Made the Most Controversial Film of the Decade.* New York: Broadway Books, 1997.

Hwong, Lucia. "Political Commitment in Filmmaking: Oliver Stone." *Third Rail: A Review of International Arts and Literature* 9 (1988): 35.

Kagan, Norman. *The Cinema of Oliver Stone.* New York: Continuum, 1995.

Kinney, Judy Lee, "Gardens of Stone, Platoon and Hamburger Hill: Ritual and Remembrance." In *Inventing Vietnam: The War in Film and Television,* edited by Michael Anderegg. Philadelphia: Temple University Press, 1991.

Mackey-Kallis, Susan. *Oliver Stone's America: "Dreaming the Myth Outward."* Boulder, Colo.: Westview Press, 1996.

McGilligan, Pat. "Point Man." *Film Comment* 23 (January/February 1987): 11–20.

Nill, Dawn M. "Oliver Stone's Defense of JFK." *Communication Quarterly* (spring 1998): 127.

"Oliver Stone." In David Breskin, *Inner Views: Filmmakers in Conversation.* New York: Faber and Faber, 1997.

"Oliver Stone." In George Hickenlooper, *Reel Conversations: Candid Interviews with Film's Foremost Directors and Critics.* Secaucus, N.J.: Citadel Press, 1991.

"Oliver Stone: Wakeup Cinema." In *Past Imperfect: History According to the Movies,* edited by Mark Carnes. New York: Henry Holt, 1995.

Pfeifer, Chuck. "Oliver Stone." *Interview,* February 1987.

Queenan, Joe. "Compensate History's Reel Victims." *Wall Street Journal,* April 17, 1998.

Riordan, James. *Stone: The Controversies, Excesses, and Exploits of a Radical Filmmaker.* New York: Hyperion, 1995.

Rosenbaum, Ron. "The Pissing Contest." *Esquire,* December 1997.

Rowland, Mark. "Stone Unturned." *American Film* 16 (March 1991): 40–43.

Salewicz, Chris. *Oliver Stone: The Making of His Movies.* New York: Thunders Mouth, 1997.

Sandler, Adam. "'Killers' Raises Concerns." *Variety,* March 15–21, 1999.

Schiff, Stephen. "The Last Wild Man." *New Yorker,* August 8, 1994.

Schweizer, Peter. "Bad Imitation." *National Review,* December 31, 1998.

Singer, Michael. *The Making of Oliver Stone's* Heaven and Earth. Boston: Charles E. Tuttle, 1993.

Smith, Gavin. "Oliver Stone: Why Do I Have to Provoke?" *Sight and Sound* 4 (December, 1994): 8–12.

Stone, Oliver. *A Child's Night Dream: Oliver Stone.* New York: St. Martin's Press, 1997.

———. "A Filmmaker's Credo: Some Thoughts on Politics, History, and the Movies." *Humanist* 56 (September/October 1996): 3–6.

———. "A Filmmaker's Credo: Some Thoughts on Politics, History, and the Movies." In *Mass Politics: The Politics of Popular Culture,* edited by Daniel M. Shea et al. New York: St. Martin's Press, 1999.

———. "Who Defines History? Oliver Stone's Address to the National Press Club." *Cineaste* 19 (winter 1992): 23–24.

Sturken, Marita. "Reenactment, Fantasy, and the Paranoia of History: Oliver Stone's Docudramas." *History and Theory* 36 (December 1997): 64–79.

"Through the Looking Glass: A Critical Overview of Oliver Stone's *JFK.*" *Cineaste* 19 (winter 1992): 8–43.

Weiner, Jon. "Who Killed Oliver Stone?" *The Nation,* November 30, 1998.

Wills, Garry. "Dostoyevsky behind a Camera." *Atlantic,* July 1997.

Wilmington, Michael. "Oliver Stone and *Born on the Fourth of July.*" In *Movie Talk from the Front Lines: Filmmakers Discuss Their Works with the Los Angeles Film Critics Association.* Jefferson, N.C.: McFarland, 1995.

Winkler, Karen. "Oliver Stone Wins Some Converts at a Meeting of Historians." *Chronicle of Higher Education,* January 17, 1997.

Wolf, Jaime. "Oliver Stone Doesn't Want to Start an Argument." *New York Times Magazine*, September 21, 1997.

AUDIOVISUAL MATERIALS

"The Film 'Nixon' As History and Commentary." Purdue University Public Affairs Video Archives, West Lafayette, Ind., 1997.

"Kennedy School of Government Forum Event: Oliver Stone." John F. Kennedy School of Government, Harvard University, Cambridge, Mass., 1992.

"Oliver Stone: Filmmaker Oliver Stone Speaks at the National Press Club on His Film 'JFK' on January 14, 1992." National Public Radio, Washington, D.C., 1992.

Oliver Stone: Inside Out. Produced and directed by Joel Sucher and Steven Fischler. Pacific Street Producers Group, Inc., 1992.

The Oliver Stone Connection: A Musical Trip into the Celluloid World of Oliver Stone. Universal City, Calif., 1998.

"Oliver Stone on Moral Amnesia." National Public Radio, Washington, D.C., 1987.

Contributors

STEPHEN E. AMBROSE is the author of numerous books, including *Nixon* (Touchstone Press, 1996), *Rise to Globalism: American Foreign Policy since 1938* (Viking/Penguin, 1997), *Citizen Soldiers: The U.S. Army from the Normandy Beaches to the Bulge to the Surrender of Germany, June 7, 1944–May 7, 1945* (Diane Publishing, 1999), and *Lewis and Clark: Voyage of Discovery* (National Geographic Society, 1998).

DAVID T. COURTWRIGHT is professor of American history, film and history, and medical history at the University of North Florida. He is the author of *Violent Land: Single Men and Social Disorder from the Frontier to the Inner City* (Harvard University Press, 1996) and *Dark Paradise: Opiate Addiction in America before 1940* (Harvard University Press, 1982) and a coauthor of *Addicts Who Survived: An Oral History of Narcotic Use in America* (University of Tennessee Press, 1989).

JACK E. DAVIS is assistant professor of history and director of environmental studies at the University of Alabama at Birmingham. He is the author of *Race against Time: Culture and Separation in Natchez since 1930* (Louisiana State University Press, forthcoming). Davis is currently working on a biography of Florida writer and environmentalist Marjory Stoneman Douglas.

JAMES R. FARR is professor of history at Purdue University. A John Simon Guggenheim Fellow in 1998–1999, he is the author of three books on French history and labor history and is currently finishing a fourth on a celebrated murder trial in seventeenth-century France. Farr teaches courses on film and history.

MARTIN S. FRIDSON is director of global high-yield strategy at Merrill Lynch & Co. He was called "the dean of the high-yield bond market" in conjunction with being voted onto the Institutional Investor All-America research team. Fridson has been a guest lecturer at the graduate business schools of Babson, Columbia, Dartmouth, Duke, Fordham, Georgetown, Harvard, MIT, New York University, Notre Dame, Rutgers, and Wharton, as well as at the Amsterdam Institute of Finance. He is the author of *It Was a Very Good Year: Great Investment Moments of the Twentieth Century* (Wiley, 1997) and *Investment Illusions: A Savvy Wall Street Pro Explodes Popular Misconceptions about the Market* (Wiley, 1996).

DAVID HALBERSTAM is the author of many books, including *The Best and the Brightest* (Fawcett Crest, 1969), *The Children* (Alfred A. Knopf, 1998), *The Fifties* (Random House, 1996), and *The Powers That Be* (Dell, 1986).

LE LY HAYSLIP is the author of *When Heaven and Earth Changed Places: A Vietnamese Woman's Journey from War to Peace* (NAL/Dutton, 1993) and *Child of War, Woman of Peace* (Doubleday, 1996). Oliver Stone's film *Heaven and Earth* dealt with her experiences in Vietnam and the United States.

MICHAEL L. KURTZ is professor of history and political science and dean of the Graduate School at Southeastern Louisiana University. He is the author of *Crime of the Century: The Kennedy Assassination from a Historian's Perspective* (University of Tennessee Press, 1982; rev. ed., 1993).

WALTER LAFEBER is professor of history at Cornell University and the author of numerous books, including *Inevitable Revolutions: The United States in Central America* (W. W. Norton, 1983), *The New Empire: An Interpretation of American Expansion, 1860–1998* (Cornell University Press, 1963), *The Panama Canal: The Crisis in Historical Perspective* (Oxford University Press, 1989), and *The Clash: A History of U.S.-Japanese Relations* (W. W. Norton, 1997).

GEORGE S. MCGOVERN served as U.S. senator from South Dakota and as the Democratic Party's candidate for president of the United States in 1972. Among his publications are *The Great Coalfield War* (University Press of Colorado, 1996), *The New Patriotism* (Pantheon, 1992), and *Terry: My Daughter's Life and Death Struggle with Alcoholism* (NAL/Dutton, 1999).

RANDY ROBERTS is professor of history at Purdue University. He is author or editor of numerous books, including *John Wayne: American* (University of Nebraska Press, 1997), *When the Dominos Fell: America and Vietnam: 1945–1990* (Diane Publishing, 1998), *My Lai: A Brief History with Documents* (Bedford Books, 1998), and *Winning Is the Only Thing: Sports in America since 1945* (Johns Hopkins University Press, 1989).

ROBERT A. ROSENSTONE is professor of history at the California Institute of Technology. He is the author or editor of *Visions of the Past: The Challenge of Film to Our Idea of History* (Harvard University Press, 1995), *Revisioning History: Film and the Construction of a New Past* (Princeton University Press, 1995), *Romantic Revolutionary: A Biography of John Reed* (Alfred A. Knopf, 1975), and *Mirror in the Shrine: American Encounters with Meiji Japan* (Harvard University Press, 1988).

ARTHUR M. SCHLESINGER, JR., is the author of numerous books, including *A Thousand Days: John F. Kennedy in the White House* (Fawcett Crest, 1965), *The Imperial Presidency* (Replica Books, 1998), *The Disuniting of America: Reflections on a Multicultural Society* (W. W. Norton, 1993), and *The Cycles of American History* (Houghton Mifflin, 1999).

ROBERT BRENT TOPLIN is professor of history at the University of North Carolina at Wilmington. He is the author or editor of nine books, including *History by Hollywood: The Use and Abuse of the American Past* (University of Illinois Press, 1996) and *Ken Burns' The Civil War: Historians Respond* (Oxford University Press, 1996). He is also editor of film reviews for the *Journal of American History* and editor for media with *Perspectives*, the publication of the American Historical Association. Toplin was a principal creator of several historical dramas that appeared nationally on PBS television and the Disney Channel, and he has made numerous appearances on the History Channel and c-span, commenting on movies and history.

DAVID WELKY is completing his doctoral work at Purdue University, where he is writing a dissertation about radio, film, and American popular culture during the Great Depression.

Index

Hinson, Hal, 191
Hinton, Dean, 102
Hiss, Alger, 211, 212
Historians' Fallacies (Fischer), 136
History
   definition of, 6–7, 28, 31, 47, 204, 215,
      292
   portrayal of in film, 6, 7, 8, 17, 27–39
   and role of historian, 90, 136, 147
Hitchcock, Alfred, 43, 126, 277
Ho, A. Kitman, 84
Hoffman, Abbie, 26, 61
Hofstadter, Richard, 14, 62, 215
Holbrook, Hal, 125
Hoover, J. Edgar, 51, 290
Hopkins, Anthony, 16, 45, 88, 208, 215,
   255
Hopkins, Jerry, 154, 240
Horne, Douglas, 176
Howard, Larry, 295
Howard, Lisa, 253, 269
Huberty, James, 197
Hume, James J., 176
Hunt, E. Howard, 14, 205, 252, 253, 254
Hussein, Saddam, 55, 61

Icahn, Carl, 124
In Retrospect (McNamara), 15, 119, 263
Inside the Oval Office (Doyle), 258

Jansen, David, 114
JFK
   artistic techniques in, 10, 13, 53, 85,
      166, 170–71
   conspiracy theory in, 11–15, 16, 30, 43,
      167, 168, 172–73, 174, 213, 214, 279–
      85
   criticism of, 11–12, 13–14, 41, 43, 85, 87,
      166, 169–70, 171–74, 251, 279, 285–86,
      292–93
   historical accuracy in, 11–16, 30, 36–37,
      48, 84, 85–86, 90, 166–67, 170, 172–
      77, 213–14
   impact of, 5, 174, 175, 177, 214, 259–60,
      296
   message of, 8, 63, 87, 166, 168, 171, 176,
      228, 298

plot of, 84–85, 167–68, 213
praise of, 170
and release of assassination
   documents, 21, 62, 174, 177, 259–60,
   296
research for, 83–84, 87
Vietnam War issues in, 4, 15–16, 21, 23,
   84, 85, 86–87, 88, 90, 168–69, 176–
   77
   See also under Kennedy, John F.
JFK and Vietnam (Newman), 261
Joe, 226
Johnny Got His Gun, 135
Johnson, Hugh, 289, 291
Johnson, Lyndon B.
   and civil rights, 278
   and JFK assassination, 12, 174, 175, 213,
      260, 269, 283, 296
   and Vietnam War, 17, 55, 84, 85, 86,
      116, 144, 168–69, 177, 209, 226, 264
Jones, Tommy Lee, 83, 168, 169, 183, 189,
   198, 242, 244
Jordan, Winthrop, 147
Joyce, William, 175
Jung, Carl, 56, 158

Kael, Pauline, 107, 145
Kallstrom, James, 50
Kamen, Stan, 75
Karnow, Stanley, 119
Kauffmann, Stanley, 122
Kenneally, Patricia, 152, 240
Kennedy (Sorensen), 263
Kennedy, John F.
   assassination of, 12, 14, 15, 60–61, 62,
      64, 83, 88, 90, 173, 177, 204–9, 213,
      215, 253, 257, 260, 279–88, 292, 293–
      97
   and Cuban issues, 85, 206, 252–53, 264,
      266, 268, 269, 270, 287
   popularity of, 145, 146, 172, 210, 211
   portrayal of in *JFK,* 11, 84–86, 90, 172,
      176, 278, 288–89
   and Vietnam War, 4, 15–16, 21, 37,
      85, 86–87, 88, 90, 174, 176–77, 206,
      209, 213, 261, 262, 263, 264, 269,
      270

Romero, Archbishop Oscar, 32–33, 35,
94, 97, 98, 99, 100, 109, 220
Roosevelt, Franklin, 45, 58, 60, 259, 289,
290–91
Roosevelt, Kermit, 267
Rosenbaum, Ron, 258
Rosenstone, Robert A.
on filmmaker as historian, 26–39, 153,
172
Stone's response to, 44, 46, 47–49, 57
Rothschild, Paul, 239
Ruby, Jack, 287, 293
Russell, Harold, 138
Russell, Richard, 175, 260
Russo, Perry Raymond, 173, 274, 285
Ryan, Meg, 150

Safire, William, 203, 250
Salem, Kario, 50
Salisbury, Harrison, 251
Salvador
criticism of, 19, 95, 98–99, 103, 107–8,
219
historical accuracy in, 19, 32–33, 35, 97,
99–100, 101–2, 103, 221, 222
message of, 5, 8, 20, 29, 37, 95
plot of, 35–36, 95–97, 99, 100–102, 106
praise of, 19–20, 96, 107
Sarkis, Najwa, 74
Sarnoff, David, 272
Savage, Bill, 191
Savage, John, 96, 102
Saving Private Ryan, 229
Scaife, Richard Mellon, 259
Scarface, 21, 42, 75, 93, 107, 231, 233
Schama, Simon, 109, 147, 148
Scheer, Robert, 53, 251
Schindler, Oskar, 45
Schlesinger, Arthur M., Jr.
on *JFK* and *Nixon*, 212–16
Stone's response to, 263, 266, 269, 289,
291–92
Schoenmann, Ralph, 273
Schwarzman, Stephen, 126
Scorsese, Martin, 74
Scott, George C., 203, 250

Scott, Hugh, 250
Secret Team, The (Prouty), 282
Securities and Exchange Commission
(SEC), 127–28, 129, 130
Seizure, 74
Seligman, Daniel, 127, 130
Seven Days in May (Knebel), 60–61
Seven Pillars of Wisdom, 46, 52
Shad, John, 127, 128
Shakespeare, William, 40, 45, 207
Shaw, Clay, 167–68, 169, 170, 171, 172,
272–75, 277, 288
Sheen, Charlie, 76, 77, 111, 122, 123, 124,
231, 235
Sheen, Martin, 20, 76, 236
Sherak, Thomas, 124
Sherrill, Patrick Henry, 197
Shipler, David, 181
Shnayerson, Michael, 199
Sibert, James, 176
Siddons, Bill, 153
Simon, Art, 171
Simon, John, 121
Simpson, Joe, 192
Siskel, Gene, 107
Sizemore, Tom, 189
Sklar, Zachary, 9, 83, 271
Sloan, Bill, 295
Smathers, George, 256
Smith, Al, 291
Smith, Bernard, 130
Smith, Walter Bedell, 265
Sobel, Robert, 131
Sorensen, Ted, 263
Spencer, Saundra, 176
Spiesel, Charles, 173, 272–73
Sporkin, Stanley, 128
Stallone, Sylvester, 76, 115
Stamp, Terence, 130
Staples, Brent, 43
Starr, Paul, 143
Stegner, Wallace, 193
Stevenson, Adlai, 253, 279
Stone, Jacqueline Goddet, 67, 68, 297
Stone, Louis, 20, 42, 67, 68, 73, 87, 106,
128, 140, 146, 231, 232, 233, 236, 265